THE SPCK BIBLE GUIDE

Parting the Red Sea
Miracle is one theme of Exodus 14 when
Moses parts the Red Sea, allowing
God's people to leave Egypt and begin their
journey to the Promised Land (see page 30).

THE SPCK BIBLE GUIDE

An illustrated survey of all the
books of the Bible – their
contents, themes and teachings

Henry Wansbrough

Originally published in the
United States of America in 2011 by
Metro Books
An imprint of Sterling Publishing
387 Park Avenue South
New York
NY 10016

First published in Great Britain in 2013

Society for Promoting Christian Knowledge
36 Causton Street
London SW1P 4ST
www.spckpublishing.co.uk

British Library Cataloguing-in-Publication Data
A catalogue record for this book is available from
the British Library

Conceived, designed and produced by
Quarto Publishing plc
The Old Brewery
6 Blundell Street
London N7 9BH

Project Editor Chelsea Edwards
Art Director Caroline Guest
Designer Susi Martin
Picture Research Sarah Bell
Copy Editor Liz Jones
Proofreader Claire Waite Brown
Indexer Helen Snaith
Creative Director Moira Clinch
Publisher Paul Carslake

ISBN 978–0–281–06851–7

Printed by 1010 Printing International Ltd., China

10 9 8 7 6 5 4 3 2 1

Contents

THE NEW TESTAMENT 220

Foreword

The Bible was written thousands of years ago, in different languages, by people living in pre-industrial, mostly agricultural societies. The following pages are designed to serve as your roadmap to the foreign land that is the Bible. It is intended as your travel-guide, pointing out some of the significant sights and explaining their significance in their own context and for us today.

The Bible contains a wide range of literature: stories, poetry, wisdom and letters, composed by dozens of people, used, re-used, adapted, enlarged and commented on over hundreds of years. It has comforted and challenged human beings around the world for thousands of years. Rich and poor, famous and infamous, farmer and scientist, poet and labourer have all found comfort and wisdom in reading it. Its language has affected our modern languages, and the message of the Bible has changed the lives of individuals and of civilisations. Our modern concepts of justice, tolerance, love and human rights all grow out of this book as it has been read and put into practice.

The message of the Bible is that God has revealed himself to human beings in order to invite us into his friendship. This has been a gradual process, taking place over centuries. It is still going on, as we ourselves, individually and collectively, penetrate more fully into the meaning of this revelation in words and deeds. As we read the Bible we learn more about ourselves, our good and bad instincts, our own achievements and our own failures, about the world and about our relationship to the divine power that guides the world. Such knowledge comes to us not only through the words spoken by God's messengers, but also in the history of God's guidance of his people, as they were brought step by step to a deeper appreciation of the truth. Recognising that this deepening of understanding is God's own gift to us, guided by the Holy Spirit among us, we are enabled to respond more fully to the divine offer of friendship. The purpose of this volume is to help towards a fuller understanding of the Book of all Books.

History begins
History is the theme in the Bible's first chapter, when God created the heavens, the earth, and humanity, and history begins (see page 18).

About this book

This book is designed to help a modern reader of the Bible. Would you like to follow the moral teachings of the Bible? Do you want to know what the Bible has to say on prayer? Are you eager to learn about the biblical view of history – and of God's plans expressed in prophecy?

The key to this book is that every chapter of the Bible is summarised briefly and then colour-coded according to theme. It acts like a knowledgeable friend to guide you through the cultural and historical contexts, making it easy to grasp the meaning and purpose of any section, while seeing how it all fits into the bigger picture.

Those reading the Bible can use this book as an introduction and guide. It will help them see the forest for the trees, granting an overall sense of where they are and where they are going. It will help keep travellers in this foreign land from getting lost and, in fact, will help them feel at home.

Notes on the translation of the Bible

This book may be used with any good translation of the Bible. The quotations of the Bible used in this text are taken from the New Revised Standard Version. This was a revision of the King James Version of the Bible, first published in 1611. Over the course of centuries the English language has evolved and made the KJV less easy to understand. Better manuscripts have also been discovered, and advances have taken place in biblical scholarship. The NRSV (published 1989), prepared by an ecumenical body of scholars, has become the most widespread of all English versions.

Joshua
Overview

I   The Entry into Canaan 1:1–5:12
 a Preparations 1:1–2:24
 b Crossing the Jordan 3:1–5:12
II Conquest of Canaan 5:13–12:24
 a The Territory of Benjamin 5:13–9:27
 b Conquest of the South 10:1–43
 c Conquest of the North 11:1–23
 d Recapitulation 12:1–24
III Distribution of the Land to the Tribes 13:1–21:45
IV Life in Canaan 22:1–24:33
 a Joshua's Final Speech 23:1–16
 b The Assembly at Shechem 24:1–31

Introductions
Each of the 74 books of the Bible is given a general introduction, including an overview of the book's structure.

Joshua
Overview

I   The Entry into Canaan 1:1–5:12
 a Preparations 1:1–2:24
 b Crossing the Jordan 3:1–5:12
II Conquest of Canaan 5:13–12:24
 a The Territory of Benjamin 5:13–9:27
 b Conquest of the South 10:1–43
 c Conquest of the North 11:1–23
 d Recapitulation 12:1–24
III Distribution of the Land to the Tribes 13:1–21:45
IV Life in Canaan 22:1–24:33
 a Joshua's Final Speech 23:1–16
 b The Assembly at Shechem 24:1–31

The Book of Joshua describes the conquest of Canaan by the Israelites under Joshua and the distribution of territories to the tribes. Both of these are artificial; they belong to a genre of literature common in the ancient world: the victory inscription. Many such inscriptions exist, thanking the national deity for an overwhelming victory, often described in exaggerated terms. The impression is given of a lightning campaign overwhelming the whole country. In fact the conquests described are almost entirely confined to the territory of Benjamin, with a minor victory over the kings of the south and the conquest of Hazor in the north. The description of the distribution of the land to the tribes is in fact largely theoretical.

Chapter 1

Joshua takes Moses' place as the leader of the Israelites. Joshua tells them that they will soon cross the Jordan River – so they need to be prepared.

Chapter 1: Commentary

This chapter gives a double introduction: Joshua is introduced as the successor of Moses, with the same leadership and the same powers. An introduction is also given to the theme of the Deuteronomic History: success depends on fidelity to the Law of the Lord.

Chapter 2

Joshua sends two spies to Jericho. They stay with a prostitute named Rahab, who hides them. They promise to spare her when the Israelites conquer the city.

Chapter 2: Commentary

Jericho was one of the first cities in the world. It has a 10,000-year-old stone tower. Its strong walls were destroyed some 900 years before Joshua. The author assumes that Joshua captured the city near the Jordan. The story of Rahab may be based on some local cult.

Chapter 3

When the priests, carrying the Ark, step into the Jordan River, God halts the water. While the priests stand in the channel, the rest of the Israelites cross the river on dry ground.

Chapter 3: Commentary

The crossing of the Jordan under Joshua's command mirrors the crossing of the Red Sea at its beginning under Moses' command. The Passover at the end mirrors the Passover at the beginning. Just as Moses sent envoys ahead (Numbers 13), so Joshua sends spies. The manna now ceases (5:12), and normal life resumes.

Chapter 4

Twelve large stones gathered from the middle of the Jordan are piled as a memorial of the crossing. When the priests leave the Jordan River, the water starts flowing again.

Chapter 4: Commentary

'Gilgal' means 'ring' or 'circle'. More familiar is the Aramaic form, Golgutha/Golgotha. Two explanations of the name are given, one as a circle of stones (4:21), one as the scene of ritual circumcision (5:4).

Commentaries
Short commentaries discuss significant or difficult portions of the text, explaining the historical or cultural background, or significant theological issues.

Chapter 2: Commentary

Jericho was one of the first cities in the world. It has a 10,000-year-old stone tower. Its strong walls were destroyed some 900 years before Joshua. The author assumes that Joshua captured the city near the Jordan. The story of Rahab may be based on some local cult.

Theme finder
Each of the chapters is assigned between one and three themes, coded by colour and number.

⑧		⑰	
The Israelites then circumcise all the men and celebrate Passover. For the first time, the Israelites eat some Canaanite food. The manna stops coming.			Chapter **5**

Chapter summaries
Each chapter of the Bible is summarized.

⑧		⑰	
The Israelites march around Jericho once a day for six days, and then seven times on the seventh day. Then the walls of Jericho fall down. The Israelites conquer Jericho.			Chapter **6**

Many of the stories given here, especially those of the territory of Benjamin, are etiological myths, that is, they explain features of the landscape or local customs, and are founded on these rather than on historical evidence. They are valuable in showing the trust in the Lord, and in his servant Joshua. Joshua is the designated successor to Moses, and is seen as continuing his work. However, the actual historical evidence is difficult to interpret. Apart from the contemporary destruction of Hazor, archaeology does not provide any confirmation of the settlement of the Hebrews in Canaan.

Rahab
When Joshua sent spies to Jericho, they visited the prostitute Rahab. She protected the spies, and so when the Israelites conquered Jericho and slaughtered its populace, they spared both her and her family.

Once when Joshua was near Jericho, he looked up and saw a man standing before him with a drawn sword in his hand. Joshua went to him and said to him, 'Are you one of us, or one of our adversaries?' He replied, 'Neither; but as commander of the army of the Lord I have now come.' And Joshua fell on his face to the earth and worshipped, and he said to him, 'What do you command your servant, my Lord?'
Joshua 5:13–14

Chapter 6: Commentary
Two accounts of the processions are interwoven. The military operation is turned into a liturgical procession.

Chapter 7: Commentary
Dedication of the spoils to the Lord designates the war as a Holy War. There is no evidence that such wholesale genocide ever occurred. More likely it is simply an expression of post-exilic xenophobia, prohibiting the vulnerable post-exilic community from mixing with the local people (Ezra 9; Nehemiah 10:31). The story is presented as explaining a feature of the landscape (verse 26).

Chapter 8: Commentary
The story of the capture of Ai (ai is Hebrew for 'ruin') explains the great ruin near the ancient sanctuary of Bethel; the city was destroyed several hundred years before Joshua. Alternatively, it may be a displaced account of an attack on Bethel itself.

⑧		⑰	
The Israelites then circumcise all the men and celebrate Passover. For the first time, the Israelites eat some Canaanite food. The manna stops coming.			Chapter **5**

⑧		⑰	
The Israelites march around Jericho once a day for six days, and then seven times on the seventh day. Then the walls of Jericho fall down. The Israelites conquer Jericho.			Chapter **6**

⑨		⑰	
Achan steals some of the spoils from Jericho, rather than destroying it. As a consequence, the Israelites lose a battle at Ai. Achan and his family are stoned to death for his theft.			Chapter **7**

⑪		⑰	
The Israelites successfully conquer the small city of Ai. Joshua builds an altar on Mount Ebal, offers sacrifices and the blessings and cursings of the covenant are read aloud.			Chapter **8**

Key to themes

Every chapter of the Bible is summarised briefly and colour-coded according to theme. The 18 themes that have been applied to the texts will provide the reader with an overall sense of the primary point or points of each chapter. For more information about each of the themes, see pages 10–13.

Praise	*1*
Forgiveness	*2*
Moral teaching	*3*
Mourning	*4*
Poetry	*5*
Parables	*6*
Prophecy	*7*
Miracles	*8*
Judgement	*9*
Love	*10*
Worship	*11*
Prayer	*12*
Apocalypse	*13*
Contract	*14*
Angels and demons	*15*
Inventory	*16*
History	*17*
Wisdom literature	*18*

Fold-out page: key to the themes
Opposite page 287, you'll find a fold-out page containing an at-a-glance key to the colour and number system used to identify the themes. Keep this page open as you use this book, or until you become familiar with the key.

Once when Joshua was near Jericho, he looked up and saw a man standing before him with a drawn sword in his hand. Joshua went to him and said to him, 'Are you one of us, or one of our adversaries?' He replied, 'Neither; but as commander of the army of the Lord I have now come.' And Joshua fell on his face to the earth and worshipped, and he said to him, 'What do you command your servant, my Lord?'
Joshua 5:13–14

Selected quotations
There are important quotations from the biblical books.

About the themes

Prophet in peril
When Daniel refused to pray to anyone but God, Darius threw him to the lions in Daniel 6. History becomes that chapter's dominant theme (see page 202).

An angel appears
Gabriel reveals the future to the prophet Daniel in Daniel 9. That chapter's themes include Prophecy, Prayer, and Apocalypse (see page 202).

The division of the Bible into chapters and verses was not part of the original writing. The chapter divisions were first introduced by Stephen Langton, Archbishop of Canterbury (d. 1228). The verse divisions were first introduced by Santes Pagnini in 1527. Not all Bibles agree about these divisions; the Hebrew text and the Greek divisions of the Bible are sometimes at odds with each other. This is particularly difficult in the Psalms, because on some occasions the Greek and Hebrew texts divide the psalms differently. The chapter divisions do not always correspond to the sense units which we discern today. In this volume the chapter-headings, by R. P. Nettelhorst, keep to the biblical chapter divisions for the convenience of readers who prefer to read a chapter at a time.

The Bible contains many different kinds of writing. Before you start to read it is often useful to know what sort of text you are about to read. The various themes, also catalogued by R. P. Nettelhorst, have been reduced to 18, but this is only a rough guide to the principal sense of a passage. 'Inventory' includes genealogies, lists of materials used for building the Temple, census records, lists of priests, territories and conquests. 'History' includes anything written as history, though it may not be history in the modern sense of the word. It includes also fiction, such as the story of Jonah or of Tobit, which teach serious moral messages in the guise of history. 'Moral teaching' includes the Laws stemming from Moses, the words of Jesus and Paul's instructions and encouragement to local Christian communities.

Following is a key to the coloured tabs and the themes they relate to, with a little contextual information about each one.

Praise

People praise God by describing his wonderful characteristics, and by recounting all the great things he has done for them, their loved ones or their nation. Praise is commonly offered to God in response to his actions: because he delivered an individual or a group from some trouble, or simply in general recognition of God as creator and daily benefactor. Praise serves to help people avoid taking life and its joys for granted.

Mourning

Mourning is an outward expression of sorrow in the face of personal or national suffering, loss and disaster. It is often linked with hope for a better future. Mourning is often expressed in poetry and it is often ritualised. It is commonly directed to God as a complaint, with the request and hope, stated or unstated, that God will respond and alleviate the cause of the mourning, and restore prosperity, peace and joy.

Forgiveness

Throughout the Bible, the guilty regularly beg God for mercy when they realise they are being punished for a crime. God is willing to grant them relief. In response, the guilty turn from their wickedness, begin living righteously, and apologise. But God grants his forgiveness first. God's forgiveness is an undeserved kindness that he graciously bestows on those who are still his enemies. God even forgives those who continue to return to the same sin, every time they ask.

Poetry

Poetry is an expression of emotions in a memorable and ornately structured way. While many cultures rhyme sounds in their poetry, the poetry of the Bible rhymes concepts instead. Poetry impacts the heart more than the head, and so will be most common in prayers, in praise and in lamentation. It is found throughout the Bible, both in the Old and New Testaments. The Psalms, the Proverbs and most of the prophecies of the Bible are poetry.

Moral teaching

The moral teaching in the Bible explains how people should treat one another and includes, among other things, all the commandments and legal texts of the Bible. It also includes Jesus' words to his disciples, instructions about prayer and the qualifications of deacons and pastors. It includes the beatitudes and the comforting words of encouragement offered to those going through difficult times. The moral teachings are summed up in the single command to love one another.

Parables

Parables and fables are short, memorable stories. They appear throughout the Bible. Fables use animals and plants as the main characters, while parables use people. Parables and fables have a moral. They are not designed just for entertainment, but to teach and to bring about a change in behaviour. In most instances, parables and fables have but a single point to make. Jesus regularly taught by using parables and, in fact, most of the parables in the Bible came from him.

Prophecy

A prophecy is usually a warning that God's judgement is coming. It describes future events. Most, though not all, prophecies in the Bible are poetic. The descriptions are often cryptic and make more sense following the predicted events than before them. Prophecies are rarely heeded. Prophecy comes from God through his spokespeople, the prophets. Prophecy shows up throughout the Bible, both in the Old and New Testaments, and not just in the books traditionally labelled as 'prophets'.

Love

According to Jesus, loving God and loving people summarises all the commandments. People do not harm those they love. Love, therefore, is the overall point of the Bible. Ideally, love means desiring what is best for others, regardless of their behaviour. Love describes emotions ranging from sexual desire to the feelings of parents, children, siblings and friends for one another. It also refers to the obligations that exist within covenant relationships, such as the one between God and Israel.

Miracles

Although it is common to think of miracles as a violation of natural law, modern theologians generally reject that as a definition. God seems no more willing to violate the natural laws than he is to violate the moral laws. Miracles are actually simply the intervention of the divine in human affairs in ways that are spectacular and noticeable, as when God parted the Red Sea, Jesus turned water into wine or an outnumbered Israelite army defeated its enemies.

Worship

Worship is about focusing on God through ritual. In a general sense, every aspect of life may be counted as part of worship. However, worship is usually more specifically about the sacrifices, the offering of prayers, public assemblies for praise or thanks and the celebration of the feast days. It includes the Temple, the altars, the equipment and even the clothing of the priests. Worship includes fasting, circumcision, abstaining from certain foods and keeping the Sabbath.

Judgement

Judgement is the deserved punishment rendered to those guilty of violating contracts, relationships, laws, regulations and customs. God judges his people when they violate the agreements they have made with him, just as governments judge those who break the laws of the land, and just as parents punish their children who misbehave. Judgement is always in the context of a relationship with God, governments or individuals. God's judgements have a corrective and redemptive purpose.

Prayer

Prayer happens when people talk to God. It happens when people let him know how they feel and what they want and need. Sometimes it is formal and public; other times it is informal and private. Human beings seek God's counsel and aid, they offer thanks for personal and national deliverance, and they beg forgiveness for personal and corporate sins. Prayers move and influence God and move and influence the one who is praying.

Apocalypse

During times of suffering and oppression, apocalyptic literature expressed the desire for judgement against those responsible. Apocalypse expresses the hope that God will establish a kingdom of righteousness and justice. It was a style of literature common in the last century BC and the first century AD. Apocalypse appears in the Old Testament prophets, including sections of Daniel, Ezekiel and Isaiah. In the New Testament, the Book of Revelation stands as the primary example of apocalypse.

Inventory

Inventory includes all the lists in the Bible, whether of genealogies, names and numbers of people, their property, the land allotments of tribes, tax records, donations, building materials for the Temple, ceremonies, soldiers or exiles. The lists demonstrated for the Bible's original readers that the Bible's stories were about their relatives. That the stories included mundane details demonstrated God's concern, not just for nations and empires, but for individuals and the affairs of everyday life.

Contract

Contracts are formal, legally binding agreements or promises made between individuals, between nations and between God and his people. An older term used by theologians for the contracts of the Bible is 'covenant' or 'testament'. Thus, the entire Bible is divided into two contracts, called the Old and New Testaments. The contractual nature of God's relationships explains how people in the Bible related to God and why God acted towards them the way that he did.

History

History is the story of what happened in the lives of people and nations, arranged more or less chronologically. In the Bible, history explains the significance of past events in the lives of God's people, with both corporate and individual implications. As Paul would write in the New Testament, 'These things happened to them as examples and were written down as warnings for us, on whom the culmination of the ages has come'. (1 Corinthians 10:11).

Angels and demons

The good supernatural beings who serve as God's emissaries are called angels. The demons and Satan are apparently angels who turned evil and rebelled against God. The angels, the demons and Satan are minor characters in the Bible. Only three angels – Michael, Gabriel and Raphael – are even given names. The words 'Satan' and the 'Devil' are designations, not names. Only once do female angels appear in the Bible (Zechariah 5:9), and many angels do not have wings.

Wisdom literature

Wisdom literature explains how to live well. It is generally intensely practical, explaining how to conduct oneself, or how to face the inevitable dilemmas and trials of life. It consists of stories that illustrate the importance of good choices, essays about the meaning of life and proverbial sayings. In the Bible, wisdom literature includes the Books of Proverbs and Job, some of the Psalms, Ecclesiastes, James and the Joseph story in Genesis.

Tower of Babel
Israel in Bondage and the Tower of Babel,
nineteenth-century painting by Caimi.

The Old Testament

The Jewish and the Christian communities took some time to settle which books belonged to the sacred text that gave us God's word in a special and normative way. Both communities independently – but more or less simultaneously – reached their conclusions in the course of the second Christian century, though the Christian tradition did not become fully steady for another two or three hundred years. The Hebrew Bible was divided into three sections: the Law, the Prophets and the Writings. The Christian Bible also included several books (and parts of books) which existed only in Greek. Acting on some remarks of St Jerome, who is credited with the first translation of the whole Bible into Latin (AD 405), Luther excluded these Greek portions from his Canon of Scripture, a move that has been observed in many Protestant traditions until the present day.

The order in which the Old Testament is given in this volume corresponds to the Greek Bible, namely histories, wisdom then prophets. Histories includes many different kinds of writing. Some is barely history at all, but would today be classified as myth or legend, which does not prevent it being a true expression of God's word and teaching. The stories of the first ancestors of Israel can be described as folk history, handed down for many centuries by word of mouth. For the later histories serious sources, such as court records, were used; these are often confirmed by court records of other neighbouring civilisations, such as Assyria, Egypt and Babylon. But all historical writing has a purpose, and in these cases the purpose is to understand and interpret God's dealings with the people of Israel. Towards the end of the histories come three little books, which again are barely historical, but each carries an important message in historical form: Tobit, Judith and Esther. In the Hebrew arrangement two of these are numbered among the Writings, while Judith is not included in the Hebrew Bible at all. At the very end come the two Books of Maccabees, which exist only in the Greek.

The wisdom literature is the least homogeneous collection of writings, including a large number of different kinds of writing. Prominent in this collection are prayers, and particularly the Psalms, the prayers of Israel's worship, praise and sorrow, reflecting Israel's response to the LORD, in joy, anxiety and suffering, throughout the course of its history. Some of the psalms were composed well before King David, some only shortly before the birth of Christ. They really do reflect the whole gamut of Israel's life. Included in the wisdom literature are also collections of down-to-earth proverbs and reflections on life and how to get on in the world, many of them uplifted by the knowledge that all true wisdom and all true success comes from God. More aggressive are the two books that rail against God, Job and Ecclesiastes, which question the whole meaning of life and the accepted

Hebrew framework of values. The believers who gathered the books of the Bible together were firm enough in their faith to also include these challenges to conventional thinking and theology. Buried among the books of this collection are half-a-dozen delightful love poems, the Song of Songs, which have always been seen as poetic celebrations of the love between God and Israel.

The final section of the Old Testament – and here the Greek and Hebrew Bible coincide again – consists of the books of the prophets. Shadowy groups of prophets had been known in Israel since the beginning of the monarchy, but during the monarchy they develop into the conscience of Israel, voicing the LORD's warning of the disasters provoked by continuous idolatry, profiteering, materialism and injustice. In the eighth century the sayings of these prophets began to be recorded, perhaps initially only by oral memory, to be later written down under the names of great prophetic figures. We cannot be sure that all the sayings attributed to these figures in fact stem from them, for other similar sayings seem to have accrued, which many scholars see as reflecting the conditions and problems of later ages. They provide valuable evidence of the divine guidance offered, often fruitlessly, to the straying people of God during these ages. For Christians they also provide a foretaste of the hopes and expectations of the reign of God which was to be fulfilled in the Messiah.

Genesis

Overview

In the Hebrew Bible this book is named after its first words, *breshit*, 'In the beginning'. 'Genesis' comes from the Greek for 'origin'.

The first 11 chapters of the book contain stories that explain the world as it is. It is the creation of an all-powerful God, who has fashioned human beings in his own image to master and care for the world. The stories explain how human failure and its dreadful consequences come to be in the world, though the loving God is always ready to forgive. The imagery is very similar to that of Babylonian legends of origin, but the picture of God and the position of human beings in the world is very different. Like many myths of origin, these stories are historical in form; however, crucially they guide the reader to an understanding of the present state of affairs.

There follows a folk history, the story of the origin of the family of nomads who would later become the nucleus of the Israelites, bringing God's

---

17

Chapter 1

God creates the universe over the course of six days, then rests on the seventh.

Chapter 1: **Commentary**

This account of creation is arranged logically, not historically: first, the framework of light and darkness. Then the three basic elements: sky, sea and earth. Then the fixed things in each: plants and stars. Then moving objects in each: fish, birds and animals. Finally the climax: man and woman, made in the image of God.

17

Chapter 2

God creates Adam and Eve and puts them in the Garden of Eden, warning them that they can eat from every tree but one: the Tree of the Knowledge of Good and Evil.

Chapters 2 and 3: **Commentary**

These chapters explain how there can be evil in the world: the temptation of the woman and the man to think they can know better than God. They are naked and defenceless, and are cast out of their garden of perfection. God does not desert them, but covers their shame and promises that evil will not prevail for ever. What was the basic sin? Was it pride or independence? Other stories put the basic evil as jealousy (Cain and Abel) or pride (the tower of Babel).

---

9   **15**   **17**

Chapter 3

Adam and Eve eat fruit from the only forbidden tree, become mortal and God expels them from the Garden of Eden to keep them away from the Tree of Life.

---

9   **16**   **17**

Chapter 4

God sends Cain, one of Adam and Eve's sons, into exile after Cain murders Abel, one of his brothers; Cain then marries, builds a city and has many descendants.

blessing to all nations. It is an epic story of three heroes, Abraham, Isaac and Jacob, comprised of family adventures, heroic and unheroic episodes and incidents explaining names and customs. Through it all runs the thread of the promise to Abraham of numberless descendants and a land that they would possess as their own. Finally comes the epic story of Joseph, the hero who brought his family down to Egypt, where they would settle for hundreds of years.

The stories of Abraham and his family were handed down from generation to generation before finally being recorded, perhaps as late as the fourth century BC. Three sets of characteristics can be discerned. Two are easily distinguished: the writer known as the Yahwist uses the name 'Yahweh' or 'the LORD' for God, and presents a warm and affectionate image of God. The Elohist uses the common word 'Elohim' for God, and shows a God more distant and concerned with morality. The priestly author supplements these two with stories about the rituals and religious customs of the Jews.

Chapter 6: **Commentary**

The 'sons of God' is a traditional expression for the angels. This strange fragment may come from a myth about an attempt to gain immortality by sexual means. Many cultures have a story of a flood. Here the world has become so wicked that God has no alternative to cleansing it by the flood; leaving only the faithful Noah and his family to carry on the human race. Two versions of the story are combined in this account.

He waited another seven days, and again he sent out the dove from the ark; and the dove came back to him in the evening, and there in its beak was a freshly plucked olive leaf; so Noah knew that the waters had subsided from the earth. Then he waited another seven days, and sent out the dove; and it did not return to him any more.

Genesis 8:10–12

Chapter 9: **Commentary**

Why did Noah curse his grandson, Canaan? This is a story that explains the inferior status of the Canaanites, later conquered by Abraham's descendants. Leviticus 18:8 suggests that 'saw his nakedness' may mean that Ham had sexual intercourse with Noah's wife; this would explain the curse.

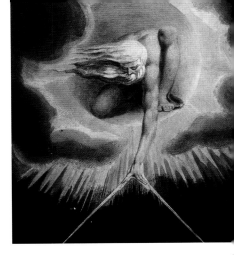

Creation of the universe
The Bible begins with God creating the universe. In contrast to the Babylonian myths of the day, the Bible is unconcerned with explaining the origin of God.

16
A genealogy from Adam to Noah, including Methuselah, who is said to live longer than anyone else in the Bible: a remarkable 969 years.

Chapter **5**

9 **17**
God is dismayed by the behaviour of the human race and decides to drown everyone except Noah, whom he orders to build a large ship for himself, his family and all the animals.

Chapter **6**

9 **17**
After Noah, his family and the animals enter the large ship he built, 40 days of rain cover the world with water, drowning everyone except for those on the ship.

Chapter **7**

17
After nearly a year spent aboard ship, Noah and his family, with the animals, disembark and Noah thanks God for their survival by offering him a sacrifice.

Chapter **8**

14 **17**
God makes a contract with the human race, sealed with a rainbow, that he will never destroy the world with a flood again; then Noah gets drunk and curses his grandson, Canaan.

Chapter **9**

16
A genealogy of the descendants of Noah's three sons, Shem, Ham and Japheth.

Chapter **10**

9   **16**

Chapter

11

Noah's descendants construct the city and tower of Babel: God confuses their language, so that they scatter across the world. Shem's genealogy ends with Abram.

7   **17**

Chapter

12

God sends Abram to the land of Canaan, promising him future blessings. After a famine in Canaan, Abram and his wife have an adventure in Egypt.

7   **17**

Chapter

13

Abram settles west of the Jordan River, while his nephew Lot moves east, near Sodom. God promises Abram descendants as numerous as 'the stars in the sky'.

14   **17**

Chapter

14

Abram gathers an army and attacks the Mesopotamian conquerors of Sodom, rescuing his nephew Lot. In thanks, Abram gives Melchizedek, king and priest of Salem, a tenth of the spoils.

14

Chapter

15

God makes a contract with Abram, assuring him that he will have a child who will become his heir, rather than his servant, Eliezer of Damascus.

17

Chapter

16

Unable to bear children, Abram takes Sarai's servant Hagar as a second wife. Hagar gives birth to a son, Ishmael, creating conflict between Hagar and Sarai.

7   **14**

Chapter

17

God establishes circumcision as the sign of the covenant between Abram and God and changes Abram's name to Abraham and Sarai's name to Sarah.

7   **15**   **17**

Chapter

18

God and two angels arrive at Abraham's home and he invites them to dinner. God reveals his intention to destroy Sodom for its wickedness.

Chapter 12: **Commentary**

God's promise to Abram is basic to the whole story of the Bible, and is the ground of Jewish and Christian hope. The blessing is not only for Abram's family, but extends to all nations. Abram's faith in God's fidelity against all likelihood (as he had no son and heir) is the model of Christian faith. There are two other versions of this promise, in chapters 15 and 17. In the latter, circumcision is instituted as a sign of faith in God's promise.

Immediately afterwards, Abram risks losing his wife to Pharaoh. The same story is told twice more, once of Abraham at Gerar (chapter 20) and once of Isaac at Gerar (chapter 26). This is typical of folk history.

'I will make of you a great nation, and I will bless you, and make your name great, so that you will be a blessing. I will bless those who bless you, and the one who curses you I will curse; and in you all the families of the earth shall be blessed.'

Genesis 12:2–3

Chapter 14: **Commentary**

Melchizedek is traditionally taken to be the priest-king of Jerusalem. Because he is not said to be descended from any human being, he is taken by the Letter to the Hebrews to be the forerunner of Christ. Abraham's payment of a tithe to him is interpreted as showing the superiority of Christ's priesthood to the priesthood of the line of Abraham. This little incident does not fit any known period of history.

Chapter 18: **Commentary**

This visit of the three supernatural figures who seem to merge into one is seen by many early Christian writers as a prefiguring of the Trinity. In the early books of the Bible the 'Angel of the LORD' often seems to be a manifestation of God himself. Some details of the story are a play on Isaac's name, understood to mean 'smile' or 'laugh'.

Chapter 19: **Commentary**

Several details of this story (Lot's wife as a pillar of salt) are used to explain the eerie features of the landscape around the Dead Sea. It is unclear whether the final sin of the inhabitants of Sodom is a sexual one or an affront to the sacred duty of hospitality.

Then the LORD rained on Sodom and Gomorrah sulphur and fire from the LORD out of heaven; and he overthrew those cities, and all the Plain, and all the inhabitants of the cities, and what grew on the ground. But Lot's wife, behind him, looked back, and she became a pillar of salt.

Genesis 19:24–26

Chapter 22: **Commentary**

This startling story of the ultimate trial of Abraham's faith is told with agonising dramatic tension. Child-sacrifice was common in the neighbouring cultures, and was even superstitiously practised in Israel. This story may be a way of showing that it must never happen.

And said, 'By myself I have sworn, says the LORD: Because you have done this, and have not withheld your son, your only son, I will indeed bless you, and I will make your offspring as numerous as the stars of heaven and as the sand that is on the seashore. And your offspring shall possess the gate of their enemies, and by your offspring shall all the nations of the earth gain blessing for themselves, because you have obeyed my voice.'

Genesis 22:16–18

Chapter 23: **Commentary**

At last Abraham acquires some territory, in fulfilment of God's promise. The elaborate oriental courtesy disguises some hard bargaining about rights and obligations. Documents of sale at that time always mention the trees included in the purchase.

Chapter 25 **Commentary**

Jacob was a trickster until he was converted by the experience at the River Jabbok (chapter 32), outwitting first his brother Esau (here and in chapter 27), then his uncle Laban. At that time, outsmarting someone seems to have been more valued than honesty. In the story the two brothers represent the neighbouring nations of Israel and Edom, often at war with each other.

---

⑨ ⑮ ⑰

Lot and two of his daughters leave Sodom before it is destroyed, but his wife doesn't make it. Then Lot's two daughters get him drunk so he'll impregnate them.

Chapter **19**

---

⑰

Abraham lies to King Abimelek about his relationship to Sarah. But in a dream, God reveals the truth, so Abimelek sends Abraham and Sarah away, with gifts of sheep, cattle and slaves.

Chapter **20**

---

⑭ ⑰

Sarah finally gives birth to a son, Isaac. After he is weaned, she forces Abraham to send Hagar and Ishmael into exile. Meanwhile, Abraham makes a treaty of peace with Abimelek.

Chapter **21**

---

⑪ ⑰

God tests Abraham by ordering him to sacrifice Isaac as a burnt offering on a mountain, but at the very last minute, God makes Abraham substitute a ram in Isaac's place.

Chapter **22**

---

④ ⑭ ⑰

After Sarah dies at the age of 127, Abraham purchases some land and a cave in Hebron from Ephron the Hittite and buries her there.

Chapter **23**

---

⑰

Abraham sends one of his servants to the village of Nahor to find a wife for his son Isaac. The servant returns with Rebecca, the sister of Laban.

Chapter **24**

---

⑯ ⑰

Abraham remarries and has many more children before finally dying at the age of 175. Esau, Isaac's firstborn son, sells his birthright to his brother Jacob in exchange for a bowl of stew.

Chapter **25**

⑭   ⑰

Chapter
26

When a famine arises where Isaac lives, God makes a covenant with him and tells him not to go to Egypt. So Isaac goes to Garar and lies to Abimelek about his relationship with Rebecca.

⑰

Chapter
27

Esau is murderously angry after Jacob tricks his father Isaac into giving him, rather than Esau, his blessing. So Rebecca sends Jacob off to live with her brother Laban.

⑦   ⑭   ⑰

Chapter
28

On the way to Laban, Jacob dreams of a ladder to heaven and God promises him future blessings. Jacob vows to worship God and give him a tenth of his future earnings.

Chapter 26: **Commentary**

Isaac is a shadowy character. Apart from this story, told in chapters 12 and 20 of Abraham, most of our information concerns controversies over wells and water-rights. Isaac seems to have settled in the north of the Negeb, tough and dry country but habitable.

Reside in this land as an alien, and I will be with you, and will bless you; for to you and to your descendants I will give all these lands, and I will fulfil the oath that I swore to your father Abraham. I will make your offspring as numerous as the stars of heaven, and will give to your offspring all these lands; and all the nations of the earth shall gain blessing for themselves through your offspring ...
Genesis 26:3–4

Chapter 28: **Commentary**

The ladder in Jacob's dream mirrors the vast stepped towers used as temples in Mesopotamia. The stone that he consecrates by anointing is presumably the cult-stone of the Israelite sanctuary of Bethel ('house of God').

Then Jacob made a vow, saying, 'If God will be with me, and will keep me in this way that I go, and will give me bread to eat and clothing to wear, so that I come again to my father's house in peace, then the LORD *shall be my God, and this stone, which I have set up for a pillar, shall be God's house; and of all that you give me I will surely give one-tenth to you.'*
Genesis 28:20–22

Jacob's ladder
Jacob dreamt that he saw angels going up and down a ladder into heaven when God promised to take care of him while he was away from his homeland.

Chapter 29: **Commentary**

Laban is able to trick Jacob by giving him the wrong daughter because by the time she removes her bridal veil it is too dark to see. Jacob's own trick on Laban relies on a primitive belief in a link between what was visible during mating and the resultant offspring.

Chapter 31: **Commentary**

The household idols function as title-deeds. Rachel sides with her husband in tricking her father by hiding the idols and pretending she is too indisposed to stand up.

So Jacob took a stone and set it up as a pillar. And Jacob said to his kinsfolk, 'Gather stones,' and they took stones, and made a heap; and they ate there by the heap. Laban called it Jegar-sahadutha: but Jacob called it Galeed. Laban said, 'This heap is a witness between you and me today.' Therefore he called it Galeed ...

Genesis 31:45–48

Chapter 32: **Commentary**

Jacob's mysterious wrestling with God or the Angel of God in the form of a water-spirit occasions his conversion. Peniel, where it occurs, means 'the face of God'. God blesses him with a new nature and a new name (Israel means 'man seeing God'), but retains the mystery of the divinity by refusing to give his own name.

Chapter 34: **Commentary**

The story of treachery, attached to the mention of Shechem in 33:18, has been explained as a hint that these two sons of Jacob never went down to Egypt. In fact the tribe of Simeon was soon absorbed into Judah, and the priestly tribe of Levi never had any territory of its own.

---

⑩ **⑰**

Jacob works seven years for his uncle Laban in order to marry Rachel. But Laban tricks him into marrying her sister Leah, too. Leah bears him four sons, but Rachel remains childless.

Chapter **29**

⑰

Rachel's servant Bilhah and Leah's servant Zilpah also marry Jacob. Leah, Bilhah and Zilpah give birth to six more sons and a daughter before Rachel finally bears Joseph.

Chapter **30**

⑭ **⑰**

After working for about 20 years for Laban, Jacob and his family sneak off to Canaan. An angry Laban pursues them, but finally makes a peace treaty with Jacob.

Chapter **31**

⑰

A worried Jacob sends messengers bearing gifts to his brother Esau to let him know that he's coming. Jacob spends a night wrestling God, who changes Jacob's name to Israel.

Chapter **32**

⑰

When Jacob finally meets up with his brother Esau, he discovers that Esau has forgiven him. Jacob and his family then settle down near the city of Shechem.

Chapter **33**

⑨ **⑭** **⑰**

The prince of Shechem kidnaps Jacob's daughter Dinah and rapes her. Jacob's sons Simeon and Levi rescue their sister and kill everyone in Shechem.

Chapter **34**

④ **⑭** **⑯**

Rachel dies giving birth to her second son, Benjamin. She is buried in Bethlehem. Altogether, Jacob has 12 sons. Jacob's father Isaac dies at the age of 180.

Chapter **35**

⑯

A genealogy lists all of Esau's children, along with their descendants. Esau is also called Edom, and his nation, formed of his descendants, has many kings.

Chapter **36**

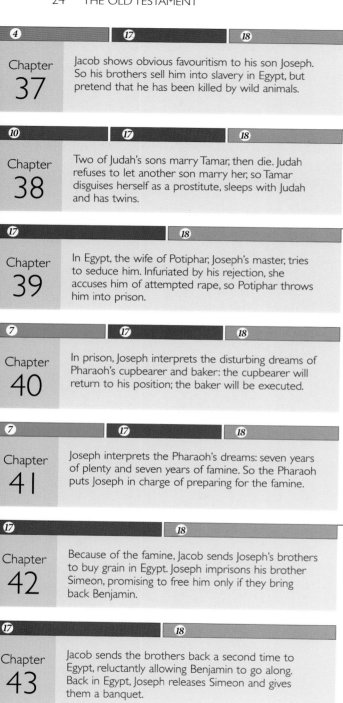

④ **⑰** **⑱**

Chapter 37

Jacob shows obvious favouritism to his son Joseph. So his brothers sell him into slavery in Egypt, but pretend that he has been killed by wild animals.

⑩ **⑰** **⑱**

Chapter 38

Two of Judah's sons marry Tamar, then die. Judah refuses to let another son marry her, so Tamar disguises herself as a prostitute, sleeps with Judah and has twins.

⑰ **⑱**

Chapter 39

In Egypt, the wife of Potiphar, Joseph's master, tries to seduce him. Infuriated by his rejection, she accuses him of attempted rape, so Potiphar throws him into prison.

⑦ **⑰** **⑱**

Chapter 40

In prison, Joseph interprets the disturbing dreams of Pharaoh's cupbearer and baker: the cupbearer will return to his position; the baker will be executed.

⑦ **⑰** **⑱**

Chapter 41

Joseph interprets the Pharaoh's dreams: seven years of plenty and seven years of famine. So the Pharaoh puts Joseph in charge of preparing for the famine.

⑰ **⑱**

Chapter 42

Because of the famine, Jacob sends Joseph's brothers to buy grain in Egypt. Joseph imprisons his brother Simeon, promising to free him only if they bring back Benjamin.

⑰ **⑱**

Chapter 43

Jacob sends the brothers back a second time to Egypt, reluctantly allowing Benjamin to go along. Back in Egypt, Joseph releases Simeon and gives them a banquet.

⑰ **⑱**

Chapter 44

Joseph has one of his servants secretly sneak a valuable cup into Benjamin's bag, then accuses them of theft. His brother Judah pleads to take Benjamin's punishment.

Chapter 37: **Commentary**

The story of Joseph will continue until the end of the Book. Two versions of Joseph's deportation to Egypt are combined: the sons of Jacob want to kill the cheeky teenager, but Reuben persuades them to cool him off in a well, from where he is kidnapped by Midianites. The sons of Israel, guided by Judah, sell him to Ishmaelites.

Chapter 38: **Commentary**

If a married man dies without an heir, his nearest male relative must get his widow pregnant to provide an heir. Wanting to keep the property for himself, Onan avoids getting Tamar pregnant. Tamar courageously takes the matter into her own hands, and Judah, intending to have a one-night fling, does his duty, not realising that the veiled prostitute is his daughter-in-law.

Chapter 39: **Commentary**

A similar story occurs in ancient Egyptian literature, in which a wife attempts to seduce her husband's handsome younger brother. It may be that the story entered the Bible at a later date, when Egyptian Wisdom literature was current in Israel.

One day, however, when he went into the house to do his work, and while no one else was in the house, she caught hold of his garment, saying, 'Lie with me!' But he left his garment in her hand, and fled and ran outside. When she saw that he had left his garment in her hand and had fled outside, she called out to the members of her household and said to them, 'See, my husband has brought among us a Hebrew to insult us! He came in to me to lie with me, and I cried out with a loud voice; and when he heard me raise my voice and cry out, he left his garment beside me, and fled outside.'
Genesis 39:11–15

Chapter 42: **Commentary**

Hearers of this tale, knowing more than the actors, can enjoy the irony of Joseph's brutal revenge. There is also a certain doubling-up, which suggests that two versions may have been combined. The sack-trick would hardly have worked twice.

And their father Jacob said to them, 'I am the one you have bereaved of children: Joseph is no more, and Simeon is no more, and now you would take Benjamin. All this has happened to me!'
Genesis 42:36

And he wept so loudly that the Egyptians heard it, and the household of Pharaoh heard it.

Joseph said to his brothers, 'I am Joseph. Is my father still alive?' But his brothers could not answer him, so dismayed were they at his presence.

Genesis 45:2–3

He blessed Joseph, and said, 'The God before whom my ancestors Abraham and Isaac walked, the God who has been my shepherd all my life to this day, the angel who has redeemed me from all harm, bless the boys; and in them let my name be perpetuated, and the name of my ancestors Abraham and Isaac; and let them grow into a multitude on the earth.'

Genesis 48:15–16

Chapter 48: **Commentary**

Jacob places the two boys 'between his knees', a rite of paternal adoption. This explains why the two main northern tribes, closely related to each other, have this special status, though by birth they are only grandsons of Jacob.

Chapter 49: **Commentary**

The blessings pronounced by Jacob foretell the future of the tribes, and are a valuable assessment of the condition of each of them. The idea of a 12-tribe league was a later development. In the blessing Judah is already the leader, which suggests that the blessings describe conditions at the time of King David.

But Joseph said to them, 'Don't be afraid. Am I in the place of God? Even though you intended to do harm to me, God intended it for good, in order to preserve a numerous people, as he is doing today. So have no fear; I myself will provide for you and your little ones.' In this way he reassured them, speaking kindly to them.

Genesis 50:19–21

17   **18**

Joseph finally reveals his true identity to his brothers, then sends for Jacob and their families to be brought back to Egypt to live in prosperity with him.

Chapter
45

16   **17**   **18**

Jacob and his whole family travel to Goshen in Egypt, where Joseph and his father Jacob are finally reunited.

Chapter
46

17   **18**

Joseph presents his father to Pharaoh, who guarantees their safety and prosperity. Meanwhile, Joseph reduces most of the Egyptians to permanent serfdom.

Chapter
47

17   **18**

Jacob's father adopts Joseph's sons, Manasseh and Ephraim, granting the rights of the firstborn to the second-born Ephraim instead of Manasseh.

Chapter
48

16   **17**   **18**

Jacob then pronounces a blessing on each of his 12 sons. Just before his death, he asks to be buried in Abraham's tomb in Hebron.

Chapter
49

4   **17**   **18**

After 70 days of official mourning, Joseph, his brothers and representatives of Pharaoh take Jacob's body to Hebron and bury it. Joseph dies at the age of 110.

Chapter
50

Joseph's identity
Joseph finally revealed his identity to his brothers. They were not entirely happy to learn that he was alive and well.

Exodus

Overview

The Book of Exodus describes the formation of a people, the People of God. Under the leadership of Moses, from being cowed and hopeless serfs in a powerful, well-organised and hostile country a rabble of escaped slaves became a coherent nation with a constitution, a protector and a purpose. The covenant made with them by God and the way of life dictated by it would shape Israel down through the ages. At the breaking and renewal of the covenant their God revealed himself to them as a loving God of forgiveness who would remain faithful and would continue to save them from their infidelities and rebellions.

This book, fundamental to Israel's way of life, consists of folk history and laws. It is impossible to re-establish the exact historical events of the departure from Egypt. Israel retained the memory of the 'strong right arm of the LORD' which forced

Moses in a basket
Moses' mother placed him in a basket and then put him in the Nile near where Pharaoh's daughter regularly bathed.

17

Chapter 1	After Joseph and all his brothers die, the Israelite population grows rapidly. To control the Israelite population growth, the Pharaoh decrees the death of all male Israelite babies.

17

Chapter 2	After rescuing him from a reed basket, Pharaoh's daughter raises Moses as her own. Moses later kills an Egyptian, flees to Midian, marries and lives as a shepherd.

Chapter 2: **Commentary**

Stories of miraculous preservation in infancy are told of many great figures in history. This story is linked to the explanation of the name 'Moses' by means of the verb *masah*, to draw out, for Moses was drawn out of the water. In fact the name is more likely explained as a shortened version of a name often compounded with a divine name, as in Ra-moses or Tut-moses.

When she could hide him no longer she got a papyrus basket for him, and plastered it with bitumen and pitch; she put the child in it and placed it among the reeds on the bank of the river. His sister stood at a distance, to see what would happen to him.

The daughter of Pharaoh came down to bathe at the river, while her attendants walked beside the river. She saw the basket among the reeds and sent her maid to bring it. When she opened it, she saw the child. He was crying, and she took pity on him. 'This must be one of the Hebrews' children,' she said.

Exodus 2:3–6

Pharaoh to let them go and frustrated attempts to recapture them, but their numbers, their route and the date remain obscure. The most likely Pharaoh of the Exodus is Ramses II (1290–1224 BC), the powerful and long-lived monarch whose monuments are still visible in Egypt today. Above all, they remembered their experience of God on Mount Sinai, a manifestation of God described in terms of earthquake, thunder and lightning, when God took them once and for all to himself, giving them a covenant and law by which to live as his own people. The earliest code of law, the laws of a nomadic people, still wandering in the desert of Sinai, is laid down in the Book of the Covenant. The basic aims of these laws are to honour and worship this awesome God, and to treat all human beings with respect as his chosen ones.

Chapter 3: **Commentary**

There are two accounts of the call of Moses, here and in chapter 6:2–13. Both centre on the awe that inspired and invigorated Moses for his task. To give a name is a sign of trust and friendship. The name given here is too awesome and too intimate to be pronounced, but the meaning of the name is unclear. All Hebrew names were explained (not always accurately) in terms of a similar word. The Greek version of the Bible understands the name by the verb 'to be', so 'The one who is'.

God said to Moses, 'I AM WHO I AM. He said further, 'Thus you shall say to the Israelites,: "I AM has sent me to you".'

God also said to Moses, 'Thus you shall say to the Israelites, "The LORD, the God of your ancestors – the God of Abraham, the God of Isaac and the God of Jacob – has sent me to you".'

'This is my name forever, the name you shall call me from generation to generation.'

Exodus 3:14–15

Moses meets God
When Moses sees the burning bush he is told to take off his sandals, for he is standing on holy ground.

 8   17

God speaks to Moses from a burning bush and sends him to Egypt to rescue the Israelites from slavery. God identifies himself as the LORD, the God of Abraham, Isaac and Jacob.

Chapter
3

8	**17**
Chapter **4**	Moses returns to Egypt able to perform three miracles. God tries to kill Moses' uncircumcised son, forcing his wife to circumcise him in order to save his life.

8	**12**	**17**
Chapter **5**	Moses and Aaron asks Pharaoh to let the people take a three-day journey into the wilderness in order to sacrifice to the LORD. Pharaoh refuses and oppresses the slaves even more.	

7	**16**
Chapter **6**	God reassures Moses that eventually Pharaoh will let the Israelites go, despite Moses' serious doubts. A genealogy of Moses' family follows.

8	**9**
Chapter **7**	An 80-year-old Moses turns his staff into a snake, then brings the first plague: all the water in Egypt turns into blood. Pharaoh refuses to let the people go.

8	**9**
Chapter **8**	The second plague: frogs. The third plague: gnats. The fourth plague: flies. And still the Pharaoh refuses to let the people go.

8	**9**
Chapter **9**	The fifth plague: the livestock all die. The sixth plague: boils on everyone. The seventh plague: hail. But Pharaoh repeatedly refuses to let the Israelites go.

Chapter 5: **Commentary**

The stubbornness of Pharaoh and the increasing drama of the demonstrations of God's power serve to show the impossibility of resisting the divine will. It appears as though Pharaoh is deliberately hardened to demonstrate God's power, but in biblical thought no distinction is made between God causing and God allowing.

God also spoke to Moses and said to him: 'I am the LORD. I appeared to Abraham, Isaac and Jacob as God Almighty, but by my name "The LORD" I did not make myself known to them. I also established my covenant with them, to give them the land of Canaan, the land in which they resided as aliens. I have also heard the groaning of the Israelites, whom the Egyptians are holding as slaves, and I have remembered my covenant.

Say therefore to the Israelites, "I am the LORD, and I will free you from the burdens of the Egyptians and deliver you from slavery to them. I will redeem you with an outstretched arm and with mighty acts of judgement."'

Exodus 6:2–6

Chapter 7: **Commentary**

The number and content of the Plagues of Egypt vary in different biblical accounts (compare Psalm 78 and Wisdom 11). Here they are presented in three groups of three, leading up to the final plague. They are based on an intensification of occurrences natural to the region, such as the discolouration and flooding of the Nile, and the proliferation of insects. There is a certain amount of duplication: the cattle are killed twice, and mosquitoes and horseflies may overlap. They serve to show the relative helplessness of the Egyptian magicians.

Then Moses and Aaron went out from Pharaoh; and Moses cried out to the LORD concerning the frogs that he had brought upon Pharaoh. And the LORD did as Moses requested: the frogs died in the houses, the courtyards, and the fields. And they gathered them together in heaps, and the land stank. But when Pharaoh saw that there was a respite, he hardened his heart, and would not listen to them, just as the LORD had said.

Exodus 8:12–15

The Plagues of Egypt
God sent a series of ten plagues against the Pharaoh of Egypt, creating both human and financial disaster.

So Moses stretched out his staff over the land of Egypt, and the LORD brought an east wind upon the land all that day and all that night; when morning came, the east wind had brought the locusts. The locusts came upon all the land of Egypt and settled on the whole country of Egypt, such a dense swarm of locusts as had never been before, nor ever shall be again. They covered the surface of the whole land, so that the land was black; and they ate all the plants in the land and all the fruit of the trees that the hail had left; nothing green was left, no tree, no plant in the field, in all the land of Egypt.

Exodus 10:13–15

Chapter 11: **Commentary**

Is God here murderously unfair? The folk history may have exaggerated and generalised a much more limited event. The inclusion of the firstborn of animals suggests confusion with the Israelite ritual of voluntarily offering the firstborn to God in recognition of divine power over all fertility and life.

Chapter 12: **Commentary**

The account of the Passover is in fact a list of instructions for the observance of the festival, or rather what was originally two festivals. The Passover is built upon an ancient nomadic festival at the first full moon of spring, when nomads offered to their god a prime member of the flock to win protection for the rest, a protection registered by the blood on the door posts. They then set out on the journey from their winter to their summer pastures. Israel adopted this festival to commemorate their great 40-year journey. To this was later joined the feast of unleavened bread, marking the beginning of the agricultural barley-harvest; this can have occurred only after their arrival in Canaan. The number of 600,000 fighting men would represent a total of several million people, which hardly fits the rest of the story. It may be taken from a later census, or simply exaggerated. Alternatively, the word translated 'thousand' may mean also 'family', which would give 600 families.

8 | **9**

The eighth plague: locusts. Pharaoh agrees to let the men go, but God is not satisfied. The ninth plague brings darkness, and once again the Pharaoh tells Moses no.

Chapter
10

8 | **9**

For the tenth plague Moses warns Pharaoh that all the firstborn of Egypt will die at midnight, while all the Israelites will be spared. Pharaoh refuses to listen.

Chapter
11

4 | **8** | **11**

God establishes the Passover ceremony to remind his people of the Exodus from Egypt. After the firstborn die, Pharaoh tells them to go and worship their God.

Chapter
12

8 | **17**

The Israelites leave Egypt, with God moving ahead of them, appearing as a pillar of cloud by day and a pillar of fire by night.

Chapter
13

Meeting before Pharaoh
Moses and Aaron stood before Pharaoh and demanded that he let the Israelites leave Egypt to worship the LORD.

Crossing the sea
After the winds blew all night long, a passage through the sea opened, allowing the Israelites to escape from the pursuing Egyptian army.

Chapter 14: **Commentary**

The Hebrew text specifies the crossing of the Sea of Reeds. There are many shallow, reedy lakes where the Suez Canal now runs. The expression 'Red Sea' comes only from the Greek version. The basis of the account is probably the crossing of such a reedy lake. A miraculous strong wind lowered the level of the lake sufficiently for the Hebrews to get across. When the wind ceased the Egyptian chariotry, unused to water, was overwhelmed and panicked. As Miriam's triumph-song states, 'Horse and rider he has thrown into the sea.'

Chapter 16: **Commentary**

The story about manna is based on a sweet secretion from the tamarisk tree, which grows on Sinai. The linkage of the story to the Sabbath indicates the hand of the priestly writer, probably during or after the Babylonian Exile. Exhausted quails are often found on Sinai during the migration season. The story stresses God's loving care for his people.

⑧   **⑰**

Chapter **14**

When Pharaoh realises the Israelites are not returning, he sends his army after them. God parts the Red Sea so the Israelites can escape, then drowns the pursuing Egyptian army.

①   **⑤**   **⑧**

Chapter **15**

Moses and the Israelites sing to the LORD. Then Miriam, Moses' sister, sings and dances. Three days later Moses tosses a piece of wood into a bitter spring to make it drinkable.

⑧

Chapter **16**

In the Desert of Sin the people wish for food like they'd enjoyed in Egypt. So God sends them quails for meat and provides manna each morning for bread.

Chapter 20: **Commentary**

The Ten Commandments sum up a way of life founded on honour for the one God and respect for all human beings. If read positively, rather than negatively, they express a whole system of values of a caring society, alert to the needs of families and individuals.

The traditional Jewish arrangement of
the Ten Commandments is as follows:

1. I am the LORD your God
2. You shall have no other gods before me; make no idols
3. Do not misuse God's name
4. Remember the Sabbath and sanctify it
5. Honour your father and mother
6. Do not murder
7. Do not commit adultery
8. Do not steal
9. Do not bear false witness
10. Do not covet

Chapter 21: **Commentary**

Many of these laws also appear in other contemporary Near Eastern law-codes. The way they are framed shows that they grow out of individual decisions and case-lore. They receive an enhanced value as the laws and customs decreed by God for his own people. They insist particularly on the value and self-respect owed to every individual. This Code of the Covenant chiefly concerns a society of herders and shepherds, not yet settled in their own land. The principle of proportionate compensation, 'an eye for an eye and a tooth for a tooth' (verse 24), is designed to limit vengeance. In the New Testament Jesus will outlaw revenge altogether.

Chapter 23: **Commentary**

The three great pilgrimage festivals which will be centred on the Temple at Jerusalem are Unleavened Bread, the beginning of Harvest and Ingathering at the end of the agricultural year. The prohibition of boiling a young goat in its mother's milk (verse 19) outlaws a Canaanite magical practice; it has become the basis of kosher regulations in Judaism.

Chapter 24: **Commentary**

The covenant is doubly ratified, firstly by the verbal acceptance by all the people, which is marked by the 12 standing stones, one for each tribe. Then it is ritually ratified by the sacrifices. Blood is the sign of life, and to scatter the blood over the altar (symbolising God) and the people signifies a sharing of life. The whole is completed by another visit of Moses to the awesome presence of the LORD on the mountain, from which he returns in chapter 32.

---

8   **17**

When Moses strikes the rock at Horeb, water gushes out despite the Israelites' worries. The Israelites defeat the Amalekites as long as Moses holds his staff over his head.

Chapter
17

8   **17**

Moses' father-in-law Jethro visits, bringing Moses' wife Zipporah and his sons with him. He also helps Moses set up an organisation for governing the Israelites.

Chapter
18

14   **17**

Moses and the people travel into the desert and camp in front of Mount Sinai. God calls Moses up to the mountain top, but warns the people of Israel to wait below.

Chapter
19

3   **14**

On top of the mountain, God speaks the Ten Commandments to Moses and makes a point to prohibit idol-making; God also explains how to properly construct altars.

Chapter
20

3   **14**

God regulates the treatment of Hebrew servants, explains how to handle personal injuries and establishes the principle of eye for eye, limiting the harshness of penalties.

Chapter
21

3   **14**

God gives Moses laws regarding property, compensation for losses and regulated sexual behaviour, and establishes protection for foreigners, widows and orphans.

Chapter
22

3   **14**

God demands impartial justice. He establishes the six-day work week and three annual festivals: Unleavened Bread, Harvest and Ingathering. God prohibits treaties with the Canaanites.

Chapter
23

8   **14**   **17**

Moses, Aaron, Nadab, Abihu and 70 elders of Israel go up on Mount Sinai to have a meal with God and confirm their covenant with him.

Chapter
24

11

Chapter
25

God asks the Israelites to bring Moses the materials to build a Tabernacle. God explains how to make the Ark of the Covenant, the Table and the Lampstand.

11

Chapter
26

God instructs the Israelites on how to make his Tabernacle, which will serve as a portable Temple for worshipping God.

11

Chapter
27

God tells the Israelites to build an altar for the burnt offerings and explains all the utensils that it will need; he also describes how to make the Lampstand oil.

11

Chapter
28

God explains how to make the priestly clothing: the *ephod*, a breastpiece of gold with its 12 gems, the robes, the tunics and even the undergarments.

11

Chapter
29

God specifies how the priests have to be consecrated over seven days: the clothing, the anointing, the sacrifices, the blood, the special bread and the drink offerings.

11

Chapter
30

God specifies the design of the incense altar, the incense, the anointing oil and the bronze washbasin. Every Israelite has to pay a half-shekel tax for the Tabernacle.

11

Chapter
31

God picks Bezalel and Oholiab to manufacture all the materials needed for worshipping God. Then God gives Moses two tablets of stone bearing the Ten Commandments.

9   **17**

Chapter
32

Moses discovers the Israelites worshipping a calf idol and partying. He smashes the tablets and the idol. Then the Levites slaughter 3,000 and God sends a plague.

Chapter 25: **Commentary**

The instructions about the sanctuary, and their fulfilment in chapters 35–40, are far too complicated for any portable desert sanctuary. They refer to the Temple eventually built at Jerusalem, and constitute a statement that the liturgical furnishings of the Temple were and always had been an integral part of the covenant. Some elements may, of course, go back to the portable Tent of Meeting in the desert.

'You shall further command the Israelites to bring you pure oil of beaten olives for the light, so that a lamp may be set up to burn regularly. In the tent of meeting, outside the curtain that is before the covenant, Aaron and his sons shall tend it from evening to morning before the LORD. It shall be a perpetual ordinance to be observed throughout their generations by the Israelites.'

Exodus 27:20–21

Chapter 32: **Commentary**

The journey through the desert is sometimes seen as a honeymoon period of perfect fidelity, sometimes as a period of testing and rebellion. Here the latter motif predominates, for Israel's idolatry breaks the fundamental first commandment. The 'golden calf' is so called to belittle it. The cult object will have been a bull, in the Near East a frequent image of the divinity for its strength and life-potency. Gods are often depicted standing on bulls.

When Joshua heard the noise of the people as they shouted, he said to Moses, 'There is a noise of war in the camp.'
But he said,
'It is not the sound made by victors,
or the sound made by losers;
it is the sound of revellers that I hear.'
As soon as he came near the camp and saw the calf and the dancing, Moses' anger burned hot, and he threw the tablets from his hands and broke them at the foot of the mountain. He took the calf that they had made, burned it with fire, ground it to powder, scattered it on the water, and made the Israelites drink it.

Exodus 32:17–20

Chapters 33–34: **Commentary**

Shocked by the disgraceful behaviour of the people, Moses intercedes for them and begs to see the glory of the LORD. No human being can see God and live, but the LORD passes before Moses and at last reveals the meaning of the sacred name YHWH, calling out, 'A God of tenderness and compassion, rich in forgiveness'. This is the concept of God that shaped Israel; it is quoted and referred to again and again throughout the Bible.

Breaking the law
While Moses was with God on Mount Sinai for 40 days, the Israelites turned to idolatry. In fury upon his return, Moses smashed the tablets with the Ten Commandments.

Chapter 40: **Commentary**

The cloud is the symbol of the divine presence. The same phenomenon will be repeated at Solomon's dedication of the Temple in 1 Kings 8, and in Isaiah's vision in the Temple in Isaiah 6. The same imagery occurs in the column of cloud that led the Israelites through the desert.

---

2 **12**

Moses begs God to forgive the Israelites, which he does. Then Moses asks to see God's glory, but God only lets him see his back.

Chapter
33

3 **8** **17**

God tells Moses to make replacements for the two smashed stone tablets and then to meet him back on Mount Sinai so he can rewrite the Ten Commandments for him.

Chapter
34

11

The people bring the materials that they need for building the Tabernacle and associated items. Then Bezalel, Oholiab and other skilled people set to work.

Chapter
35

11 **16**

The Israelites donate more material than the workers need. The building and design of the Tabernacle is given in great detail.

Chapter
36

11 **16**

Bezalel makes the Ark of the Covenant; the details of its materials, shape and size are given. Others construct the Table, Lampstand and the Altar of Incense.

Chapter
37

11 **16**

The other workers build the Altar of Burnt Offering, the Basin for Washing and the Courtyard. There is a detailed listing of the materials used.

Chapter
38

11 **16**

Skilled workers at last make all the priestly garments. Once everything has been manufactured, Moses inspects it, then blesses the people for their hard work.

Chapter
39

8 **11**

God tells Moses to set up the Tabernacle, consecrate the priests and place the tablets of the law inside the Ark of the Covenant. Then the glory of God fills the Tabernacle.

Chapter
40

Leviticus

Overview

The Book of Leviticus codifies Israel's liturgical response to God, and is vital in showing how Israel understood and responded to the holiness of God. It is called 'Leviticus' because the tribe of Levi was the priestly tribe, the custodians of the ritual of sacrifice and the annual feasts that provided the rhythms of Israel's life. Israel's view of life and of its relationship to God circled around the ritual of sacrifice.

The first part of the book prescribes the preparation and investiture of the priests who perform much of the ritual of sacrifice. The second part classifies the familiar elements of life into clean

---

II

Chapter 1

Moses is to sacrifice a burnt offering: the sort of animal to be burnt is based on how much the one making the sacrifice can afford.

II

Chapter 2

God explains the requirements for a grain offering.

II

Chapter 3

God explains the requirements for a fellowship offering.

II

Chapter 4

God explains the requirements for a sin offering. The animal to be sacrificed varies depending upon who has sinned: priest, community or citizen.

3 **II**

Chapter 5

God explains that anyone who does not bear witness when asked has to make a sin offering. Those who sin unintentionally have to make a guilt offering.

Chapter 1: **Commentary**

The first three chapters describe the ritual for the three basic types of sacrifice: an animal completely burnt, a cereal offering of which part is given to the priests and an offering that is shared between God and the offerer. This last is ritual slaughter of an animal for food, with the recognition that all life, represented by the blood, is a gift of God. The gesture of laying hands on the head of the animal signifies the identification of the offerer with the animal.

If the offering is a burnt-offering from the herd, you shall offer a male without blemish; you shall bring it to the entrance of the tent of meeting, for acceptance in your behalf before the LORD. You shall lay your hand on the head of the burnt-offering, and it shall be acceptable in your behalf as atonement for you. The bull shall be slaughtered before the LORD; and Aaron's sons the priests shall offer the blood, dashing the blood against all sides of the altar that is at the entrance of the tent of meeting. The burnt-offering shall be flayed and cut up into its parts.

Leviticus 1:3–6

Chapter 4: **Commentary**

A sin committed inadvertently may seem a contradiction in terms, but it was still felt that it could violate the natural order, especially if it transgressed the rules of clean and unclean. Carelessness can also be culpable.

and unclean. Many of these rules are based on obvious principles of hygiene, others on ancient superstitions whose meaning is obscure to us. The third part is called the Holiness Code, a set of rules by which Israel expresses its awareness that the processes of life and death are awesome, especially linked to the divine holiness.

Although the rituals prescribed in this book are ancient and often mysterious, the book itself and its instructions probably reached its final form at the end of the Babylonian Exile, perhaps as late as the fifth century BC. Its ascription to Moses and its position among the first books of the Bible shows its importance for Israel's life and attitudes.

Chapters 6: **Commentary**

The daily offering in the Temple was an essential witness to Israel's continuing loyalty to God. It was interrupted only by the Sack of the Temple by Nebuchadnezzar and the desecration of the Temple by Antiochus Epiphanes. It permanently ceased only at the Sack of the Temple by the Romans in AD 70.

Then Moses said to Aaron, 'This is what the LORD meant when he said:
    "Through those who are near me
I will show myself holy;
and before all the people
I will be glorified."'
    And Aaron was silent.

Leviticus 10:3

Chapter 11: **Commentary**

Many of these taboos are built on theories of hygiene, but also reflect the Israelite map of life (as the eating of dogs is abhorrent in many modern societies). Scavengers and reptiles are particularly avoided, and the only fish allowed are those that can be preserved by salting.

Chapter 12: **Commentary**

The law of uncleanness after childbirth is in fact a way of protecting women from sexual molestation at an important moment. Male circumcision, originally a puberty ritual of cleanliness, became a sign of belonging to the People of God, so an expression of faith.

11 The guilt offering also applies for someone who deceives a neighbour. Detailed regulations regarding burnt offerings, grain offerings and sin offerings. — Chapter 6

11 God explains the guilt offering and fellowship offering. He prohibits eating fat and blood, and decides what sacrificed portions belonged to the priests. — Chapter 7

11 God has Moses ordain Aaron and his sons as God's priests; the ceremony of ordination is described in detail. — Chapter 8

11 Aaron and his sons perform a series of sin offerings, burnt offerings, fellowship offerings and grain offerings. Then fire comes and consumes the burnt offerings. — Chapter 9

3 9 11 Nadab and Abihu offer the wrong incense, so God kills them. Then Moses warns Aaron and his sons not to drink alcohol while serving in the Tabernacle. — Chapter 10

3 16 God lists the animals that the Israelites can eat, such as cows and grasshoppers, as well as those they can't eat, such as pigs and reptiles. — Chapter 11

3 Women were ceremonially unclean for 40 or 80 days after giving birth, depending on the child's gender. Sons have to be circumcised on the eighth day after birth. — Chapter 12

3

Chapter
13

God explains how to handle someone who comes down with a skin disease like leprosy. God also explains what to do about mould that might appear on fabric.

3

Chapter
14

After someone has been cleansed from a skin disease or fabric mould, the priest certifies it and then offers sacrifices.

3

Chapter
15

God explains what to do about bodily discharges of various sorts – such as blood, pus or semen – and the sacrifices to be offered as part of the cleansing ritual.

3

Chapter
16

Once a year on the Day of Atonement, the high priest enters the Most Holy Place to offer a sacrifice for the collective sins of the Israelite people.

3   **11**

Chapter
17

Sacrifices are to be performed only by the official priests and only at the Tabernacle. Eating blood or animals found dead is prohibited.

3

Chapter
18

The Israelites must not act like the Egyptians or Canaanites, and various sexual practices are forbidden. The Israelites must not sacrifice their children to the god Molek.

3

Chapter
19

God reiterates and expands upon the Ten Commandments, adding prohibitions against various occult practices. He tells them to love others, respect the aged and treat foreigners well.

Chapter 13: **Commentary**

The biblical concept of 'leprosy' is far wider than the modern diagnosis of *Microbacterium leprae*. It applies also to various skin diseases and mould or fungus on walls or fabrics. The purpose of the regulations is to avoid contagion. Freedom from the condition must be certified by a qualified person.

Chapter 15: **Commentary**

The regulations surrounding the life-giving processes of sex show the sacredness of this participation in the divine gift of life, as well as limiting sexually transmitted diseases and protecting the rights of women.

Chapter 16: **Commentary**

The ceremonies of the annual Day of Atonement combine several rituals. The expulsion of the scapegoat is a very ancient symbol of the expulsion of evil. The blood of sacrifice sprinkled on altar and on the people is a symbol of the renewal and sharing of life. Fasting is a symbol of repentance: if you are upset, you don't feel like eating.

Chapter 17: **Commentary**

The Code of Holiness (chapters 17–26) is the latest part of the book, probably post-exilic. It sets Israel apart from other nations, instructing them how to share in the holiness of God.

'You shall rise before the aged, and defer to the old; and you shall fear your God: I am the LORD.
'When an alien resides with you in your land, you shall not oppress the alien. The alien who resides with you shall be to you as the citizen among you; you shall love the alien as yourself, for you were aliens in the land of Egypt: I am the LORD your God.'
Leviticus 19:32–34

The Tabernacle
God gave the Israelites detailed instructions for how to build a tent for worship and sacrifice, and explained the details of how to dress the priests.

'For six days shall work be done; but the seventh day is a sabbath of complete rest, a holy convocation; you shall do no work: it is a sabbath to the LORD throughout your settlements.'

Leviticus 23:3

3

God explains the penalties that must be exacted for the violations of any of God's laws, repeating many of the prohibitions previously listed.

Chapter
20

3   **11**

Priestly behaviour is constrained: they are limited in whom they can marry and how they can behave when someone dies. The handicapped cannot become priests.

Chapter
21

11

Ceremonially unclean priests are excluded from sacrificial services. Food dedicated to God can only be consumed by priests and their families. Certain sacrifices are forbidden.

Chapter
22

Chapter 25: **Commentary**

The Sabbatical Year. As each seventh day is a day of rest for man, so each seventh year is a day of rest for the soil, and a recognition that all produce comes from the LORD. In the Jubilee Year (so called from *yobel*, trumpet, which announced the year), every Hebrew slave was to be set free, all debts cancelled and all land to revert to its ancestral owners. At different periods both these years will have been observed more or less faithfully.

11

The appointed Israelite holy days: the Sabbath, the Passover and Unleavened Bread, First Fruits, Festival of Weeks, Festival of Trumpets, Day of Atonement and the Festival of Tabernacles.

Chapter
23

3   **9**   **11**

Twelve loaves of bread sit on a table in the Tabernacle. God orders the execution of a man guilty of blasphemy and reiterates several other laws.

Chapter
24

'If you follow my statutes and keep my commandments and observe them faithfully, I will give you your rains in their season, and the land shall yield its produce, and the trees of the field shall yield their fruit. Your threshing shall overtake the vintage, and the vintage shall overtake the sowing; you shall eat your bread to the full, and live securely in your land. And I will grant peace in the land, and you shall lie down, and no one shall make you afraid; I will remove dangerous animals from the land, and no sword shall go through your land.'

Leviticus 26:3–6

3

Every seventh year the fields must not be ploughed or harvested. Every fiftieth year debts must be cancelled, land returned to its original owners and slaves freed.

Chapter
25

3   **14**

God promises blessing and prosperity for the Israelites if they keep his laws, punishments for disobedience and forgiveness for confession of sin and repentance.

Chapter
26

Chapter 27: **Commentary**

This appendix was added after the Exile. The ban, *herem*, of verses 28–29 was intended to prevent the contamination of Israel by other nations and customs, and to recognise that victory comes from God. It has often been dismissed as a mere theoretical ruling, but it is mercilessly applied in 1 Samuel 15:33.

3

God explains the regulations about dedicating something to God and the cost of redeeming it. He also explains what cannot be redeemed.

Chapter
27

Numbers

Overview

The Greek title of the Book as 'Numbers' is derived from the census at beginning and end. More apt is the Hebrew title, taken from the first words of the book, 'In the desert', for the book describes chiefly the wanderings of Israel through the desert, and the incidents there that contributed to the traditions and later lifestyle of the people after the settlement in Canaan. Some of the material, including ancient magical practices, may date from

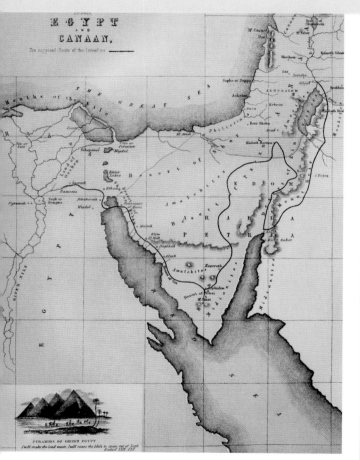

The wandering
The Israelites left the region of Goshen in Egypt and wandered in what is today called the Sinai Peninsula for 40 years. The black line on the map shows the route taken by the tribe.

Chapter 1: **Commentary**

Much of the material reflects a date later than the Exodus. Like many numbers given in the Bible, the numbers are symbolic rather than historical. The figures would represent a total population of two million. The 12 tribes are also a later construct: not all of them came out of Egypt. The tribe of Judah seems to have been formed later from several sub-groups.

The LORD spoke to Moses in the wilderness of Sinai, in the tent of meeting, on the first day of the second month, in the second year after they had come out of the land of Egypt, saying: 'Take a census of the whole congregation of Israelites, in their clans, by ancestral houses, according to the number of names, every male individually; from twenty years old and upwards, everyone in Israel able to go to war. You and Aaron shall enrol them, company by company. A man from each tribe shall be with you, each man the head of his ancestral house.'

Numbers 1:1–4

16

Chapter

1

Moses takes a census of the Israelite men 20 years old and older by tribes, for a total of 603,550, excluding the tribe of Levi.

an early period; other stories reflect David's conquests and empire; still other legislation comes from priestly legislation after the return from Exile. Altogether the book constitutes a rich inventory of the customs and concerns of the people of Israel. Particularly significant for Israel's hopes is the incident of Balaam (chapters 22–24).

Miriam, the sister of Moses
Miriam, Moses' sister who helped hide him while he was a baby, led the Israelites in celebratory song, and also challenged his leadership of the Israelites (Numbers 12).

'I hereby accept the Levites from among the Israelites as substitutes for all the firstborn that open the womb among the Israelites. The Levites shall be mine, for all the firstborn are mine; when I killed all the firstborn in the land of Egypt, I consecrated for my own all the firstborn in Israel, both human and animal; they shall be mine. I am the LORD.'

Numbers 3:12–13

Chapter 5: **Commentary**

Wives suspected of committing adultery were subjected to barbaric trials, which survived into the Middle Ages.

'Speak to the Israelites: "When a man or a woman wrongs another, breaking faith with the LORD, that person incurs guilt and shall confess the sin that has been committed. The person shall make full restitution for the wrong, adding one-fifth to it, and giving it to the one who was wronged."'

Numbers 5:6–7

16

Whenever the Israelites pause in their travels towards the Promised Land, the 12 tribes set up camp surrounding the Tabernacle, three to a side.

Chapter
2

16

Moses counts the Levites and the firstborn male Israelites. There are 273 more firstborn Israelites than there are Levite males; the excess have to pay five shekels each.

Chapter
3

16

Moses counts the Kohathite branch of the Levites and assigns them their duties. The same is then done for the Gershonite and Merarite Levitical branches.

Chapter
4

3

The ceremonially unclean sit outside the Israelite camp. Restitution must be made to those who have been wronged. A husband suspecting his wife of infidelity has certain options.

Chapter
5

3   **5**   **11**

Chapter 6

An Israelite can take a Nazirite vow to abstain from fermented beverages, grapes, raisins and haircuts. They must avoid dead bodies. The priests offer a blessing.

11   **16**

Chapter 7

During the 12 days it takes for the Tabernacle to be dedicated and opened for worship, each of the tribes bring gifts of silver, gold and animals for sacrifice.

11

Chapter 8

The Levites are consecrated to God's service in a public ceremony. Only Levites between the ages of 25 and 50 are allowed to serve in the Tabernacle.

8   **11**

Chapter 9

During the second year out from Egypt the people celebrate Passover. Then God's cloud covers the newly dedicated Tabernacle. The Israelites resume their travels only when the cloud lifts.

16

Chapter 10

Two silver trumpets are made to call the community together and to break camp. After God's cloud lifts, the Israelites leave the Sinai and travel for three days.

7   **9**

Chapter 11

The people complain about the food, and Moses intercedes for them. God sends his spirit on 70 of the Israelite elders to help Moses.

'The LORD bless you and keep you;
the LORD make his face to shine upon you
and be gracious to you;
the LORD lift up his countenance upon you
and give you peace.
So they shall put my name on the Israelites, and I
will bless them.'

Numbers 6:24–27

Chapter 6: **Commentary**

Nazir means 'to set apart'. The uncut hair is a symbol of strength dedicated to the LORD; abstention from grapes signifies avoidance of all luxury; the strict rules of cleanliness resemble those of priestly consecration.

Chapter 9: **Commentary**

Throughout the Bible a cloud is often a symbol of the presence of God, moving mysteriously and unpredictably. When Solomon dedicates the Temple, it is filled with such a cloud, symbolising the divine presence (1 Kings 8). When the presence of God leaves the Temple at the Exile, it is in a cloud (Ezekiel 10). At the Transfiguration of Jesus, he is covered with a bright cloud (Matthew 17).

On the day the tabernacle was set up, the cloud
covered the tabernacle, the tent of the covenant;
and from evening until morning it was over the
tabernacle, having the appearance of fire. It was
always so: the cloud covered it by day and the
appearance of fire by night. Whenever the cloud
lifted from over the tent, then the Israelites would
set out; and in the place where the cloud settled
down, there the Israelites would camp.

Numbers 9:15–17

So Moses said to the LORD, 'Why have you treated
your servant so badly? Why have I not found
favour in your sight, that you lay the burden of all
this people on me? Did I conceive all this people?
Did I give birth to them, that you should say to me,
"Carry them in your bosom, as a nurse carries a
sucking child", to the land that you promised on
oath to their ancestors? Where am I to get meat to
give to all this people? For they come weeping to me
and say, "Give us meat to eat!" I am not able to
carry all this people alone, for they are too heavy
for me.'

Numbers 11:11–15

Chapters 13–14: **Commentary**

This is a composite narrative. The original describes a reconnaissance into Canaan; most of the envoys give an unfavourable report, and a half-hearted attack fails. A Deuteronomic addition (14:13–25) allows the tribe of Caleb to enter from the south, though the majority of Israel entered from the east, north of the Dead Sea. A further addition (13:21, 14:26–38) sends the expedition to the far north, a few kilometres short of Damascus.

And they came to the Wadi Eshcol, and cut down from there a branch with a single cluster of grapes, and they carried it on a pole between two of them. They also brought some pomegranates and figs. That place was called the Wadi Eshcol, because of the cluster that the Israelites cut down from there. At the end of forty days they returned from spying out the land.

Numbers 13:23–25

And they told him, 'We came to the land to which you sent us; it flows with milk and honey, and this is its fruit. Yet the people who live in the land are strong, and the towns are fortified and very large; and besides, we saw the descendants of Anak there. The Amalekites live in the land of the Negeb; the Hittites, the Jebusites and the Amorites live in the hill country; and the Canaanites live by the sea, and along the Jordan.'

Numbers 13:27–29

Chapter 16: **Commentary**

The punishment of rebellion. Sheol is the underworld, the abode of the dead, where all lead a powerless half-life, unable even to praise God. Belief in life after death is not developed until 2 Maccabees 7 and Daniel 12, though it is hinted in several of the Psalms.

2	9	17

Moses marries a Cushite, so Miriam and Aaron complain about Moses' leadership. God tells them that Moses is rightfully in charge and gives Miriam leprosy for a week.

Chapter 12

17		

Moses sends 12 men to explore Canaan, one from each tribe. Ten say it is impossible to conquer Canaan, but Joshua and Caleb disagree.

Chapter 13

The grapes of Canaan
They cut off a branch bearing a single cluster of grapes. Two of them carried it on a pole between them (Numbers 13:23).

2	9	12

The Israelites want to give up and return to Egypt. Therefore God tells them that those more than 20 years old will die in the wilderness.

Chapter 14

3	9

Additional regulations: atonement for faults of inadvertence. Sabbath-breaking is punished by death.

Chapter 15

9	

Korah, Dathan and Abiram rebel against Moses' authority, and are punished by being swallowed up by the earth.

Chapter 16

8 **17**

Chapter
17

God puts an end to the grumbling against Moses and Aaron once and for all when, out of 12 labelled staffs, only Aaron's sprouts, buds and produces almonds.

11

Chapter
18

Only Aaron and his descendants can be priests. The other Levites serve as support staff. No priests or Levites are allowed to own any land.

11

Chapter
19

A red heifer is sacrificed. Its ashes are put in a ceremonially clean place, to be mixed, as needed, in water to 'cleanse' those who have touched the dead.

4 **17**

Chapter
20

Moses' sister Miriam dies. After the Edomites forbid the Israelites passage through their land, Moses' brother Aaron dies.

9 **17**

Chapter
21

The capture of Arad in the northern Negeb desert. Israel's grumbling brings on a plague of serpents, checked by a magical remedy.

8 **17**

Chapter
22

On his way to curse the Israelites for Moab's king Balak, Balaam's donkey talks to him. Then an angel warns Balaam to speak only God's words.

5 **7** **17**

Chapter
23

Balaam pronounces two blessings on the Israelites instead of curses. An angry Balak takes Balaam to a different spot and orders him to curse them.

5 **7** **17**

Chapter
24

Instead of a curse, once again, Balaam offers a blessing. An angry Balak sends Balaam away unpaid, so Balaam pronounces four more blessings upon the Israelites.

Moses spoke to the Israelites; and all their leaders gave him staffs, one for each leader, according to their ancestral houses, twelve staffs; and the staff of Aaron was among theirs. So Moses placed the staffs before the LORD in the tent of the covenant. When Moses went into the tent of the covenant on the next day, the staff of Aaron for the house of Levi had sprouted. It put forth buds, produced blossoms, and bore ripe almonds.

Numbers 17:6–8

Chapter 19: **Commentary**

Red is the colour of blood, and so of life. This and some other magical rites were adopted from the surrounding peoples, for example trial by ordeal (5:16–28) and the scapegoat (Leviticus 16:5–10).

Chapter 20: **Commentary**

Moses striking the rock is described also in Exodus 17. His punishment seems disproportionate to his fault. Perhaps his real fault was so grave that it was suppressed out of reverence for this great leader.

Chapter 21: **Commentary**

This sympathetic magic, snake to ward off snake, is attached to the ancient bronzeworks of Timnah, near Elath, where such copper snakes have been found. It is also the origin of the sign of medical care still used today. The stories of conflict with Transjordan cause historical difficulties: there were no kings of Moab at the time, and the country was not sufficiently inhabited or organised to prevent passage. There may be some reading back from the later continuous conflicts between Israel and the territories of Moab and Edom.

Chapter 22: **Commentary**

The story of Balaam is full of irony and humour. Such professional seers were known in Mesopotamia, but not all their donkeys found speech, let alone instructed their masters. Balaam's final oracle is already redolent of royal messianic promises (24:17) and of the conflict with the Philistines (24:24).

God is not a human being, that he should lie,
  or a mortal, that he should change his mind.
Has he promised, and will he not do it?
  Has he spoken, and will he not fulfil it?
See, I received a command to bless;
  he has blessed, and I cannot revoke it.

Numbers 23:19–20

The LORD said to Moses, 'Go up this mountain of the Abarim range, and see the land that I have given to the Israelites. When you have seen it, you also shall be gathered to your people, as your brother Aaron was, because you rebelled against my word in the wilderness of Zin when the congregation quarrelled with me.

Numbers 27:12–14

Chapter 28: **Commentary**

These regulations about festivals must be post-exilic, when the Jewish community in the Holy Land was gathered within convenient distance of Jerusalem. But these and all the other regulations are anachronistically attributed to Moses, even though there was no fixed sanctuary in his time, as a way of showing that the whole Jewish way of life was a consequence of the establishment of the People of God at the time of the Exodus.

⑨ ⑰

Leaders of the people engage in idolatrous worship. Phinehas spears a couple in the act of idolatrous fertility rites.

Chapter **25**

⑯

After the plague, Moses takes a second census of the Israelites. Everyone counted in the first census had died during the 40 years of wandering.

Chapter **26**

③ ⑰

The daughters of Zelophehad are the first women to be given inheritance rights. Joshua is appointed as leader in succession to Moses.

Chapter **27**

③ ⑰

A summary of the regular offerings and sacrifices: the daily, weekly and monthly sacrifices, along with those for Passover and the Festival of Weeks.

Chapter **28**

Aaron's staff that blossomed
After Korah's rebellion against Moses and Aaron, God had Moses collect 12 staffs, one each from the leader of every Israelite tribe. Only the staff of Aaron blossomed.

①

Chapter **29**

A summary of the offerings and sacrifices on the Festival of Trumpets, the Day of Atonement and the Festival of Tabernacles.

③

Chapter **30**

Vows are usually unbreakable, but the father of an unmarried woman, or the husband of a married woman, can disavow any vow she makes when he first learns about it.

⑨   **⑰**

Chapter **31**

The Israelites kill every male Moabite and Midianite, including King Balak and the prophet Balaam, and take their women, children, and livestock as spoils.

⑰

Chapter **32**

The tribes of Reuben, Gad and Manasseh are allowed to settle east of the Jordan when their men agree to fight alongside the other tribes until all Canaan is conquered.

Chapter 30: **Commentary**

The regulations of this chapter reflect the continuing inferior status of women, but do at least provide some independent security for them.

When a man makes a vow to the LORD, or swears an oath to bind himself by a pledge, he shall not break his word; he shall do according to all that proceeds out of his mouth.

Numbers 30:2

Chapter 31: **Commentary**

The regulations about dedication of captives and spoil to the LORD reflect the post-exilic concern to avoid contamination with the religion of surrounding peoples. They remained theoretical, and there is no evidence that they were generally put into practice.

Passover Seder
Every year the Israelites were to remember how God rescued them from Egyptian slavery and brought them to their Promised Land.

Hebrew holidays Names (English, Hebrew)	Dates (Hebrew and Modern)
Sabbath, Shabbat	every seven days
Passover, Pesach	15–16 Nisan (March–April)
Festival of Weeks, Pentecost, Shavuot	6–7 Sivan (May–June)
Festival of Trumpets, Rosh Hashana	1 Tisri (September–October)
Day of Atonement, Yom Kippur	9 Tisri (September–October)
Festival of Tabernacles, Booths, Succot	15–21 Tisri (September–October)

The Jewish calendar is a lunar calendar. Therefore, the dates of the holidays vary from year to year on our common Gregorian calendar, which is a solar calendar.

Balaam and his donkey
Balaam's donkey stopped in its tracks because it saw an angel blocking the path. Balaam beat the donkey, who then explained why he was refusing to budge.

'You shall take possession of the land and settle in it, for I have given you the land to possess. You shall apportion the land by lot according to your clans; to a large one you shall give a large inheritance, and to a small one you shall give a small inheritance; the inheritance shall belong to the person on whom the lot falls; according to your ancestral tribes you shall inherit.

'But if you do not drive out the inhabitants of the land from before you, then those whom you let remain shall be as barbs in your eyes and thorns in your sides; they shall trouble you in the land where you are settling. And I will do to you as I thought to do to them.'

Numbers 33:53–56

'The towns that you give to the Levites shall include the six cities of refuge, where you shall permit a slayer to flee, and in addition to them you shall give forty-two towns.

Numbers 35:6

16   *17*

A summary of the Israelites' journeys from the time they leave Egypt until they stand on the plains of Moab across from Jericho.

Chapter
33

16

The boundaries of Canaan. One man from each tribe is to help Eleazar and Joshua in the distribution of land.

Chapter
34

16

The Levites grant certain towns scattered throughout the nation. Six of those towns became Cities of Refuge for those guilty of involuntary manslaughter.

Chapter
35

3

The daughters of Zelophehad are required to marry only members of their own tribe, so that their father's property does not end up being transferred to another tribe.

Chapter
36

Deuteronomy

Overview

Faced with the threat of the growing power of Babylon, King Josiah of Judah mounted a great reform movement in 612 BC, centralising religious activity on Jerusalem and abolishing the contaminated and possibly idolatrous ceremonies of local shrines. In the course of the restoration of the Temple a book was produced from the Temple, which was acclaimed as a second version of the Law of Moses. It is impossible now to re-establish the age or extent of this book; it may be the product of the short-lived reform of King Hezekiah, half a century earlier. This version of the Law, faithful to the original, but adapted to a more advanced and stable form of civilisation, is the basis of the Book of Deuteronomy. The book is indebted to three different periods: the Law descended from Moses himself, the period of Josiah's reform on the eve of the Exile, and the period of the Exile itself. It probably even reached its final form after the return from Exile, for some of the

---

Chapter 1

Forty years after leaving Egypt, Moses explains how the Israelites ended up wandering in the wilderness until only Joshua and Caleb remained of the original group.

Chapter 1: **Commentary**

The travelogue of the first three chapters resumes the data of Numbers 13, 14 and 21, stressing the repeated rebellions of Israel, which will be an emphasis throughout the book. It was a time of testing and repeated failure.

Chapter 2

Moses summarises their history from leaving Kadesh Barnea until they defeated Sihon, king of Heshbon.

Surely the LORD your God has blessed you in all your undertakings; he knows your going through this great wilderness. These forty years the LORD your God has been with you; you have lacked nothing.

Deuteronomy 2:7

Chapter 3

Og is also defeated. So the lands of Sihon and Og are given to the tribes of Reuben and Gad. Moses cannot enter the Promised Land. Joshua will take his place.

Chapter 4

God will judge the Israelites if they disobey, but they could be forgiven. God is great and loves them. Bezer, Ramoth and Golan become Cities of Refuge.

For what other great nation has a god so near to it as the LORD our God is whenever we call to him? And what other great nation has statutes and ordinances as just as this entire law that I am setting before you today?

Deuteronomy 4:7–8

laws are adapted to a small community such as that huddled around the restored but restricted city of Jerusalem.

The pattern of the book provides the theme for the so-called Deuteronomic History, the main segment of the historical works of the Bible, running from the beginning of Joshua to the end of the Books of Kings. These were composed and edited to show the same pattern of the relationship between Israel and God, a cycle of Israel's infidelity, punishment by foreign invaders, repentance and rescue by God. This pattern is seen to be repeated time after time in the story of the Chosen People. It is pointed at intervals throughout these History Books. The passages where the editor of the Histories points the lesson are phrased in the characteristic, repetitive style of the Book of Deuteronomy itself, and must stem from the same school of thought.

Chapter 6: Commentary

Verses 4–6 are the central confession and prayer of Judaism, the *shema*, recited daily by every pious Jew. It is quoted also by Jesus as the chief of all the commandments, on which all others depend.

Hear, O Israel: The Lord is our God, the Lord alone. You shall love the Lord your God with all your heart, and with all your soul, and with all your might. Keep these words that I am commanding you today in your heart. Recite them to your children and talk about them when you are at home and when you are away, when you lie down and when you rise. Bind them as a sign on your hand, fix them as an emblem on your forehead, and write them on the doorposts of your house and on your gates.
Deuteronomy 6:4–9

Moses and the covenant
The Book of Deuteronomy was the formal contract that transferred ownership of Israel from Egypt to God.

③		⑭	
After repeating the Ten Commandments, Moses reminds them that he has become their mediator with God because they didn't want to hear God's voice any more.			Chapter 5

③		⑭	
Moses tells the people to love God and to keep his commandments, teaching them to their children and future generations.			Chapter 6

③   **⑭**

Chapter

7

Moses orders the Israelites to destroy both the Canaanites and their religion. God chooses the Israelites because he loves them; he will bless their obedience and punish their disobedience.

③   **⑭**

Chapter

8

The Israelites must not forget about God after they become prosperous in their new land. Moses warns that if they forget God, God will punish them.

③   **⑭**

Chapter

9

God gives Canaan to the Israelites not because they are righteous, but because the Canaanites were wicked. In fact the Israelites have a history of disobedience too.

③   **⑭**   **⑰**

Chapter

10

Moses reminds the Israelites how he replaced the Ten Commandments after smashing them. God is powerful. The people must love him and love each other.

Chapter 7: **Commentary**

There is no evidence that this brutal destruction was ever carried out. The legislation (also given in chapter 20) is probably post-exilic and merely theoretical, reflecting the fear of the vulnerable, fervent and tight-knit post-exilic community of being dissipated through contamination by the people around them. The archaeology of the period of entry into Canaan shows little sign of conquest; it was probably a result of gradual infiltration rather than military power.

*For the L*ORD *your God is bringing you into a good land, a land with flowing streams, with springs and underground waters welling up in valleys and hills, a land of wheat and barley, of vines and fig trees and pomegranates, a land of olive trees and honey, a land where you may eat bread without scarcity, where you will lack nothing, a land whose stones are iron and from whose hills you may mine copper. You shall eat your fill and bless the L*ORD *your God for the good land that he has given you.*

Deuteronomy 8:7–10

Harvesting the land
Moses tells the people to harvest the plentiful land and bless God for what he has provided.

You shall love the LORD *your God, therefore, and keep his charge, his decrees, his ordinances, and his commandments always.*

Deuteronomy 11:1

3 · 14 · 11

God blesses obedience and curses disobedience. When they enter the land, they must proclaim those blessings from Mount Gerizim and the curses from Mount Ebal.

Chapter
11

Chapter 12: **Commentary**

The Deuteronomic Code repeats earlier laws in a more developed form, adapted to settled civilisation. The emphasis is on religious observance and centralisation around the Temple of Jerusalem. Josiah's reforms set out to abolish the superstitions and idolatry of the local shrines by such centralisation, but worship only in Jerusalem would be practicable only for the small post-exilic community.

3 · 14

The Israelites must worship only the Lord, only in the prescribed way and only at the prescribed place. They must never add to or subtract from God's laws.

Chapter
12

You must diligently observe everything that I command you; do not add to it or take anything from it.

Deuteronomy 12:32

3 · 14

If a prophet predicts the future and performs miracles, but encourages the worship of other gods, then he should be ignored and all who worship other gods must be destroyed.

Chapter
13

3 · 14

Only certain animals, birds and fish can be eaten. The Israelites must give one-tenth of their income for the support of Levites, foreigners, orphans and widows.

Chapter
14

3 · 14

Every seven years all debts must be cancelled and all slaves must be freed. Slaves cannot be sent away empty-handed. Firstborn male animals are to be sacrificed.

Chapter
15

Chapter 16: **Commentary**

The Passover was originally celebrated as a family festival. Its centralisation on Jerusalem was a major feature of King Josiah's reform. Other novelties are: no mention of blood smeared on the doorposts (this would suit only a festival at home) and the linkage to the Week of Unleavened Bread, the beginning of the barley harvest.

3 · 14

They must celebrate the holy days, they must appoint honest judges and officials in every town and they must never set up Asherah poles or sacred stones.

Chapter
16

Chapter 18: **Commentary**

Priests of the local shrines would have been made redundant by the centralisation of the cult. If they wish to retain their priestly position they must move to Jerusalem. The chapter also seeks to outlaw superstitious practices like child sacrifice, which is evidenced in crises throughout Israel's history. The expectation of another prophet like Moses (verses 15, 18) was an important element of the hopes of Israel at the time of Jesus. In the Gospel of Matthew, Jesus is presented as this Second Moses.

3 · 14

Defective animals must not be sacrificed. Worshippers of other gods must die. The Tabernacle priests are the highest court. The Israelite king must be subject to the laws.

Chapter
17

3 · 14

The superstitious practices of the neighbouring peoples are forbidden. The LORD will send another prophet like Moses, who will guide them into all truth.

Chapter
18

3	14

Chapter **19**

At least three Cities of Refuge are to be established west of the Jordan. Boundary stones must not be moved. One witness is not enough to convict anyone of a crime. False witnesses are to receive punishment.

3	14

Chapter **20**

Only those willing and unafraid, without entanglements, are allowed to fight in war. Peace treaties can be arranged with distant nations, but not with the Canaanites.

3	14

Chapter **21**

Unsolved murders require the sacrifice of an animal. Firstborn rights are established. Israelites can marry women they capture in war. Rebellious sons can be executed.

3	14

Chapter **22**

There are laws regarding the care of lost animals, rooftops, seeds, animal husbandry, clothing, adultery, rape and false accusations of infidelity.

3	14

Chapter **23**

Some can be excluded from the Israelites' assembly for defects of birth. Escaped slaves seeking refuge must be protected, vows kept, the poor protected and gleaning (collecting leftover crops) permitted.

3	14

Chapter **24**

Remarriage after divorce is regulated. Those recently married must not go to war for a year. Kidnappers are to be executed. Foreigners, orphans and widows must be protected.

3	14

Chapter **25**

No more than 40 lashes. Widows without sons must marry their husband's brother. A woman loses her hand if she grabs a man's genitals during a fight. Amalekites must die.

3	14

Chapter **26**

Offerings of first fruits and tithes must be given to God in gratitude for his provision. The Israelites must carefully obey God's commands, since they voluntarily agreed to them.

Then the officials shall address the troops, saying, 'Has anyone built a new house but not dedicated it? He should go back to his house, or he might die in the battle and another dedicate it. Has anyone planted a vineyard but not yet enjoyed its fruit? He should go back to his house, or he might die in the battle and another be first to enjoy its fruit. Has anyone become engaged to a woman but not yet married her? He should go back to his house, or he might die in the battle and another marry her.' The officials shall continue to address the troops, saying, 'Is anyone afraid or disheartened? He should go back to his house, or he might cause the heart of his comrades to fail like his own.'

Deuteronomy 20:5–8

You shall not see your neighbour's donkey or ox fallen on the road and ignore it; you shall help to lift it up.

Deuteronomy 22:4

The death of Moses
Because he disobeyed God's command, God did not let Moses live to see the Israelites enter the Promised Land.

Chapter 23: **Commentary**

In a state of primitive biological science, human and crop fertility could be a special worry. Sacred prostitution at the local mountain shrines is frequently condemned by the prophets. 'Dog' (verse 19) is a contemptuous term for a male prostitute.

Chapter 25: **Commentary**

The levirate law (*levir* meaning 'brother-in-law') was a means of preserving the name and inheritance of a family member, particularly important when there was no awareness of life after death. The spitting underlines the shame of refusing this fraternal duty.

The LORD will make you the head, and not the tail; you shall be only at the top, and not at the bottom—if you obey the commandments of the LORD your God, which I am commanding you today, by diligently observing them, and if you do not turn aside from any of the words that I am commanding you today, either to the right or to the left, following other gods to serve them.

Deuteronomy 28:13–14

Chapter 28: **Commentary**

Blessings and curses for fidelity or failure are an important feature of the pattern of Near Eastern alliances between overlord and vassal, on which Deuteronomy is structured. The threats towards the end of this chapter envisage the Babylonian Exile, which the author saw as the direct result of Israel's infidelity to the covenant.

When all these things have happened to you, the blessings and the curses that I have set before you, if you call them to mind among all the nations where the LORD your God has driven you, and return to the LORD your God, and you and your children obey him with all your heart and with all your soul, just as I am commanding you today, then the LORD your God will restore your fortunes and have compassion on you, gathering you again from all the peoples among whom the LORD your God has scattered you.

Deuteronomy 30:1–3

Chapter 32: **Commentary**

This noble poem contrasts God's unfailing care for Israel with Israel's own infidelity and repeated failures. But the absence of any clear allusion to the Exile suggests that it was written before that catastrophic reversal.

Chapter 33: **Commentary**

The Blessings of Moses correspond to the situation of the tribes at a later date than the Blessings of Jacob in Genesis 49. Judah stands at the head, followed by the priestly tribe of Levi, but the emphasis is on the northern tribes. They are full of affectionate allusions to the tribal circumstances.

Chapter 34: **Commentary**

The account of the death of Moses excludes any claim that Moses was author of the Pentateuch in any literary sense. He was, of course, under God the author in the sense that he led the movement made up of the People of God, whose constitution it prescribes. Some hold that Moses is a composite personality and that no single person led the whole movement.

3 **14**

Upon crossing the Jordan, the Israelites must go to Mount Ebal, write the law on plaster-coated stones, build an altar, curse lawbreakers and sacrifice fellowship offerings.

Chapter
27

3 **9** **14**

Blessings come upon the Israelites for obedience and curses for disobedience. Continued disobedience would ultimately result in the Israelites being exiled from their land.

Chapter
28

3 **14** **17**

Because of all the wonders that they had seen since leaving Egypt, the Israelites must obey God's commands. Otherwise, God will send them into exile.

Chapter
29

2 **14**

If the curses come, the Israelites can always beg God's forgiveness. Moses calls upon the heavens and earth to bear witness to this treaty between Israel and God.

Chapter
30

3 **14** **17**

Since Moses is about to die, Joshua will take his place. Every seven years, when debts are forgiven, the Law of God must be read to the Israelites.

Chapter
31

5 **7** **14**

Moses recites a song that calls on the heavens to bear witness that God is great, but that the Israelites are wicked and will suffer punishment before repenting.

Chapter
32

5 **7** **14**

Moses pronounces a blessing, in the form of a poem, upon each of the 12 tribes of Israel.

Chapter
33

17

Moses climbs Mount Nebo, sees the Promised Land and dies. God himself buries Moses. Then the Israelites mourn his death for 30 days.

Chapter
34

Joshua
Overview

The Book of Joshua describes the conquest of Canaan by the Israelites under Joshua and the distribution of territories to the tribes. Both of these are artificial; they belong to a genre of literature common in the ancient world: the victory inscription. Many such inscriptions exist, thanking the national deity for an overwhelming victory, often described in exaggerated terms. The impression is given of a lightning campaign overwhelming the whole country. In fact the conquests described are almost entirely confined to the territory of Benjamin, with a minor victory over the kings of the south and the conquest of Hazor in the north. The description of the distribution of the land to the tribes is in fact largely theoretical.

Chapter 1: **Commentary**

This chapter gives a double introduction: Joshua is introduced as the successor of Moses, with the same leadership and the same powers. An introduction is also given to the theme of the Deuteronomic History: success depends on fidelity to the Law of the Lord.

(17)

Chapter 1

Joshua takes Moses' place as the leader of the Israelites. Joshua tells them that they will soon cross the Jordan River – so they need to be prepared.

Chapter 2: **Commentary**

Jericho was one of the first cities in the world. It has a 10,000-year-old stone tower. Its strong walls were destroyed some 900 years before Joshua. The author assumes that Joshua captured the city near the Jordan. The story of Rahab may be based on some local cult.

(17)

Chapter 2

Joshua sends two spies to Jericho. They stay with a prostitute named Rahab, who hides them. They promise to spare her when the Israelites conquer the city.

Chapter 3: **Commentary**

The crossing of the Jordan under Joshua's command mirrors the crossing of the Red Sea at its beginning under Moses' command. The Passover at the end mirrors the Passover at the beginning. Just as Moses sent envoys ahead (Numbers 13), so Joshua sends spies. The manna now ceases (5:12), and normal life resumes.

(8)   **(17)**

Chapter 3

When the priests, carrying the Ark, step into the Jordan River, God halts the water. While the priests stand in the channel, the rest of the Israelites cross the river on dry ground.

Chapter 4: **Commentary**

'Gilgal' means 'ring' or 'circle'. More familiar is the Aramaic form, Golgultha/Golgotha. Two explanations of the name are given, one as a circle of stones (4:21), one as the scene of ritual circumcision (5:4).

(8)   **(17)**

Chapter 4

Twelve large stones gathered from the middle of the Jordan are piled as a memorial of the crossing. When the priests leave the Jordan River, the water starts flowing again.

Many of the stories given here, especially those of the territory of Benjamin, are etiological myths, that is, they explain features of the landscape or local customs, and are founded on these rather than on historical evidence. They are valuable in showing the trust in the Lord, and in his servant Joshua. Joshua is the designated successor to Moses, and is seen as continuing his work. However, the actual historical evidence is difficult to interpret. Apart from the contemporary destruction of Hazor, archaeology does not provide any confirmation of the settlement of the Hebrews in Canaan.

Rahab
When Joshua sent spies to Jericho, they visited the prostitute Rahab. She protected the spies, and so when the Israelites conquered Jericho and slaughtered its populace, they spared both her and her family.

Once when Joshua was near Jericho, he looked up and saw a man standing before him with a drawn sword in his hand. Joshua went to him and said to him, 'Are you one of us, or one of our adversaries?' He replied, 'Neither; but as commander of the army of the LORD I have now come.' And Joshua fell on his face to the earth and worshipped, and he said to him, 'What do you command your servant, my LORD?'
Joshua 5:13–14

Chapter 6: Commentary

Two accounts of the processions are interwoven. The military operation is turned into a liturgical procession.

Chapter 7: Commentary

Dedication of the spoils to the Lord designates the war as a Holy War. There is no evidence that such wholesale genocide ever occurred. More likely it is simply an expression of post-exilic xenophobia, prohibiting the vulnerable post-exilic community from mixing with the local people (Ezra 9; Nehemiah 10:31). The story is presented as explaining a feature of the landscape (verse 26).

Chapter 8: Commentary

The story of the capture of Ai (*ai* is Hebrew for 'ruin') explains the great ruin near the ancient sanctuary of Bethel; the city was destroyed several hundred years before Joshua. Alternatively, it may be a displaced account of an attack on Bethel itself.

8	17
The Israelites then circumcise all the men and celebrate Passover. For the first time, the Israelites eat some Canaanite food. The manna stops coming.	Chapter **5**

8	17
The Israelites march around Jericho once a day for six days, and then seven times on the seventh day. Then the walls of Jericho fall down. The Israelites conquer Jericho.	Chapter **6**

9	17
Achan steals some of the spoils from Jericho, rather than destroying it. As a consequence, the Israelites lose a battle at Ai. Achan and his family are stoned to death for his theft.	Chapter **7**

11	17
The Israelites successfully conquer the small city of Ai. Joshua builds an altar on Mount Ebal, offers sacrifices and the blessings and cursings of the covenant are read aloud.	Chapter **8**

⑭   **⑰**

Chapter
9

Canaanites from Gibeon trick the Israelites into making a peace treaty. When the Israelites learn of their deception, they enslave the Gibeonites.

Chapter 9: Commentary

This story of a clever trick explains the presence of an ethnically foreign group in the middle of Benjamin territory, and their unusual status.

⑤   **⑧**   **⑰**

Chapter
10

Joshua and the Israelites rescue the Gibeonites from an attack by five kings. The Israelites conquer most of southern Canaan.

Chapter 10: Commentary

The famous miracle of the sun standing still is simply a misunderstanding. As verse 13 hints, this is a poetic exaggeration, drawn from a victory song.

⑰

Chapter
11

Joshua and the Israelites defeat most of the kings and cities of the northern part of Canaan.

On the day when the LORD gave the Amorites over to the Israelites, Joshua spoke to the LORD; and he said in the sight of Israel,
'Sun, stand still at Gibeon,
*   and Moon, in the valley of Aijalon.'*
And the sun stood still, and the moon stopped,
*   until the nation took vengeance on their enemies.*
Is this not written in the Book of Jashar? The sun stopped in mid-heaven, and did not hurry to set for about a whole day.
There has been no day like it before or since, when the LORD heeded a human voice; for the LORD fought for Israel.

Joshua 10:12–14

⑯   **⑰**

Chapter
12

A list of all the kings and their cities that the Israelites defeated and conquered.

⑯   **⑰**

Chapter
13

A list of the lands still remaining to be conquered in Canaan. The land east of the Jordan is apportioned between Reuben, Gad and half of Manasseh.

Chapter 11: Commentary

The great city of Hazor, ten times the size of Jerusalem, still controls the northern approach into Israel. Only a small part of it has been excavated, but it is the one city where archaeological evidence corroborates a sack at the time of Joshua.

⑯   **⑰**

Chapter
14

The land west of the Jordan River is apportioned by lot between the remaining nine and a half tribes. An 85-year-old Caleb receives the city of Hebron as his personal inheritance.

So Joshua took the whole land, according to all that the LORD had spoken to Moses; and Joshua gave it for an inheritance to Israel according to their tribal allotments. And the land had rest from war.

Joshua 11:23

⑯   **⑰**

Chapter
15

The land allotted to Judah is outlined, with its borders.

And Caleb said, 'Whoever attacks Kiriath-sepher and takes it, to him I will give my daughter Achsah as wife.' Othniel son of Kenaz, the brother of Caleb, took it; and he gave him his daughter Achsah as wife.

Joshua 15:16–17

⑯   **⑰**

Chapter
16

The land allotted to Ephraim is outlined, with its borders.

Then the whole congregation of the Israelites assembled at Shiloh, and set up the tent of meeting there. The land lay subdued before them. There remained among the Israelites seven tribes whose inheritance had not yet been apportioned.

So Joshua said to the Israelites, 'How long will you be slack about going in and taking possession of the land that the LORD, the God of your ancestors, has given you?'

Joshua 18:1–3

Chapter 20: **Commentary**

There was no police force in ancient Israel. It was the duty of relatives to avenge a killing. The Cities of Refuge, three east of the Jordan, three west of the river, are intended to ensure that an accidental killer lives long enough to receive fair trial, so that this fact can be established. There seems to have been an amnesty at the death of the high priest.

Therefore we said, "Let us now build an altar, not for burnt-offering, nor for sacrifice, but to be a witness between us and you, and between the generations after us, that we do perform the service of the LORD in his presence with our burnt-offerings and sacrifices and offerings of well-being; so that your children may never say to our children in time to come, 'You have no portion in the LORD.'"

Joshua 22:26–27

Chapter 23: **Commentary**

Joshua's final speech sums up the theology of Deuteronomy and the Deuteronomic History: fidelity to the commandments will ensure divine protection. Its language is thoroughly Deuteronomic.

Chapter 24: **Commentary**

The religious significance of Shechem was important, for here Abraham built an altar. This is perhaps why it was chosen as a scene for the great renewal of the covenant, by which all the elements of Israel, originally of disparate origin, were united into the worship of the LORD. A standing stone, sometimes inscribed, is normally erected as the witness of such a covenant.

16	17	Chapter
The land allotted to Manasseh is outlined, with its borders.		**17**

16	17	Chapter
The Tabernacle is erected in Shiloh. The remaining seven tribes divide the land by lot and survey it. The land allotted to Benjamin is outlined, with its borders.		**18**

16	17	Chapter
The land allotted to Simeon, Zebulun, Issachar, Asher, Naphtali and Dan is outlined, with its borders. Joshua is granted the town of Timnath Serah as his personal inheritance.		**19**

3	16	17	Chapter
The Cities of Refuge are established so that those who kill accidentally will have a place to run from the avenger of blood.			**20**

16	17	Chapter
The Levites are given towns among the other tribal possessions to inhabit, since the Levites receive no territory of their own.		**21**

17	Chapter
The men of Reuben, Gad and half the tribe of Manasseh finally return to their lands east of the Jordan. They build an altar on the border as a memorial to their union with Israel.	**22**

3	17	Chapter
Near the end of his life, Joshua reminds the Israelites to obey the laws of the LORD and to worship no other gods.		**23**

3	17	Chapter
Joshua renews the covenant between God and the Israelites. Then, at the age of 110, Joshua dies and is buried.		**24**

Judges
Overview

The Book of Judges covers the period of Israel's history between the death of Joshua and the rise of kingship in Israel. A first introduction gives a more detailed picture of the situation of these groups of immigrants, faced with established populations and forces among whom they were trying to settle; they did not all succeed in appropriating the land 'allotted' to them by Joshua. A second introduction draws the lesson that shaped this second book of the Deuteronomic History, that Israel's success or failure depended on her fidelity to the LORD. There was a cycle of infidelity, leading to punishment by invaders; then Israel repented, returned to the LORD and was rescued from the invaders. The same cycle will eventually reach its climax in the Babylonian Exile.

Chapter 1: **Commentary**

The southern tribe of Judah is treated separately. It seems to have remained separate, for it takes no part in the action of the northern tribes related in Judges 5. The tribe itself was possibly formed later from the sub-groups mentioned here. The account of the northern tribes makes clear that they were unable to conquer the great cities, and that some tribes had to be content with serf status.

Chapter 1

After Joshua's death, the Israelites renew their fight against the remaining Canaanites and conquer more territory, but they fail to get rid of all of the Canaanites.

Chapter 2: **Commentary**

The Deuteronomic editor sets out the lesson repeated throughout Israel's history: infidelity leads to punishment, then repentance leads to divine rescue. The editor sees the foreign nations as left in Canaan specifically to test Israel.

Chapter 2

At Bokim, the angel of the LORD warns the Israelites that because of their idolatry, God will not drive out all the Canaanites and so they will repeatedly face oppression.

Chapter 3: **Commentary**

The number of 12 *suphetim* corresponds to the 12 tribes of Israel. The Spirit of the LORD seizes upon each of them, imparting either military prowess or judicial wisdom. Ehud is a left-hander, so he carries his weapon on his right hip, where it is not noticed.

Chapter 3

Othniel rescues the Israelites from Aram Nahariam. Then Ehud assassinates Eglon, the king of Moab, by stabbing him in the belly. Shamgar kills 600 Philistines with an ox goad.

Chapters 4–5: **Commentary**

These two chapters recount the same victory in prose and poetry respectively; the latter is the older version. Deborah and Jael are the first military heroines in Israel. Jael's sexual role reversal is particularly striking, with first the gift of milk and then her tent peg plunged into Sisera.

Chapter 4

Deborah leads the Israelites in a successful battle against Jabin, defeating his general Sisera in battle. Jael kills a sleeping Sisera when she drives a tent peg through his head.

Within this outline the story is told by means of two groups of individuals. The first are warlike leaders, both men and women, who are stirred by the Spirit of the LORD to arise and inspire Israel to expel the invaders. They are interspersed with a second group, who are more peacetime leaders. Their Hebrew designation as *suphetim* assimilates them to the *suphetes* of some neighbouring cultures, Phoenicia and Carthage, the ruling magistrates of those places.

The book ends with growing tension, both external and internal. The strongman hero Samson manages to inflict some annoyances on the growing threat of the Philistines, until he is wiped out in a classic honeytrap. Finally, the stories of unrest in the tribes of Dan and Benjamin show the mounting anarchy and rampant immorality of the tribal groups themselves. The time is ripe for the stronger and more permanent leadership of the kings.

Barak and Deborah
Deborah, the judge of Israel, with her general Barak, lead the Israelites to victory in battle against Jabin, king of Canaan in Hazor.

Chapter 5: **Commentary**

The variety of reactions of the different tribes' willingness, hesitation or refusal to help their fellow Israelites shows the looseness of the bonds between them at this time. If there was a 12-tribe league, it was pretty ineffective.

5		17	
Deborah and Barak sing a song celebrating their victory over Jabin and his general, Sisera.			Chapter **5**

Chapter 6: **Commentary**

The story of the vocation of Gideon was probably the foundation story of the sanctuary of Ophrah (whose location is now unknown). The lowly status of Gideon and his unwillingness stress the lesson that his power comes from God, not from his own resources. Similarly, the continual reduction of his forces shows that victory belongs to the LORD.

8		9		17	
Gideon destroys his father's gods, raises an army against the oppressive Midianites, then begs the LORD to give him a sign of his favour, using fleece.					Chapter **6**

8		17	
Gideon miraculously defeats the Midianites with only 300 men after the bulk of the assembled Israelite army abandons him.			Chapter **7**

As soon as Gideon died, the Israelites relapsed and prostituted themselves with the Baals, making Baal-berith their god. The Israelites did not remember the LORD their God, who had rescued them from the hand of all their enemies on every side; and they did not exhibit loyalty to the house of Jerubbaal (that is, Gideon) in return for all the good that he had done to Israel.

Judges 8:33–35

17	
After Gideon's 300 defeat the Midianites, he makes a gold *ephod* (high priest's breastplate). After 40 years of peace, Gideon dies and the Israelites revert to worshipping Canaanite gods.	Chapter **8**

⑥	⑨	⑰

Chapter 9

Gideon's son Abimelech sets himself up as the king of Shechem after killing all but one of his brothers. With a fable, the surviving brother warns Shechem of a coming disaster.

⑨	⑰

Chapter 10

Tola leads Israel as judge for 23 years, followed by Jair for 22 years. Israel then returns to idolatry and is oppressed by Philistines and Ammonites, until it repents and seeks a leader.

⑨	⑰

Chapter 11

The people of Gilead choose Jephtha to lead them. Jephtha promises God he will sacrifice the first thing he meets after his victory. He is victorious and sacrifices his daughter.

⑨	⑰

Chapter 12

Jepthah and his fellow Gileadites fight against the tribe of Ehpraim. After he dies, Ibzan, Elon and Abdon follow him as the leaders of Israel.

⑮	⑰

Chapter 13

Manoah's wife can't get pregnant. An angel promises them a son who will be a Nazirite from birth. He will deliver Israel from the Philistines. His name is Samson.

⑧	⑨	⑰

Chapter 14

Samson marries a Philistine and tells a riddle. His threatened wife reveals the answer. Samson kills 30 Philistines to pay off a bet. Meanwhile, his wife is given to another man.

⑧	⑨	⑰

Chapter 15

When Samson discovers that his wife has been given to another, he burns down the Philistines' fields. Samson kills the Philistines who murder his wife and father-in-law.

Chapter 9: **Commentary**

Although Gideon, Abimelech's father, refused the kingship, Abimelech means 'my father is king'. Abimelech's mother was a concubine of Shechem. This entirely godless account of his reign shows the worst of kingship. However, in Jotham's fable it provides the first occasion in the Bible of the use of a nature tale as a parable of human behaviour.

Chapter 11: **Commentary**

The basis of this story may be the cult-legend of a feminine festival in Gilead. Jephtah was a successful bandit of dubious parentage. Child sacrifice was in fact occasionally practised in Israel at many periods of its history, despite its prohibition in the Law. Jephtah regards it as tolerable for the sake of fulfilling his rash vow. His message to the Ammonites shows that he recognised the existence also of other gods. This henotheism was the state of belief normal at this time: the LORD was Israel's own and only God, but this did not exclude the possibility of other nations having their own gods. The belief in monotheism (one God of the whole universe) was reached only at the time of the Babylonian Exile.

Chapter 13: **Commentary**

Samson stands out from the other figures as an individual folk hero. He merely provokes the Philistines by his antics, not bringing deliverance to Israel. His strength is connected to his levirate vow, but is almost magical, and these folk tales do not have much religious significance. Many of them are legends based on features of the landscape. The overall message is the increasing threat of the Philistines, which will soon impel the Israelites into monarchy.

Chapter 14: **Commentary**

Samson's marriage, involving occasional visits, but not permanent residence, has parallels in oriental cultures. Such an arrangement, of course, leaves plenty of room for the behaviour that results in the bawdy exchange of riddles in this chapter.

*Then he found a fresh jawbone of a donkey,
reached down and took it, and with it he killed a
thousand men.*

*And Samson said,
'With the jawbone of a donkey,
 heaps upon heaps,
with the jawbone of a donkey
 I have slain a thousand men.'*

*When he had finished speaking, he threw away
the jawbone; and that place was called Ramath-lehi.*

Judges 15:15–17

She let him fall asleep on her lap; and she called a man, and had him shave off the seven locks of his head. He began to weaken, and his strength left him.

Then she said, 'The Philistines are upon you, Samson!' When he awoke from his sleep, he thought, 'I will go out as at other times, and shake myself free.' But he did not know that the LORD had left him. So the Philistines seized him and gouged out his eyes. They brought him down to Gaza and bound him with bronze shackles; and he ground at the mill in the prison. But the hair of his head began to grow again after it had been shaved.

Judges 16:19–22

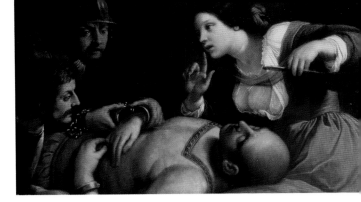

Samson and Delilah
Samson fell in love with Delilah, but she betrayed him, tricked him and turned him over to his enemies, the Philistines.

8 **12** **17**

After a night with a prostitute, Samson demolishes the city gates. Later, Delilah cuts off Samson's hair. The Philistines capture and blind him. His hair grows back and he gets his revenge.

Chapter
16

Chapter 17: **Commentary**

Micah is a shortened form of Micayehu ('Who is like the LORD?'). The story of the tribe's move to the north is told against a background of anarchy, theft, banditry, infidelity and idolatry. It contains the only clear case in the Bible of a cult image of the LORD.

11 **17**

Micah steals silver from his mother. When he returns it, she makes an idol from some of it. Micah hires a Levite from Bethlehem to serve as a priest for the idol.

Chapter
17

17

As the tribe of Dan heads off to conquer Laish, they steal the idol from Micah and ask his priest, the Levite, to join them. The priest happily goes with them to Laish.

Chapter
18

Chapter 19: **Commentary**

The story is modelled on the story of Lot at Sodom (Genesis 19:1–11). In both it is unclear whether homosexuality or the infringement of the obligations of hospitality is the greater crime. Even though this overrides the girl's rights, he is so distraught that he cuts her into 12 pieces and sends them to each of the 12 tribes, inviting them to join him in taking vengeance on the rapists.

17

A Levite spends the night in Gibeah of Benjamin, where his concubine is raped and murdered. He cuts her into 12 pieces that he distributes to each of the 12 tribes.

Chapter
19

9 **17**

The tribe of Benjamin refuses to bring the murderers to justice, so the other tribes go to war against them. They kill nearly everyone in the tribe of Benjamin.

Chapter
20

Chapter 21: **Commentary**

The two solutions in verses 1–14 and 15–23 are mutually exclusive. The latter is based on a matchmaking ritual at the grape harvest festival at Shiloh.

17

The Israelites had sworn never to give their daughters in marriage to Benjaminites, so they tell the surviving Benjaminites to kidnap their daughters for marriage, instead.

Chapter
21

In those days there was no king in Israel; all the people did what was right in their own eyes.

Judges 21:25

Ruth

Overview

This comforting tale of the ancestry of David is placed in the Hebrew Bible in its third division, among the Writings rather than the Histories. It has two motifs: to legitimate the ancestry of David and to protest against the fear of contamination of Israel by foreign customs. Such xenophobia is characteristic of the post-exilic period, when the Jews were a vulnerable community huddled around Jerusalem. The traces of Aramaic in the language of the book also suggest that the final edition of the book dates from that time, but the dating is far from certain.

Above all it is a story of fidelity, the loyalty of the widowed Ruth to her widowed mother-in-law, stranded in a foreign land, the returned love of Naomi for her daughter-in-law, the gentleness of Boaz and his dutiful respect for his family obligations. It begins in despair and hopelessness, for the widowed women have no means of support, and ends with the ample reward for their dutiful devotion.

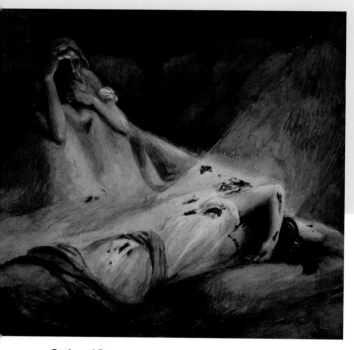

Ruth and Boaz
After the harvest festival, when Boaz found Ruth in bed with him, he knew that he had to make things right and marry her.

So she said, 'See, your sister-in-law has gone back to her people and to her gods; return after your sister-in-law.' But Ruth said,
'Do not press me to leave you
* or to turn back from following you!*
Where you go, I will go;
* where you lodge, I will lodge;*
your people shall be my people,
* and your God my God.*
Where you die, I will die—
* there will I be buried.*
May the Lord do thus and so to me,
* and more as well,*
if even death parts me from you!'

Ruth 1:15–17

17

Chapter
1

Naomi's husband and sons die while they are living in Moab. Naomi decides to return to her home in Bethlehem and her widowed daughter-in-law, Ruth, decides to go with her.

17

Chapter
2

Ruth begins gleaning in the fields of Boaz, a relative of Naomi's husband. Boaz notices Ruth and makes certain that she is protected and that she receives extra grain.

Chapter 2: **Commentary**

Boaz's generosity to Ruth shows his gentleness and courtesy, but no doubt other motives too. Her gleanings of corn amount to 25 kilos! Naomi recognises that he is one of those who have the duty to prolong the inheritance, though not necessarily the nearest relative.

The legal background to the whole book is the levirate law (Deuteronomy 25.5–10), by which the nearest male relative of a man who dies without issue must marry the widow of the dead man and raise up an heir who will prolong the dead man's name and inheritance.

Ruth and Naomi
Ruth was a Moabite, but when her husband died she returned to Bethlehem with her mother-in-law Naomi.

Chapter 3: **Commentary**

There is subtle innuendo in the euphemisms of this chapter, which may, but need not, imply sexual intercourse.

When Boaz had eaten and drunk, and he was in a contented mood, he went to lie down at the end of the heap of grain. Then she came quietly and uncovered his feet, and lay down. At midnight the man was startled and turned over, and there, lying at his feet, was a woman! He said, 'Who are you?' And she answered, 'I am Ruth, your servant; spread your cloak over your servant, for you are next-of-kin.'

Ruth 3:7–9

Chapter 4: **Commentary**

The nearest male relative agrees to buy back the land, but backs off from marrying the widow, since a resulting son would be considered son and heir of Ruth's dead husband, not of himself. In the Deuteronomic legislation the widow is to spit in the face of the relative who refuses his duty, and symbolically to unman him by taking his sandal. Here the sandal has a different significance.

17

Naomi and Ruth conspire to force Boaz to marry Ruth. On the night of the big harvest celebration, after Boaz has got drunk, he awakens to find Ruth lying beside him.

Chapter
3

16 **18**

Boaz quickly makes the necessary arrangements and marries Ruth. Their son, Obed, becomes the grandfather of King David.

Chapter
4

1 Samuel

Overview

The Books of Samuel originally formed a single continuous narrative. This was divided into two books simply for the sake of the convenience of the standard length of scrolls, a convenient point of division being the death of Saul. The First Book of Samuel relates the transition in Israel from the unsteady rule of occasional charismatic rulers, raised up to repel the threat of invasion, to the relatively stable rule of kings. Saul was anointed king to check the incursions of the Philistines, who were threatening to advance into the hill-country of Israel. His dynasty was short-lived, giving way to that of David, the model of kingship in Israel. History is written by the victors, so that the story of Saul is told from David's point of view. David is here presented as chased from the royal court as the victim of Saul's jealousy; but a close reading of the story has suggested to some that David was an unscrupulous young upstart whom Saul tried unsuccessfully to hold in check.

Chapter 1

Having problems getting pregnant, Hannah promises God that her firstborn son will be a Nazirite raised by the high priest. She becomes pregnant and fulfils her vow.

'For this child I prayed; and the LORD has granted me the petition that I made to him. Therefore I have lent him to the LORD; as long as he lives, he is given to the LORD.' She left him there for the LORD.

1 Samuel 1:27–28

Chapter 2

Hannah praises and thanks God. The high priest Eli has wicked sons who steal sacrifices and sleep with Temple prostitutes. God warns of coming judgement.

Chapter 2: **Commentary**

Hannah's song of thanksgiving is placed on her lips by the author. It is a hymn marked by the later spirituality of the Poor of the LORD. Its final reference to the king places it at least in the period of the monarchy. Mary's canticle, the Magnificat, is modelled on it, but is far more personal.

Chapter 3

God calls Samuel to become his prophet and tells him that Eli and his family are going to be judged by God.

Chapter 4: **Commentary**

The story of the Ark forms a separate cycle, in which Samuel plays no part. It is the symbol of God's awesome presence in Israel and its loss leaves Israel desolate. For its new owners it is too hot to handle. Their own god, Dagon, involuntarily bows before it, and it brings them humiliating sickness (piles). It continues to wreak havoc until it is returned to Israelite territory, where it seems to have lain neglected until rescued by David (2 Samuel 5).

Chapter 4

The Philistines capture the Ark and kill Eli's sons. Eli tumbles in shock from his chair and breaks his neck, while one of his daughters-in-law goes into labour and dies giving birth.

The book makes use of several sources. Some is still folk history: two versions are given of the sin that led to Saul's rejection. Three incompatible versions of David's first appearance are given: the shepherd-boy, the harpist and the giant-slayer. This gives way to two parallel versions of David's rise to power (chapter 24 parallels chapter 26). The purpose of these narratives is to show the hand of God, guiding history towards the Davidic monarchy by means of the fascinating and ruthless charismatic leadership of David himself. The final editor, however, weaves these stories into the greater story of the Deuteronomic History, whose message is the four-fold cycle of Israel's infidelity leading to disaster, then conversion to the LORD and rescue from the enemy. In this book the lesson is taught chiefly by the story of the loss and recovery of the Ark of the LORD.

Samuel is presented to Eli
Samuel's mother Hannah promised God that she would devote her firstborn son to God. So when Samuel was weaned, she turned him over to be adopted by the high priest, Eli.

The hand of the LORD was heavy upon the people of Ashdod, and he terrified and struck them with tumours, both in Ashdod and in its territory. And when the inhabitants of Ashdod saw how things were, they said, 'The ark of the God of Israel must not remain with us; for his hand is heavy on us and on our god Dagon.' So they sent and gathered together all the lords of the Philistines, and said, 'What shall we do with the ark of the God of Israel?' The inhabitants of Gath replied, 'Let the ark of God be moved on to us.' So they moved the ark of the God of Israel to Gath.

1 Samuel 5:6–8

Chapter 8: **Commentary**

In a major Deuteronomic set speech Samuel lays out the dangers of kingship. A king will require monetary taxes and personal service. Most of all, their demand for a king is seen as a lack of trust in the LORD as King of Israel and its protector against enemies. But in the end Samuel is instructed to give them a king. By a revelation Samuel is brought to Saul, whom he secretly consecrates king by anointing him. Then the Spirit seizes on Saul, and he is elected by the people. In a third story (chapter 11) Saul cows the people into accepting his leadership and is acclaimed king after a great victory.

9	**17**	
The Philistines place the Ark in the Temple of Dagon. Dagon repeatedly falls on his face before the Ark. After an outbreak of tumours they decide to return the Ark to the Israelites.		Chapter **5**
9	**17**	
The Ark is spontaneously brought to Beth Shemesh, on the borders of the hill-country, drawn by two cows, despite their calves being shut away. Awed by the Ark, the inhabitants send it on to Kiriath Jearim.		Chapter **6**
11	**17**	
The Ark stays in Kiriath Jearim for 20 years. Samuel grows up, leads Israel and calls the people to Mizpah to recommit themselves to the LORD. Then they defeat the Philistines.		Chapter **7**
17		
When Samuel is old, the Israelites ask him for a king. Samuel warns that the king will tax them and conscript their children as servants and warriors, but they still demand a king.		Chapter **8**

(17)

Chapter

9

One day Saul from Benjamin is looking for his father's lost donkeys. He meets Samuel, who invites him to dinner.

(17)

Chapter

10

Samuel informs Saul that the donkeys are safe, that he will become the king of Israel, and that he will prophesy. Then Samuel arranges a meeting in Gilgal, where he proclaims Saul king.

(17)

Chapter

11

The Ammonites threaten Jabesh Gilead. Saul leads an army against the Ammonites and defeats them. The people of Israel reaffirm Saul's kingship.

(9) **(17)**

Chapter

12

Samuel tells the Israelites that they have displeased God by asking for a king. So rain falls during the wheat harvest. He encourages obedience to God's commands.

(9) **(17)**

Chapter

13

The Philistines assemble for an all-out war after Jonathan attacks Geba. Saul impatiently disobeys Samuel, and Samuel predicts the end of Saul's reign.

(14) **(17)**

Chapter

14

Unaware of Saul's vow that no one would eat, Jonathan eats honey. Thanks to Jonathan, the Israelites rout the Philistines. Saul's soldiers prevent Saul from executing Jonathan for violating the vow.

As he turned away to leave Samuel, God gave him another heart; and all these signs were fulfilled that day. When they were going from there to Gibeah, a band of prophets met him; and the spirit of God possessed him, and he fell into a prophetic frenzy along with them. When all who knew him before saw how he prophesied with the prophets, the people said to one another, 'What has come over the son of Kish? Is Saul also among the prophets?'

1 Samuel 10:9–11

Chapter 12: Commentary

Samuel's rehearsal and prediction of history in his retirement speech again points to the Deuteronomic lesson that God is the king who cares for Israel. Earthly kingship will bring Israel no good in the end, but will lead them into the infidelity which will eventually result in the Babylonian Exile.

Chapter 13: Commentary

The short account of Saul's reign is ominously sandwiched between two accounts of his rejection in the LORD's name by Samuel. Neither fault seems adequately grave: Saul's impatience when his army is deserting at Samuel's failure to keep his appointment, nor Saul's failure to execute his royal prisoner of war. The impression is given of widespread and heroic victories, but modern historians tend to see this as exaggeration and reclassify Saul as a minor tribal chieftain.

Now the sons of Saul were Jonathan, Ishvi, and Malchishua; and the names of his two daughters were these: the name of the firstborn was Merab, and the name of the younger, Michal. The name of Saul's wife was Ahinoam daughter of Ahimaaz. And the name of the commander of his army was Abner son of Ner, Saul's uncle; Kish was the father of Saul, and Ner the father of Abner was the son of Abiel.

There was hard fighting against the Philistines all the days of Saul; and when Saul saw any strong or valiant warrior, he took him into his service.

1 Samuel 14:49–52

Chapter 16: Commentary

Three stories recount how David enters the scene: the anointed shepherd-boy (later he will be anointed again at Hebron as king of Judah, and then as king of all Israel), the heroic giant-slayer and the soothing minstrel. David's magnetic personality, his loyal leadership and his ruthless ambition shine through all the stories of his rise to power.

When they came, he looked on Eliab and thought, 'Surely the LORD's anointed is now before the LORD.'

But the LORD said to Samuel, 'Do not look on his appearance or on the height of his stature, because I have rejected him; for the LORD does not see as mortals see; they look on the outward appearance, but the LORD looks on the heart.'

1 Samuel 16:6–7

Chapter 18: Commentary

History is recounted by the victors. In the Bible the story is given from David's viewpoint, and David is represented as persecuted by the murderous Saul. However, the same facts can be viewed differently. Saul was not unreasonably suspicious of David's success and his ambition. No doubt the bride-price demanded by Saul was a challenge to David, and a hope on Saul's part to get his young rival killed. Saul's plan backfired.

When David had finished speaking to Saul, the soul of Jonathan was bound to the soul of David, and Jonathan loved him as his own soul. Saul took him that day and would not let him return to his father's house. Then Jonathan made a covenant with David, because he loved him as his own soul. Jonathan stripped himself of the robe that he was wearing, and gave it to David, and his armour, and even his sword and his bow and his belt.

David went out and was successful wherever Saul sent him; as a result, Saul set him over the army. And all the people, even the servants of Saul, approved.

1 Samuel 18:1–5

---

⑨ **⑰**

Saul spares Agag, the king of the Amalekites, along with some animals. Samuel tells Saul that God will replace Saul with a new king. Then Samuel executes Agag.

Chapter **15**

---

⑰

In Bethlehem, Samuel anoints David as the next king, to replace Saul. David enters Saul's service as his musician and armour bearer. David's lyre playing eases Saul's manic depression.

Chapter **16**

---

⑰

David visits his brothers in Saul's army, accepts the challenge of Goliath and kills him with a sling. The Philistine army flees in panic with the Israelites in pursuit.

Chapter **17**

---

⑩ **⑰**

David and Jonathan become friends. David joins Saul's army, advances and wins victories. Saul becomes paranoid. David becomes Saul's son-in-law after delivering 200 Philistine foreskins as a bride-price.

Chapter **18**

David the musician
After Saul was rejected by God, he was despondent. He hired David to play music in the hope that it would make him feel better.

10 **17**

Chapter 19

Saul decides to execute David. David's wife Michal helps him escape the palace when she puts an idol into his bed and tells Saul's servants that David is sick.

10 **14** **17**

Chapter 20

Jonathan confirms to David that his father is out to kill him. They promise undying friendship and Jonathan admits that he expects David to become king some day.

17

Chapter 21

David flees to Nob where the priest Ahimelech gives him bread and Goliath's sword. David seeks refuge with Achish, the king of Gath, faking insanity.

17

Chapter 22

David sends his parents to Moab for their protection, and gathers a band of freebooters. Meanwhile, Saul massacres Ahimelech and the priests who had helped David at Nob.

17

Chapter 23

David and his men defeat the Philistines attacking Keilah, but its citizens want to turn him over to Saul. David must flee and hide from Saul in the Desert of Ziph.

17

Chapter 24

When Saul goes into a cave near En Gedi to relieve himself, a hidden David cuts off a corner of his garment. David shows Saul how easily he could have killed him if he'd wanted.

Chapter 19: **Commentary**

The women of the townships and both of Saul's children, Michal and Jonathan, are clearly besotted with the handsome young warrior. Some of the stories are obviously alternative versions of the same incident: David's pact with Jonathan (chapters 19 and 20) and David's indulgence of Saul (chapters 24 and 26).

Chapter 21: **Commentary**

David's improbable story gains him not only food supplies but the emblematic trophy of Goliath's sword. Ahimelech will pay for his gullibility with his life, but cleverness was more important to David than truth, as he shows (verses 14 and 27:5–12) in his negotiations with the Philistines.

David took these words to heart and was very much afraid of King Achish of Gath. So he changed his behaviour before them; he pretended to be mad when in their presence. He scratched marks on the doors of the gate, and let his spittle run down his beard.

Achish said to his servants, 'Look, you see the man is mad; why then have you brought him to me? Do I lack madmen, that you have brought this fellow to play the madman in my presence? Shall this fellow come into my house?'

1 Samuel 21:12–15

'Now I know that you shall surely be king, and that the kingdom of Israel shall be established in your hand. Swear to me therefore by the Lord *that you will not cut off my descendants after me, and that you will not wipe out my name from my father's house.'*

So David swore this to Saul. Then Saul went home; but David and his men went up to the stronghold.

1 Samuel 24:20–22

Saul's suicide
The Philistines defeat the Israelite army and mortally wound Saul, who then chooses to kill himself.

Chapter 25: **Commentary**

David was operating a protection racket with a rich landowner *Nabal* (meaning 'brute'), who is foolish enough to refuse to pay the fee and conveniently eats himself to death. This enables David to parade his two wives, Saul's ex-wife Ahinoam and Nabal's widow (verse 43). Monogamy is not yet the norm.

Now David and his men went up and made raids on the Geshurites, the Girzites, and the Amalekites; for these were the landed settlements from Telam on the way to Shur and on to the land of Egypt. David struck the land, leaving neither man nor woman alive, but took away the sheep, the oxen, the donkeys, the camels, and the clothing, and came back to Achish.

1 Samuel 27:8–9

Chapter 28: **Commentary**

Having himself forbidden necromancy and wizards (verse 9, cf. Deuteronomy 18:11–12), but having lost his own prophet and the prophetic ephod, Saul is driven to desperation. The woman's attempts to comfort him are touching, but ineffective.

Chapter 30: **Commentary**

As the Philistine leaders would not trust David to join their forces in the north against his own people (29:4), he uses the opportunity to build up his power base in the south by distributing his spoils to the elders of Judah.

The battle pressed hard upon Saul; the archers found him, and he was badly wounded by them.
Then Saul said to his armour-bearer, 'Draw your sword and thrust me through with it, so that these uncircumcised may not come and thrust me through, and make sport of me.' But his armour-bearer was unwilling; for he was terrified. So Saul took his own sword and fell upon it.
When his armour-bearer saw that Saul was dead, he also fell upon his sword and died with him.

1 Samuel 31:3–5

⑰ Samuel dies. In Carmel, Nabal refuses to pay David his fee for the protection racket, so his wife pays instead. Nabal dies and David marries his wife. **Chapter 25**

⑰ David has the opportunity to kill a poorly guarded Saul while he sleeps. Later, from a safe distance, he lets Saul know what he could have done. Saul stops hunting David. **Chapter 26**

⑰ David and his men move into Philistine territory, joining the king of Gath's army, and he gives them Ziklag. David pretends to kill Israelites while he builds his power base by passing the spoils of his raids to the elders of Judah. **Chapter 27**

⑦ ⑰ The Philistines, with David and his men, prepare for battle against Israel. A medium at Endor contacts the dead Samuel for Saul. Samuel reveals that the Philistines will kill him. **Chapter 28**

⑰ Achish sends David and his men back to Ziklag when the other Philistine kings refuse to let David join them in their battle against the Israelites. **Chapter 29**

⑰ The Amalekites have torched Ziklag and taken their wives, children and belongings. David and his men rescue their families and property. David sends gifts to the elders of Judah. **Chapter 30**

⑨ ⑰ The Philistines defeat Israel in battle and wound Saul and kill his son Jonathan. Saul kills himself. The Philistines strip them of their armour, cut off Saul's head and pin their bodies to the wall of Beth Shan. **Chapter 31**

2 Samuel

Overview

This book represents the second half of the Samuel scroll. It recounts the reign of David, the model of Israelite monarchy. With the help of his brutal and unprincipled cousin, his general Joab, David eliminates Saul's heir and becomes king of the whole country. Having captured Jerusalem, which is the hinge between the two territories, he makes it his capital. By transferring the Ark of the Covenant there, he also makes it God's capital, the symbol of God's presence. The reign of David and the extent of his power is presented as the most glittering moment of Israel's history, though the lack of archaeological evidence has led some scholars to doubt the veracity

---

4   **5**   **17**

Chapter 1
David learns of Saul's death and the death of Jonathan. David then takes up a lament for them.

17

Chapter 2
David becomes king over Judah in Hebron, while Abner, the commander of Saul's army, makes Saul's son Ish-Bosheth king over Israel. Civil war breaks out between them.

17

Chapter 3
David grows stronger, while Ish-Bosheth grows weaker. David has several sons by his many wives in Hebron. Abner defects to David, but Joab is distrustful and murders him.

17

Chapter 4
Rekab and Baanah murder the king of Israel, Ish-Bosheth son of Saul in his bed, cut off his head and bring it to David. David executes Rekab and Baanah.

Chapter 1: **Commentary**

David's treatment of the messenger shows that the LORD's anointed is not to be tampered with. His lament over his friends, preserved in an ancient collection of poems, is a masterpiece, but it is striking that there is no mention of or allusion to God.

'O daughters of Israel, weep over Saul,
* who clothed you with crimson, in luxury,*
* who put ornaments of gold on your apparel.*
How the mighty have fallen
* in the midst of the battle!*
Jonathan lies slain upon your high places.
I am distressed for you, my brother Jonathan;
greatly beloved were you to me;
* your love to me was wonderful,*
* passing the love of women.*
How the mighty have fallen,
* and the weapons of war perished!'*

2 Samuel 1:24–27

Chapter 3: **Commentary**

Being a left-hander, Joab had the advantage of being able to use a concealed weapon unexpectedly. He makes use of this to murder Abner and, later, Amasa (20:9). Even David, though, could not control his daredevil and unscrupulous cousin. This will be made clear at Joab's revenge on Absalom, 18:10–19:9.

of this presentation. The central part of the book, the court history of David, is the most brilliant biography of any that has come down to us from the ancient world; with its intimate knowledge of the characters involved, it must depend on an eye-witness of the events it describes. However, the theme of the Deuteronomic History continues, for David's adultery with Bathsheba and his weak control of his family bring disaster in the form of Absalom's rebellion and death. The book concludes with some supplementary information.

Chapter 6: **Commentary**

The brilliant move of bringing the Ark, symbol of God's presence, to hallow his personal fiefdom at Jerusalem made David the model of messianic monarchy. This will be confirmed by Nathan's promises in 7:5–16. However, as a man of blood, he was not allowed to build the Temple, but only acquired the land for it. The awesome sanctity of the Ark is stressed by the fate of Uzzah, who presumes to patronise God by propping up the Ark which he thought was in danger of falling.

Your house and your kingdom shall be made sure for ever before me; your throne shall be established for ever.

2 Samuel 7:16

Chapter 8: **Commentary**

David here laid claim to control over a larger area than Israel held at any other time, from the Orontes in the north to the Euphrates in the east. In the absence of firm archaeological evidence to confirm this, historians have held that these claims are exaggerated, or even that David was no more than a petty chieftain.

Chapter 11: **Commentary**

Having got Uriah's wife pregnant, David attempts to persuade the cuckolded husband to sleep with his wife so that the child may be taken as his. The rules of war forbid this, so David has to compound his sin by arranging that Uriah should be killed in battle. Adultery was considered significantly more reprehensible than a single fling with an unmarried woman.

(17)

David becomes king over a united Israel. David then conquers Jerusalem, builds his palace, takes more wives and has more children. David defeats the Philistines.

Chapter **5**

(11)   **(17)**

On the first attempt to move the Ark of the Covenant from Shiloh to Jerusalem, Uzzah dies. The second attempt succeeds, but David's wife Michal criticises him for dancing before the Ark.

Chapter **6**

(7)   **(12)**   **(17)**

David wants to build a temple for the LORD, but God tells him his son will build it instead. God promises that David's kingdom will endure forever. David thanks God in prayer.

Chapter **7**

(17)

David conquers the Philistines, the Arameans, Edom, Moab, the Ammonites and Amalek. His control over Israel is firmly established.

Chapter **8**

(14)   **(17)**

David takes in Saul's handicapped son, Mephibosheth, and provides well for him and his family.

Chapter **9**

(17)

David sends a delegation to express sympathy when the king of Ammon dies. The delegation is mistreated, so David conquers Ammon and their allies, the Arameans.

Chapter **10**

(17)

While David's army is off fighting Ammon, David stays home and has an affair with Uriah's wife, Bathsheba. After she gets pregnant, he has her husband killed and marries her.

Chapter **11**

(2)   **(9)**   **(17)**

The prophet Nathan rebukes David for his affair and murder. He warns him that trouble will plague him the rest of his life. The child born to Bathsheba dies.

Chapter **12**

Chapter 13

9 | 17

Amnon rapes his half-sister Tamar. Two years later her brother Absalom kills Amnon, then flees from his father David to Talmai, the king of Geshur, where he stays for three years.

Chapter 14

2 | 17

Absalom finally arranges, through David's general Joab, to return home to Jerusalem. He reconciles with his father David.

Chapter 15

9 | 17

Absalom conspires to overthrow David. David flees Jerusalem, taking loyalists with him, but he leaves some priests, ten concubines and his advisor Hushai to undermine Absalom.

Chapter 16

9 | 17

Mephibosheth's servant Ziba claims that Mephibosheth has turned against David. Shimei, a relative of Saul's, curses David. Absalom sleeps with David's ten concubines.

Chapter 17

17

Ahithophel advises Absalom to immediately pursue David and kill him. But Hushai tells him to wait and gather an army. Absalom agrees, so Ahithophel hangs himself.

Chapter 18

4 | 9 | 17

David's army routs Absalom's army. Absalom gets tangled in tree branches by his long hair. David's general, Joab, kills him. David mourns his death.

Chapter 19

2 | 17

David returns to Jerusalem in triumph. Mephibosheth claims Ziba lied about him, so David splits the property between them. Shimei begs forgiveness for his curses.

Chapter 20

9 | 17

Sheba leads a rebellion against David. Joab leads the army against Sheba, who takes refuge in Abel Beth Maakah. The town's elders cut off his head, ending the rebellion.

Now in all Israel there was no one to be praised so much for his beauty as Absalom; from the sole of his foot to the crown of his head there was no blemish in him. When he cut the hair of his head (for at the end of every year he used to cut it; when it was heavy on him, he cut it), he weighed the hair of his head, two hundred shekels by the king's weight.

2 Samuel 14:25–26

Chapter 17: **Commentary**

The advice of David's two counsellors, one loyal, one treacherous, is given in a passage of brilliant flowery rhetoric. When Ahitophel sees that his correct analysis has been disregarded, he commits the only suicide in the Hebrew Bible, thus providing a precedent for another traitor, Judas, in the New Testament.

The battle spread over the face of all the country; and the forest claimed more victims that day than the sword.

Absalom happened to meet the servants of David. Absalom was riding on his mule, and the mule went under the thick branches of a great oak. His head caught fast in the oak, and he was left hanging between heaven and earth, while the mule that was under him went on.

A man saw it, and told Joab, 'I saw Absalom hanging in an oak.'... And ten young men, Joab's armour-bearers, surrounded Absalom and struck him, and killed him.

2 Samuel 18:8–10, 15

It was told Joab, 'The king is weeping and mourning for Absalom.' So the victory that day was turned into mourning for all the troops; for the troops heard that day, 'The king is grieving for his son.' The troops stole into the city that day as soldiers steal in who are ashamed when they flee in battle. The king covered his face, and the king cried with a loud voice, 'O my son Absalom, O Absalom, my son, my son!'

2 Samuel 19:1–4

Then the woman went to all the people with her wise plan. And they cut off the head of Sheba son of Bichri, and threw it out to Joab. So he blew the trumpet, and they dispersed from the city, and all went to their homes, while Joab returned to Jerusalem to the king.

2 Samuel 20:22

Chapter 21: **Commentary**

There now follow six supplements to the court history. We do not know what Saul did to the Gibeonites, but it provided a convenient excuse for David to exterminate Saul's family, possible rivals. No doubt this is why their clansman, Shimei, curses David as a man of blood (16:5). David kept his oath to Jonathan by allowing Meribaal, Jonathan's crippled son, to survive – under house arrest.

9 **18**

To stop a famine, David lets the Gibeonite survivors of Saul's attempted genocide execute seven of Saul's descendants. David's wars against the Philistines succeed.

Chapter
21

1 **5**

David offers up a song of praise to the LORD for his deliverance from his enemies.

Chapter
22

The cords of Sheol entangled me,
the snares of death confronted me.
'In my distress I called upon the LORD;
to my God I called.
From his temple he heard my voice,
and my cry came to his ears.'

2 Samuel 22:6–7

The God of Israel has spoken,
the Rock of Israel has said to me:
One who rules over people justly,
ruling in the fear of God,
is like the light of morning,
like the sun rising on a cloudless morning,
gleaming from the rain on the grassy land.

2 Samuel 23:3–4

The murder of Amnon
Absalom, King David's third-eldest son, murdered Amnon, David's eldest son and heir to the throne, because Amnon had raped Absalom's sister and had suffered no punishment.

Chapter 24: **Commentary**

The census may be considered sinful because it qualifies the LORD's ownership of his people. The story has a typical folkloristic motif of three alternatives and impossibly high figures: 11,000 armed men represents a total population of several million.

1 **5** **16**

David's last words, a poem in praise of God, are followed by a list of the names and deeds of David's most famous soldiers.

Chapter
23

9 **15** **17**

David sins by taking a census. God sends a plague, that stops at Jerusalem when David builds an altar and makes sacrifices on the threshing floor of Araunah, the Jebusite.

Chapter
24

1 Kings

Overview

The two Books of Kings, originally a single narrative, but too long for a single scroll, conclude the Deuteronomistic History, edited to show that fidelity to the covenant brings success and infidelity brings therapeutic punishment. Each king is judged not on political or economic success, but uniquely on religious observance. Material is drawn from the royal annals and from the cycles of the prophets Elijah and Elisha, possibly also from a cycle of stories of the Aramaean Wars. In this book the highlight is Solomon, who is praised for his divine gift of wisdom as a ruler. He is the initiator of the wisdom tradition in Israel. He built a palace and the Temple,

---

Chapter 1

David's son Adonijah tries to claim the throne of Israel for himself but fails in the attempt. David sets up his son Solomon as the next king instead.

Chapter 2

David tells Solomon to obey God's laws and take vengeance on those who wronged him. After David dies, Solomon kills Adonijah, deposes Abiathar and executes Joab and Shimei.

Chapter 3

Solomon asks God for wisdom, which he grants. When two prostitutes both claim to be the mother of a baby, Solomon tells them to cut the baby in two.

Chapter 4

A list of Solomon's officials, daily food rations and the prosperity of Israel during his rule. Solomon writes proverbs, composes songs and demonstrates a knowledge of nature.

Chapter 5

From Hiram, the king of Tyre, Solomon hires workers and supplies to build the Temple for God in Jerusalem.

Chapters 1–2: **Commentary**

David is represented as at least partly senile, manipulated by the mothers of potential royal rivals. These two chapters form the end of the Succession Narrative of 2 Samuel. Solomon ruthlessly exterminates possible rivals and David's old guard, and attempts to put the blame for his ruthlessness on David.

Chapter 3: **Commentary**

Solomon was revered as the fount of the wisdom tradition in Israel, so that several of the books of wisdom are attributed to him. His wisdom showed itself in his judgements and in his court organisation, but also in his commercial success, hence the wonder of the Queen of Sheba. He was the middleman, selling horses from Anatolia to Egypt and chariots from Egypt to Anatolia. His 'King's Highway' to Aqaba on the Red Sea is still a commercial lifeline for the Kingdom of Jordan. But he also introduced the seeds of disaster, the idolatry and hostility that would lead to the break-up of the kingdom.

Chapter 5: **Commentary**

The Israelites were not used to constructing large buildings, and Solomon had to turn to Canaanite models and Phoenician materials and craftsmen. Jerusalem was hugely enlarged, and great fortresses were built at Gezer, Hazor and Megiddo, of which much (including a standard gateway) has been uncovered by archaeologists. The relative dimensions of the Temple and Solomon's palace at Jerusalem make the former seem only a palace-chapel of the latter (floor plans of 1,200 and 5,000 square cubits, and heights of 20 and 25 cubits respectively).

developed an organised court and amassed huge wealth by trade. He also sowed the seeds of disaster by his marriage alliances, which introduced idolatry into the heart of the kingdom, and by alienating the northern tribes through forced labour. Thereafter, the schism introduced an idolatrous temple at Bethel, as king after king was condemned for failing to halt idolatry or purge the contaminated religion of the mountain fertility shrines. Towards the end of the book attention turns to the prophetic tradition of Elijah and then his successor Elisha, especially in the northern kingdom, which was supported by this rather than by the Davidic dynastic promises.

17

Solomon spends seven years building the Temple for the LORD, using large amounts of cedar and gold.

Chapter 6

16   **17**

Solomon spends 13 years building a palace for himself. A description of the Temple's furnishings is given.

Chapter 7

11   **12**   **17**

The Ark of the Covenant is placed in the Temple. Solomon formally dedicates the Temple with a prayer, many sacrifices and a festival that lasts 14 days.

Chapter 8

Jeroboam and the golden calves
Jeroboam led a successful rebellion against Rehoboam and established a new kingdom made up of the ten northern tribes.

14 **16** **17**

Chapter 9

The LORD tells Solomon that his throne will endure forever if his descendants are obedient to God. Solomon conquers enemies, builds ships and marries Pharaoh's daughter.

16 **17**

Chapter 10

The Queen of Sheba visits Solomon on hearing about his wisdom. Solomon acquires great wealth through his extensive trade with neighbouring countries.

17

Chapter 11

Solomon marries foreign women, builds temples for their gods and make sacrifices to them. As a judgement against Solomon, Jeroboam will take ten tribes of Israel from Rehoboam.

9 **17**

Chapter 12

Solomon dies. His son Rehoboam becomes king. Ten of the tribes rebel, making Jeroboam their king. Jeroboam establishes temples in Bethel and Dan, with golden calf idols.

7 **17**

Chapter 13

A prophet tells Jeroboam that someday Josiah will burn human bones on the altar he's built in Bethel. The prophet then dies on his way home because he believes a lie.

7 **17**

Chapter 14

Ahijah predicts the death of Jeroboam's son and the destruction of his kingdom. Pharoah invades Jerusalem and plunders it. Nadab succeeds Jeroboam. Abijah succeeds Rehoboam.

When the queen of Sheba had observed all the wisdom of Solomon, the house that he had built, the food of his table, the seating of his officials, and the attendance of his servants, their clothing, his valets, and his burnt-offerings that he offered at the house of the LORD, there was no more spirit in her. So she said to the king, 'The report was true that I heard in my own land of your accomplishments and of your wisdom.'

1 Kings 10:4–6

Chapter 12: **Commentary**

Despite the warning of Jeroboam's rebellion, supported by the prophet Ahijah, the young bloods suggested only a coarse retort ('loins' in verse 10 is a euphemism) to the request from the northerners for more equable treatment. Political independence was followed by religious independence, for the northerners could not pay homage at the Temple of their rivals. The shrine and 'calf' (bull) at Bethel is denounced by Hosea and Amos, and was destroyed in the reforms of Josiah.

While Jeroboam was standing by the altar to offer incense, a man of God came out of Judah by the word of the LORD to Bethel and proclaimed against the altar by the word of the LORD, and said, 'O altar, altar, thus says the LORD: "A son shall be born to the house of David, Josiah by name; and he shall sacrifice on you the priests of the high places who offer incense on you, and human bones shall be burned on you." '

1 Kings 13:1–2

Judah did what was evil in the sight of the LORD; they provoked him to jealousy with their sins that they committed, more than all that their ancestors had done. For they also built for themselves high places, pillars, and sacred poles on every high hill and under every green tree; there were also male temple prostitutes in the land. They committed all the abominations of the nations that the LORD drove out before the people of Israel.

1 Kings 14:22–24

Solomon and the Queen of Sheba
The Queen of Sheba visited Solomon and was impressed by his wealth and wisdom.

Ahab son of Omri did evil in the sight of the LORD more than all who were before him. And as if it had been a light thing for him to walk in the sins of Jeroboam son of Nebat, he took as his wife Jezebel daughter of King Ethbaal of the Sidonians, and went and served Baal, and worshipped him. He erected an altar for Baal in the house of Baal, which he built in Samaria. Ahab also made a sacred pole. Ahab did more to provoke the anger of the LORD, the God of Israel, than had all the kings of Israel who were before him.

1 Kings 16:30–33

Chapter 18: **Commentary**

Queen Jezebel, daughter of the priest-king of Tyre, becomes proverbial as an evil influence. The status of the bands of prophets whom she slaughters is unclear. They have appeared before this: 'Saul among the prophets' (1 Samuel 19:20). They appear in several towns (2 Kings 2:3–7) and at the royal court mouthing prophecies to please the king (1 Kings 22). This is an important background to the named prophets of the Bible. The rivalry of the prophets of Baal shows that monotheism has no firm grip at this time.

Chapter 19: **Commentary**

Prophets from Moses, through Jeremiah to Jonah, attempt to evade the unrewarding office of pronouncing the LORD's punishments. The fact that here the LORD is manifested in 'a sound of silence' rather than tempest does not mean that the content of the message will be gentle, as the bloodshed of Hazael and Jehu will show.

Chapter 21: **Commentary**

The crime of Ahab and Jezebel is aggravated by several features. Naboth was legally forbidden to alienate his ancestral land. The king should be God's representative in championing the rights of the poor and helpless, instead of which Naboth is falsely accused of blasphemy, so that his now-ownerless land reverts to the king.

Chapter 22: **Commentary**

Micaiah's vision of God seated on his throne, surrounded by his heavenly court, is the ancestor of a series of such biblical scenes: Job 1–2, Isaiah 6, Ezekiel 1, Daniel 7 and finally Revelation 4–5. Ahab obviously senses that at first Micaiah is sarcastically parroting the court prophets.

17

Abijah, king of Judah, rules briefly and is succeeded by Asa who worships the LORD faithfully, allies with Ben-Hadad and fights wars with Baasha, king of Israel.

Chapter 15

17

After two years, Baasha assassinates Nadab. Zimri assassinates his son Elah. Omri assassinates Zimri and establishes Samaria as his capital. His son Ahab marries Jezebel.

Chapter 16

7   8   17

Elijah the prophet predicts drought, then hides from Ahab, first near a brook, then with a widow in Zarephath, near Sidon, who is miraculously fed. Elijah resurrects her dead son.

Chapter 17

7   9   17

After three years, Elijah has a contest on Mount Carmel to see who should be worshipped: the LORD or Baal. Baal loses, so Elijah has Baal's prophets killed. Then the drought ends.

Chapter 18

7   17

Jezebel threatens to kill Elijah, so he runs away. God reassures Elijah and tells him to pick Elisha to become Israel's next prophet. Elisha becomes Elijah's disciple and servant.

Chapter 19

7   17

Ahab defeats Ben-Hadad, the king of Aram, when he attacks Samaria, but Ahab lets him live and grants a favourable treaty. A prophet condemns Ahab for his leniency.

Chapter 20

7   17

Ahab's wife Jezebel arranges to have Naboth killed so Ahab can steal his vineyard. Elijah foretells that Ahab's descendants will die and that dogs will eat Jezebel.

Chapter 21

7   9   17

Jehoshaphat joins Ahab in an alliance against Aram to attack Ramoth Gilead. The prophet Micaiah predicts Ahab's death. Jehoshaphat and Ahab go to war anyway and Ahab dies.

Chapter 22

2 Kings

Overview

The Second Book of Kings continues the First without any real break, concluding the Elijah Cycle. The cycles of these two prophets constitute the last moments of prosperity before the accelerating decline and fall of the two states under the hammer blows first of Assyria and then Babylon.

	⑦	⑨	⑰
Chapter 1	Ahab's son Ahaziah injures himself. He sends messengers to consult Baal-zebub, the god of Ekron, about recovering. Elijah intercepts them and tells them Ahaziah will die.		

	⑦	⑧	⑨
Chapter 2	After Elijah is taken away by a fiery chariot, Elisha crosses the Jordan, purifies a bad spring and calls out bears to maul boys who made fun of his baldness.		

	⑰		
Chapter 3	Ahab's son, Joram, succeeds Ahaziah as king. He reigns 12 years. During his reign, Moab successfully revolts against Israel and gains its independence.		

	⑦	⑧	⑰
Chapter 4	Elisha miraculously helps a widow pay off her husband's creditors. Then Elisha raises a dead boy back to life, fixes a poisoned stew and multiplies loaves of bread to feed a crowd.		

	⑦	⑨	⑰
Chapter 5	Elisha heals Naaman, the commander of the king of Aram, of leprosy. Elisha refuses payment, but Gehazi secretly makes him pay. So Elisha curses Gehazi with leprosy.		

Chapter 1: **Commentary**

This is a typical folk story, with the motif of triple repetition, illustrating the danger of disrespect for the LORD's representative.

Again the king sent to him another captain of fifty with his fifty. He went up and said to him, 'O man of God, this is the king's order: Come down quickly!'

But Elijah answered them, 'If I am a man of God, let fire come down from heaven and consume you and your fifty.' Then the fire of God came down from heaven and consumed him and his fifty.

2 Kings 1:11–12

Chapter 2: **Commentary**

Elisha is presented as the heir to Elijah (receiving a double share of his inheritance, as the eldest son), just as Joshua is the heir to Moses. The parallel between the two prophets is close: both work an oil miracle for a widow, both work a water miracle with ditches, both raise a child from the dead. However, Elisha is more of a political operator than a critic of morality as Elijah was. He even seems to approve the assassination of Jehoram, and some of his miracles are mere demonstrations of power without a clear religious dimension.

As they were walking along and talking together, suddenly a chariot of fire and horses of fire appeared and separated the two of them, and Elijah went up to heaven in a whirlwind. Elisha saw this and cried out, 'My father! My father! The chariots and horsemen of Israel!' And Elisha saw him no more. Then he took hold of his garment and tore it in two.

2 Kings 2:11–12

> *The officer had said to the man of God, 'Look, even if the Lord should open the floodgates of the heavens, could this happen?' The man of God had replied, 'You will see it with your own eyes, but you will not eat any of it!' And that is exactly what happened to him, for the people trampled him in the gateway, and he died.*
>
> **2 Kings 7:19–20**

Elijah's chariot
The prophet Elijah ascends into the sky riding a chariot lifted by a whirlwind. His servant Elisha witnesses the event and becomes a prophet to replace him.

8		**17**		Chapter
Elisha makes an axe head float. He blinds an army and leads them captive to Samaria. The king of Samaria wants Elisha dead when a siege against Samaria leads to cannibalism.				**6**

7		**8**		**17**	Chapter
Elisha announces that the siege-induced famine will end. The Aramean army inexplicably retreats, leaving piles of food, which lepers discover and report to the king.					**7**

17

Chapter
8

The mother of the resurrected boy has her land restored after Gehazi tells her story to the king. Hazael murders Ben-hadad, king of Aram. Jehoram, king of Judah,

7   **9**   **17**

Chapter
9

Elisha sends a prophet to anoint Jehu king of Israel. So Jehu kills Joram king of Israel and Ahaziah king of Judah. Then he kills Jezebel, who is eaten by dogs.

When King Ahaziah of Judah saw this, he fled in the direction of Beth-haggan. Jehu pursued him, saying, 'Shoot him also!' And they shot him in the chariot at the ascent to Gur, which is by Ibleam. Then he fled to Megiddo, and died there. His officers carried him in a chariot to Jerusalem, and buried him in his tomb with his ancestors in the city of David. In the eleventh year of Joram son of Ahab, Ahaziah began to reign over Judah.

2 Kings 9:27–29

Then he went in and ate and drank; he said, 'See to that cursed woman and bury her; for she is a king's daughter.' But when they went to bury her, they found no more of her than the skull and the feet and the palms of her hands. When they came back and told him, he said, 'This is the word of the LORD, which he spoke by his servant Elijah the Tishbite, "In the territory of Jezreel the dogs shall eat the flesh of Jezebel; the corpse of Jezebel shall be like dung on the field in the territory of Jezreel, so that no one can say, This is Jezebel."'

2 Kings 9:34–37

Painted Jezebel
Jezebel, mother of Joram king of Israel, is tossed out of a window and dies on the orders of his general, Jehu, who had already killed the king and taken his place on the throne.

As soon as he had finished presenting the burnt-offering, Jehu said to the guards and to the officers, 'Come in and kill them; let no one escape.' So they put them to the sword. The guards and the officers threw them out, and then went into the citadel of the temple of Baal. They brought out the pillar that was in the temple of Baal, and burned it. Then they demolished the pillar of Baal, and destroyed the temple of Baal, and made it a latrine to this day. Thus Jehu wiped out Baal from Israel.

2 Kings 10:25–28

Chapter 11: **Commentary**

Athaliah, daughter of Jezebel and grand-daughter of the priest-king of Tyre, would be highly suspect to the Jerusalem establishment. She was also a worshipper of Baal. She swiftly eliminates all possible rivals.

So Elisha died, and they buried him. Now bands of Moabites used to invade the land in the spring of the year. As a man was being buried, a marauding band was seen and the man was thrown into the grave of Elisha; as soon as the man touched the bones of Elisha, he came to life and stood on his feet.

2 Kings 13:20–21

Chapter 15: **Commentary**

The inexorable advance of Assyria, gobbling up Mediterranean states, now reaches Israel. In a dozen years it will swallow up the northern kingdom. 'Pulu' (verse 19) is a throne-name of Tiglath-Pileser III, King of Assyria from 745–727 BC. In the Assyrian records Menahem is listed as a tributary in 738 BC, and Hoshea as having paid a heavy bribe to achieve the throne of Israel (verse 30).

He did what was evil in the sight of the LORD; he did not depart from the sins of Jeroboam son of Nebat, which he caused Israel to sin.

In the days of King Pekah of Israel, King Tiglath-pileser of Assyria came and captured Ijon, Abel-beth-maacah, Janoah, Kedesh, Hazor, Gilead, and Galilee, all the land of Naphtali; and he carried the people captive to Assyria.

2 Kings 15:28–29

Athaliah
Judah's sole queen came to the throne by mass murder and ended her reign by herself being murdered.

		Chapter 10

9 **17**

Jehu slaughters the remainder of Ahab's family, kills the worshippers of Baal, demolishes Baal's temple and turns Baal's altar and sacred stones into a latrine.

	Chapter 11

17

In Judah, Ahaziah's mother Athaliah kills all but one of the royal sons and makes herself queen. Seven years later, Joash becomes king after a successful rebellion against Athaliah.

	Chapter 12

17

Joash rules 40 years. He refurbishes the Temple in Jerusalem, then strips its gold to pay Hazael to stop his attack on Jerusalem. After Joash's murder, his son Amaziah becomes king.

		Chapter 13

7 **17**

Jehoahaz rebels against Hazael, king of Aram. During the reign of his son Jehoash, Elisha dies after predicting Jehoash will defeat Aram three times. Hazael is succeeded by his son, Ben-hadad.

	Chapter 14

17

Amaziah king of Judah unsuccessfully fights against Israel. He is assassinated. His son Azariah becomes king. Jeroboam II becomes king of Israel and restores its borders.

		Chapter 15

9 **17**

Azariah has leprosy, so his son Jotham rules. Ahaz follows Jotham. In Israel, Shallum assassinates Zechariah. Menahem assassinates Shallum. Pekah assassinates Pekahiah. Hoshea assassinates Pekah.

(17)

Chapter 16

Ahaz worships idols and sacrifices a son. When Rezin king of Aram and Pekah king of Israel march against him, he pays Tiglath-Pileser king of the Assyrians to fight them.

(9) **(17)**

Chapter 17

As God's judgement against their idolatry, Shalmaneser king of Assyria attacks and conquers Samaria, capital of Israel, and deports king Hoshea and the upper class to Assyria.

(11) **(17)**

Chapter 18

Hezekiah king of Judah restores the worship of the LORD. Judah celebrates Passover for the first time as a pilgrimage festival at Jerusalem. Sennacherib king of Assyria threatens Jerusalem and lays siege to it.

Chapter 16: **Commentary**

The shameful behaviour of Ahaz is presented as the reason why Judah also now pays tribute to Assyria. The dismantling of the Solomonic altar and replacement by an Assyrian altar would also be a recognition of the superiority of the Assyrian gods.

Chapter 17: **Commentary**

Hoshea, 'like a dove, silly and without sense' (Hosea 7:11) defaulted on his tribute and turned to Egypt for help. After the Fall of Samaria the Deuteronomic editor gives an extended reflection on the reasons for the disaster: infidelity in worship and failure to observe the Law. The Assyrian policy was to unite their empire by exchange of populations to break down ethnic identities. Nevertheless, at least traces of Yahwism remained.

Chapter 18: **Commentary**

For his religious reforms Hezekiah is given higher praise than any king since David. Assyrian records also note that in 701 BC Sennacherib besieged 46 cities of Judah and shut Hezekiah up 'like a bird in a cage'. On the accounts of the Assyrian embassy and withdrawal, see Isaiah 36–39, where the same story is told.

Sennacherib's army dies
Hezekiah and Judah survive thanks to a plague that devastates the Assyrian king's army, forcing an end to Jerusalem's siege.

Hezekiah received the letter from the hand of the
messengers and read it; then Hezekiah went up to the
house of the LORD and spread it before the LORD. And
Hezekiah prayed before the LORD, and said: 'O LORD
the God of Israel, who are enthroned above the
cherubim, you are God, you alone, of all the
kingdoms of the earth; you have made heaven and
earth. Incline your ear, O LORD, and hear; open your
eyes, O LORD, and see; hear the words of Sennacherib,
which he has sent to mock the living God.

2 Kings 19:14–16

Chapter 21: **Commentary**

The reign of Manasseh was the longest of any in Judah, but
both his own and the Assyrian records stress that he was a
loyal subject of Assyria. The placing of a statue of Asherah,
the Canaanite fertility goddess, was a desecration.

Chapter 22: **Commentary**

This 'Book of the Law' is at the heart of Josiah's reform.
It was probably the Book of Deuteronomy, or at least the
core of the work, which expresses the same spirit. The
nucleus of it could date from the previous reform of
Hezekiah. The most striking aspect of the reform was
the abolition of the suspect local, syncretistic cults and
the centralisation of worship in Jerusalem, but also the
abolition of Assyrian astral cults and Canaanite fertility
rites. Josiah also destroyed the suspect northern shrine
at Bethel. Passover had always been a family festival,
celebrated at home; its centralisation around Jerusalem
was integral to the reform.

Chapter 23: **Commentary**

Assyrian power was broken by Babylon in 612 BC. Egypt
seized the opportunity to advance across the Euphrates.
Josiah was killed at the battle of Carchemish, attempting
to block Pharoah Neco.

Chapter 24: **Commentary**

With the invasion of Nebuchadnezzar of Babylon, the final
stage of the subjugation of Judah begins, with a series of
rebellions, punished by deportations – first the nobles and
armament manufacturers (verse 14), then 'the rest of the
people' (25:11). It is impossible to know how many were
left behind, but the Book of Lamentations shows that
some worship continued in the ruins of the Temple.

⑦	⑫	⑰	
Hezekiah prays for help and the prophet Isaiah predicts deliverance. Sennacherib's army dies of a plague and he leaves. Back home, two of Sennacherib's sons assassinate him.			Chapter **19**

⑦	⑧	⑫	
Hezekiah becomes ill and miraculously recovers. Hezekiah shows Babylonian envoys his wealth. Isaiah predicts the Babylonian conquest. Hezekiah dies. His son Manasseh succeeds him.			Chapter **20**

⑨	⑰	
Manasseh worships false gods, sacrifices a son, practises divination, consults mediums and murders. His son Amon is assassinated. Amon's son Josiah replaces him.		Chapter **21**

⑦	⑰	
During Josiah's renovations of the Temple, the priests find 'the Book of the Law'. The female prophet Huldah warns that Judah will be judged, but not during Josiah's lifetime.		Chapter **22**

⑪	⑰	
Josiah removes all the idols and once again celebrates Passover. He dies when he goes to war with Pharaoh Necho at Megiddo. Jehoiakim becomes king and pays Necho tribute.		Chapter **23**

⑨	⑰	
Nebuchadnezzar king of Babylon conquers Judah. Jehoiakim rebels. When Jehoichin becomes king after Jehoiakim dies, Nebuchadnezzar replaces him with Zedekiah.		Chapter **24**

⑨	⑰	
Zedekiah rebels, so Nebuchadnezzar attacks, kills his sons, blinds him and takes him away. Nebuchadnezzar destroys Jerusalem and the Temple, exiling all but the poor to Babylon.		Chapter **25**

1 Chronicles

Overview

In the Greek Bible the Books of Chronicles are called *Paraleipomena*, or 'things left out'. The title 'Chronicles' comes from the Latin of Jerome in the late fourth century. They cover much the same ground as the Books of Samuel and Kings, with a good deal of supplementary information. In fact they are a rewriting of the previous historical account from a different point of view. The Books of Samuel and Kings were part of the great Deuteronomic History, whose theme was that success depended on fidelity to the LORD, and infidelity was punished by failure and the chastisement by enemies. The viewpoint of Chronicles is focused on the Temple and its liturgy, both David and Solomon being lavishly

16	17	
Chapter 1	The genealogies of Noah's sons, Japheth, Ham and Shem, including the descendants of Abraham, Ishmael, Esau's sons and the kings of Edom.	
Chapter 2	Israel, also known as Jacob, has 12 sons. The genealogy of Israel's son Judah.	
Chapter 3	The genealogy of David, listing those who become kings down to the Babylonian Exile, and his descendants after the Babylonian Exile.	
Chapter 4	The genealogies of the other clans of Judah and the genealogy of Simeon.	
Chapter 5	The genealogies of Reuben, Gad and the half-tribe of Manasseh.	

Chapters 1–9: Commentary

These chapters consist almost entirely of lists of names. Many of the names are in fact place names, showing relationships between villages. The importance of these lists is not the names themselves but the stress that the post-exilic people of God form the legitimate heirs of ancient Israel. David's tribe of Judah is especially stressed (chapter 3), for David will be represented as a sort of second Moses, an almost messianic figure forming and leading his people. The Levites also receive special emphasis (5:27–6:66), as do the liturgical functionaries of Jerusalem (chapter 9).

Jabez was honoured more than his brothers; and his mother named him Jabez, saying, 'Because I bore him in pain.' Jabez called on the God of Israel, saying, 'Oh that you would bless me and enlarge my border, and that your hand might be with me, and that you would keep me from hurt and harm!' And God granted what he asked.

1 Chronicles 4:9–10

praised because they were the founders of the Temple liturgy. Thus the intensely human portrait of David and the whole sad story of his weak dealings with his dysfunctional family is omitted. No word is said of the sordid squabbles over the succession to David. Solomon's dalliance with his foreign wives and their idolatrous gods is passed over in silence. Kings are assessed not on their fidelity to the covenant, as in 1–2 Kings, but on their devotion to the Temple liturgy. The author is fascinated by the details of Temple liturgy, and the various offices of priests and Levites. He repeatedly underlines the joy of the Temple festivities and the generosity of the faithful people to the Temple.

Chapter 10: **Commentary**

The first king of Israel gets short shrift. We hear only of his disobedience, disgrace and death, for he is mentioned only as a dark background to contrast with the light of David.

So Saul died for his unfaithfulness; he was unfaithful to the LORD in that he did not keep the command of the LORD; moreover, he had consulted a medium, seeking guidance, and did not seek guidance from the LORD. Therefore the LORD put him to death and turned the kingdom over to David son of Jesse.

1 Chronicles 10:13–14

Chapters 11–20: **Commentary**

The purpose of these chapters is less to recount the story of David, already told in the Books of Samuel, than to show that Israel was united under his inspired leadership.

Chapter 13: **Commentary**

This chapter on the transfer of the Ark to Jerusalem really shows the author's purposes. The simple but awesome little country procession described in 2 Samuel 6 is transformed into a magnificent spectacle, a festival for 'all Israel' with orchestras and liturgical splendour. The author describes not so much what happened as what should have or must have happened.

The genealogies of Levi and its various clans, along with the towns that are allotted to them from the other tribes.

Chapter 6

The genealogies of Issachar, Benjamin, Naphtali, Manasseh, Ephraim and Asher.

Chapter 7

The genealogies of Benjamin, focusing on the line of King Saul.

Chapter 8

The list of several of those who are first to return to Jerusalem following the Babylonian Exile, followed by a genealogy of King Saul.

Chapter 9

The Philistines attack Israel. King Saul and his sons fight them and die in battle. Saul dies because he was 'unfaithful' to the LORD.

Chapter 10

David becomes king in place of Saul and conquers the Jebusite city of Jerusalem and makes it his own. A list of David's best soldiers, along with some of their exploits.

Chapter 11

A list of those who join David while he is hiding from Saul at Ziklag. A listing of how many people join David in Hebron when they make him king over all Israel.

Chapter 12

David begins to move the Ark of the Covenant from Kiriath Jearim to Jerusalem, but when Uzzah is killed during the process, he leaves it in the house of Obed-Edom the Gittite.

Chapter 13

16   **17**

Chapter
14
Hiram, king of Tyre, supplies David with what's needed for building a palace in Jerusalem. David marries several women and has many children. He repeatedly defeats the Philistines.

16   **17**

Chapter
15
David brings the Ark of the Covenant to Jerusalem, carried by the Levites. David dances before the Ark, but his wife, Michal, despises him for it.

5   **11**

Chapter
16
At the Tabernacle, there are sacrifices and music. Asaph and his associates praise the LORD. The priests continue daily sacrifices at the high place in Gibeon.

7   **12**

Chapter
17
God will not let David build a permanent Temple. God promises him an everlasting kingdom and throne. His son will build the Temple, instead. David offers thanks to God.

16   **17**

Chapter
18
A list of David's military victories over the Philistines, Moabites, Arameans, Edomites, Ammonites and Amalekites. A list of important government officials.

17

Chapter
19
Hanun, the new king of Ammon, insults David's messengers, leading David to attack and conquer him. David also subjugates the Arameans who had allied with the Ammonites.

17

Chapter
20
David captures Rabbah, the capital of Ammon, and fights against the Philistines at Gezer and Gath.

9   **15**   **17**

Chapter
21
David takes a census of Israel despite Joab's opposition. God sends a plague against Israel that stops when David purchases the threshing floor of Araunah and offers a sacrifice.

Chapter 15: Commentary

The great ceremony and massive procession, interrupted to underline David's international success, now continues.

Chapter 17: Commentary

The secret of David's greatness is still his personal relationship with God and God's promise to him. This account keeps close to its model in 2 Samuel 7, but significantly omits any mention of failure and punishment (2 Samuel 7:14), and stresses (verse 14) that the Temple and the sovereignty belong not to David but to God. Nowhere is there a hint of David's adultery with Bathsheba and his murder of her husband.

'I will appoint a place for my people Israel, and will plant them, so that they may live in their own place, and be disturbed no more; and evildoers shall wear them down no more, as they did formerly, from the time that I appointed judges over my people Israel; and I will subdue all your enemies. Moreover, I declare to you that the LORD will build you a house.'

1 Chronicles 17:9–10

Again there was war at Gath, where there was a man of great size, who had six fingers on each hand, and six toes on each foot, twenty-four in number; he also was descended from the giants. When he taunted Israel, Jonathan son of Shimea, David's brother, killed him.

1 Chronicles 20:6–7

Then Ornan said to David, 'Take it; and let my lord the king do what seems good to him; see, I present the oxen for burnt-offerings, and the threshing-sledges for the wood, and the wheat for a grain-offering. I give it all.'
But King David said to Ornan, 'No; I will buy them for the full price. I will not take for the LORD what is yours, nor offer burnt-offerings that cost me nothing.'

1 Chronicles 21:23–24

Chapter 22: Commentary

Subtle but significant changes slip into the account of the building of the Temple and its arrangements. The work is now done by foreigners (verse 2), not by forced labour gangs of Israelites, whose resentment led to the split of the kingdom. David's tribute to the LORD is enormously increased (verse 14). In the following chapters, which have no parallel in the earlier account, the throngs of Temple servants and their detailed duties show a nation wholly intent on the liturgical worship of their sovereign.

'With great pains I have provided for the house of the LORD one hundred thousand talents of gold, one million talents of silver, and bronze and iron beyond weighing, for there is so much of it; timber and stone too I have provided. To these you must add more. You have an abundance of workers: stonecutters, masons, carpenters, and all kinds of artisans without number, skilled in working gold, silver, bronze, and iron. Now begin the work, and the LORD be with you.'

1 Chronicles 22:14–16

David did not count those below twenty years of age, for the LORD had promised to make Israel as numerous as the stars of heaven. Joab son of Zeruiah began to count them, but did not finish; yet wrath came upon Israel for this, and the number was not entered into the account of the Annals of King David.

1 Chronicles 27:23–24

Chapter 28: **Commentary**

David himself was not allowed to build the Temple, since his wars had made him a man of blood. In the original account this charge referred to his annihilation of the family of Saul, potential rivals (2 Samuel 16:7–8). However, he makes all possible preparations: not only does he purchase the land for the Temple (as in 2 Samuel), but he hands over vast quantities of precious building materials and makes detailed preparations for the liturgy, of which he could be regarded as the real founder. A talent is roughly 30 kilos.

---

16 **17**

David declares that the future Temple will be built on that threshing floor. Then he makes extensive preparations for building it, giving Solomon and the leaders of Israel instructions.

Chapter **22**

16 **17**

David makes Solomon king before he dies. He counts the Levites, organises them, and puts them in charge of helping Aaron's descendants minister at the future Temple.

Chapter **23**

16 **17**

David organises Aaron's descendants. The various Aaronic families will have to take turns at the Temple. The Levitical families will also have to take turns at the Temple.

Chapter **24**

16 **17**

David organises the musical service at the Temple, determining who will perform and when – and what each family will be placed in charge of.

Chapter **25**

16 **17**

A list of the families and individuals who are to serve as gatekeepers. A list of the treasurers and other government officials.

Chapter **26**

16 **17**

A list of the heads of families. A list of the commanders of the army and its divisions that serve on a rotating basis. A list of the tribal leaders and other government officials.

Chapter **27**

16 **17**

David reiterates his desire to build a Temple and then he gives a detailed overview of his design for the Temple.

Chapter **28**

5 **12** **17**

David and other wealthy people in Israel make large donations for the future Temple. David praises God. Solomon is acknowledged as the next king. Then David dies.

Chapter **29**

2 Chronicles

Overview

This Second Book of Chronicles provides a rollercoaster history of the Kingdom of David until the end of the monarchy. Written after the return from Exile, it is not surprising that it shows little interest in the northern kingdom of Israel, and all the emphasis is on the southern kingdom of Judah, to which the Exiles returned. The same interests in liturgical activity and Temple worship as in the first Book remain constant, and the same interpretation of history by means of speeches of the participants points the lessons. Success depends on fidelity to

---

Chapter 1

After Solomon becomes king, God grants him wisdom, so he can better govern the people of Israel. God also gives him wealth and honour.

Chapter 2

Solomon orders the building of the Temple. Hiram king of Tyre supplies the wood and skilled labour. Solomon conscripts non-Israelites to do much of the hard, unskilled labour.

Chapter 3

Solomon then builds the Temple. A list of the materials used in its construction.

Chapter 4

A detailed list of the Temple's furnishings and the materials used in making them.

Chapter 1: **Commentary**

It is puzzling that, after all the preparations for building the Temple as God's residence at Jerusalem, Solomon should go off to sacrifice at the Tent of Meeting at Gibeon, a short distance north of Jerusalem. Furthermore, his personal visit described in 1 Kings, resulting in a revelatory dream, is transformed into a national procession. The gift of wisdom is seen as the highest gift for a ruler. In Solomon's case it also implies the gift to acquire the wealth for building the Temple and endowing the liturgy. As verses 16–17 show, his wealth was gained by acting as middleman between the chariots of Egypt and the horses of Cilicia.

Chapter 3: **Commentary**

The account of the building of the Temple is much shorter than in 1 Kings 6–7. Of course that Temple no longer existed after the Exile, and the author is more interested in the details of the liturgy, and especially the part to be played by the Levites, who did not exist in Solomon's day.

liturgical norms: some rulers begin well but succumb to pride, while others begin badly but finally convert. The basic pattern conforms to that of the Books of Kings, but there are numerous additions, often quite developed, which are unattested in other historical works. Whether they are authentic history or not we cannot now judge. As they stand, these express the chronicler's understanding of history, but they may well be based on real historical events about which we are otherwise uninformed.

The Temple
With a capital city for the nation, Solomon finally replaced the wandering Tabernacle when he built a permanent Temple in Jerusalem.

When Solomon had ended his prayer, fire came down from heaven and consumed the burnt-offering and the sacrifices; and the glory of the LORD filled the temple. The priests could not enter the house of the LORD, because the glory of the LORD filled the LORD's house. When all the people of Israel saw the fire come down and the glory of the LORD on the temple, they bowed down on the pavement with their faces to the ground, and worshipped and gave thanks to the LORD, saying, 'For he is good,
    for his steadfast love endures for ever.'

2 Chronicles 7:1–3

'When I shut up the heavens so that there is no rain, or command the locust to devour the land, or send pestilence among my people, if my people who are called by my name humble themselves, pray, seek my face, and turn from their wicked ways, then I will hear from heaven, and will forgive their sin and heal their land. Now my eyes will be open and my ears attentive to the prayer that is made in this place.'

2 Chronicles 7:13–15

11   **17**

Once the Temple has been built, the Ark of the Covenant is brought there and set in the Most Holy Place. There are sacrifices and celebrations. God's glory fills the Temple.

Chapter
5

1   **11**   **12**

Solomon pronounces a blessing on the assembled people, praises God and offers a prayer of dedication.

Chapter
6

1   **14**   **17**

Fire consumes the sacrifices and the glory of God fills the Temple. The celebration lasts for weeks. God promises to bless Solomon if he remains faithful, and curse him if he doesn't.

Chapter
7

17

Solomon enslaves the non-Israelites within Israel's borders, builds a palace for his wife, Pharaoh's daughter, performs sacrifices to the LORD, builds a trading fleet and grows wealthy.

Chapter
8

Hezekiah's sign from God
God gave Hezekiah a sign that he would be healed from his illness: the shadow on the stairs moved backwards ten steps.

⑰	
Chapter **9**	The Queen of Sheba visits Solomon because of his wisdom. She praises him and the prosperity of his kingdom. Solomon dies after reigning for 40 years.

⑨		⑰
Chapter **10**	The ten tribes north of Judah rebel against Solomon's son Rehoboam because he refuses to lighten their tax burden. So they set up a rival kingdom under Jeroboam.	

⑰	
Chapter **11**	God prevents Rehoboam from attacking Israel. Most of the Levites and priests leave Israel and move to Judah. Rehoboam has many wives and children.

⑦		⑨		⑰
Chapter **12**	The Egyptian Pharoah Shishak attacks Jerusalem. The prophet Shemiah proclaims it is God's judgement. A state of war exists between Rehoboam and Jeroboam until Rehoboam dies.			

Chapter 9: **Commentary**

The chronicler presents Solomon in all his glory, but says no word about the diminution of his empire or about his foreign wives and the idolatry they introduced, as recounted in 1 Kings 11. The author is similarly silent about the first revolt of Jeroboam and Ahijah's prophecy of the division of the kingdom. This removes any trace of legitimacy of Jeroboam's action. A major difference between the accounts of Kings and Chronicles is the absence of interest in the history of the northern kingdom in the latter. The Levites from the north desert the idolatrous national shrine there and flee to the southern kingdom (11:13–17). For the post-exilic community, grouped around the Temple in Judah, the history of the northern kingdom of Israel lay in the distant past.

The young men who had grown up with him said to him, 'Thus should you speak to the people who said to you, "Your father made our yoke heavy, but you must lighten it for us"; tell them, "My little finger is thicker than my father's loins. Now, whereas my father laid on you a heavy yoke, I will add to your yoke. My father disciplined you with whips, but I will discipline you with scorpions."'
2 Chronicles 10:10–11

Chapter 12: **Commentary**

The parallel account in 1 Kings 14 mentions Pharaoh Shishak's pillaging of the Temple, but says no word about the king's repentance at the prophet's warning, which enabled Rehoboam to regain his strength. The same will occur two centuries later when Sennacherib invades and the repentance of the wicked King Hezekiah spares Jerusalem from total destruction (chapter 32). The moral message is clear.

Chapter 13: **Commentary**

This confrontation between Abijah and the illegitimate northern king with an army double the size is not recorded in the Books of Kings. The author stresses that victory is due to the legitimate worship of the one and the idolatry of the other. A similar victory of the reforming Asa's army of half a million over the million Cushite (Ethiopian) invaders follows (14:8–14). By contrast, when Asa shows mistrust in the LORD by allying himself with the Aramaeans, and refuses to listen to the prophet Hanani, he is stricken with disease and dies (16:1–12).

The Spirit of God came on Azariah son of Oded. He went out to meet Asa and said to him, 'Listen to me, Asa and all Judah and Benjamin. The LORD is with you when you are with him. If you seek him, he will be found by you, but if you forsake him, he will forsake you. For a long time Israel was without the true God, without a priest to teach and without the law. But in their distress they turned to the LORD, the God of Israel, and sought him, and he was found by them.

2 Chronicles 15:1–4

Then Micaiah said, 'I saw all Israel scattered on the mountains, like sheep without a shepherd'; and the LORD said, 'These have no master; let each one go home in peace.' The king of Israel said to Jehoshaphat, 'Did I not tell you that he would not prophesy anything favourable about me, but only disaster?'

2 Chronicles 18:16–17

Chapters 19–20: **Commentary**

The judicial reforms of Jehoshaphat and the miraculous intervention of the LORD in battle that follows are not attested by history. Jehoshaphat's speeches, the liturgical formalities and the joyful worship are typical of the chronicler. However, these are no more than narrative details. The whole incident serves well the chronicler's lesson of the reward of fidelity.

(17) Abijah, Rehoboam's son, becomes king of Judah. He criticises the northern tribes for following Jeroboam, then defeats Jeroboam in battle. He has many wives and children. — **Chapter 13**

(17) After Abijah dies, his son Asa becomes king, enjoys ten years of peace, eliminates high places, builds up Judah's defences and successfully defends Judah against the Cushites. — **Chapter 14**

(17) Asa removes idols, swears allegiance to the LORD and deposes his grandmother Maakah as queen mother because she set up an Asherah pole. — **Chapter 15**

(7) (9) (17) Asa allies with Ben-Hadad, king of Aram, against Israel. When the prophet Hanani criticises Asa for relying on Aram, Asa imprisons him. Asa dies from disease after turning to doctors rather than the LORD. — **Chapter 16**

(16) (17) Jehoshaphat removes the high places and Asherah poles. He sends Levites to teach the people from the Book of the Law. He keeps a large standing army and fortifies the country. — **Chapter 17**

(7) (9) (17) Ahab asks Jehoshaphat to fight against Ramoth Gilead. The prophet Micaiah prophesies disaster: Ahab will die. Neither Jehoshaphat nor Ahab listen and Ahab dies. — **Chapter 18**

(7) (17) The prophet Jehu prophesies against Jehoshaphat. Jehoshaphat appoints judges from the Levites, priests and heads of Israelite families to settle disputes and administer justice. — **Chapter 19**

⑦ **⑫** **⑰**

| Chapter **20** | The Moabites and Ammonites attack Jehoshaphat. He prays and Jehaziel prophesies victory. He builds trading ships with Ahaziah, king of Israel. Eliezer predicts their destruction. |

'O our God, will you not execute judgement upon them? For we are powerless against this great multitude that is coming against us. We do not know what to do, but our eyes are on you.'

2 Chronicles 20:12

⑦ **⑰**

| Chapter **21** | Jehoram becomes king. He kills his brothers, marries one of Ahab's daughters and worships other gods. Edom and Libnah revolt and the prophet Elijah prophesies his death. |

When Jehoram had ascended the throne of his father and was established, he put all his brothers to the sword, and also some of the officials of Israel. Jehoram was thirty-two years old when he began to reign; he reigned for eight years in Jerusalem. He walked in the way of the kings of Israel, as the house of Ahab had done; for the daughter of Ahab was his wife. He did what was evil in the sight of the LORD.

2 Chronicles 21:4–6

Jehoshaphat leading Judah
After prayer, Jehoshaphat led Judah to victory over the Moabites and the Ammonites who had attacked him.

⑰

| Chapter **22** | Ahaziah king of Judah is killed with Joram king of Israel when Jehu rebels against Joram. Ahaziah's mother, Athaliah, kills all but Joash and sets herself up as queen of Judah. |

Chapter 23: **Commentary**

This version of the removal of Athaliah is typical of the chronicler's minor adjustments of history: the foreign mercenaries of 2 Kings 11 are replaced by Levites because foreigners should not be allowed in the sanctuary. The trumpeters are joined by cantors leading hymns.

⑰

| Chapter **23** | Seven years later, when Joash is eight, Jehoida leads a coup against Athaliah, kills her, and Joash becomes king. Jehoida eliminates idolatry throughout Judah. |

Chapter 24: **Commentary**

The reforms of Joash are attested also in 2 Kings 12, and the Aramaean invasion. There, however, the Aramaeans are bought off by the gift of the Temple treasure. Here, Joash's infidelity is more drastically punished by his lingering death. Defeat of his forces by the smaller army (verse 24) underlines that it was a divine punishment.

⑦ **⑨** **⑰**

| Chapter **24** | Joash renovates the Temple, but worships idols. Zechariah prophesies against him and Joash has him stoned to death. Severely wounded in an Aramean attack, Joash is assassinated in his bed. |

So the king gave command, and they made a chest, and set it outside the gate of the house of the LORD. A proclamation was made throughout Judah and Jerusalem to bring in for the LORD the tax that Moses the servant of God laid on Israel in the wilderness. All the leaders and all the people rejoiced, and brought their tax and dropped it into the chest until it was full.

2 Chronicles 24:8–10

Chapter 26: **Commentary**

In 2 Kings 15 details are not given of the reason for Uzziah's leprosy. Here, however, it is attributed to his assumption of the priestly privilege of burning incense on the altar, which was enough to cancel out all his good work for the nation. In the Bible, 'leprosy' is a far wider term than the modern Hansen's disease, popularly known as leprosy. It includes many other skin diseases (Leviticus 13–14), for which isolation is prescribed to prevent spread of infection. As with other kings, the basic fault is seen to be pride (verse 16), though this is expressed in liturgical infringement.

Chapter 28: **Commentary**

Fuller information on the Syro-Ephraimite War of 726 BC is provided in 2 Kings 16 and Isaiah 7–9. It marks the beginning of the end, for Ahaz was compelled for his own protection to pay tribute (or a bribe) to the king of Assyria who was advancing through the Syrian territory. Although the Assyrian Empire lost power before engulfing Judah, it was their Mesopotamian successor, Babylon, who eventually destroyed Jerusalem. In the ancient world appeal to a nation for protection implied acknowledgement of the power of its gods, and so infidelity to the LORD, as Ahaz energetically shows.

He walked in the ways of the kings of Israel. He even made cast images for the Baals; and he made offerings in the valley of the son of Hinnom, and made his sons pass through fire, according to the abominable practices of the nations whom the LORD drove out before the people of Israel.

2 Chronicles 28:2–3

Chapters 29–32: **Commentary**

The energetic but short-lived reform of Hezekiah was enough to stave off Sennacherib's invasion in 701. Sennacherib overran the majority of towns in Judah, but, after the 'frank discussions' of 32:10–19, inexplicably or miraculously left Jerusalem intact. The water tunnel under Jerusalem, mentioned in 32:30, may still be seen today.

⑦ ⑨ ⑰

Amaziah executes Joash's assassins, restores the worship of the LORD in Judah, but later starts worshipping Edomite idols. He loses a war with Israel. Ultimately, he is assassinated.

Chapter **25**

⑦ ⑨ ⑰

Uzziah burns incense in the Temple. The priest Azariah challenges him, but Uzziah reacts with fury until he suddenly develops leprosy, which forces him to live out his days in isolation.

Chapter **26**

⑰

Uzziah's son Jotham rules for 16 years. Although he is faithful to the LORD, the people of Judah are not. He conquers the Ammonites.

Chapter **27**

⑦ ⑰

Ahaz worships Baal and sacrifices his children. Israel takes many people captive from Judah, until the prophet Oded says they should be released. Ahaz buys help from Assyria.

Chapter **28**

⑯ ⑰

Hezekiah rules 29 years and is faithful to God. He restores true worship and purifies the Temple.

Chapter **29**

Uzziah contracts leprosy
King Uzziah tried to present incense in the Temple, only to contract leprosy in the process.

11   **17**

Chapter
30

Hezekiah celebrates the Passover, inviting people from all over Judah and Israel to participate. They celebrate the holiday for two weeks.

16   **17**

Chapter
31

Sacred stones and Asherah poles are destroyed throughout Israel and Judah. The Israelites bring huge numbers of animals in tithe and for sacrifice to the Temple in Jerusalem.

So the couriers went from city to city through the country of Ephraim and Manasseh, and as far as Zebulun; but they laughed them to scorn, and mocked them. Only a few from Asher, Manasseh, and Zebulun humbled themselves and came to Jerusalem. The hand of God was also on Judah to give them one heart to do what the king and the officials commanded by the word of the LORD.

2 Chronicles 30:10–12

Evil king
Hezekiah's son, Manasseh, was an evil king who worshipped other gods, sacrificed his children as burnt offerings and, according to tradition, murdered the prophet Isaiah.

And the LORD sent an angel who cut off all the mighty warriors and commanders and officers in the camp of the king of Assyria. So he returned in disgrace to his own land. When he came into the house of his god, some of his own sons struck him down there with the sword. So the LORD saved Hezekiah and the inhabitants of Jerusalem from the hand of King Sennacherib of Assyria and from the hand of all his enemies; he gave them rest on every side.

2 Chronicles 32:21–22

7   **8**   **17**

Chapter
32

Sennacherib, king of Assyria, threatens Jerusalem, but a plague wipes out his army. Hezekiah recovers from illness, entertains visiting Babylonians and builds a water channel for Jerusalem.

Chapter 33: Commentary

Manasseh embraced superstition and idolatry whole-heartedly. These remained just below or just above the surface throughout the history of Israel. It is impossible now to judge how much hold they had on the popular imagination. Was the worship of the LORD the religion of a majority or a minority? To what extent was it diluted by superstition and partnership with other gods? Cult objects, fertility charms and such practices as child sacrifice are to be found in every period of the history of Israel. Manasseh's conversion after captivity in Assyria (more likely Babylon) is unattested elsewhere. It may be a theological deduction to explain his long reign of 55 years.

2   **9**   **17**

Chapter
33

Manasseh worships other gods and sacrifices his children. He repents after exile in Babylon and returns to his kingdom. His son Amnon worships false gods and is assassinated.

Chapter 34: **Commentary**

Josiah's final great reform involves purifying the whole country, but – typically of the chronicler – climaxes in the elaborate liturgical act of the Passover. Disaster strikes nevertheless, for Josiah's pride prevents him heeding the divine warning spoken by Pharaoh Necho (35:22).

7		17	
Josiah renovates the Temple and destroys the idols. Priests find the Book of the Law. The prophetess Huldah prophesies that God will judge Judah, though not during Josiah's life.			Chapter **34**

11		17	
Josiah celebrates the Passover with the people of Judah and the people of Israel who had not been deported to Assyria. Josiah fights against Pharaoh Necho and dies in battle			Chapter **35**

Chapter 36: **Commentary**

To the chronicler the material historical details are unimportant. He gives us no information about the Exile itself, concentrating on the destruction of his beloved Temple and the fulfilment of Jeremiah's prophetic warning (verse 31). The final two verses are repeated as the opening of the Book of Ezra.

7	9	17	
Necho dethrones Jehoahaz. Nebuchadnezzar replaces Jehoiakim, first with Jehoiachin and then Zedekiah. Then he destroys Jerusalem and sends the Israelites captive to Babylon.			Chapter **36**

Jerusalem burnt
Nebuchadnezzar's army destroyed the city of Jerusalem, took its people captive and burnt the Jewish Temple to the ground.

Ezra

Overview

In the Hebrew and Greek Bibles the Books of Ezra and Nehemiah form one continuous whole. They are formed from an amalgam of sources, including many possibly authentic documents of the time, loosely centred on two quite disparate leading figures. Ezra was a scribe, skilled in the Law, sent by the Persian King Artaxerxes (probably Artaxerxes I in 458 BC, but possibly Artaxerxes II in 398 BC) to regulate observance of the Law, and equipped with funds to correctly set up the sacrificial system in the renewed Temple in Jerusalem. He reads the Law to the people and provokes them to bind themselves to the it and take an oath to observe it. Nehemiah, on the other hand, was wine-taster to King Artaxerxes, and in 445 BC secured from him a commission to go to Jerusalem to sort out some administrative difficulties. In his dozen years there he supervised the rebuilding of the walls, and then reported back to the Persian court, before making a short second visit.

---

16   **17**

Chapter

1

Cyrus announces that the people of Judah and Jerusalem can return home and gives the articles Nebuchadnezzar removed from the Temple to Sheshbazzar to take back with them.

Chapter 1: **Commentary**

Cyrus the Mede conquered Babylon, 'bloodlessly', in 539 BC. His decree to free exiled peoples to return home and to restore their temples is preserved to this day in the 'Cyrus cylinder' in the British Museum in London.

In the first year of King Cyrus of Persia, in order that the word of the LORD by the mouth of Jeremiah might be accomplished, the LORD stirred up the spirit of King Cyrus of Persia so that he sent a herald throughout all his kingdom, and also in a written edict declared:

   'Thus says King Cyrus of Persia: The LORD, the God of heaven, has given me all the kingdoms of the earth, and he has charged me to build him a house at Jerusalem in Judah. Any of those among you who are of his people—may their God be with them!—are now permitted to go up to Jerusalem in Judah, and rebuild the house of the LORD, the God of Israel—he is the god who is in Jerusalem;'

               Ezra 1:1–3

The exiles return
During his first year, the Persian King Cyrus issued a decree that allowed the exiled Jewish people to return to their homeland.

The background is that after the 70 years of exile in Babylon, the conquering King Cyrus gave the Jews leave to return to their homeland. Some took advantage of this, while others remained comfortably in Babylon. By then they had settled into a way of life that was to become Judaism, marked by circumcision, observance of the Sabbath and the laws of kosher food. This way of life bound them together and marked them off from the Babylonians. When they returned to their homeland they encountered stiff opposition from those who had either stayed behind or replaced them, and did not share the same way of life. This double book is the record of how they coped with the difficulties that faced them, an invaluable witness to this crucial stage in the development of early Judaism.

Ezra returning to the Jewish homeland
Ezra, the priest and scribe, returned to the Jewish homeland and taught the Law of Moses to the returning Israelites.

Chapter 2: **Commentary**

This list occurs also in Nehemiah 7 and in the non-canonical 1 Esdras.

Chapter 3: **Commentary**

Such enthusiasm for rebuilding the Temple is belied by the prophets Haggai and Zechariah, who reproach their fellow countrymen for their slackness in the matter. They are also hampered by the disputes over their right to build the Temple, detailed in chapters 5–6. The Temple was not completed until 515 BC (6:15).

Chapter 4: **Commentary**

The returned exiles obviously provoked the local people by their determination to maintain their separateness. The documents quoted in these chapters are in Aramaic, the official language of the Persian Empire, and must be authentic. The dispute over rebuilding the walls occurred under Kings Xerxes and Artaxerxes (486–425), thus a century later than the dispute over the Temple detailed in chapters 5–6.

16 | 17

The list of the people who returned to Judah.

Chapter
2

17

The returned exiles rebuild the altar to the LORD, perform sacrifices and then begin the rebuilding of the Temple.

Chapter
3

17

Zerubbabel refuses to allow any of the non-Israelites to help them rebuild the Temple. The non-Israelites send letters to Artaxerxes king of Persia to get him to halt the rebuilding.

Chapter
4

⑰

Chapter **5**

The prophets Haggai and Zechariah encourage the people to start rebuilding again. They send a letter to King Darius explaining that Cyrus had commanded them to rebuild.

⑰

Chapter **6**

Darius discovers that they are correct and orders that the Temple be rebuilt at once. So the Temple is rebuilt and the Israelites celebrate Passover.

So the elders of the Jews built and prospered, through the prophesying of the prophet Haggai and Zechariah son of Iddo. They finished their building by command of the God of Israel and by decree of Cyrus, Darius, and King Artaxerxes of Persia; and this house was finished on the third day of the month of Adar, in the sixth year of the reign of King Darius.

Ezra 6:14–15

⑰

Chapter **7**

During the reign of Artaxerxes, Ezra comes to Jerusalem along with priests, Levites and other officials. He is to supervise the Israelites, train them and appoint judges.

Chapter 7: **Commentary**

Ezra brought with him a second wave of returning exiles. His commission was to check on observance of the Law and to deliver funds to the Temple. There is no sign that he fulfilled a further element, to set up magistrates and courts to oversee legal observance (verses 25–26). This might well have encountered difficulties from the local Persian administration, hence Nehemiah's mission. Ezra's own report on his work runs from 7:27–9:15.

⑯   **⑰**

Chapter **8**

A list of the people who went to Jerusalem with Ezra. Ezra and the people make a successful journey and offer sacrifices upon their arrival.

⑫   **⑰**

Chapter **9**

Ezra is appalled by the intermarriage of Israelites and non-Israelites. He prays for God to forgive the Israelites their many sins. He fears for the future of the people.

Chapter 9: **Commentary**

The prohibition and dissolution of marriage to the local people was intended to maintain the purity of observance of the way of life developed in Babylon and now standard in Judaism.

⑨   **⑯**   **⑰**

Chapter **10**

Ezra orders the Israelites with non-Israelite wives to divorce them. He also forces them to expel their children. There is a list of those Israelites who had married non-Israelites.

'O my God, I am too ashamed and embarrassed to lift my face to you, my God, for our iniquities have risen higher than our heads, and our guilt has mounted up to the heavens. From the days of our ancestors to this day we have been deep in guilt, and for our iniquities we, our kings, and our priests have been handed over to the kings of the lands, to the sword, to captivity, to plundering, and to utter shame, as is now the case. But now for a brief moment favour has been shown by the LORD our God, who has left us a remnant, and given us a stake in his holy place, in order that he may brighten our eyes and grant us a little sustenance in our slavery.'

Ezra 9:6–8

Ezra's tomb
According to one tradition, Ezra was buried near Basra, beside the Tigris River in Iraq.

Dedication of the replacement Temple
When the Israelites returned to Jerusalem after their 70 years of captivity, they rebuilt the Temple that Nebuchadnezzar had destroyed and dedicated it to the LORD.

Nehemiah

Overview

Nehemiah, a high official at the Persian court, received permission from Artaxerxes (probably Artaxerxes I, so in 445 BC) to improve the situation of the Jews returned from Exile in Babylon, including oversight of the rebuilding of the walls of Jerusalem. Most of the book is his report or 'memoir' on his mission (1:1–7:72a; 11:1–2; 12:27–43; 13:4–31). Included in this report are various lists: 3:1–32, the list of those who built different sections of the wall; 7:6–72a, the list of the first exiles to return (given also in Ezra 2); 10:1–40, the promises made by the community; 11:1–12:26, population lists. Another important section is Ezra's reading of the Law and its acceptance by the people, which may be considered the birth of Judaism.

Chapter 1	Nehemiah prays to God about the sorry state of Jerusalem and asks that God let him do something about it. He is the king's cupbearer.
Chapter 2	Artaxerxes, the king of Persia, sends Nehemiah to Judah to rebuild Jerusalem along with the necessary money and materials. He also makes Nehemiah the new governor.
Chapter 3	The Israelites begin rebuilding the walls. Those who were involved in the rebuilding are listed as well as the sections of the walls that they worked on.

Chapter 1: **Commentary**

Nehemiah is cupbearer to King Artaxerxes, presumably charged with testing the wine for poison. No doubt this task was combined with more administrative offices; at the notoriously formal Persian court he seems to be on intimate terms with the king. No mere footman would be charged with government for 12 years with a staff of 150. The governor of the Persian province of Yehud, resident at Samaria, not surprisingly resents this intrusion on his authority.

But when Sanballat the Horonite and Tobiah the Ammonite official, and Geshem the Arab heard of it, they mocked and ridiculed us, saying, 'What is this that you are doing? Are you rebelling against the king?'

Then I replied to them, 'The God of heaven is the one who will give us success, and we his servants are going to start building; but you have no share or claim or historic right in Jerusalem.'

Nehemiah 2:19–20

Rebuilding the city walls
When Nehemiah arrived in Jerusalem as the new governor, he quickly saw to rebuilding the city walls, completing them in only 52 days.

From that day on, half of my servants worked on construction, and half held the spears, shields, bows, and body-armour; and the leaders posted themselves behind the whole house of Judah, who were building the wall. The burden-bearers carried their loads in such a way that each laboured on the work with one hand and with the other held a weapon. And each of the builders had his sword strapped at his side while he built. The man who sounded the trumpet was beside me.

Nehemiah 4:16–18

Chapter 4: **Commentary**

The resentment of the country people at the privileged position accorded to the exiles returned to Jerusalem is a standard feature of these two books. They especially resented the transformation of the ruined city into a walled stronghold. The Jews in their turn obviously despised the local people for not observing the full Law. This division will have been cemented by Ezra's promulgation in chapter 8.

Chapter 5: **Commentary**

Resentment at the intrusion of the self-contained community of Jews from Babylon will have accentuated the economic difficulties of the beleaguered Jerusalem community.

(17)

Sanballat, Tobiah, the Arabs and the Ammonites at first ridicule the efforts to rebuild Jerusalem's walls. Soon, they threaten violence. Nehemiah arms the builders.

Chapter
4

(3)　　　(17)

Nehemiah criticises the wealthy for charging interest and enslaving some of their fellow Israelites. He gets them to cancel the debts and free their slaves.

Chapter
5

Ezra reads the Law
When Ezra read the Law of Moses to the assembled people
newly returned from exile, they celebrated for seven days.

So the wall was finished on the twenty-fifth day of the month Elul, in fifty-two days.

Nehemiah 6:15

(17)

Despite the threats against Nehemiah by those opposed to building the wall, the wall of Jerusalem is successfully rebuilt in only 52 days.

Chapter
6

(17)

The population of Jerusalem was small. The houses had not been rebuilt. Nehemiah got a list of the returned exiles and called them to an assembly in Jerusalem.

Chapter
7

Chapter 8: **Commentary**

The Book of the Law of Moses read out by Ezra was presumably the Pentateuch, possibly already in its final form. It is to this that the people commit themselves. Significantly, in this chapter the months are merely numbered, in the traditional biblical style, not named in the Persian style, as they are in Nehemiah's report.

(11) **(17)**

Ezra reads and explains the Law of Moses to the people. They celebrate for seven days.

Chapter
8

Chapter 9: **Commentary**

Confession of sin and repentance remains a standard feature of post-exilic spirituality, seen in the Book of Baruch and in many of the Psalms.

(11) **(14)** **(17)**

They confess their sins, wear sackcloth and ashes, and fast while the Book of the Law of Moses is read. They make a binding agreement to serve God faithfully.

Chapter
9

Chapter 10: **Commentary**

This agreement, headed by Nehemiah's signature, refers principally to the matters settled by his reforms, rather than to the reading of the Law by Ezra.

(14) **(16)** **(17)**

A listing of all those who made the binding agreement. The other Israelites bound themselves with a curse and an oath to worship only the LORD and to obey his commandments.

Chapter
10

Chapter 13: **Commentary**

Nehemiah's second mission seems to have been simply a tidying-up operation, a removal of abuses that had crept in. The homogeneity of the community must be secured by a single language, Hebrew, and the exclusion of local dialects (verse 24).

(16) **(17)**

One out of ten of the Israelites agree to take up residence in Jerusalem. Who will live in Jerusalem is determined by casting lots. There is a list of those who decide to live in Jerusalem.

Chapter
11

On that day they read from the book of Moses in the hearing of the people; and in it was found written that no Ammonite or Moabite should ever enter the assembly of God, because they did not meet the Israelites with bread and water, but hired Balaam against them to curse them—yet our God turned the curse into a blessing. When the people heard the law, they separated from Israel all those of foreign descent.

Nehemiah 13:1–3

(16) **(17)**

A list of the priests and Levites who returned with Zerubbabel and Joshua to Israel from Babylonian Exile. The new wall of Jerusalem is dedicated with song and sacrifice.

Chapter
12

(9) **(17)**

The Israelites exclude all those of foreign descent. Nehemiah throws Tobiah out of his home, prevents work on the Sabbath and rebukes those who married non-Israelites.

Chapter
13

Tobit
Overview

The Book of Tobit is a novel, almost a comedy, for it teaches its lessons by means of all kinds of satire, farce and absurdity, using a laughable range of exaggerated characters. The successful quest for money, the wedding and the happy ending have also earned the book the name of a 'romance'. Tobit himself is absurdly and fussily pious, set against his busy and practical wife and his timid son, who has to be gingerly led around by an

---

6

Chapter 1

Tobit introduces himself to the reader, a pious exile in Assyria, stubbornly faithful to every detail of the Law, and ensuring that everyone else observes the Law too.

6

Chapter 2

Tobit takes his siesta under the sparrows' nest and is blinded by their offerings.

1

Chapter 3

Tobit's prayer of acceptance. The reader is introduced to Tobit's cousin, Sarah, in faraway Media. We learn of her misfortunes in marriage and her desperate perseverance in prayer.

6

Chapter 4

Tobit gives his son Tobias the mission of recovering the money he has deposited with his cousin in Media.

Chapter 2: **Commentary**

Tobit is ultra-scrupulous in his observance of the Law, paying his tithes, generous to the needy, avoiding unclean food and careful to cleanse himself of defilement. This becomes absurd when he insists that the goat given to his wife as a tip must be given back in case it was stolen. And what is his reward? Blindness! This is the reverse of the pious expectations of God. But Tobit still delivers a long sermon to his son about careful legal observance before sending him off on the journey.

That same night I washed myself and went into my courtyard and slept by the wall of the courtyard; and my face was uncovered because of the heat. I did not know that there were sparrows on the wall; their fresh droppings fell into my eyes and produced white films. I went to physicians to be healed, but the more they treated me with ointments the more my vision was obscured by the white films, until I became completely blind. For four years I remained unable to see. All my kindred were sorry for me, and Ahikar took care of me for two years before he went to Elymais.

Tobit 2:9–10

angel. The story is placed in the early days of the Babylonian Exile, but it uses a mishmash of history. In a quirky way it teaches God's care for his own (in the end!), but it has also set the mark for centuries of self-mocking Jewish humour. For some centuries the earliest text seemed to be in Greek, but both Hebrew and Aramaic fragments have now been discovered.

6

Tobias bumps into Raphael, an angel posing as a well-travelled, unemployed Israelite. Raphael offers to act as guide to Tobias at a drachma a day. Tobit brushes aside his wife's entreaties to keep him at home.

Chapter
5

6

Guided by Raphael, Tobias sets out. He is frightened by a big fish, and hears the ominous story of Sarah's marital mishaps. Raphael teaches him some useful magic against demons.

Chapter
6

6

A warm welcome unites the cousins, Tobias learns that it is his right and duty to marry Sarah, and a dinner-party celebrates the meeting.

Chapter
7

Chapter 5: **Commentary**

Raphael seems to have no scruples about telling a few white lies in order to get alongside Tobias. (Perhaps conventions about telling a straight truth do not apply to angels.) This is the most extended biblical stay of an angel in human form. God is imagined as surrounded by the 'sons of God', courtiers who carry out his will. These powers do not necessarily have any visible form. Normally angels merely manifest themselves, give their message and vanish. Any mention of their appearance serves to stress their heavenly nature.

Chapter 6: **Commentary**

The magical use of parts of the fish goes against the general condemnation of magical practices in the Bible. Despite such condemnations, magic and superstition certainly existed in Israel alongside Yahwism, even to the extent of child sacrifice, though we cannot tell how widespread it was. Even Saul broke his own prohibition. Perhaps the novelistic character of the story explains its presence here and in the case of Sarah's misfortunes.

Chapter 7: **Commentary**

By the levirate law (Deuteronomy 25:5) the nearest male relative of a man who marries and dies childless must marry the widow and raise up an heir to the dead man's name. So Tobias, and Tobias alone, is obliged to marry Sarah.

Tobias curing his father's blindness
When Tobias and the angel returned from their journey, Tobias used the fish's gall bladder to restore his father's sight.

1

6

Chapter
8

The happy couple pray before bed, while Sarah's father digs a grave in which to hide evidence in case anything goes wrong. This turns out to be unnecessary, and they celebrate with a meal.

6

Chapter
9

Raphael is despatched to collect the money, and the guests gather for the wedding feast.

6

Chapter
10

Tobias' parents worry about his failure to return from his gap year. After 14 days of wedding celebrations Tobias decides it is time to go home, and sets off, laden with useful wedding presents.

6

Chapter
11

The homecoming of the young couple, piloted by Raphael. Tobias successfully operates on his father's eyes, restoring his sight. Tobit's gratitude to God.

6

Chapter
12

Tobit prepares to pay Raphael for his services, but Raphael discloses his true identity, to the awestruck confusion of his clients.

1

Chapter
13

Tobit's concluding song of gratitude, thanking God for his release and praying for the rebuilding of Jerusalem.

6

Chapter
14

The aftermath: Tobit gives his son final instructions and dies at the age of 112. Tobias himself dies at the age of 117, rejoicing over the destruction of Nineveh.

Chapter 11: **Commentary**

Tobit's blindness seems to be based on a kind of glaucoma. It is described as white spots on the eyes. After treatment with the magical fish gall bladder medicine these can be blown away (6:8), though in 11:11 Tobias peels away a film from the corners of his father's eyes, a sort of primitive cataract operation.

Next, with both his hands he peeled off the white films from the corners of his eyes. Then Tobit saw his son and threw his arms around him, and he wept and said to him, 'I see you, my son, the light of my eyes!' Then he said, 'Blessed be God, and blessed be his great name, and blessed be all his holy angels. May his holy name be blessed throughout all the ages.'

Tobit 11:13–14

Chapter 13: **Commentary**

Only three angels are named in the Bible: Gabriel ('the Strength of God'), Michael ('Who is like God') and Raphael ('the Healing of God'). They are all powers of God, by which God acts in the world. Michael is the warrior power of God, confronting evil. Gabriel gives God's message to human beings, as at the Annunciation to Mary; 'angel' means 'messenger'.

Chapter 14: **Commentary**

At the height of the Assyrian Empire, Tobit on his deathbed correctly foresees the fall of Assyria (609 BC) and of Babylon (539 BC). In the manner of post-exilic prophecy he also predicts the universalism of the messianic age when all nations will come to draw salvation from a renewed and glorious Jerusalem.

Judith

Overview

The Book of Judith is a book of contrasts. It is not a historical story, for the story does not fit the circumstances or the geography of any period of history. Nebuchadnezzar (1:1) was king of Babylon, not of Nineveh in Assyria. Holofernes is a Persian name, and a certain Holofernes is known only as an officer of Artaxerxes III, a couple of centuries after Nebuchadnezzar. No city of Bethulia is known to have existed. Furthermore, it seems to be situated in Samaria, from where the Israelites were expelled long before Nebuchadnezzar. There may be some event behind it, but in this case the story is retold with staggering carelessness and inaccuracy. More likely, the story is a model tale, an edifying fiction, built around the classic honeytrap and the contrast between the two chief characters. Without any overt divine intervention, it illustrates God's help for those who trust in him, even in a desperate situation, to rectify a situation by means of human action.

The main contrast is, of course, between Judith and Holofernes: the triumph of Holofernes' brutality in the first seven chapters, and the triumph of Judith's beauty in the second seven has suggested that the title of the book should be 'The

Continues >

Chapter 1: **Commentary**

Verse 1 is such a muddle historically (Nebuchadnezzar was king of Babylon, not Assyria nor Nineveh; no king called Arphaxad is known to history) that it almost seems a deliberate statement to show that the book is not to be regarded as history. Similarly, Holofernes' route in chapter 2 must be a deliberate geographical jumble.

Chapter 3: **Commentary**

Holofernes ruthlessly disregards all the friendly, welcoming gestures and pleas for mercy. It is ironic that the welcoming procession that greets his arrival (verse 7) will be repeated to greet his severed head in 15:12.

6

The vast military might of Nebuchadnezzar, 'king of Nineveh'. He threatens all the kings of the West, who spurn his messengers. He then makes an example of Arphaxad and advances into Persia.

Chapter 1

6

Nebuchadnezzar's chief general, Holofernes, advances with a gigantic army, and lays waste to most of the countries to the west, travelling by a very roundabout route.

Chapter 2

6

The coastal cities of Ascalon and Azotus sue for peace – in vain. Holofernes ravages their territories and comes to rest opposite Scythopolis, within range of Judea.

Chapter 3

Beast and Beauty'. The name 'Judith' simply means 'the Jewess', and she is the personification of Jewish piety, careful about all observances, prayerful, chaste and fearless. Holofernes, by contrast, is the personification of evil, an unbeliever, concentrated as much on sexual rapacity as on military conquest. A second contrast is between the puny Jewish nation and the might of Assyria, over which Judaism triumphs with the help of God. A third contrast is between the timid Jewish men, cowering behind the walls of their besieged city and unable to devise any solution, and the courageous woman, who sallies forth, single-handed against the might of the Assyrian Empire, and returns with the head of their leader. Perhaps the most dominant contrast is the sexual role reversal of the modest woman over the braggart male.

The book may well date from the nationalistic period of the late second century BC. The prominence of both Pharisaic observances and Hellenistic customs fits this period, though the first mention of the Book is in the Letter of Clement to the Corinthians at the end of the first century AD. A valuable secondary motif is that the action takes place in Samaria, now inhabited by a mixed race, detested by all 'right-minded' Jews, and that the pagan enemy is warned of the overwhelming protective power of God by Achior, a gentile sage, who later converts to Judaism. There is, then, a concern for the gentiles too.

No Hebrew text of Judith exists, but the Greek version is clearly a translation from Hebrew or Aramaic. The book was part of the Greek Bible, the original Bible of the Christian Church, but was never accepted into the Hebrew canon, perhaps because of the irregular conversion of Achior.

6

Chapter 4

All the Israelites living in Judea panic and converge on the Temple of Jerusalem in prayer.

Chapter 4: **Commentary**

Such earnest prayer and fasting in the Temple is the chief sign in the book of a piety based on the Temple. Is it a play on the desecration of the Temple by the Syrian king Antiochus Epiphanes in 169 BC? Such Pharisaic piety and observance is a feature of the book (see 9:1), and especially of Judith's own conduct.

6

Chapter 5

Holofernes calls a council of war. Achior, an Ammonite leader, warns him of the power of the God of Israel, but is scornfully rejected by Holofernes' advisors.

6

Chapter 6

Achior is bundled up and dumped by the attackers outside Bethulia. The inhabitants of Bethulia flee in panic, but return, untie Achior and make him welcome.

Chapter 6: **Commentary**

Achior, the Ammonite mercenary, may be a reminiscence of the famous non-Jewish sage Ahikar (who appears also in the Book of Tobit). He stands in the line of other non-Jews who recognise and warn about the strength of the Jewish God. In 14:10 he is converted to Judaism and circumcised, though according to later Jewish regulations he should have been baptised as well.

6

Chapter 7

Holofernes lays siege to Bethulia until supplies and water are running out. The young men are all for surrendering, but Uzziah persuades them to trust in God and hold out for another five days.

Judith remained as a widow for three years and four months at home where she set up a tent for herself on the roof of her house. She put sackcloth around her waist and dressed in widow's clothing. She fasted all the days of her widowhood, except the day before the sabbath and the sabbath itself, the day before the new moon and the day of the new moon, and the festivals and days of rejoicing of the house of Israel.

Judith 8:4–6

6

Chapter 8

The faithful widow Judith makes her first appearance. She summons the elders, assures them that God is only testing them and promises a daring and startling plan to solve the problem.

Judith with the head of Holofernes
When all the men of Bethulia are too scared to act, Judith ensnares Holofernes in a honeytrap and cuts off his head.

She came close to his bed, took hold of the hair of his head, and said, 'Give me strength today, O Lord God of Israel!' Then she struck his neck twice with all her might, and cut off his head. Next she rolled his body off the bed and pulled down the canopy from the posts. Soon afterwards she went out and gave Holofernes' head to her maid, who placed it in her food bag. Then the two of them went out together, as they were accustomed to do for prayer. They passed through the camp, circled around the valley, and went up the mountain to Bethulia, and came to its gates.

Judith 13:7–10

Chapter 16: Commentary

The erotic language of the description of Judith's approach to Holofernes (especially verse 9) is a delicious contrast to the propriety of her demure modesty and meticulous observance of the Law. It is the height of the irony that runs throughout the book.

12 Judith's prayer to the Lord for strength against the enemy, so that she may show that God champions those who trust in him.	**Chapter 9**
6 Judith sallies forth in all her finery, accompanied only by her maid and a supply of kosher food. The Assyrians are immediately star-struck by her incomparable beauty.	**Chapter 10**
6 Judith meets Holofernes, flatters him outrageously and promises to lead him all the way to Jerusalem, provided that she is allowed out each night to pray on her own.	**Chapter 11**
6 For three nights Judith goes out early to purify herself and pray. On the fourth evening Holofernes orders a private banquet and prepares to make Judith his own.	**Chapter 12**
6 **12** After dining too well, Holofernes falls asleep on the bed. With a quick prayer Judith cuts off his head, pops it into her maid's food bag and bears it triumphantly back to Bethulia.	**Chapter 13**
6 Achior identifies the head as genuine and, emboldened by this trophy, the Jews sally forth against the Assyrians. Holofernes' majordomo discovers his master's dead body.	**Chapter 14**
6 Israelites from all the surrounding country join in to pursue and massacre the Assyrians. The high priest and elders of Israel congratulate Judith, who also receives Holofernes' booty as her own.	**Chapter 15**
6 Judith's hymn of thanksgiving. She dedicates Holofernes' spoils to God, lives the life of a celebrity and dies at the age of 105.	**Chapter 16**

Esther

Overview

The Book of Esther tells the story of a young Jewish woman who becomes queen of Persia and saves her people from destruction. The book is named after her. Although she had a Hebrew name, 'Hadassah', she is better known by her Persian name, 'Esther'. This is a Hebraised form of 'Ishtar', a pagan fertility goddess. It is a straightforward story of intrigue, violence and vengeance at the fairy-tale royal court. Though a basis in history is not impossible, no such events are attested in any historical record. The storyline is somewhat far-fetched, but the main characters are wittily depicted. There is, however, no mention of important factors in Jewish belief and practice, such as the Temple, the Law, food rituals or covenant. God is never mentioned in the Hebrew version, though it is clear that God is in the background, watching over his people and directing the course of events to their advantage.

17

Chapter

1

King Xerxes has a party and asks his queen, Vashti, to dance for his guests. She refuses and so he deposes her.

17

Chapter

2

King Xerxes has a contest to find a replacement for Vashti and selects Esther, the cousin of Mordecai. Mordecai uncovers an assassination plot against Xerxes.

17

Chapter

3

Mordecai offends Haman, an official of Xerxes, by not bowing down to him. So Haman decides to kill Mordecai and all the Jews. Xerxes orders their extermination.

12   **17**

Chapter

4

Mordecai begs Esther to do something about it. The prayers of Mordecai, of Esther and of all Israel, asking for heavenly help.

Then Memucan said in the presence of the king and the officials, 'Not only has Queen Vashti done wrong to the king, but also to all the officials and all the peoples who are in all the provinces of King Ahasuerus. For this deed of the queen will be made known to all women, causing them to look with contempt on their husbands, since they will say, "King Ahasuerus commanded Queen Vashti to be brought before him, and she did not come." This very day the noble ladies of Persia and Media who have heard of the queen's behaviour will rebel against the king's officials, and there will be no end of contempt and wrath!'

Esther 1:16–18

Chapter 2: **Commentary**

Though often described as a beauty contest, the selection of the new queen was not made on a catwalk, but rather in the bedroom. All the women selected from the kingdom as the potential new queen were taken into the king's harem. He then slept with each of them in turn and only afterwards decided that Esther would take the place of his old queen, Vashti. Those not selected to be queen remained a part of his harem.

(17) Esther, arrayed in her full beauty, invites the King and Haman to a banquet. Meanwhile, Haman runs up a 50-cubit gallows on which to hang Mordecai.

Chapter 5

(17) Haman is humiliated when he is forced to help honour Mordecai for uncovering the assassination plot against the king. Then he leaves for Esther's banquet.

Chapter 6

(17) At the banquet Esther protests the loyalty of the Jews, blaming Haman for false accusation. The king has Haman hanged on the gallows that Haman had erected for Mordecai.

Chapter 7

(17) Xerxes gives Mordecai Haman's job and gives Haman's property to Esther. Xerxes allows the Jews to fight their enemies. The Jews celebrate and many people convert to Judaism.

Chapter 8

(17) The Jews defeat their enemies. Every year since then, the Jews celebrate Purim to remember their victory over those who would have destroyed them.

Chapter 9

(17) Increased prosperity of both King Xerxes and his minister Mordecai. Mordecai attributes to God the welfare of Israel. Tailpiece dates the translation of the book into Greek to 114 BC.

Chapter 10

The longer Greek version of the book contains six more passages (107 verses in total, normally printed in italics), which somewhat change the character of the book, making it more explicitly religious, stressing the presence of God and the effectiveness of prayer. It also generalises the hostility between Jews and Gentiles, which in the Hebrew text is a personal vendetta between Mordecai and Haman.

The author of this story is unknown. It is set at the court of Xerxes (or Ahasuerus in Persian), the King of Persia from 486 to 464 BC, and linguistically the Hebrew text of the Book fits well into the latter part of that century. Two of the Greek passages (the highly rhetorical letters in chapters 3 and 8) are in sophisticated Greek and may well stem from Alexandrian Jewry. The other additions could have originated in Hebrew or Aramaic, and fit well into the second or first centuries BC.

Then Mordecai returned to the king's gate, but Haman hurried to his house, mourning and with his head covered. When Haman told his wife Zeresh and all his friends everything that had happened to him, his advisers and his wife Zeresh said to him, 'If Mordecai, before whom your downfall has begun, is of the Jewish people, you will not prevail against him, but will surely fall before him.'

While they were still talking with him, the king's eunuchs arrived and hurried Haman off to the banquet that Esther had prepared.

Esther 6:12–14

Chapter 9: **Commentary**

The Jewish holiday Purim grows out of the events described in the Book of Esther. According to the story, Haman, a member of Xerxes' royal government, decided to destroy all the Jews in the Persian Empire on a day that was chosen by casting lots. The Hebrew word for 'lots' is *purim*. Today, Jewish people celebrate the holiday by reading the Book of Esther in the synagogue. Each time Haman's name is mentioned, the congregation makes loud noises to drown out the sound of his name. Afterwards, a festive meal is enjoyed by all.

Esther and Xerxes
Queen Esther comes before King Xerxes and reveals the evil plot of Haman to slaughter all the Jews in the Persian Empire.

1 Maccabees

Overview

This First Book of Maccabees is straightforward Hellenistic history, using good information and some documents, and covering the period 175 to 135 BC, a period in which Judaism was struggling for its survival against the varying success at attempted political and religious domination by the powerful Syrian kingdom to the north. The author wished to show the legitimacy of the Hasmonean royal line, sprung from Mattathias and his son, Simon the Maccabee, replacing the Davidic royal line and the Oniad priestly line. This is done by showing their dedication and success in countering the attempts of the Syrian kings Antiochus IV Epiphanes and his successors to wipe out Judaism from the empire. The most likely date of writing is the very end of the second century BC.

The conventions of Hellenistic history writing are employed, such as the use of artificial speeches put into the mouths of important characters to explain the significance of events. It is also biblical history, in that it stresses the workings of God through human means within history, rewarding virtue and punishing vice. It is often enriched by prayers and prayerful reflection, and is supported

---

17

Chapter 1

Antiochus Epiphanes emerges as a successor of Alexander the Great; he invades Israel, installs a Syrian citadel in Jerusalem, desecrates the Temple and prohibits Jewish legal observance.

17

Chapter 2

The rebellion of Mattathias and his zeal for the Law. His attack on a Jew who conforms to Antiochus' sacrificial requirements, the refusal of loyal Jews to fight on the Sabbath and the death of Mattathias.

17

Chapter 3

Judas the Maccabee takes over the leadership. Syrian invasion under the command of Lysias. The Jewish army gathers together and prays at the ancient shrine of Mizpah.

Chapter 1: **Commentary**

The stronghold built at the high point of Jerusalem, the Acra, would remain an irremovable thorn in the flesh of the Jews for many years, unassailable and dominating the Temple, situated lower on the same hill. It eventually became the palace of Herod the Great, and subsequently the residence of the Roman governor. It still dominates the Jaffa Gate of Jerusalem.

Chapter 2: **Commentary**

Careful observance of Sabbath regulations was part of the way of life developed in the Babylon Exile and brought back on the return to Jerusalem and Judea. In this case the regulation is not to depart more than 1,000 cubits from home, which would preclude most military operations. A few verses later, however, the Jews realise from this heroic inaction that such self-restraint will cost them their whole way of life.

by a series of seemingly authentic documents, which are fully quoted. Although the interest centres unashamedly on the Maccabee family, the only serious bias is that the author somewhat underplays the importance of a party within Judaism who were perfectly willing to assimilate Hellenistic culture. The author, however, does not attempt to conceal either Jewish failures or Jewish treachery. This period of Jewish history is remarkable in that it is devoid both of any expectation of a Davidic Messiah and of prophecy. The lack of a prophet seems to have been acutely felt (4:46). God remains remote and transcendant, manifest only in the guidance of history and in victory or defeat in battle. This impersonality or remoteness is reinforced by abstention from using the name of God; it is replaced either by a personal pronoun or by 'Heaven', where God was thought to reside.

Although both Origen and Jerome attest that they knew a Hebrew text of this book, the two Books of Maccabees were never part of the Hebrew Bible, nor are they of the Protestant canon, but they are included in the Greek Septuagint.

Chapter 8: **Commentary**

In the second century BC Roman interest and power in the eastern Mediterranean area was increasing. The chief moments were the Treaty of Apamaea in 188, which neutralised the power of Antiochus III, and the bequest of the kingdom of Asia Minor to Rome in 133 BC. The Romans were happy to foster any little states that might provide annoyance to the control of the major powers in that area, though the alliances with the Jews do not seem to have amounted to much. In the course of the next century Rome came to dominate, and largely to own, the whole territory.

Battle of Emmaus
The decisive victory of Judas the Maccabee over the Syrian forces.

⑰

Chapter **9**
Death of Judas at the Battle of Beer-Zaith. His brother Jonathan takes over the leadership of the resistance, against opposition from the Syrian occupying forces, who are eventually defeated.

⑰

Chapter **10**
Two rival parties of the Syrians compete for support from Jonathan and the Jews. Letters from both parties to Jonathan. Demetrius II taunts Jonathan into battle and is soundly defeated.

⑰

Chapter **11**
Uneasy alliance of the Syrian kings with Jonathan. They confirm him as high priest, but battles continue against various parties of the divided Syrians.

⑰

Chapter **12**
Jonathan renews the alliance with Rome and also allies himself with Sparta. He attempts to isolate the Syrian stronghold, but is tricked into negotiating at Ptolemais, where he is taken prisoner.

⑰

Chapter **13**
Simon the Maccabee takes over the leadership and attempts to negotiate for Jonathan's release, but Jonathan is killed. Simon strengthens the fortresses of Judea and frees Judea from the Syrian yoke.

⑰

Chapter **14**
Simon renews the alliances with Sparta and Rome and receives an elaborate eulogy from the Jewish people.

⑰

Chapter **15**
The new Syrian king, Antiochus VII, becomes hostile to Simon and eventually repudiates any alliance with him and sends an army to harass Judea.

⑰

Chapter **16**
Simon defeats the Syrian general, but is lured to a banquet in the fortress of Dok, above Jericho, where he is treacherously killed. He is succeeded as high priest by his son John.

Then Jonathan and Simon took their brother Judas and buried him in the tomb of their ancestors at Modein, and wept for him. All Israel made great lamentation for him; they mourned for many days and said, 'How is the mighty fallen, the saviour of Israel!'

1 Maccabees 9:19–21

Chapter 10: **Commentary**

The Maccabees themselves avoided the title of 'king' and ruled as high priest and ethnarch (literally 'ruler of the nation'), presumably in recognition that the royal title traditionally belonged, for example in the Psalms, to God alone. Moreover, by their ancestry they lacked any claim to the royal title, for their rule was founded entirely on their dedication and military prowess. The title of 'king' was later revived, but under the Roman domination the high priest was again the ethnarch.

... the Jews entered it with praise and palm branches, and with harps and cymbals and stringed instruments, and with hymns and songs, because a great enemy had been crushed and removed from Israel. Simon decreed that every year they should celebrate this day with rejoicing. He strengthened the fortifications of the temple hill alongside the citadel, and he and his men lived there.

1 Maccabees 13:51–52

Chapter 14: **Commentary**

After a quarter-century of struggles, Simon Maccabeus at last achieved independence again for Judea in 142 BC by the expulsion of the Syrian garrison from the citadel of Jerusalem and by the liberation of Gezer. He received the appointment as ethnarch, religious and political ruler of the people. The new era was marked by counting the years from this date. He also minted his own coinage, a typical sign of independence. He was murdered in 136 BC, but his dynasty continued.

2 Maccabees

Overview

The First and Second Books of Maccabees are not one continuous history. This second book begins with two introductory letters encouraging Egyptian Jews to celebrate the Feast of Dedication of the Temple. It then gives a version of a work of Jason of Cyrene, covering part of the same ground as the first book, but in a quite different manner. The flowery and rhetorical preface makes clear that the author's purpose is to entertain and to profit the reader rather than to give a meticulous account of the events. The history concentrates on showing God's protection of his people and his sanctuary, the reward of fidelity to the Law, the punishment of impiety and the effectiveness of prayer. So it includes accounts of marvels, dreams and visions, signs and portents, and heavenly riders supporting the Jews in battle. It stresses the endurance and successes of the heroes, and the vain boasting of their demonised opponents. Both first and second halves end with the gruesome death of a wicked persecutor of God's people and Temple, Antiochus and Nicanor respectively. Occasionally Jewish failures or reverses, of which we know from 1 Maccabees, are simply omitted. Hellenistic rhetoric is prominent, both in the speeches of the participants and in the author's own little sermons. How much of this dramatic presentation stems from Jason, the original author, and how much from the compiler, we have no means of knowing.

The dates both of Jason's work and of the epitome of it are unknown. They could have been produced anywhere in the Hellenistic Jewish world. The first of the accompanying letters, however, is dated to 124 BC, soon after the events it recounts. Doctrinally, the book is important for its teachings on the resurrection of the dead, on prayer for the dead and on the intercession of the saints.

Chapter 1: **Commentary**

The lurid account of the death of Antiochus IV differs from that given in 9:28 and in 1 Maccabees. The author has drawn the story from the death of Antiochus III, who died after attacking the temple of Artemis.

17

Two letters from the Jews of Jerusalem and Judea to those of Egypt, encouraging them to keep Sukkoth. The second letter describes the death of the Antiochus and the preservation of the sacred fire.

Chapter

1

Chapter 2

The second letter, continued: the preservation of other relics, the sacred fire and Nehemiah's library. Also the compiler's preface, explaining the sense and purpose of the book.

Chapter 3

Heliodorus, agent of the Syrian king, advances against the Temple to despoil it. He is attacked by a heavenly horse and rider. When he recovers, he is converted to the LORD.

Chapter 4

Intrigues over the high priesthood and the introduction of Hellenism into Judea under Antiochus Epiphanes. One claimant, Onias, is murdered, the other, Menelaus, remains in power.

Chapter 5

Jason attempts to seize power in Jerusalem and slaughters his own countrymen. Antiochus responds by pillaging the Temple, with Menelaus as his guide.

Chapter 6

Antiochus bans the observance of the Jewish Law. The Temple is desecrated and becomes the scene of ritual orgies. The noble martyrdom of Eleazar, who refuses to eat pork flesh.

Chapter 7

The noble martyrdom of the Seven Brothers, encouraged by their heroic mother.

Chapter 8

Judas Maccabaeus rallies the Jews to oppose the Syrian desecrations and assembles an army, and massacres Nicanor's forces. The army of Timotheus and Bacchides is also massacred.

Chapter 9

King Antiochus, hearing the news, swears terrible vengeance on the Jews, but is struck by a wasting disease and dies in agony, having designated his son Antiochus V as his successor.

Chapter 2: **Commentary**

The author wants to show that the basic emblems of Judaism remained, though the Tent of Meeting ceased to exist in the time of Solomon, and the Ark was pillaged at the Sack of Jerusalem. Nehemiah's library is also a fiction to stress the continuity of the history.

Chapter 3: **Commentary**

Interventions of heavenly warriors in support of the Jews are a feature of 2 Maccabees, as in 5:4, 10:29 and 11:8. Victory is a gift of God. Visible interventions from heaven are common also in contemporary apocalyptic writings.

Chapter 6: **Commentary**

Such dramatic accounts of martyrdom, with the final speech of the martyrs, as in 7 and 14:37–46, become both a basis for a theology of martyrdom and a model for the accounts of early Christian martyrs.

*When the battle became fierce, there appeared to
the enemy from heaven five resplendent men on
horses with golden bridles, and they were leading
the Jews. Two of them took Maccabeus between
them, and shielding him with their own armour
and weapons, they kept him from being wounded.
They showered arrows and thunderbolts on the
enemy, so that, confused and blinded, they were
thrown into disorder and cut to pieces.*

2 Maccabees 10:29–30

Chapter 12: **Commentary**

The Jews had long believed that the dead continued in a
miserable and powerless half-life in Sheol. But a belief that
God would never abandon his own was developing, first
as a yearning, then as a conviction. This book and the
contemporary Daniel 12:2–3 proclaim a resurrection of
the dead, which seems to be a full bodily resurrection (see
7:9). This passage also supports the idea of prayer by the
living for the dead. At the same time, in Hellenistic Judaism,
a belief in the immortality of the soul appears.

*For if he were not expecting that those who had
fallen would rise again, it would have been
superfluous and foolish to pray for the dead. But if
he was looking to the splendid reward that is laid
up for those who fall asleep in godliness, it was a
holy and pious thought. Therefore he made
atonement for the dead, so that they might be
delivered from their sin.*

2 Maccabees 12:44–45

Chapter 15: **Commentary**

Judas' dream of the intercession by Onias and Jeremiah
is the first evidence for a belief in the intercession of the
sacred dead on behalf of God's people who are still living.
The epilogue by the compiler is typical of contemporary
historical works in Greek and Latin literature. The ideal is
to entertain and edify at the same time. The apology is a
mere convention.

The Temple is cleansed and an annual festival instituted. The struggle to rid Judea of the foreigners continues successfully, with the help of heavenly warriors. — **Chapter 10**

The freedom struggle continues. With heavenly help the Syrian regent, Lysias, is defeated and sues for peace. The Jewish Law is reinstated, with the added approval of Rome, allied to the Jews. — **Chapter 11**

More victories for the Jews. All the Jewish casualties are found to be carrying superstitious charms. There is sacrifice and prayer for the dead, which shows belief in the resurrection for the holy dead. — **Chapter 12**

Further victories of the Jews. The execution of Menelaus the persecutor. By successful operations of the Jews and rebellion at home, Antiochus V is brought to negotiate an uneasy peace. — **Chapter 13**

Alcimus, a renegade high priest, invites the Syrians back into Judea. Nicanor, the Syrian general, makes peace with Judas, but the king insists that Judas must be slain, and war is renewed. Heroic suicide of Razis. — **Chapter 14**

Nicanor brazenly attacks on the Sabbath, but is defeated and killed. His head is hung from the Citadel, and the victory is commemorated by the Day of Mordecai. Compiler's epilogue. — **Chapter 15**

The expulsion of Heliodorus from the Temple
As Heliodorus entered the Temple to plunder it, he was struck down by an angel and paralysed.

Job
Overview

The Book of Job raises in its most acute form the problem of the undeserved suffering of the righteous. At least the main part of the poem makes no appeal to previous biblical revelation, and the drama is set in the distant and mythical land of Uz, out of reach of biblical revelation. While Job's 'comforters' (he more often seems to regard them as his tormentors) suggest that his suffering is deserved because of deliberate, or at least indeliberate, sin, Job rejects all such easy solutions and forcefully protests his innocence. While he rails against the injustice of God, he simultaneously clings to the God who torments him. The easier solution of a life after death, in which all wrongs are put right, is not yet available to him, though he also, in a memorable passage, voices his conviction that he will eventually be vindicated. One interpretation of the final speeches

---

18

Chapter 1

Job, a righteous man, loses his wealth and children when God gives Satan permission to attack him. Job accepts his loss and does not lose his trust in God.

Chapter 1: **Commentary**

The 'sons of God' here are the heavenly court. Among them one, the Satan, has the specific task of testing human beings. The name means 'the accuser', and despite his cheeky dialogue with the LORD, Satan is not yet necessarily a fallen or evil angel.

18

Chapter 2

God gives Satan permission to take Job's health and still Job does not curse God, despite his wife telling him he should. His friends Eliphaz, Bildad and Zophar arrive to offer comfort.

Then Satan answered the LORD, 'Does Job fear God for nothing? Have you not put a fence around him and his house and all that he has, on every side? You have blessed the work of his hands, and his possessions have increased in the land. But stretch out your hand now, and touch all that he has, and he will curse you to your face.'

Job 1:9–11

---

5 | **18**

Chapter 3

Job finally speaks to his friends. He tells them that he wishes that he had never been born or at least had died at birth. He expresses his utter misery.

---

5 | **18**

Chapter 4

Eliphaz tells him that the innocent are not destroyed; God destroys only the wicked. Of course, no humans are really good.

Chapter 4: **Commentary**

Eliphaz is the first of the wise men from the East to try to explain to Job why he is suffering. As they come from the East, these wise men have no knowledge of the revelation to Israel, and use only natural wisdom.

and experience of God is that human beings cannot understand and have no right to question divine dispositions. To the end the problem of suffering remains tantalisingly unsolved. This straightforward reading of the book would situate it conveniently in the period of the Exile when a second generation of exiles was questioning why they should be subjected to the penalties deserved by their parents' infidelity.

In the wisdom literature Job is neither the first nor the last dramatisation of this intractable problem, drawing as it does upon many predecessors in the wisdom of the ancient Near East. There are, however, problems about the composition and integrity of the book. These indicate that it may have undergone expansion and rewriting in the course of its history.

5	18	
Eliphaz tells Job that while fools and wicked people lose everything, if Job will just repent of his crimes, then God will restore him to prosperity.		Chapter **5**

5	18	
Job wishes that God would just kill him and he tells his friends that they are not helpful at all. He hasn't done anything wrong. Can his friends show him what he has done wrong?		Chapter **6**

5	18	
Job points out that his lifespan is brief. Even if he had misbehaved, why couldn't God just forgive him since he's going to be dead soon anyhow, no matter what.		Chapter **7**

5	18	
Bildad responds: Job's words are worthless. Is God unjust? The blameless don't suffer, only the wicked suffer.		Chapter **8**

'What are human beings, that you make so much of them,
  that you set your mind on them,
visit them every morning,
  test them every moment?
Will you not look away from me for a while,
  let me alone until I swallow my spittle?
If I sin, what do I do to you, you watcher of humanity?
  Why have you made me your target?
  Why have I become a burden to you?
Why do you not pardon my transgression
  and take away my iniquity?
For now I shall lie in the earth;
  you will seek me, but I shall not be.'

Job 7:17–21

Chapter 7: **Commentary**

Traditionally, in Israel's wisdom, God watches over human beings to care for them. Job complains that God's scrutiny is crippling.

Job's suffering
Job lost his children, his wealth and his health but refused to turn against God, even though he could not explain why Job was suffering.

5 **18**

Chapter

9

Job responds: How can I argue with God? But I am innocent and so yes, God does destroy both the innocent and the guilty. God is unjust. If only someone could arbitrate between us.

5 **18**

Chapter

10

Job continues: God, why have you done this to me? Why did you let me be born if it was going to end this way? Why can't you just leave me in peace, since I'll be dead soon?

5 **18**

Chapter

11

Zophar replies: Job, you're ignorant and arrogant. How dare you question God? Of course you're guilty. If you were righteous, you wouldn't be suffering. So repent. Then all will be well with you.

The argument
Job argued with his friends Eliphaz, Bildad and Zophar over the cause of his suffering. They believed suffering only came as a result of evil behaviour, but Job disagreed.

Chapter 9: **Commentary**

Job comes to the state of doubting even his own innocence, and then abandons all idea of divine justice, accusing God of being a tyrannical bully.

'How then can I answer him,
*   choosing my words with him?*
Though I am innocent, I cannot answer him;
*   I must appeal for mercy to my accuser.*
If I summoned him and he answered me,
*   I do not believe that he would listen to my voice.*
For he crushes me with a tempest,
*   and multiplies my wounds without cause;*
he will not let me get my breath,
*   but fills me with bitterness.*
If it is a contest of strength, he is the strong one!
*   If it is a matter of justice, who can summon him?*
Though I am innocent, my own mouth would condemn me;
*   though I am blameless, he would prove me perverse.'*

Job 9:14–20

Chapters 12–14: **Commentary**

At the end of this first cycle of discussions, Job finally explodes, again confidently asserting his innocence and protesting that God is an all-powerful tyrant. And yet he seeks refuge in God. He knows that after death there is no coming back to life, and yet for day after day of his service he would wait for relief, would wait for God's call (14:13–14).

'Your maxims are proverbs of ashes,
*   your defences are defences of clay.*
Let me have silence, and I will speak,
*   and let come on me what may.*
I will take my flesh in my teeth,
*   and put my life in my hand.*
See, he will kill me; I have no hope;
*   but I will defend my ways to his face.'*
Job 13:12–15

'But you are doing away with the fear of God,
*   and hindering meditation before God.'*
Job 15:4

'I have heard many such things;
*   miserable comforters are you all.*
Have windy words no limit?
*   Or what provokes you that you keep on talking?*
I also could talk as you do,
*   if you were in my place;*
I could join words together against you,
*   and shake my head at you.*
I could encourage you with my mouth,
*   and the solace of my lips would assuage your pain.'*
Job 16:2–5

---

5 · 18

Job replies: Indeed, Zophar, you know everything. It's so easy to judge when you're not suffering. God can do whatever he wants and people cannot resist him.

Chapter **12**

5 · 18

Job continues: I know the same things you know. But I'm innocent. If I could stand before God, I would prove it.

Chapter **13**

5 · 18

Job continues: Life is short and full of trouble. What is the point of God doing this to me now when I'll be dead soon?

Chapter **14**

5 · 18

Eliphaz responds: Job, you're wrong. God destroys the wicked. Their prosperity is short-lived. If you're right and good people can suffer, then what's the point of being good?

Chapter **15**

5 · 18

Job responds: You're not comforting me at all; in fact, you're only making me feel worse. I'm innocent. I've lost everything. And you're just compounding my misery.

Chapter **16**

5 · 18

Job continues: I'm destroyed, my life is ruined and only the grave awaits me.

Chapter **17**

5 · 18

Bildad responds: Job, you don't know what you're talking about. Only the wicked, those who don't know God, suffer horribly.

Chapter **18**

5 | **18**

Chapter
19

Job responds: Why do you keep on adding to my misery? Even if I have done something wrong, why is that your concern? But in fact, God has mistreated me for no good reason.

5 | **18**

Chapter
20

Zophar responds: Though the evil person might prosper for a while, in the end, God will bring him down and punish him as he deserves, making him suffer horribly.

5 | **18**

Chapter
21

Job responds: Why don't you pay attention to what I say and what has happened to me? Bad things can happen to good people and good things to bad people. God does whatever he wants.

5 | **18**

Chapter
22

Eliphaz responds: Do you really think God is punishing you for being good? God is righteous and you're not. So repent and then he'll forgive you and restore your fortunes.

5 | **18**

Chapter
23

Job wishes that he could present his innocence. But he can't oppose God or do anything to stop God's actions against him.

5 | **18**

Chapter
24

Job wishes that it was as his friends suggest; that the wicked were swiftly punished by God when they misbehaved. But in reality, justice doesn't always happen.

5 | **18**

Chapter
25

Bildad responds: God is powerful and humans are weak and wicked.

5 | **18**

Chapter
26

Job responds: You have done nothing to help me or make me feel better.

Chapter 19: **Commentary**

Job's spirit seems at last to be broken; he merely begs his friends for sympathy. Then comes his strongest assertion of hope: although he has not reached the concept of life after death, he is convinced that somehow he will be vindicated. In Israelite Law the 'redeemer' is a family member bound to come to the help of a family member in trouble. 'In my flesh' (verse 26) is a first indication of the bodily resurrection, an idea that will become fully explicit only later in the Bible.

'O that my words were written down!
O that they were inscribed in a book!
O that with an iron pen and with lead
they were engraved on a rock for ever!
For I know that my Redeemer lives,
and that at the last he will stand upon the earth;
and after my skin has been thus destroyed,
then in my flesh I shall see God,
whom I shall see on my side,
and my eyes shall behold, and not another.
My heart faints within me!'

Job 19:23–27

'Will any teach God knowledge,
seeing that he judges those that are on high?
One dies in full prosperity,
being wholly at ease and secure,
his loins full of milk
and the marrow of his bones moist.
Another dies in bitterness of soul,
never having tasted of good.
They lie down alike in the dust,
and the worms cover them.'

Job 21:22–26

Chapter 23: **Commentary**

In his desperation Job challenges God to a lawsuit, despite knowing that he cannot win it.

'As God lives, who has taken away my right,
  and the Almighty, who has made my soul bitter,
as long as my breath is in me
  and the spirit of God is in my nostrils,
my lips will not speak falsehood,
  and my tongue will not utter deceit.
Far be it from me to say that you are right;
  until I die I will not put away my integrity
from me.
I hold fast my righteousness, and will not let it go;
  my heart does not reproach me for any of my days.'
                                    Job 27:2–6

Job's complaint
Job complains to both God and his friends about how badly they are treating him.

Chapter 28: **Commentary**

This great poem on wisdom falls into three stanzas, separated by the refrain of verse 12 and 20. First, human ingenuity; second, the transcendence of true wisdom; third, the divine origin of the wisdom that is 'fear of the LORD'.

'But where shall wisdom be found?
  And where is the place of understanding?
Mortals do not know the way to it,
  and it is not found in the land of the living.'
                                    Job 28:12–13

Chapters 29–31: **Commentary**

Job ends his defence by contrasting his former happiness with his present misery and by vigorously protesting his innocence.

Chapters 32–37: **Commentary**

Elihu appears and disappears abruptly, with only a lame excuse. He alone has a Jewish name ('he is my God') and ancestry; he uses a different style and vocabulary. His solution pre-empts the final speeches of God. It is possible that these chapters are a later insertion to bring the dialogues closer to orthodox theology.

5	18	
Job continues: God has mistreated me. Why do you keep repeating meaningless platitudes about how God makes the wicked suffer?		Chapter **27**

5	18	
A poem in praise of wisdom. Where can wisdom be found?		Chapter **28**

5	18	
Job continues: I wish my life could be the way it used to be, when I was happy and prosperous and people respected me.		Chapter **29**

5	18	
Job continues: Instead, my life is miserable – and stupid, insignificant people are berating me.		Chapter **30**

5	18	
Job continues: I've been a good person and I didn't deserve to have these bad things happen to me. If I'd been bad, it would have made sense.		Chapter **31**

5	18	
Job's friends give up on him. Elihu, a young man who has been listening to the discussion between Job and his friends, decides that he has something to say.		Chapter **32**

End of suffering
Job thanked God for the return of his health, for a new family and for renewed prosperity.

5 | **18**

Chapter **33**

Elihu claims to be upright and wise. He says that Job is wrong to claim innocence, and wrong about suffering unjustly. God makes people suffer only to make them repent.

5 | **18**

Chapter **34**

Elihu continues: God repays people for what they do: he punishes the evil. So Job is a sinner and a rebel.

5 | **18**

Chapter **35**

Elihu continues: God is unaffected by human sin and has never responded to the just complaints of the oppressed, so why would you expect him to answer your worthless charges?

5 | **18**

Chapter **36**

Elihu continues: God helps the righteous and punishes the wicked in order to get them to turn back to God. God does whatever he wants, so we can't ever tell him he's wrong.

5 | **18**

Chapter **37**

Elihu continues: God is beyond our understanding, and he only does what is right. He is just in all his dealings.

5 | **18**

Chapter **38**

God responds to Job from the storm: You don't know what's going on. So here are some questions: Do you understand how I created the universe? Do you comprehend its laws?

*'There they cry out, but he does not answer,
    because of the pride of evildoers.
Surely God does not hear an empty cry,
    nor does the Almighty regard it.
How much less when you say that you do not see
him, that the case is before him, and you are
waiting for him!
And now, because his anger does not punish,
    and he does not greatly heed transgression ...'*
Job 35:12–15

Chapters 38–39: **Commentary**

Suddenly the drama enters into the sphere of Israelite revelation, for God is named 'the LORD', who makes himself known in the storm, the standard vehicle of revelation in Israel. This revelation contains no answers to Job's questions, but goes beyond them, showing that human wisdom falls short of any explanation. Human wisdom can explain suffering no more than it can explain how the world comes to be. The divine wisdom and power are overwhelming and beyond human comprehension. Job is simply overwhelmed into silence (40:4–5).

'Will you even put me in the wrong?
  Will you condemn me that you may be justified?
Have you an arm like God,
  and can you thunder with a voice like his?
'Deck yourself with majesty and dignity;
  clothe yourself with glory and splendour.
Pour out the overflowings of your anger,
  and look on all who are proud, and abase them.
Look on all who are proud, and bring them low;
  tread down the wicked where they stand.
Hide them all in the dust together;
  bind their faces in the world below.
Then I will also acknowledge to you
  that your own right hand can give you victory.'

Job 40:8–14

Chapters 40–41: **Commentary**

In myth Behemoth and Leviathan are symbols of
overpowering cosmic evil. In this lyrical presentation of
divine power they are shrunk to the hippopotamus and
crocodile respectively, monsters whom no human being
can control, but the playthings of the LORD. Job again
concedes his own impotence (42:2–6).

Chapter 42: **Commentary**

After the great revelation of divine power and wisdom the
prose conclusion is perhaps somewhat tame, for Job's
restoration is hardly adequate to remove the problem.
Like other great biblical figures, Abraham and Moses, Job
himself becomes the intercessor for his friends. His wealth
is so vast that even his daughters receive inheritance rights.

*After the LORD had spoken these words to Job, the
LORD said to Eliphaz the Temanite: 'My wrath is
kindled against you and against your two friends;
for you have not spoken of me what is right, as my
servant Job has. Now therefore take seven bulls and
seven rams, and go to my servant Job, and offer up
for yourselves a burnt-offering; and my servant Job
shall pray for you, for I will accept his prayer not to
deal with you according to your folly; for you have
not spoken of me what is right, as my servant Job
has done.'*

Job 42:7–8

5		**18**	
God continues: Can you tell me all about goats? Donkeys? Wild oxen? Ostriches? Horses? Hawks?		Chapter **39**	

5		**18**	
God continues: Are you ready to correct me? Job has nothing to say. God continues: If you were powerful like me, you could save yourself. So how powerful are you? Can you control Behemoth?		Chapter **40**	

Sacrificing for his friends
*Job performs sacrifices for his friends so God will forgive
them. Their arguments about God's motives and practices
had been wrong, while everything Job had said was right.*

6		**19**	
God continues: can you control the monster Leviathan?		Chapter **41**	

6		**19**	
Job responds: I know that you can do anything and know everything, while I am powerless and incredibly ignorant. God blesses Job and warns his friends that they were wrong. Job prays for their forgiveness.		Chapter **42**	

Psalms

Overview

The final editor of the Book of Psalms arranged the various Psalms into five sections, perhaps imitating the five divisions of the Law: Genesis, Exodus, Leviticus, Numbers and Deuteronomy.

I   Book 1 – 1–41 – Genesis

II   Book 2 – 42–72 – Exodus

III Book 3 – 73–89 – Leviticus

IV   Book 4 – 90–106 – Numbers

V   Book 5 – 107–150 – Deuteronomy

Note: The numbering of the Psalms differs, for the Greek Psalm 9 is divided into Psalms 9 and 10 in the Hebrew; this creates a knock-on effect until Psalm 148. In this translation, the New Revised Standard Version, the Hebrew numbering is used.

The Psalter is the book of Israel's religious poetry, prayers and praise to God, though of course by no means the only prayers of the Bible. The Psalms express every mood in Israel's encounter with God, from joy to sorrow, and from confidence to despair. Theoretically attributed to King David, in fact they stem from every period of Israel's history: some ancient Canaanite prayers adapted to praise Israel's God, some prayers from the Jerusalem monarchy, laments from the time of the Babylonian Exile and wisdom poems from the later, post-exilic period. Mindful that Jesus himself must have prayed for them, the Christian tradition has adopted them, and sees Christ praying in them. Hebrew poetry does not rhyme, as many English poems do, and has no set rhythm. The poetic rhythm is provided by a balance of ideas expressed in parallel. This parallelism appears chiefly in three forms: synonymous (two lines repeating the same idea: 'It is he who set it on the seas/on the waters he made it firm'), antithetical (balancing positive and negative: 'Calm your anger and forget your rage/Do not fret, it only leads to evil') and synthetic (an idea followed by a fuller statement: 'O gates lift high your heads/Grow higher, ancient doors'). Psalm 32 is an excellent example of parallelism.

The Psalms are prayers of joy and sorrow, praise and repentance, celebration and reflection – a prayer for every occasion. Some are full of joy and noisy exhilaration, others give voice to depression and worry. Each psalm has been categorised and this is noted above each summary.

Book 1 (Psalms 1–41)

Wisdom Psalms

Psalm 1

The righteous who obey God's law are blessed, in contrast to the wicked.

Psalm 1: **Commentary**

Placed at the head of the Psalter, a contrast between the joy of the righteous and the misery of the wicked, illustrated respectively by a well-watered tree and unstable chaff.

Rather than three separate behaviours or individuals, the nature of Hebrew poetry reveals a single individual and a single idea. 'Counsel of the wicked', 'way of sinners' and 'seat of mockers' are all parallel or synonymous concepts meaning simply: 'those who behave wrongly'.

The nearest equivalent to rhyme in these poems is the use of acrostics – a line, verse or group of verses beginning successively with each letter of the alphabet in turn. This effect is very difficult to reproduce in translation. The prime example is Psalm 119, in which groups of eight verses begin with each letter in turn.

The arrangement of the Psalter is somewhat haphazard. We do not know how the Psalms were collected or preserved, or how they were used in Israelite worship. Some Psalms are obviously public, processional songs; others are intimate and private prayers. Some have a refrain or choral response, while others imply an instrumental accompaniment. At some stage the Psalter was arranged in five books. Attached to the end of the last Psalm of each book is a cry of praise to God (Psalms 40, 71, 88, 105), rising to a great paean of praise at the very end, Psalms 148–150. At the seams between books a Davidic, or messianic, Psalm is often placed.

Illuminated manuscript
A handwritten page of the first Psalm, dating from the fourteenth century, shows King David, the traditional author of many Psalms, playing a harp.

Psalm 2: **Commentary**

A coronation song, mocking the rebellions that often occurred when a new king arose. The king is adopted as God's son. This Psalm is quoted several times in the New Testament with reference to Jesus as God's Son.

Psalm 3: **Commentary**

A morning prayer of confidence in God despite persecution.

Royal Psalms for a king of David's line	
The nations may rise up against God and his appointed king, but God will rebuke them. The nations would be wise to submit to God and his appointed king.	Psalm 2

Confidence Psalms	
I have many enemies; but I believe God will protect me. Please God, destroy my enemies and protect me.	Psalm 3

Confidence Psalms

Psalm 4

I am suffering. Please God, relieve my distress and bring me joy once again. I am not an idolater. I know only you can help me, God.

Psalm 4: **Commentary**

A tranquil evening prayer of thanksgiving for protection.

Confidence Psalms

Psalm 5

God, I need your help; save me from my enemies. I know you will judge the wicked and protect the righteous because you are righteous.

Psalm 5: **Commentary**

A morning prayer of confidence, contrasting the happiness of those whom God protects with the fate of evil-doers.

Laments: individual

Psalm 6

Please God, show me mercy. I'm in anguish. How long before you deliver me and rescue me from my enemies? I know you've heard my prayer and will answer it.

Psalm 6: **Commentary**

Sorrow for sin and a prayer for forgiveness. Verse 5, 'Sheol': the Hebrew word for the abode of the dead, where the dead live a wretched, powerless existence, unable even to praise God.

Confidence Psalms

Psalm 7

I trust you, God. If I'm guilty, then may I be punished. But if not, then punish my enemies instead. I know you are just and will punish my enemies and so I praise you for it.

Psalm 7: **Commentary**

A protestation of innocence and of confidence in divine protection against enemies.

Hymns of praise: God in nature

Psalm 8

God, compared to you and the universe you've made, human beings are insignificant. And yet you care about us and made us rulers over that universe. You're wonderful!

Psalm 8: **Commentary**

Praise for the creator who has made human beings the crown of creation, little less than the angels, superior to all the beasts of land, air and sea, crowned with glory and honour, and able to praise the creator. In the Psalms the attitude to creation is always one of praise and wonder at God's continuously holding all things in being.

Confidence Psalms

Psalm 9

Praise to God for all he has done and for his justice. Please continue to judge my enemies and all those who are opposed to you.

Psalm 9: **Commentary**

Praise for God, as champion of the poor and the needy. The psalmist rejoices, confident in God's protection against oppressive nations. In the Greek version this Psalm runs on continuously into Psalm 10 (which upsets the numbering until Psalm 148). The acrostic runs straight through both Psalms, but the approach of Psalm 9 is broader, on a national scale, whereas Psalm 10 is more individual.

Confidence Psalms

Psalm 10

Why have you been so slow to rescue us from our wicked enemies? Look how evil they are! Please do something about them. We know you care about those who suffer.

Psalm 10: **Commentary**

Praise for God, as champion of the poor and the needy. The psalmist describes the plots of the wicked, but asserts confidence in God's protection.

Confidence Psalms

Psalm 11

Since I take refuge in the LORD, why do you tell me to run away? The LORD will take care of the righteous, but destroy the wicked, because he is just.

Psalm 11: **Commentary**

Enthroned in heaven, God keeps his eye on the world and protects his loyal friends from the bowshots of the wicked.

Psalm 12: **Commentary**

Confidence in the protection of the Lᴏʀᴅ, who is as true to his promises as silver refined in a furnace, against the lying tongues of the wicked.

Confidence Psalms

Lᴏʀᴅ, help us because we can't believe anyone else. The poor are suffering. But what God says is trustworthy. God will take care of us and protect us from the wicked.

Psalm 12

Psalm 13: **Commentary**

A little song of confidence: fourfold 'How long?', threefold request, threefold 'I trusted', 'I shall rejoice', 'I will sing'.

Confidence Psalms

How long do I have to be miserable, God? Please answer me and rescue me. I trust your unfailing love, rejoice in your salvation and will sing praise to you.

Psalm 13

Psalm 14: **Commentary**

The folly of denying the existence of God, when God watches over those who seek him. This Psalm must have been especially popular, for it occurs almost identically as Psalm 53.

Confidence Psalms

Only fools don't believe in God. Everyone is wicked, but God will protect the righteous. We will rejoice when the Lᴏʀᴅ rescues his people Israel.

Psalm 14

The creator cares
The psalmist wonders how the God who made the sun, moon and stars could care for human beings, who seem so insignificant in the vastness of the universe.

Wisdom Psalms

Psalm 15

Who will live with God? Those who do the right thing, speak the truth, abhor wrongdoers, keep their promises, reject bribes and give to the poor without charging interest.

Confidence Psalms

Psalm 16

Protect me, God. You have given me everything that is good in my life. Thank you for your instructions and for your care. You will protect me from death and make me happy.

Confidence Psalms

Psalm 17

LORD, please hear my prayer and vindicate me. I am not a liar and I have followed your ways. Protect me and destroy my enemies who are falsely accusing me.

Royal Psalms for a king of David's line

Psalm 18

I love you LORD, you are my rock. Thank you for rescuing me from my enemies. You always rescue the humble and righteous because of your perfect, flawless ways.

Hymns of praise: God in nature, Wisdom Psalms

Chapter 19

The sky above displays God's glory and power to everyone. God's law is perfect and gives us life and protects us from going the wrong way.

Royal Psalms for a king of David's line

Psalm 20

May God grant all your requests and give victory to the king who trusts in God rather than in his own power.

Royal Psalms for a king of David's line

Psalm 21

The king rejoices because God has granted his requests and given him victory. The king trusts God. God will destroy the king's enemies.

Laments: individual

Psalm 22

God, I beg for help, but no help comes. Everyone is against me. I will praise you in front of everyone once you take care of me, which will encourage others when they face problems.

Psalm 15: **Commentary**

A wisdom Psalm: the integrity and loyalty required to enter God's house. This outlines a demanding programme for the moral life.

Psalm 16: **Commentary**

The LORD is my portion and cup. At all times he gives me comfort. He will never yield me up to Sheol.

Psalm 17: **Commentary**

A confident appeal: the LORD protects his friends like the apple of his eye against the circle of lions ready to claw and the young lion crouched in hiding.

Psalm 18: **Commentary**

A Psalm attributed to David in 2 Samuel 22. It consists of two poems joined by a bridge, verses 20–27, which attests the psalmist's loyalty. The first poem is concentric, meaning that the following lines are balanced: 1 and 10; 2 and 9; 3 and 8; 4 and 7; 5 and 6. The second poem (verses 28–50) is full of the imagery of war.

Psalm 19: **Commentary**

This Psalm consists of two independent parts, different in subject and metre, each praising the glory of God. The first praises God in the heavens, after the manner of Babylonian hymns to the sun, the second praises the LORD in the Law.

Psalm 20: **Commentary**

A royal prayer before battle. Some trust in chariots or horses, but we trust in the name of the LORD.

Psalm 21: **Commentary**

A royal Psalm, possibly a coronation song, since it mentions crowning. Victory over foes would also fit such an occasion, for the accession of a new king was often the occasion for subject peoples to rebel.

Psalm 22: **Commentary**

The Psalm speaks of the servant of the LORD, trusting in the LORD through persecution, suffering and humiliation. His eventual vindication brings glory to God before all nations. There is striking similarity to the Song of the Suffering Servant in Isaiah 53. Placed on the lips of Jesus crucified, several of the details of the Passion are described in the terms of this Psalm.

Psalm 23: **Commentary**

The LORD as the good shepherd. It is alluded to not only in the parable of the Good Shepherd in John 10, but also in the story of the Feeding of the Five Thousand on the green pastures beside the waters of Lake Galilee.

Thanksgivings: individual

The LORD cares for his people and he supplies all their needs, just as a shepherd takes care of his sheep.

Psalm
23

Psalm 24: **Commentary**

The conditions for entry into the Temple. The final verses suggest a liturgy of the LORD entering his Temple, possibly a commemoration of the entry of the Ark into the Temple, though we know of no such liturgy.

Wisdom Psalms, Psalms for a public liturgy

Everything belongs to God and he made it all. The righteous can come before God and receive God's blessing. God is strong and powerful, so be encouraged.

Psalm
24

Psalm 25: **Commentary**

A confident prayer for forgiveness, this is an alphabetical Psalm. The need to sustain the strict acrostic form perhaps dictates the somewhat incoherent order of ideas.

Confidence Psalms

I trust God. Teach me to live the right way. You, God, are good. You guide me, and you forgive me when I do the wrong thing. Please take care of me in my loneliness and affliction.

Psalm
25

Psalm 26: **Commentary**

A protestation of innocence, but at the same time a plea for God's mercy and redemption. It is saved from complacency by the psalmist's awareness of the need for God's help to live out this innocence.

Confidence Psalms

Vindicate me, God, because I am innocent and blameless, so don't destroy me like the bloodthirsty who plot evil.

Psalm
26

Psalm 27: **Commentary**

An ardent prayer, full of visual imagery, to keep close to the LORD, to see the LORD's face and to live in the presence of the LORD in his Temple.

Confidence Psalms

The LORD is my light and salvation, so I have nothing and no one to fear. Please protect me and don't reject me. I know you'll take care of me and I'll see your goodness.

Psalm
27

Psalm 28: **Commentary**

A prayer under threat, ending on a note of firm confidence. The central part is an appeal for vengeance, a reminder that in Old Testament morality vengeance was merely limited to the amount of the offence. It was not until the teaching of Jesus that all revenge was outlawed by the demand for unlimited forgiveness.

Laments: individual, confidence psalms

LORD, don't ignore me; show me mercy. Repay the wicked for their evil. Thank you for helping me. I praise you with joy.

Psalm
28

Psalm 29: **Commentary**

One of the most ancient of the Psalms, using the imagery for God of storm, thunder and earthquake, the powers of nature. All this is perceived as the voice of the LORD (seven times). The Canaanite god, Baal, is just such a divinity. This Psalm was possibly a hymn to Baal, whose imagery was transferred to the praise of the God of Israel.

Hymns of praise: God in nature

Ascribe glory and power to the LORD, who shakes the world with thunder and storm, rules over all and blesses his people with peace.

Psalm
29

Psalm 30: **Commentary**

An individual song of thanksgiving for deliverance from some life-threatening danger.

Thanksgivings: individual

Thank you LORD for saving me from my enemies, when I was at my lowest ebb. I called for mercy and you showed me mercy, turning my sadness to dancing.

Psalm
30

Thanksgivings: individual

Psalm 31

LORD, I have taken refuge in you, I am in distress, consumed by anguish. Be merciful to me. I'm trusting in you. You are good, a shelter to all. We can all trust and praise you.

Thanksgivings: individual

Psalm 32

Those who are forgiven are blessed. I was miserable until I told you about my sins and you forgave me. You will protect me in my troubles and I can rejoice in you.

Hymns of praise: God in nature

Psalm 33

Sing joyfully to the LORD! His word is faithful and true; he made the universe and no one can thwart his plans. The LORD takes care of his own and only the LORD can really help us.

Wisdom Psalms

Psalm 34

When I sought the LORD, he delivered me from all my fears. So taste and see that the LORD is good and listens to the righteous. They may have troubles, but the LORD will rescue them.

Psalm 31: **Commentary**

A prayer for deliverance, this Psalm is marked by the repeated appeal to God's 'steadfast love', that unfailing family love, the basis of God's relationship with his people. The early part of the Psalm has a balancing structure:
1–5 Confident prayer for help.
6–8 Declaration of trust in the LORD.
9–13 Lament.
14–15 Declaration of trust in the LORD.
16–18 Confident prayer for deliverance.
After this comes thanksgiving for deliverance (19–24).

Be gracious to me, O LORD, for I am in distress;
my eye wastes away from grief,
my soul and body also.
For my life is spent with sorrow,
and my years with sighing;
my strength fails because of my misery,
and my bones waste away.
I am the scorn of all my adversaries,
a horror to my neighbours,
an object of dread to my acquaintances;
those who see me in the street flee from me.
I have passed out of mind like one who is dead;
I have become like a broken vessel.
For I hear the whispering of many –
terror all around! –
as they scheme together against me,
as they plot to take my life.

Psalms 31:9–13

Psalm 32: **Commentary**

A cry of joy at God's forgiveness.

Psalm 33: **Commentary**

A joyful song of thanksgiving for God's total care for creation. God created by his word, and continues to guide creation in all its details. The Psalm is again a celebration of the 'steadfast love' of the LORD, bracketed by the concept in verses 5 and 22. It is marked also by the post-exilic awareness that God's plan of salvation is for all nations.

Psalm 34: **Commentary**

An acrostic Psalm in the wisdom tradition, each couplet beginning with a successive letter of the Hebrew alphabet. After an extended invitation to praise the LORD, it lays down guidelines for good conduct. This consists chiefly in a vivid awareness of the presence and attention of the LORD.

David asks for mercy
In Psalm 38 David begged God to relieve his suffering, which he recognised as a punishment from God for his sins.

Psalm 35: **Commentary**

This confident appeal for help against enemies falls into three sections, each of which ends with an expression of thanksgiving for deliverance (verses 10, 18, 27–28).

Psalm 36: **Commentary**

A prayer of confidence in the LORD: whatever the schemes of evil-doers may threaten, the steadfast love of the LORD (verses 5, 7, 10) will continue to support those who are loyal to him.

Psalm 37: **Commentary**

An alphabetical wisdom Psalm, this is built on the conventional assumption that virtue brings its own reward – 'yet a little while and the wicked will be no more' (verse 10) a morality rightly questioned by the Book of Job.

Psalm 38: **Commentary**

A strange and touching Psalm, for the psalmist stands before the LORD thoroughly conscious of his sin, his foul and festering wounds, his throbbing heart, but still a deaf man who hears nothing. Yet he admits his sin and longs to be close to the LORD, his salvation.

Psalm 39: **Commentary**

The psalmist is conscious of his sin, but especially of the insubstantiality of his life. The solution of eternal life has not yet been revealed, but all his hope is in the LORD, that somehow he may be delivered from his transgressions and smile again before he departs to be no more.

Psalm 40: **Commentary**

A hymn of praise for God's deliverance and the privilege of declaring to all God's faithfulness and steadfast love. The central verses 6–8 reflect on the value of obedience, an open ear, over mere sacrifice. In the New Testament the Letter to the Hebrews 10:5–7 reads 'a body' for 'an open ear' and applies the lesson to the incarnation and sacrifice of Christ. The last five verses of this Psalm are used again independently in Psalm 70.

Psalm 41: **Commentary**

A prayer of confidence in time of sickness, with a wry reflection on seemingly friendly visitors who confidently expect the worst (verses 5–10). For the Christian there is additional poignancy in the use of verse 9 by Jesus to refer to his betrayer. The blessing at the end of the Psalm concludes the First Book of Psalms.

Thanksgivings: individual

LORD, fight against those who fight against me. How much longer will I have to suffer? I'm tired of your silence. I want to praise you and thank you for deliverance.

Psalm **35**

Confidence Psalms

The wicked have no fear of God; all they do is plot evil. But your love is never-ending and people can take refuge in you. Protect me from the wicked; I know they will be destroyed.

Psalm **36**

Wisdom Psalms

Don't envy the wicked. Their time is short. Instead, trust the LORD. The righteous will prosper, while the wicked won't. The LORD will deliver the righteous from their troubles.

Psalm **37**

Laments: individual

I am overwhelmed by my guilt. My body is falling apart. I'm in enormous pain. I confess my sin; please don't forsake me. Rescue me, please.

Psalm **38**

Laments: individual

I tried to keep silent, but I couldn't hold it in. Life is fleeting. Remove your scourge from me. Hear my cry for help. And let me enjoy my life once again.

Psalm **39**

Thanksgivings: individual

I waited patiently for the LORD to hear me and rescue me from my problems. When he did, he restored my joy. I tell everyone about you. May my enemies be destroyed.

Psalm **40**

Confidence Psalms

The LORD takes care of those who take care of the weak. Heal me, because I've sinned. My enemies plot against me. Even my closest friend rejects me. Restore me so I can repay them.

Psalm **41**

Book II (Psalms 42–72)

Psalms 42–43: **Commentary**

These Psalms were probably originally one Psalm, separated for some liturgical purpose. The two halves conclude with the same refrain, and each contains the same lament, 42:9 and 43:2. The sevenfold reference to 'my soul', the deepest and most intimate element of human personality, intensifies the passionate longing to come close to God.

Psalm 44: **Commentary**

A prayer for deliverance from disaster, sharply contrasting God's former championship (verses 1–8) with the persecution now being undergone (verses 9–25). The protestations of loyalty to the covenant mean that the likely persecution is that of the Maccabean period, for the Babylonian Exile was accepted as the punishment for infidelity. What has happened to the LORD's steadfast love?

Psalm 45: **Commentary**

A royal wedding song, praising the military prowess of the king and the beauty and distinction of his bride – but hardly a mention of God. After the end of the Israelite monarchy this Psalm must have retained its place in the Psalter through the messianic sense attached to the kingship and the promise of worldwide dominion for all generations.

Psalm 46: **Commentary**

A hymn in three sections, the second and third ending with the same refrain, this Psalm celebrates the peace flowing from the spring of Gihon in the midst of Jerusalem, the symbol of God's presence in his holy habitation. The first stanza details the turmoil in nature, the third the turmoil of war; but the heart of the Psalm is the second stanza, the peace of Jerusalem.

Psalm 47: **Commentary**

The first of a number of Psalms celebrating the kingship of the LORD. The conquest of the peoples of Canaan becomes symbolic of God's kingship over all the peoples of the world in this noisy Psalm of celebration with clapping, singing and trumpets.

Psalm 48: **Commentary**

The Hill of Zion is not by nature the mightiest of mountains. However, when David brought the Ark up to Jerusalem, the presence of God made it beautiful, the joy of all the earth. From this sovereign presence the justice of God prevails in all the world. Verse 8, Tarshish is a name of uncertain meaning. It has been understood to indicate Tarsus or Tartessos. The sense may be 'a very distant place'. Solomon acquired ivory, apes and peacocks from Tarshish – all products of India. 'Ships of Tarshish' may mean strong, ocean-going vessels.

Psalm 49: **Commentary**

A wisdom poem, meditating on the certainty of death for rich and poor alike. No man can buy his own ransom, but God will ransom the psalmist from death. The doctrine of resurrection from the dead had not yet been formulated, but already there is a feeling that somehow the love of God admits of no separation.

But God will ransom my soul from the power of Sheol,
*   for he will receive me. Selah.*
Do not be afraid when some become rich,
*   when the wealth of their houses increases.*
For when they die they will carry nothing away;
*   their wealth will not go down after them.*
Though in their lifetime they count themselves
happy – for you are praised when you do well for
yourself – they will go to the company of their
ancestors, who will never again see the light.
Mortals cannot abide in their pomp;
*   they are like the animals that perish.*

Psalms 49:15–20

David admits his guilt
The prophet Nathan confronted David for his adultery with Bathsheba. David confessed his sin and begged forgiveness in Psalm 51.

Psalm 50: **Commentary**

This Psalm proclaims the judgement of God on vain and empty sacrifice. From the earliest times the prophets pronounced the vanity of formal but soulless liturgy. Now, in a court scene, God proclaims how pointless it is without fidelity to the demands of the covenant.

Psalm 51: **Commentary**

This noble expression of repentance is often attributed to David at his contrition after adultery with Bathsheba and the murder of her husband. However, the rebuilding of the walls of Jerusalem (verse 18) makes sense only after their destruction 400 years after David. The new heart and spirit (verse 10) must reflect the prophecy of Ezekiel 18:31.

Psalm 52: **Commentary**

First the psalmist describes the deceitful braggart, plotting destruction all day long. Then some light relief in the mockery of the righteous. Finally the reversal: while the braggart is uprooted, the psalmist is as deeply rooted as the olive tree. The olive is well known for its slow growth and endless fruitfulness, taking 30 years to reach full maturity and then bearing fruit for many centuries.

Wisdom Psalms

Why be troubled by your problems? Why put your trust in money? Death comes to all. Trusting in yourself or your money is foolish. Only God can redeem you from death.

Psalm
49

Prophetic exhortations

God says, 'I already own all the animals, so I don't need your sacrifices. Just thank me and I'll deliver you. But you wicked have no right to recite my laws, since you don't keep them.'

Psalm
50

Laments: individual

God, have mercy on me! I've sinned against you. Please clean me and make me pure once again. Deliver me from my guilt. My broken spirit is the only sacrifice you want.

Psalm
51

Wisdom Psalms

You are evil and deceitful and boastful. You are a disgrace and God will destroy you. You trusted in your wealth instead of in God. But I trust in God and so I will praise him forever.

Psalm
52

Confidence Psalms

Psalm 53

Only fools don't believe in God. Everyone is wicked, but God will protect the righteous. We will rejoice when the LORD rescues his people Israel.

Thanksgivings: individual

Psalm 54

God, please save me. Those who don't care about God are attacking me. I will sacrifice in thanks when you save me from my troubles and let me look triumphantly over my enemies.

Laments: individual

Psalm 55

God, please answer my prayer. I'm in anguish. I want to hide and run away. Someone that was once my friend has become my enemy. Destroy my enemies. I trust you, God.

Laments: individual

Psalm 56

My enemies are after me. They never let up. When I'm afraid, I look to God and my fear leaves me. What can people do to me when God stands by me? I thank God for saving me from death.

Laments: individual

Psalm 57

Have mercy on me, God. I'm trusting you to vindicate me. My enemies are like lions. They plot against me. But I will praise you, God, because you are powerful and you love me.

Imprecations

Psalm 58

The rulers are unjust and oppressive; they've been wicked from birth. God, destroy them! Make them vanish! The righteous will rejoice when at long last they are avenged.

Laments: Individual

Psalm 59

God, deliver me from my enemies! I'm innocent. When you punish them, don't kill them. I want them to remember their crimes and know that God is in charge. I can rely on you.

Psalm 53: **Commentary**

This Psalm is almost identical to Psalm 14. Only the divine name is different.

Psalm 54: **Commentary**

A lovely poem about divine protection, in which the hostility of the foes is perfectly mirrored by God's care:
Verse 1 – Save me by your Name.
Verse 3 – The insolent against me.
Verse 3 – Seek my life.
Verse 3 – Do not set God before them.
Verse 4 – God is my helper.
Verse 4 – Upholder of my life.
Verse 5 – My enemies.
Verse 6 – Thanks to your Name.

Psalm 55: **Commentary**

A prayer for rescue from persecution and harassment. The enemy is at one moment a single treacherous friend, at another a gang patrolling the city walls. In either case escape from Jerusalem into the peaceful solitude of the Judean desert would be a welcome respite.

Psalm 56: **Commentary**

A confident request for help in persecution, anchored in the repeated refrain, 'In God I trust, I am not afraid, what can flesh do against me?'

Psalm 57: **Commentary**

Again a prayer for rescue from persecution, imagined as man-eating lions, sharp swords and pitfalls in the path. But the dimension is now cosmic: in the refrain (verses 5 and 11) God is exalted above the clouds or the heavens and his glory over the earth. His praise too will be among the nations.

Psalm 58: **Commentary**

A bitter prayer that unjust judges may be annihilated – with rich and explicit imagery. It is not merely that the harm they do should cease, but that the just may positively rejoice in their discomfiture. This is not a Christian Psalm, but is shot through with the sentiments of revenge that Jesus sought to transcend.

Psalm 59: **Commentary**

A more cheerful Psalm of confidence in persecution, with two refrains, one about the persecutors (verses 5–6 and 14–15), the other of confidence (verses 9 and 17). The persecutors are represented as prowling dogs. Instead of praying unyieldingly for their destruction, the psalmist here at least suggests that they may be left as a laughing stock to deter others.

Psalm 60: **Commentary**

After a crushing defeat, described in terms of earthquake, the psalmist prays to make his own the traditional enemies of post-exilic Judah. Judah is his sceptre, but the northern territory of Ephraim his helmet, and outlying lands his washbasin, the earth beneath his shoe or simply the object of his triumph. Perhaps this is simply asking that God may reclaim for himself the whole earth.

Psalm 61: **Commentary**

This simple short prayer falls into two halves: 'Hear my prayer' (verses 1–4), the prayer of an exile to return to Zion, and 'You have heard my vows' (verses 5–8), a prayer for the endless reign of the messianic king. The final petition for 'steadfast love and faithfulness' is fulfilled in the prologue of the Gospel of John, 'grace and truth have come through Jesus Christ'.

Psalm 62: **Commentary**

This Psalm has two distinct parts. The first (verses 1–8) is a declaration of trust. It revolves around two short refrains: the first refrain proclaims that God is my rock and my salvation. Against this the assailants fruitlessly batter as against a leaning wall or a tottering fence – little hope of success there! The second refrain renews the hope with gratitude and trust. The second part of the Psalm (verse 9–12) is a wisdom pronouncement, contrasting human strength with divine power.

Psalm 63: **Commentary**

The third in this little series of Psalms of confidence comes peacefully to rest in the sanctuary, 'in the shadow of your wings' where 'your right hand holds me fast'.

Psalm 64: **Commentary**

The psalmist prays that those who are planning harm may find the tables turned on them so thoroughly that they become an example to all people.

Psalm 65: **Commentary**

A springtime song, rejoicing in the blessings of the Temple, and rejoicing in God's gift of the beauty of the short-lived Judaean spring.

Psalm 66: **Commentary**

This joyful song is permeated with delight at forgiveness and the release from Exile in Babylon, the second Exodus. The psalmist pledges his loyalty, sacrifice and praise.

Laments: communal, Thanksgivings: communal

You have rejected us, God. But now, please restore us, and save us from our enemies. Go out with our armies and fight. Give us victory against the enemies of Israel.

Psalm **60**

Confidence Psalms, Hymns of God's kingship

Hear my prayer. You're my refuge. Protect me. Protect the king. I will always praise you and I promise to fulfil all my vows to you.

Psalm **61**

Confidence Psalms, Imprecations

I can rest secure in God, a rock that will never be shaken. My salvation and honour depend on God and I know I can trust him. He is powerful and his love will never fail.

Psalm **62**

Confidence Psalms

I earnestly seek God, like a thirsty person looking for water. I know I can rely on you and that you will overcome my enemies.

Psalm **63**

Imprecations

God, protect me from my enemies who plot injustice. I know you will destroy them and turn their evil plans against them. The righteous will rejoice and rest securely in you.

Psalm **64**

Hymns of praise: God in nature

God, people will praise you in Zion, because you forgave us and answered our prayers. You provided us with what we need to live, giving us our water and food in abundance.

Psalm **65**

Thanksgivings: communal

Israel should praise God for what he's done for them before. I will bring sacrifices to the Temple and fulfil my vows. Thank you for your forgiveness and for listening to my prayers.

Psalm **66**

Thanksgivings: communal

Psalm
67

May God give us what we don't deserve and may the peoples of the world praise God. Give us what we need and bless us.

Psalms for a public liturgy

Psalm
68

May God destroy his enemies. May the righteous rejoice. You care for the powerless. You will save us from all our troubles and bring us victory. Therefore, we praise you.

Laments: communal

Psalm
69

Save me, God! My problems are overwhelming. You know I'm foolish and you know my guilt. Forgive and rescue me because you love me. My thanks are better than sacrifice.

Thanksgivings: individual

Psalm
70

Hurry up and rescue me from those who are trying to harm me. May they suffer the harm instead. May all those who seek your help rejoice. Don't delay in rescuing me.

Confidence Psalms

Psalm
71

I've depended on you all my life. So don't abandon me now that I'm old. Save me from my enemies. I always have hope. I will tell everyone about your righteous acts.

Royal Psalms for a king of David's line

Psalm
72

May the king be righteous and just. May he and his people prosper. May he deliver those who suffer and may he live a long time.

Psalm 67: **Commentary**

A simple little song with three refrains, celebrating God's blessings on the earth and calling all people to praise God.

Psalm 68: **Commentary**

A processional song of victory, poetically celebrating the processions and victories of Israel's history, describing the composition of the solemn procession itself, and coming to a climax of universal praise.

Psalm 69: **Commentary**

The Psalm is one of lamentation, by a sufferer who feels that he is being persecuted for his loyalty to God, but retains a conviction that his sacrifice is pleasing to God and that God will somehow listen to him. The New Testament sees in this Psalm a prophecy of the Passion of Christ, and quotes from it not only 'It is zeal for your house that has consumed me' (verse 9; John 2:17) but also in the Passion narrative itself 'in my thirst they gave me vinegar to drink' (verse 21; Mark 15:36).

Psalm 70: **Commentary**

This Psalm duplicates the final verses of Psalm 40.

Psalm 71: **Commentary**

In old age the psalmist leans contentedly on God, seeing that God has been his help from his mother's womb. He praises God continually, for, despite his troubles, God will raise him up from the earth (verse 20) – a hint of the resurrection.

Do not cast me off in the time of old age;
do not forsake me when my strength is spent.
Psalms 71:9

Psalm 72: **Commentary**

This messianic Psalm sings of the reign of peace and justice which the king will introduce, revered by all from sea to sea, attentive to the needs of the poor and blessed by all. Even the land will respond with abundant harvests. The final blessing concludes the Second Book of Psalms.

Book III (Psalms 73–89)

Psalm 73: **Commentary**

A wisdom Psalm about the fate in store for the proud, as the psalmist endeavours to puzzle out how it is that the wicked prosper while the righteous suffer. The solution of bliss in heaven if not on earth, is not yet available to him. A nobler solution is company with God already in this world: 'I am continually with you; you hold me by my right hand' (verse 23).

Psalm 74: **Commentary**

A lament for the Temple. How is it that he who crushes Leviathan's heads, who rules the night and the day, can allow the Temple to be so brutally destroyed? A cry to the LORD to defend his own.

Psalm 75: **Commentary**

A simple statement of retribution on wrongdoing, for God himself is the judge. It may be that this Psalm is deliberately placed after the previous Psalm, to show that those who desecrated the Temple will not go unpunished.

Psalm 76: **Commentary**

An English translation of this Psalm fails to convey its full meaning, for it circles around two dominant concepts, the awesome terror of the LORD, the Holy One of Israel, resplendent and made known in Judah, and the poor and humble of the earth, those especial favourites of the LORD, who fall under his particular patronage.

Psalm 77: **Commentary**

An agonised prayer of doubt: has the right hand of the Most High changed? The psalmist recalls the wonder of overwhelming power shown in the crossing of the Red Sea in the time of Moses and Aaron, and wonders why God does not answer prayer as he did in the days of old.

Wisdom Psalms

God is good to Israel, but it bothers me how the wicked prosper. It makes me wonder if there's any reason to be good. God, I trust you to give everyone what they deserve.

Psalm
73

Laments: communal

Why are you angry with us, God? We're suffering and there is no sign of you. How long will it be before you rescue us? You saved us in the past, so save us now.

Psalm
74

Laments: communal

We praise you God, for all the wonderful things you've done; you judge the wicked in your own way, in your own time, in your own place, and exalt the righteous when you please.

Psalm
75

Hymns of praise: God in Zion

God is well known in Israel. His power is unassailable, his enemies are defeated and the oppressed are rescued. Keep the promises you make to God. All should fear him.

Psalm
76

Hymns of praise: God in history

When I asked God to solve my problems, nothing happened. No matter how much I prayed, I didn't feel any better. All I can do is remember how God rescued his people in times past.

Psalm
77

When God is silent
The author of Psalm 77, illustrated by a young woman in prayer, asked for help from God. Even though nothing has changed and she feels no peace, she trusts God anyway.

Jerusalem destroyed
The destruction of Jerusalem traumatised the ancient Israelites and forced them to become more faithful to the LORD.

Hymns of praise: God in history	
Psalm **78**	God gave his laws to prevent rebellion. Ephraim broke those laws so God judged him. But God chose Judah and picked David, who has led them with integrity.
Hymns of praise: God in history	
Psalm **79**	God, Jerusalem has been destroyed, your people slaughtered, and your Temple defiled. How long will you stay angry with us? Please rescue us and destroy our enemies.
Hymns of praise: God in history	
Psalm **80**	Restore us, God. How much longer will you be angry with us? Your land has been devastated. Rescue us and we will not turn from you.
Psalms for a public liturgy	
Psalm **81**	Sing praises to God. God rescued Israel from Egypt, warning them to worship him alone. But they didn't and so now he has judged them. If they repent, God will forgive.

Psalm 78: **Commentary**

A meditation on the glorious deeds of the LORD for Israel in the past, the vacillating rebelliousness of Israel during the 40 years in the desert, God's anger and repeated patient corrections and how God rejected the northern shrine of the Ark at Shiloh and chose David as his servant. A meditation on history from the Deuteronomic viewpoint.

Psalm 79: **Commentary**

A cry for help and forgiveness after the destruction of Jerusalem. Why should the nations be allowed to taunt the LORD for his apparent inability to rescue his people?

Psalm 80: **Commentary**

A meditation on the Vineyard of Israel, once so flourishing and now ravaged by the boar from the forest. Verses 4, 5, 8, 15 and 20: 'LORD God of hosts', an ancient title of God, referring perhaps to God's military power, perhaps to the angelic hosts.

Psalm 81: **Commentary**

A processional song for a festival of the new moon, with a reminder of God's intervention to save Israel in Egypt and of Israel's disobedience. Would that Israel's obedience would provoke a new intervention of power.

Psalm 82: **Commentary**

A mythical scene, in which God is pictured as judging lesser gods, the powers that rule the world. They do not give justice to the weak and oppressed, and so will themselves be punished. There is perhaps also some reflection on human judges.

Hymns of God's kingship, Laments: communal

God presides over the kings of the world, kings who believe they are gods but are unjust. You're not really gods. You're just arrogant mortals who will die for your evil behaviour.

Psalm **82**

Psalm 83: **Commentary**

The psalmist prays that all the nations who plot against God's people may be destroyed like the nations that attempted to oppress them in the time of the Judges. Let them be scattered like chaff, driven away by God's tempest.

Hymns of praise: God in history, Laments: communal

God, do something: your enemies are plotting to destroy Israel. Treat them like you've treated your enemies before. Let them know who you are: the only God over all the world.

Psalm **83**

Psalm 84: **Commentary**

A contented Psalm of welcome to God's house. A blessing on those who dwell in God's house, a blessing on pilgrims to God's house, a blessing on those who trust in the LORD.

Thanksgivings: communal, Psalms for a public liturgy

God, where you dwell is beautiful! How blessed are those who live there, and even those who only visit. A moment in Jerusalem is better than a lifetime anywhere else.

Psalm **84**

Psalm 85: **Commentary**

A prayer that God's wrath may turn away, concluding with a prophecy of the fulfilment of God's steadfast love and faithfulness in the messianic reign of peace. Verse 3 shows God's anger and his jealousy as anthropomorphisms. God is likened to a spouse reacting to the infidelity of a spouse. This anger is no outburst of temper, but is always corrective, to bring Israel back to fidelity.

Laments: communal

You've forgiven your people before. Please forgive us once again. Don't be angry with us forever. Salvation is close to those who worship God. He will be good to the righteous.

Psalm **85**

Psalm 86: **Commentary**

This Psalm begins and ends with a prayer of confidence in God's loving mercy, verses 1–7 and 14–17. The centre is a plea for a faithful and undivided heart (verse 11). Several of the verses of the Psalm are drawn from other Psalms.

Confidence Psalms

God, please answer me: my enemies are coming. But I am faithful to you, so give me joy and make me obedient. You are compassionate, merciful and gracious. Destroy my enemies.

Psalm **86**

Psalm 87: **Commentary**

When King David installed the Ark in Jerusalem God chose it as his holy city. Now citizens of all nations are to be registered as citizens of Jerusalem, to share in its blessings. A universalist, post-exilic Psalm.

Hymns of praise: God in Zion

The city of Zion belongs to God and God belongs to the whole world: to Egypt, Babylon, Philistia, Tyre and Cush. They will all sing to God and be treated as if they were born in Zion.

Psalm **87**

Psalm 88: **Commentary**

The most desolate of all the Psalms, without a ray of hope. Three times the psalmist calls to the LORD, at night, every day, in the morning (verses 1, 9, 13), but there seems to be no reply, and the Psalm ends in darkness as it began.

Laments: individual

I am overwhelmed by my problems night and day. Why don't you do something, God? Can I praise you when I'm dead? Why have you rejected me? I'm all alone.

Psalm **88**

Psalm 89: **Commentary**

A song of praise to God's power and his protection of Israel, this Psalm gives us perhaps the oldest record of God's promise to David of a messianic king who will be God's son. But why has this promise been soiled, and his throne hurled to the ground? When will it be fulfilled?

Hymns of praise: God in history, Laments: communal

God, your love is forever. You promised to always care for David and his descendants, but now you've punished him. How much longer before you rescue him and our nation?

Psalm **89**

Book IV (Psalms 90–106)

Moses on Mount Sinai
In Psalm 90, Moses asked God for compassion in the face of human frailty and sin, both his own and that of the people of Israel in the wilderness.

Psalm 90: **Commentary**

A wisdom reflection on life's impermanence, dominated by the image of the short-lived freshness of grass in the morning, with a plea for wisdom and the loving favour of God.

Psalm 91: **Commentary**

A prayer of confident repose in the LORD, promising divine protection against a series of paired dangers: the terror and the arrow, pestilence and destruction, the lion and the adder, the young lion and the serpent. In the account of the testing of Jesus verse 11 is neatly chosen by the Tempter as a challenge to God's saving care (Matthew 4.6). In verses 1–2 God is invoked under four different ancient names: Elyon (the Most High), Shaddai (God of the Mountains), YHWH (the intimate personal name of Israel's God) and Elohim (the common name for God).

Psalm 92: **Commentary**

Praise for God's gifts of strength like the young wild ox (or 'rhinoceros' in the Greek) and stability like the great cedars of Lebanon. This Psalm is entitled 'for the Sabbath', perhaps because the sacred name, 'the LORD', occurs seven times.

Psalms 93, 95, 96, 97, 98, 99: **Commentary**

A group of Psalms celebrating the kingship of the LORD. The earthly king in Israel was seen only as the LORD's delegate and representative; the real ruler of Israel was the LORD himself. The ultimate delegate was to be the Messiah, bringing the reign of God to its fulfilment.

Psalm 93 is a very ancient, originally Canaanite, Psalm contrasting the LORD's power and glory with that of the mythical waters of chaos, held back by divine power from imploding the universe.

Psalm 95 is an invitation to prayer, and especially an invitation to greater fidelity than was shown by the Israelites in the desert wanderings. Its use in Hebrews 4:1–11 is the basis of the view of the Christian life as pilgrimage.

Psalm 96 was perhaps a processional chant, as was its parallel in 1 Chronicles 16:23–33, celebrating God's power over creation.

Psalm 97 is a celebration of God's kingship under the images of light and fire, purifying and enlightening.

Psalm 98 The joy of God's kingly rule, which brings salvation and justice to the whole world.

Psalm 99 concentrates on the holiness of the LORD. In the Book of Isaiah the LORD is 'the Holy One of Israel', an awesome title, for God is totally other, inviting at once the contrasting qualities of an awed fear and a warm love.

Confidence Psalms, Wisdom Psalms

| Psalm 90 | You were God before the world existed but our lives are short and your punishment is heavy. Relent! How long before you forgive us? May your favour rest on us. |

Confidence Psalms

| Psalm 91 | God will protect those who belong to him. If he is your refuge, then no harm can befall you. God will save us because we love him. He will answer our prayers. |

Confidence Psalms

| Psalm 92 | It is good to praise the LORD and make music to him. His acts are great: he blesses the righteous and judges the wicked. God's enemies perish, but the righteous flourish. |

Hymns of praise: God in nature, Hymns of God's kingship

| Psalm 93 | God reigns in power; he has existed forever. He is more powerful than the ocean waves. His laws are firmly established forever. |

Psalm 94: **Commentary**

A hymn to God as judge of the universe. First, some wisdom reflections on God's judgement against the wicked (verses 1–15). Then an application to the psalmist himself of the LORD as a stronghold of justice in his favour.

Happy are those whom you discipline, O LORD,
and whom you teach out of your law,
giving them respite from days of trouble,
until a pit is dug for the wicked.
                                    Psalms 94:12–13

Psalm 100: **Commentary**

A simple, joyful and much loved little Psalm, consisting of seven invitations to praise the LORD, interspersed with reasons for doing so.

A Psalm of thanksgiving.
Make a joyful noise to the LORD, all the earth.
Worship the LORD with gladness;
come into his presence with singing.
Know that the LORD is God.
It is he that made us, and we are his;
we are his people, and the sheep of his pasture.
                                    Psalms 100:1–3

The Ark of the Covenant
The LORD was pictured as sitting enthroned between the cherubim on the Ark of the Covenant, which was kept in the Temple in the Most Holy Place (Psalm 99:1).

Confidence Psalms , Wisdom Psalms

The LORD avenges. So how long will the wicked endure? God's discipline brings wisdom. God will judge the wicked and restore the righteous. I can take joy in God's unfailing love.

Psalm **94**

Hymns of God's kingship, Pilgrimage Psalms

Come, let us sing for joy to the LORD. He is greater than all gods; he made both land and sea. Worship him and obey him, unlike our ancestors who suffered for their disobedience.

Psalm **95**

Hymns of God's kingship, Psalms for a public liturgy

Sing a new song to the LORD. God is great and worthy of our praise. May the heavens, earth and all creation rejoice before the LORD, who will judge the world in righteousness.

Psalm **96**

Hymns of God's kingship

God is in control. His power is irresistible. May those who love the LORD hate what is evil. God will protect the righteous, so rejoice in the LORD and praise him.

Psalm **97**

Hymns of God's kingship

Sing a new song to the LORD. He has revealed himself to the world. He shows love and faithfulness to Israel. Shout for joy, all of creation. He will judge the world in righteousness.

Psalm **98**

Hymns of God's kingship

The LORD is in control. He is powerful, he loves justice. God spoke to his priests in the past and answered their prayers. God punishes and forgives. So worship God.

Psalm **99**

Hymns of praise

Shout for joy to the LORD. He made us and we belong to him. He loves us forever and will always be good to us. There is much to be thankful for.

Psalm **100**

Wisdom Psalms

Psalm
101

I will sing of your love and justice, Lᴏʀᴅ. As king, I promise to conduct myself well, and to put the evil in their place. So when will you help me?

Laments: individual

Psalm
102

Please answer my prayer, Lᴏʀᴅ. I'm suffering and need your help now. Rescue me from my enemies. You are in charge. You made the universe. It will end but you will not.

Thanksgivings: communal

Psalm
103

Praise the Lᴏʀᴅ, who forgives sin, revealed himself to Moses, is compassionate like a father and understands that we are weak, ephemeral mortals. But God is forever.

Hymns of praise: God in nature

Psalm
104

Praise the Lᴏʀᴅ for his power and his gifts: for the rain, the sun and moon, for wine and food – all that he has provided for both people and animals. I will praise God all my life.

Hymns of praise: God in history

Psalm
105

Praise the Lᴏʀᴅ. Remember what he did: his miracles, his covenant with Abraham and his descendants. Remember he brought Israel from Egypt to the Promised Land.

Hymns of praise: God in history

Psalm
106

We have sinned, just as our ancestors did, but although God punished them over and over, he also rescued them over and over. So God will rescue us, too.

Psalm 101: **Commentary**

This is a wisdom Psalm, praising two qualities. The first, *hesed*, is the quality of selfless love, a family love that will never give up on another family member. The second, *mishpat*, is fair judgement. In this Psalm it is allied to completeness or integrity, excluding anything wayward or slipshod. Such are the qualities that the psalmist asks God to set before him.

Psalm 102: **Commentary**

With vivid imagery the psalmist sees all as transitory, as the grass under the hot sun, or as worn-out clothes. He is overcome also by the loneliness of a pelican, an owl, a bird perched on a roof. In the strong central section (verses 12–22) he prays for the restoration of liberty to Zion.

Psalm 103: **Commentary**

The Lᴏʀᴅ is compassion and love, ever ready to forgive weak, transitory human beings. In return we can offer only our praise and gratitude.

Psalm 104: **Commentary**

A warm appreciation of the creator, watching over the valleys, their birds and predatory beasts, human beings at their labours, even the sea monsters he made to play with, this Psalm bears striking similarity to the Egyptian Hymn to the Sun of Pharaoh Akhenaton. Both express the same delicate love of nature and gratitude towards the creator.

Psalm 105: **Commentary**

A historical Psalm, a celebration of the covenant promised to Abraham, and gratitude for God's care of Israel in Egypt, including the plagues and the Exodus. It is an entirely happy poem, with no hint of Israel's stubbornness or disobedience.

Psalm 106: **Commentary**

In sharp contrast to the previous Psalm, this poem reflects on the constant disobedience and rebellion of Israel during the wanderings in the desert of the Exodus, answered by God's constant corrections and forgiveness. They failed at every turn, but still he kept his covenant with them. This Psalm concludes the Fourth Book of the Psalter.

Like a bird alone
This illustration from a page of an ancient, handwritten Psaltar appears in Psalm 102, where the psalmist compared himself to birds that are alone and in distress.

Book V (Psalms 107–150)

Psalm 107: **Commentary**

Let them thank the LORD for his steadfast love! Four scenes of dire emergency where the LORD has helped: lost in the desert, prisoners in a dungeon, sickness, storm at sea. Each is described in similar sequence: the need – the resolution – the thanks. Finally, a more tranquil scene of cultivation and harvest.

Let them thank the LORD for his steadfast love,
  for his wonderful works to humankind.
For he satisfies the thirsty,
  and the hungry he fills with good things.
                                    Psalms 107:8–9

Psalm 108: **Commentary**

A positive and cheerful hymn of praise, composed from the combination of Psalm 57:8–11 followed by Psalm 60:5–12.

Psalm 109: **Commentary**

A comprehensive curse, which leaves no aspect of the life of the psalmist's enemy untouched; a model for any future curse. Attempts have been made to Christianise it by suggesting that verses 6–19 are quoting the curse of the psalmist's enemies, a lame and ineffective subterfuge. At this stage of revelation it was still felt that God would support his own by damning their enemies.

Psalm 110: **Commentary**

A Psalm celebrating the messianic installation of the priest-king of Jerusalem, probably indebted to the pre-Davidic ritual of Jebusite Jerusalem. The first three verses express God's oath in support of the king, the fourth his appointment as priest. Verse 7 refers to the part played in the coronation ritual by the water of the Spring of Gihon, as in 1 Kings 1:38–40. In the New Testament this Psalm is the most quoted of all the Psalms, to illustrate the elevation of Christ to God's right hand at the Resurrection.

Wisdom Psalms

Give thanks to the LORD. Those God has rescued have many stories about how bad things were before he rescued them. God is good, merciful, and he forgives.

Psalm 107

Thanksgivings: individual

I will praise God with music. May God's glory cover the earth. May he save us from our enemy Edom and grant us victory.

Psalm 108

Imprecations

God, please don't remain silent. Instead, curse my enemy. May he suffer horribly for all the bad things he ever did to me and for all his other evil deeds.

Psalm 109

Royal Psalms for a king of David's line

The LORD told the king that he would make his enemies his footstool. He announced that the king is a priest like Melchizedek. God will use the king to judge the nations.

Psalm 110

Mighty works of God
The psalmist recounts all of God's mighty works on behalf of the Israelites, including rescuing them from Egypt.

Psalm 111: **Commentary**

A perfectly alphabetical Psalm of enthusiastic gratitude, summing up the benefits conferred on Israel by God's compassionate love, his covenant protection, his gift of the Law, the fear of his Name and the divine wisdom.

Psalm 112: **Commentary**

This alphabetical Psalm may be placed here to pair with Psalm 111. It is, however, a wisdom statement, detailing the material and spiritual advantages of fear of the LORD. In the wisdom literature, God's blessing was held to grant material prosperity as well as spiritual, though the prophetic tradition regarded the poor as special recipients of the LORD's favour.

Psalm 113: **Commentary**

The Psalm celebrates the LORD's rule over the whole world and all its nations. The LORD pays special attention to his favourites, the poor and needy. The same sentiments are prominent in Mary's Canticle of the Magnificat (1 and 13). 'Alleluia' or 'Hallelujah' is Hebrew for 'Praise the LORD'; 'Ya' is a short form of the sacred name. Psalms 113–118 all begin 'Alleluia/Hallel', and are known as the Lesser Hallel. They were sung at the three great annual pilgrimage festivals, and especially Passover. The 'Great Hallel' has been used to describe either Psalms 120–136 or simply Psalm 136.

Psalm 114: **Commentary**

This short Psalm celebrates two water-crossings wrought by the power of the LORD, the crossing of the sea that marked the beginning of the Exodus, and the crossing of the River Jordan, which marked the end of the journey. The last verse also mentions the gift of water when Moses struck the rock in the desert (3). At this stage the Greek and Hebrew numbering becomes still more confusing: Hebrew 114 and 115 constitutes Greek 113, then Hebrew 116 divides into Greek 114 and 115. Thereafter the Greek numbering reverts to being Hebrew-minus-1. We continue to follow the Hebrew numbering.

Psalm 115: **Commentary**

The first half of this Psalm reiterates the diatribes of Second Isaiah against Babylonian idolatry, stressing the folly of fashioning for worship a god who cannot perceive. The second half repeats blessings on the sons of Israel and the sons of Aaron.

Thanksgivings: individual, Wisdom Psalms

| Psalm 111 | Praise the LORD! His works are great. He is compassionate and takes care of his people. God's laws are permanently established. Fearing God is the beginning of wisdom. |

Wisdom Psalms

| Psalm 112 | Praise the LORD! The children of those who worship God will become powerful and prosperous. The righteous will never be afraid of bad news. But the wicked will suffer. |

Hymns of praise, Prophetic exhortations

| Psalm 113 | Praise the LORD! May the LORD be praised forever and everywhere. No one is like the LORD. He cares for the powerless and rescues those who are suffering. |

Hymns of praise: God in history

| Psalm 114 | When Israel came from Egypt, the waters of the Red Sea and the Jordan River fled. Why? Because God made them flee, just as he brought water from the rocks in the wilderness. |

Hymns of praise

| Psalm 115 | Praise the LORD for his love and faithfulness. The nations around Israel worship powerless idols. But Israel worships the LORD, who is powerful and who will rescue us. |

Psalm 116: **Commentary**

The Psalm is bound together by the triple 'I call on the LORD's name' in verses 4, 13 and 17, which makes the division of the Greek version less likely. It is all about trust in the LORD and gratitude to the LORD for hearing the psalmist's prayer, an intimate and heartfelt thanks, expressed in raising the cup and in the vows and thanksgiving sacrifice.

Psalm 117: **Commentary**

Short as this Psalm is, it is rich in material for prayer. The first couplet calls on the whole world, all nations and people, to praise the LORD – a reflection of the post-exilic universalism. The second couplet is centred on God's generous love and truth, that pair – translated 'grace and truth' in the prologue of St John – that reach their fulfilment in Jesus Christ.

Psalm 118: **Commentary**

A processional chant moving towards the sanctuary, this Psalm begins with several choral responses, and ends with grateful movement towards the altar. It is clear that the psalmist at the centre of the chant has been delivered from some trial or enemies by the LORD's right hand, and is giving his own thanks.

Psalm 119: **Commentary**

By far the longest chant of the Psalter, this Psalm is an alphabetic *tour de force*, each group of eight verses beginning with a new letter. It is a wisdom Psalm, celebrating the gift of the Law to Israel. The Law is God's greatest gift to Israel, since it shows how Israel must live in order to be God's people. It therefore reveals God's own nature, and to obey the Law is a loving response to a gift made in love. Obedience to the Law gives Israel its reason for existence and its dignity. Each law, statute, ordinance – many such interchangeable words are used – is therefore a special gift to be treasured.

Psalms 120–134, Songs of Ascents: **Commentary**

These songs were sung by pilgrims as they went up to Jerusalem for the pilgrimage festivals. This would be an occasion of great joy, as pilgrims, coming from minority situations in the scattered diaspora outposts among the gentiles, met up with members of their own religious family. They are short, straightforward, easily memorable songs that could be retained and sung without difficulty on the journey.

Psalm 120: **Commentary**

A song of gladness to be free from the vexations of Gentiles. Meshech is near the Black Sea; Kedar is part of the desert people of Nabataea.

The Word of God is read in a synagogue
This pious scene shows the gift of God's laws being shared.

Thanksgivings: individual

I love the LORD because he answered my prayer and rescued me from my problems. I will praise him forever, thank him and fulfil my vows.

Psalm
116

Hymns of praise

All the people on earth should praise the LORD for his great love and everlasting faithfulness.

Psalm
117

Psalms for a public liturgy

Give thanks to the LORD because he is good and his love lasts forever. When I was suffering and prayed to God, he answered my prayer and rescued me.

Psalm
118

Wisdom Psalms

Those who keep God's laws will be blessed; those who don't will suffer the consequences of their folly. God's laws are perfect and wonderful. They make our lives good.

Psalm
119

Pilgrimage Psalms

LORD, please rescue me from those who are deceitful. Rescue me from those who hate peace and prefer war.

Psalm
120

Pilgrimage Psalms

Psalm 121

My help comes from the LORD, who made the universe. He watches over Israel and he watches over you to protect you from all harm, forever.

Psalm 121: **Commentary**

The LORD will protect the pilgrims from the dangers of the journey, even though they themselves sleep.

Pilgrimage Psalms

Psalm 122

I was happy when I learned we were going to God's house. And now we're here! May there always be peace in Jerusalem. I will pray for its security and prosperity.

Psalm 122: **Commentary**

A triple prayer for the peace of Jerusalem, playing on the popular etymology of the name as 'city of peace'.

Pilgrimage Psalms

Psalm 123

As slaves look to their master, so we look to God, waiting for him to show us mercy. We've endured contempt for long enough.

Psalm 123: **Commentary**

A heartfelt statement of commitment to the LORD in Jerusalem. The singers compare themselves to devoted servants, male and female.

Pilgrimage Psalms

Psalm 124

If the LORD hadn't been on our side we'd have been destroyed. Praise the LORD for rescuing us. He is the one who made the universe.

Psalm 124: **Commentary**

Relief at deliverance from the dangers of the journey, imagined as flash floods or bird snares.

Pilgrimage Psalms

Psalm 125

Those who trust the LORD are as secure as the mountain on which Jerusalem sits. May the LORD do good to those who do good, and punish the evil as they deserve.

Psalm 125: **Commentary**

A prayer of confidence in Jerusalem, free at last from all foreign domination.

Pilgrimage Psalms

Psalm 126

When the LORD restored our fortunes, it was like we were dreaming. We were so happy! Those who go out sowing seed with tears will reap a harvest with joy.

Psalm 126: **Commentary**

The laughter, song and amazement at deliverance from slavery, as unexpected as streams in the desert.

Pilgrimage Psalms, Wisdom Psalms

Psalm 127

Unless the LORD is involved in the building of a house or watching over it, it's a waste of time. Having many children is a gift from the LORD that blesses and protects a person.

Psalm 127: **Commentary**

A reflection on Jerusalem, city of the LORD, and the need of his protection for prosperity and progeny.

Pilgrimage Psalms, Wisdom Psalms

Psalm 128

Those who obey the LORD are blessed by him: their work and families prosper. So may Jerusalem be blessed by the LORD and may Israel know peace.

Psalm 128: **Commentary**

Gratitude for the blessing of family and children, and a prayer for Jerusalem.

Psalm 129: **Commentary**

Relief from persecution, and a prayer that the persecutors may wither like grass scorched on a roof.

Psalm 130: **Commentary**

A prayer for forgiveness, longing for the LORD as the night-watchman longs for daybreak.

Psalm 131: **Commentary**

Hope and dependence on the LORD, as a helpless child on its mother.

Psalm 132: **Commentary**

The Song of the Ark of the Covenant. The LORD's oath of a dynasty for David corresponds to David's oath to place the Ark in Jerusalem.

Psalm 133: **Commentary**

Joy in fraternal harmony compared to the scented oil of festival meals, or the dew of the majestic Mount Hermon.

Psalm 134: **Commentary**

A prayer for blessing in the Temple at night.

Psalm 135: **Commentary**

A composite Psalm of praise, drawing on many others, particularly 95, 115 and 136.

> *For I know that the LORD is great;*
> *our LORD is above all gods.*
> *Whatever the LORD pleases he does,*
> *in heaven and on earth,*
> *in the seas and all deeps.*
> *He it is who makes the clouds rise at the end*
> *of the earth;*
> *he makes lightnings for the rain*
> *and brings out the wind from his storehouses.*
> **Psalms 135:5–7**

Psalm 136: **Commentary**

A litany of gratitude for God's wisdom in creation and for his care of Israel at the Exodus, sung with a repeated refrain.

Pilgrimage Psalms

Israel has long suffered oppression, but the LORD has granted her victory. May those who hate Israel suffer and never be blessed by the LORD.

Psalm 129

Pilgrimage Psalms

Answer my prayer. God forgives. I'm waiting for you and put my hope in you. Israel can be confident because God's love never fails. The LORD will rescue his people.

Psalm 130

Pilgrimage Psalms

I'm not arrogant, I don't concern myself with great matters. My ambition is small, like that of a child. Israel can forever hope in the LORD.

Psalm 131

Pilgrimage Psalms

Remember all that David suffered, all his promises, so that the LORD's Temple could be built. For David's sake, therefore, do not reject Israel's king. Bless Israel and its king.

Psalm 132

Pilgrimage Psalms, Wisdom Psalms

It is wonderful if people can live together in harmony. That is when the LORD has given his blessing.

Psalm 133

Pilgrimage Psalms

May all those who work in the Temple during the night praise the LORD. And may the LORD, the creator of the universe, bless you.

Psalm 134

Hymns of praise

The LORD rescued Israel from its enemies in Egypt, in the wilderness, and in the Promised Land. The LORD is real and powerful, but idols are powerless, manmade trinkets.

Psalm 135

Hymns of praise: God in history, Wisdom Psalms

Give the LORD thanks for his power, for his victories over Israel's enemies, from the Pharaoh in Egypt to Sihon and Og. The LORD's love endures forever.

Psalm 136

Laments: communal, Imprecations

Psalm 137

During our Exile in Babylon we wept while our conquerors tried to make us sing for them. LORD, remember what they did to us. Destroy them like they have destroyed us.

Hymns of praise

Psalm 138

I will praise you, LORD. May all the kings of the earth praise you. Though you are high and mighty, you care about the lowly. Rescue me from my troubles and vindicate me.

Confidence Psalms, Wisdom Psalms

Psalm 139

LORD, you are all-powerful, all-knowing, and there's nowhere I can hide from you. You created me and know everything about me. Destroy the wicked. Wash away my sin.

Confidence Psalms

Psalm 140

Rescue me from my enemies who are plotting against me. Protect me. I know you give the poor justice. Surely the righteous will praise you.

Confidence Psalms, Wisdom Psalms

Psalm 141

Answer my prayer quickly. Keep me from sin. I know the wicked will perish, but I'm looking to you to rescue me from my enemies. May my enemies suffer instead of me.

Laments: individual

Psalm 142

LORD, I need mercy. I'm in desperate trouble. Please listen to me and rescue me from my enemies. Then the righteous will praise you because you've been good to me.

Hymns of praise: God in history, Laments: individual

Psalm 143

I depend on your righteousness and faithfulness to bring me relief. I'm suffering. Answer my prayer quickly. Rescue me from my enemies. Teach me to do your will.

Psalm 137: **Commentary**

The impossibility of praising the LORD on the alien soil of the Babylonian Exile – and a cry for brutal vengeance.

If I forget you, O Jerusalem,
  let my right hand wither!
Let my tongue cling to the roof of my mouth,
  if I do not remember you,
if I do not set Jerusalem
  above my highest joy.

Psalms 137:5–6

Psalm 138: **Commentary**

A song of praise to God's steadfast love (verses 2 and 8), from the kings of the earth and the lowly alike.

Psalm 139: **Commentary**

The psalmist rejoices in God's intimate knowledge of his whole being and every thought and deed from before his conception, wherever he may be. He prays to ally his mind with that of God.

Psalm 140: **Commentary**

A prayer for rescue from enemies, alternating with complete trust in the LORD.

Psalm 141: **Commentary**

A prayer for protection against evil and against getting involved with evil-doers.

Psalm 142: **Commentary**

A lone voice cries out to the LORD for deliverance from a dire situation of persecution.

Give heed to my cry,
  for I am brought very low.
Save me from my persecutors,
  for they are too strong for me.
Bring me out of prison,
  so that I may give thanks to your name.
The righteous will surround me,
  for you will deal bountifully with me.

Psalms 142:6–7

Psalm 143: **Commentary**

In the knowledge that no one is just in God's sight, the psalmist appeals to the LORD's steadfast love for rescue as in the days of old.

Psalm 144: **Commentary**

The first part of the Psalm is woven largely from other Psalms, especially the Davidic Psalm 17. Thereafter it is a prayer for happiness in family life.

Psalm 145: **Commentary**

Making generous use of quotations from other Psalms, this final alphabetical Psalm thanks the LORD for the multiple blessings he has bestowed on his creation.

Psalm 146: **Commentary**

The first Psalm of the final Hallel, this contrasts the reliability of divine generosity with transitory human help. It ends with six statements ('the LORD…') of blessings conferred by the LORD on those in need.

Psalm 147: **Commentary**

Is this last praise before the final Hallel single, double or triple? The Greek Bible starts a new Psalm at verse 12, and there also seems to be a new beginning at verse 7. It may be seen as celebrating the recovery after the return from the Exile. If it is seen as three appeals to praise, the first concerns the healing of the exiles, the second agricultural prosperity, the third security and peace.

Psalms 148–150: **Commentary**

A final great triple paean of praise. Psalm 148 invites all the elements of creation to praise the LORD. Psalm 149 rejoices in freedom from enemies. Psalm 150 invites the noisy praise of the full ancient orchestra.

Let everything that breathes praise the LORD!
Praise the LORD!

Psalms 150:6

Thanksgivings: individual

Praise the LORD who helps me train for war. You are loving and kind; why do you even care about ephemeral humans? Rescue me from my enemies. Then I will praise you.

Psalm **144**

Thanksgivings: individual

LORD, you should be praised for your power, love and compassion. You exist forever and forever keep your promises. You take care of those who put their trust in you.

Psalm **145**

Hymns of praise

Praise the LORD and trust him, rather than humans who will soon die. The LORD made the universe. He takes care of the oppressed and powerless. He feeds the hungry.

Psalm **146**

Hymns of praise

Praise the LORD who restored the fortunes of the Israelites after their Exile. He brings the rain and provides food for all. Only to Israel has the LORD revealed his law.

Psalm **147**

Hymns of praise: God in nature

May everyone and everything in heaven and everyone and everything on earth praise the LORD. The LORD has restored his people.

Psalm **148**

Hymns of praise: God in nature

Praise the LORD with a new song. Let Israel praise him with music and dance. May their praise of the LORD inflict vengeance on their enemies.

Psalm **149**

Hymns of praise: God in nature

Praise the LORD for his power and his greatness with music and dancing. May everything that breathes praise the LORD.

Psalm **150**

Free at last
In Psalm 142 David asked God to set him free from the prison of his problems, suffering, fear and worry.

Proverbs

Overview

Collections of wise sayings, proverbs and admonitions abound in the literature of the countries surrounding Israel, both in Egypt and in Mesopotamia. These are sometimes collections of moral stories and rules of life, instructing young courtiers about behaviour at court, and often more earthy and general reflections on life in general. For Israel the East was the treasury of wisdom; the wise men who attempt to explain Job's sufferings to him come from the East, as do the wise men, or magi, who follow the star to Bethlehem. Professional wise women are known before Solomon (1 Samuel 28; 2 Samuel 14), but King Solomon was the first to set up a structured royal court with its advisers and staff, drawing on Egyptian models. This will have included a school for scribes and courtiers, for the wisdom literature stresses that the wise should seek instruction (Proverbs 1.5; 2.4–5; 12.15). Solomon himself had a formidable reputation for wisdom, both in giving wise judgements and in practical wisdom, which won him material success and wealth.

3	5	18

Chapter 1	The purpose of the Proverbs is to make people wise. Don't listen to those who entice you to do wrong. Instead, listen to wisdom, which offers you a long and happy life. Don't be a fool.

Chapter 1: **Commentary**

Translated, the Hebrew word 'proverbs' includes a wide variety of sayings, riddles, parables and images – any saying whose meaning can be discerned only with thoughtful reflection. The fear of the LORD, 'the beginning of knowledge', implies receptivity, reverence and awe towards the holiness and transcendence of God. This introduction, Proverbs 1–9, is the latest part of the book, probably post-exilic.

Let the wise also hear and gain in learning,
* and the discerning acquire skill,*
to understand a proverb and a figure,
* the words of the wise and their riddles.*
Proverbs 1:5–6

Wisdom and Folly are both personified as offering guidance in life to the wise or unwary (Proverbs 8:1–9:18), with very different results. Many of the wise sayings in the wisdom literature have no connection with religion or faith, but simply show deep good sense, reflecting a cynical and secular society, often allied to compassion for the poor and unfortunate. The special contribution of wisdom in Israel was the awareness that all true wisdom comes from God (Proverbs 2:6). The beginning of wisdom is the fear of the LORD (Proverbs 1:7; 9:10), that is, a reverent openness to God's revelation. God's wisdom is seen in creation (Proverbs 3:19), and personified Wisdom declares that she was created before the oldest of his works and delights to be with human beings (8:22–31). This personification of Wisdom as responsible for creation, distinct from, yet united to God, will be expanded in the later Wisdom books (Baruch 3:9–4.4; Wisdom 7:22–8:1).

King Solomon
King Solomon, noted for his wisdom, is traditionally seen as the author of the Book of Proverbs.

> *Trust in the LORD with all your heart,*
> *and do not rely on your own insight.*
> *In all your ways acknowledge him,*
> *and he will make straight your paths.*
> **Proverbs 3:5–6**

Chapter 5: **Commentary**

Just as Wisdom (which in Hebrew and Greek is feminine) is personified as a woman, so Folly, its opposite, is represented as a woman. In the Bible the covenant between God and Israel is represented as a marriage bond; so adultery is often the symbol of infidelity to the Law, and virginity the symbol of fidelity to the covenant.

| 3 | 5 | 18 |

If you follow the way of wisdom, you'll know to do what's right, instead of what's wrong. Choosing wisdom will protect you from many easily avoidable problems.

Chapter
2

| 3 | 5 | 18 |

The way of wisdom will prolong your life and grant you peace and prosperity. God used wisdom to make the universe, so don't lose sight of wisdom. Wisdom will protect you.

Chapter
3

| 3 | 5 | 18 |

Wisdom is valuable: it's worth whatever you have to pay to get it. Be wise and be righteous. Don't be foolish and wicked. Wisdom is the road to life; folly is the road to death.

Chapter
4

| 3 | 5 | 18 |

Wisdom will protect you from adultery; adultery may seem like fun at first, but in the end, it only leads to embarrassment and loss. Adultery will destroy your life.

Chapter
5

3	5	18

Chapter 6

Don't be foolish. Work hard, like the ant. Don't be lazy. People will forgive someone who steals bread because they're starving. An adulterer will forever be disgraced.

3	5	18

Chapter 7

Be wise. Avoid the fate of the foolish young man I saw having an affair with a married woman. He wasn't the first one she seduced. And the affair destroyed him.

3	5	18

Chapter 8

Wisdom is offering to help you. God created wisdom before he made anything else, and it was by wisdom that he created the universe. So listen to wisdom.

How long will you lie there, you sluggard?
When will you get up from your sleep?
A little sleep, a little slumber,
a little folding of the hands to rest –
and poverty will come on you like a thief
and scarcity like an armed man.

Proverbs 6:6–11

Chapter 8: **Commentary**

The poem on wisdom (8:22–31) in creation is one of several in the wisdom literature, especially Job 28, Sira 24, Wisdom 7:22–8:1 and Baruch 3:9–4:4. The reference to the creation story of Genesis 1 is clear: God is shown as creating by his wisdom, but wisdom itself is not created in the same sense; a different verb is used in the Hebrew, which may be translated as 'engendered' or 'possessed'. Wisdom personified is presented as distinct from but closely united with God, the artisan of all God's works.

Solomon's judgements
Solomon, the traditional author of Proverbs, was well known for his wisdom and learning and for rendering enlightened judgements.

When he established the heavens, I was there,
  when he drew a circle on the face of the deep,
when he made firm the skies above,
  when he established the fountains of the deep,
when he assigned to the sea its limit,
  so that the waters might not transgress his command,
when he marked out the foundations of the earth,
  then I was beside him, like a master worker;
and I was daily his delight,
  rejoicing before him always,
rejoicing in his inhabited world
  and delighting in the human race.

Proverbs 8:27–31

3	5	18

Chapter 9

Wisdom may be more difficult at first, but it offers genuine security and joy. Folly claims to offer a shortcut to security and joy, but the ways of folly really lead only to death.

5	18

Chapter 10

Wise children are a joy to their parents, but foolish ones bring them grief. Wisdom brings wealth, but folly brings poverty. Trouble destroys the foolish, but the wise will survive.

Chapter 10: **Commentary**

This collection of two-line proverbs is attributed to Solomon because of his reputation for wisdom. They are sayings, witty and down-to-earth, concerning family life, work, wealth and reputation. These are typical products of oral culture, folk wisdom to which many parallels exist in the wisdom collections of the surrounding cultures. Here, however, there is a repeated awareness that God is the source of all wisdom, and that wisdom is a blessing from God.

Chapter 12–21: **Commentary**

Many of these neat sayings represent a man's world, the world of small peasantry, where hard work, self-reliance and trustworthiness are the only means of survival and a moderate degree of comfort. The sayings all present a masculine view. A woman's place is subordinate but important, for a gracious woman brings honour to her husband (11:16) and a good wife is the crown of her husband (12:4). There is a sense that the woman of the house has some moral authority; only a fool despises his mother (15:20).

Fools show their anger at once,
but the prudent ignore an insult.
Proverbs 12:16

Wealth hastily gained will dwindle,
but those who gather little by little will increase it.
Proverbs 13:11

Those who spare the rod hate their children,
but those who love them are diligent to discipline them.
Proverbs 13:24

The heart knows its own bitterness,
and no stranger shares its joy.
Proverbs 14:10

The simple believe everything,
but the clever consider their steps.
Proverbs 14:15

A soft answer turns away wrath,
but a harsh word stirs up anger.
Proverbs 15:1

The human mind plans the way,
but the LORD directs the steps.
Proverbs 16:9

A friend loves at all times,
and kinsfolk are born to share adversity.
Proverbs 17:17

5	18	Chapter 11
Pride leads to disgrace, but humility brings wisdom. The righteous survive problems. Gossip is destructive. Both nations and individuals depend upon wisdom for their survival.		

5	18	Chapter 12
Discipline may seem unpleasant, but in the end, discipline is what will make you successful. For the best life, watch your tongue, persevere, work hard and be honest.		

5	18	Chapter 13
Spend time with the wise and you'll start to become wise; spend time with fools and you'll start to become foolish. Trouble is the lot of those who are wicked and stupid.		

5	18	Chapter 14
Simple-minded people believe everything they hear; those who are wise are a bit more discerning. Be careful. Consider the potential consequences of the choices you make.		

5	18	Chapter 15
Speak kindly, rather than harshly, if you want to fix problems. Think about what's most likely to be effective long-term, rather than what feels good in the moment.		

5	18	Chapter 16
God is the only one really in control. People may think their motives are pure, they may believe they're doing the right thing, but most of the time they're just fooling themselves.		

5	18	Chapter 17
It's better to be poor and at peace, than wealthy and facing strife. And it's better to face an angry mother bear than to spend time with a fool. A real friend will always love you.		

5	18

Chapter 18

Fools don't really care about the facts, they just want to win the argument. Get all the facts before deciding what to do. Find and hold onto your real friends.

A fool's lips bring strife, and a fool's mouth invites a flogging.

Proverbs 18:6

5	18

Chapter 19

If you are careful, work hard, watch your tongue and in general practise good self-control, you'll live longer and be more successful than those who don't.

The words of a whisperer are like delicious morsels; they go down into the inner parts of the body.

Proverbs 18:8

5	18

Chapter 20

Don't lose your temper, don't be lazy. Be respectful of those with power on their side. Let God avenge you, don't do it yourself. Plan for the future carefully.

A king's anger is like the growling of a lion, but his favour is like dew on the grass.

Proverbs 19:12

5	18

Chapter 21

You're better off doing the right thing to begin with than having to ask for forgiveness later. Justice brings joy to the righteous, even as it terrorises the wicked.

Who can say, 'I have made my heart clean; I am pure from my sin'?

Proverbs 20:9

It is better to live in a corner of the housetop than in a house shared with a contentious wife.

Proverbs 21:9

5	18

Chapter 22

Your reputation is a precious thing, worth more than any other possession. What people first learn to do is what they will tend to keep on doing ever after. Discipline is important.

Chapter 22: **Commentary**

Several of the sayings in this collection have a marked similarity to the sayings collected in the Wisdom of Amenemope, a collection of sayings in 30 chapters (compare 22:20) made by an Egyptian sage *c.* 1100 BC, perhaps a century earlier than Solomon. However, there need not be any direct link.

5	18

Chapter 23

Watch yourself around those with power. Don't make wealth your priority. Avoid fools. Discipline your children. Obey your parents. Don't get drunk all the time.

Train children in the right way, and when old, they will not stray.

Proverbs 22:6

5	18

Chapter 24

Don't envy the wicked and foolish. In the end, you'll be better off with wisdom. Don't let your problems get the best of you. Help those you see struggling. God is in control.

Do not withhold discipline from your children; if you beat them with a rod, they will not die. If you beat them with the rod, you will save their lives from Sheol.

Proverbs 23:13–14

Do not rejoice when your enemies fall, and do not let your heart be glad when they stumble, or else the LORD will see it and be displeased, and turn away his anger from them.

Proverbs 24:17–18

Chapter 25: **Commentary**

This second collection of proverbs is linked to King Hezekiah, who reigned in Jerusalem from 716–687 BC, and instituted a religious reform. They are less antithetical than the previous collection: a second line often continues the idea rather than opposing it.

A word fitly spoken
* is like apples of gold in a setting of silver.*
Like a gold ring or an ornament of gold
* is a wise rebuke to a listening ear.*
Proverbs 25:11–12

The unjust are an abomination to the righteous,
* but the upright are an abomination to the wicked.*
Proverbs 29:27

Chapter 30: **Commentary**

The Sayings of Agur present non-Israelite wisdom, for Massa is in Arabia. Some of them, however, such as 30.9, are clearly Yahwistic. Numerical sayings are common also in the prophetic literature; the accent always falls on the concluding line.

Chapter 31: **Commentary**

King Lemuel, like Agur, is unknown. It is notable that the king's mother is listed regularly in the biblical records of the kings of Israel and Judah. This, and the final alphabetical poem on the perfect wife, do provide a counterbalance to the strongly negative view of women shown in the book, although there is heavy emphasis on the usefulness of the wife to her husband.

5 · **18**

The ways of kings and the powerful are hard to predict. Be circumspect, speak softly and respectfully and don't visit them too frequently. Be kind to your enemies.

Chapter **25**

5 · **18**

Fools are trouble, so stay away from them if you can. The lazy will find any excuse to avoid work. Gossip is destructive. Beware of flattery.

Chapter **26**

5 · **18**

You don't know the future, so be careful about boasting about what hasn't happened yet. Let other people praise you, but don't let it go to your head. Be loyal. Be careful out there.

Chapter **27**

5 · **18**

Being foolish and wicked is a punishment in itself. Wisdom and righteousness can be its own reward. Guilt is a never-ending torment.

Chapter **28**

5 · **18**

Wisdom will bring joy and prosperity, but folly will bring sorrow and destruction. Accept correction and become better for it. Hold your temper. Discipline your children.

Chapter **29**

5 · **18**

It's best to be neither too poor nor too rich. Besides, you'll never be fully satisfied. You'll always want something more. Only God fully satisfies.

Chapter **30**

5 · **18**

Kings shouldn't get drunk. A virtuous woman is to be treasured and will make the man who finds her happier than any other man. She'll create prosperity for herself and for her family.

Chapter **31**

Ecclesiastes

Overview

Almost everything about this book has been debated: authorship, date, structure, meaning – even the title. It claims to be authored by a king in Jerusalem, whose success, riches and wisdom suggest Solomon as author (1:12–2:12); but the Persian and Aramaic linguistic elements make this impossible, for they point to a date half a millennium later, after the Exile. Authorship by Solomon must be a literary fiction, although attribution to Solomon accounts for its position in the Bible, between Proverbs and the Song of Songs, both attributed to the same author.

The modern title of the book, 'Ecclesiastes' is one possible translation, through the Greek, of the Hebrew title 'Qoheleth'. It may mean 'man of the assembly', or possibly 'gatherer or leader of the assembly' or even 'preacher'. Possibly the name means 'gatherer (of sayings)'. The structure of the

---

5	18

Chapter 1

Life seems to lack meaning because everything repeats. So I'm going to see if I can figure out the meaning of life. It's not wisdom: the more you know, the sadder you'll be.

5	18

Chapter 2

So I tried to find the meaning of life in endless pleasures, but life was still meaningless because no matter what, I'm going to die, whether I'm wise or foolish.

5	18

Chapter 3

There is a time for everything that happens: things come and go. And so we gain nothing from our work. We're no better than the animals: we live, we breathe and then we die.

5	18

Chapter 4

The world is filled with suffering and all accomplishment is due to envy. It's better not to be alone, but no matter what you accomplish, people will soon forget you. Life is meaningless.

Chapters 1–2: **Commentary**

The quasi-autobiographical details of these chapters present the author as King Solomon. The name 'Qoheleth' is allied to the verb for 'assemble'; it may designate his function as drawing the community together or as gathering together these wise words.

Chapter 3: **Commentary**

The purpose of this scintillating series of contrasts remains obscure. Is it to say that everything is fixed and unchangeable in life, or that nobody knows the answers?

What gain have the workers from their toil? I have seen the business that God has given to everyone to be busy with. He has made everything suitable for its time; moreover, he has put a sense of past and future into their minds, yet they cannot find out what God has done from the beginning to the end. I know that there is nothing better for them than to be happy and enjoy themselves as long as they live; moreover, it is God's gift that all should eat and drink and take pleasure in all their toil. I know that whatever God does endures for ever; nothing can be added to it, nor anything taken from it; God has done this, so that all should stand in awe before him.

Ecclesiastes 3:9–14

book, if it has one, is hard to follow. There are three firm passages, the 'catalogue of times' (3:1–8), the series of comparisons (7:1–29), and the poetic unit on old age (12:1–7). Apart from these passages, the reader is left with a series of reflections, often immediately contradicting each other, on whether or not life is meaningless, whether or not conventional wisdom is being endorsed, whether or not the fate of man and beast is identical. It is not clear whether these contradictions have been inserted by an editor to correct the original writing. It is even unclear whether the final verses of the book, on the fear of God as the whole of human duty, clarify the lesson of the book or were added later to correct it. The fact that this book was accepted into both the Jewish and the Christian canons of scripture is a reassurance that even within the world of faith such questioning has its place.

Do not give heed to everything that people say, or you may hear your servant cursing you; your heart knows that many times you have yourself cursed others.

Ecclesiastes 7:21–22

Chapter 7: **Commentary**

This repeated formula, 'Better A than B', is a common way of arguing in the moral reasoning of the period.

Chapter 12: **Commentary**

The splendid allegorical description of advancing age underlines Qoheleth's message of hopelessness. It is disputed whether the final six verses of the book are Qoheleth's own summary or a warning by a later editor.

The end of the matter; all has been heard. Fear God, and keep his commandments; for that is the whole duty of everyone. For God will bring every deed into judgement, including every secret thing, whether good or evil.

Ecclesiastes 12:13–14

5	18	
If you make a promise to God, keep it. Wealth is meaningless, too. The more you have, the more you want. You'll never be satisfied and in the end, you die and can't take it with you.		Chapter **5**

5	18	
Maybe you can enjoy yourself for a while, but you'll never be satisfied, no matter how much you get. And no one can reveal the meaning of life or the future.		Chapter **6**

5	18	
There's no such thing as 'the good old days'. Good comes to the bad and bad to the good. So don't be so bad that you suffer, but don't be so good that you don't have any fun.		Chapter **7**

5	18	
Obey the powerful; you'll have an easier life. And try to enjoy yourself; you'll never figure out what it all means. Anyone who claims he has it all figured out is wrong.		Chapter **8**

5	18	
No matter what you do, no matter how you live, in the end you're going to die. Time and chance happen to everyone. Life has no guarantees. You can do everything right and still lose.		Chapter **9**

5	18	
People get promoted who don't deserve it. Good things happen to fools. Of course, if you do everything wrong, if you are a fool, you increase your chances of things going badly.		Chapter **10**

5	18	
So be wise in your ventures, but there is still no guarantee that you'll succeed.		Chapter **11**

5	18	
Enjoy your life while you're young. When you're old, it won't be as much fun. But it's all meaningless, because in the end, whether you're good or bad, God will judge you.		Chapter **12**

Song of Songs

Overview

Note: This is a proposed division of the songs, though not the only possible arrangement. In the Hebrew original the masculine and feminine forms are more clearly marked than in English translations.

In origin, these love songs are purely secular, celebrating the love of two young people, full of *double entendre* and sexual innuendo. The book is attributed to Solomon because in the third song the man is depicted as Solomon in all his glory – an allegorical description, for Solomon the wise and successful king, with innumerable wives and concubines, was obviously typical of the successful lover. This certainly does not suffice to yield either date or authorship of the poems. They depict their love-making by means of the conventions and imagery of love poetry from Egypt and Mesopotamia, as early as the second millennium BC. In fact, the two represent the archetypal lovers whom the reader or hearer overhears and looks in upon as they express their timeless love for each other. All the emotions of love-making are represented: seeking and finding, parting and reuniting, teasing and soothing, frustration and joy.

5	10	18

Song 1

The two lovers express their love and admiration for each other in short, complimentary speeches. Finally the chorus gives the charge not to disturb them.

5	10	18

Song 2

The girl describes how her lover approaches her, little by little, until they are joined. Then she describes how she finds him in the city. The chorus again gives the charge not to disturb them.

5	10	18

Song 3

The girl (or the chorus) describes the approach of her lover as King Solomon in all his glory on his wedding day.

5	10	18

Song 4

The man depicts his lover's body, part by part, in striking metaphors, then as a secret, enclosed, exotic garden of sweet-smelling flowers. She invites him in. He accepts eagerly and enters the garden.

Song 1: **Commentary**

The *dramatis personae* are the two lovers and an imaginary chorus of the daughters of Jerusalem, invoked by both of them. The girl comments on the darkness of her complexion from looking after the sheep, but it is unclear whether this is considered to enhance or detract from her good looks.

Song 2: **Commentary**

The orchard and flowers are allegorical features of Egyptian love poetry. Various among them were considered aphrodisiacs, such as raisins (raisin cakes were used in the worship of fertility goddesses), mandrakes and pomegranates.

You have ravished my heart, my sister, my bride,
   you have ravished my heart with a glance of your
   eyes, with one jewel of your necklace.
How sweet is your love, my sister, my bride!
   how much better is your love than wine,
   and the fragrance of your oils than any spice!
                              Song of Songs 4:9–10

5	10	18

The girl describes how her lover comes to visit her, but then runs off. As she seeks him she is set upon by the city guards. To the chorus she describes her lover, part by part, in similarly striking metaphors.

Song 5

5	10	18

The man praises his lover again, each part in detail. Then, to the chorus, he praises her loveliness again in detail.

Song 6

How does this love poetry find its way into the Bible? There is no mention at all of God in the Song. It has been claimed that the Bible would be defective if it did not at some point give due space to that most elemental of human emotions, the love of man and woman. In fact, since at least the time of Rabbi Aqiba in the early second century AD, when the Jewish canon of scripture was being formed, the book has been seen in Judaism as an allegory of the undying love of God for Israel, and in Christianity as an allegory of the undying love of Christ for his Church, as taught by Ephesians 5:23–26. Allusions to and quotations from these songs have been common in love-poetry and music throughout the Christian centuries.

The Shulamite
The beloved woman of the Song of Songs was identified as a 'Shulamite' in 6:13, perhaps identifying her hometown, or perhaps as belonging to Solomon.

Song 5: **Commentary**

The sexual symbolism is again unmistakeable. The sudden disappearance may suggest a dream sequence, in which the watchmen are the custodians of propriety.

Song 7: **Commentary**

The name 'Shulam' is a feminine form of 'Solomon'. It is appropriate that the description of a dancer should begin with her feet.

*Let us go out early to the vineyards,
    and see whether the vines have budded,
whether the grape blossoms have opened
    and the pomegranates are in bloom.
There I will give you my love.
The mandrakes give forth fragrance,
    and over our doors are all choice fruits,
new as well as old,
    which I have laid up for you, O my beloved.*
Song of Songs 7:12–13

Song 8: **Commentary**

The songs end at 8:7, and are followed by four independent additions.

5	10	18

The girl invites her lover to the secret garden and offers him her love.

Song 7

5	10	18

Alternating snatches of song between the two, expressing their love for each other.

Song 8

Wisdom

Overview

The Book of Wisdom claims to have been written by King Solomon, but this is a literary fiction. It really means that the wisdom contained in it expresses the Jewish tradition of wisdom that stems from Solomon. It was originally written in Greek, not Hebrew, by Jews who had settled in the great city of Alexandria in Egypt, renowned for its Greek culture. It was there that the Bible was first translated into Greek, for the Jews of the city had lost the knowledge of their original national language. It is perhaps the latest book of the Old Testament, written only a few years before the birth of Jesus. It is shaped by Greek culture and tradition, sharply hostile to the Egyptians, dwelling on what they had done to the ancestors of these Jews, over 1,000 years earlier, at the time of the Exodus under Moses.

18

Chapter

1

God's wisdom fills the whole world, and invites all well-intentioned people to a share in divine wisdom. God created life, and offers us immortality.

Chapter 1: **Commentary**

'The spirit of the LORD fills the world.' This is not yet the Christian teaching on the Holy Spirit, but is leading towards it. The author is acutely aware that God controls and directs history through the divine spirit, for the spirit of God is present everywhere.

18

Chapter

2

The dreariness of life without God. The jealous sneers of the godless against the upright who claim to be children of God. Death came into the world by the envy of the Devil.

Chapters 2–4: **Commentary**

The primitive belief in the Bible about existence after death was that the dead person lived a sort of powerless half-life in Sheol. Later develops a conviction that God will not desert those whom he loves, expressed in Job and the Psalms. In the second century BC this develops into a belief in full bodily resurrection (Daniel 12:2). Among the Greek-speaking Jews this is expressed as immortality of the soul. The soul will stay safe in the hands of God.

18

Chapter

3

A contrast between the upright and the godless. The upright are tested like gold in a furnace, and their hope is rich with immortality.

18

Chapter

4

The godless cannot understand the hopes of the upright and merely mock them. But if the upright die young, they are carried off to be with God.

This book is especially valuable for its teaching on life after death and the immortality of the soul, for the Jews had only recently come to believe that our life in God continues after physical death. The second part (chapters 6–9) is a rich meditation on divine wisdom. God created the universe in and by his wisdom, but what is the relationship between God and this divine wisdom? The third part is a brilliant satire on the folly of worshipping idols. It uses the stories of the escape of the Hebrews from the Egyptians at the time of the Exodus, contrasting the favour shown by God to the Hebrews and the punishment of the Egyptians. But God's will to save all people is especially stressed.

Chapter 6: **Commentary**

Solomon prayed for the gift of wisdom (1 Kings 3). He was renowned as the founder of the wisdom tradition in Israel, and many proverbs and wise sayings were attributed to him.

Chapter 7: **Commentary**

God seemed to be too distant and awesome to dirty his hands by creating the world, so he is said to create through his wisdom. But what is the relationship of wisdom to God? Here a list of 21 qualities of wisdom suggests that wisdom itself is divine. In verses 25–26 the author is struggling to find an image for this relationship. In the New Testament (especially Colossians 1:15) these images are applied to the incarnation of God's wisdom in Christ.

18

The remorse of the godless when they realise that their joys are vain and disappear without trace, while the upright are rewarded by God.

Chapter **5**

18

Solomon's praise for wisdom, and the rewards of those who reflect on wisdom and honour wisdom.

Chapter **6**

18

Solomon's praise of wisdom. From his earliest childhood he sought wisdom above all gifts. Wisdom is the reflection of the eternal light and the image of divine goodness.

Chapter **7**

18

How Solomon courted Wisdom to make her his spouse so that she would share his life and his search for immortality.

Chapter **8**

12

Solomon's prayer for wisdom and the holy Spirit in ruling God's people as God's representative when he became king.

Chapter **9**

5   *17*

How wisdom was at work in the story of the Exodus from Egypt, God protecting his faithful ones from oppression, leading them across the Red Sea to freedom.

Chapter **10**

5   *17*

A contrast: for the Hebrews pure water from the rock in the desert, for the Egyptians foul muddy water and assaults from the wild animals that they worshipped.

Chapter **11**

5   *17*

God's lenient punishment of the idolatrous inhabitants of Canaan to bring them to their senses and to belief. God's generosity towards Israel.

Chapter **12**

18

Chapter
13

A satire on a woodcarver who makes his own image of his god and then prays to it and worships it.

18

Chapter
14

The folly of worshipping a piece of wood. Images serve only as a reminder of the dead. Idolatry leads to evil, murderous and disgusting behaviour.

18

Chapter
15

It is foolish to worship idols of pottery or silver, especially models of loathsome animals. Human beings are above such creatures.

5   **17**

Chapter
16

A series of contrasts: the Plagues of Egypt brought grisly punishment on the Egyptians but salvation to Israel: frogs, locusts and hail.

5   **17**

Chapter
17

More contrasts from the Plagues of Egypt: darkness and death on the Egyptians brought light and freedom to Israel.

5   **17**

Chapter
18

God's word came down to destroy the Egyptians, but God raised up a deliverer for Israel.

5   **17**

Chapter
19

The contrast between the deliverance of Israel at the crossing of the Red Sea and the fate of their pursuers, the punishment of their own harsh treatment of the Israelites.

Again, one preparing to sail and about to voyage over raging waves calls upon a piece of wood more fragile than the ship that carries him. For it was desire for gain that planned that vessel, and wisdom was the artisan who built it; but it is your providence, O Father, that steers its course, because you have given it a path in the sea, and a safe way through the waves, showing that you can save from every danger, so that even a person who lacks skill may put to sea.
Wisdom 14:1–4

Chapter 15: **Commentary**

The ancient Egyptians worshipped gods in the form of animals: Khnum, the god of the dead, as a ram; Thoth, the god of wisdom, as a baboon or an ibis. This form of animal-worship especially disgusted the Jews.

Chapter 16: **Commentary**

This poetic dramatisation of the events of the Exodus builds on the earlier traditions to make a contrast between Israel and their oppressors. The same events that brought misery to the Egyptians brought salvation to Israel.

Chapter 19: **Commentary**

The 'dry land' and the 'green plain' are poetic exaggerations. In Exodus 15 the phenomenon that enabled Moses and his group to cross the 'Reed Sea' (the Hebrew name for it) was an east wind. This would have lowered the water level of the reedy lake sufficiently for the Hebrews to cross it. When the wind miraculously dropped, the water returned and the pursuing Egyptian chariots got bogged down. As Miriam sang in her very ancient victory song, 'Horse and rider he has thrown into the sea' (Exodus 15:1, 21).

For the whole creation in its nature was fashioned anew, complying with your commands, so that your children might be kept unharmed. The cloud was seen overshadowing the camp, and dry land emerging where water had stood before, an unhindered way out of the Red Sea, and a grassy plain out of the raging waves, where those protected by your hand passed through as one nation, after gazing on marvellous wonders. For they ranged like horses, and leapt like lambs, praising you, O Lord, who delivered them.
Wisdom 19:6–9

Worshipping the golden calf
The Book of Wisdom repeatedly warns against the of worshipping manmade images.

Sirach

Overview

The full title of the book is 'The Wisdom of Jesus Ben Sirach'. The standard text is in Greek, translated from Hebrew by the grandson of the author, for use by the Greek-speaking Jews of Alexandria. The original Hebrew was probably written between 190 and 180 BC, and in the last 150 years large portions of the Hebrew have been found in various places, so that now about two-thirds of the Hebrew text is known. It is also called 'Ecclesiasticus' or 'The Church Book', because it gives advice on a wide variety of moral matters. The author was obviously passionately devoted to Jerusalem and to the Law, so that he regards the Law as the expression of all wisdom, and sees its source and centre as the Temple of Jerusalem. So the first half of the book ends with a lyrical description of how wisdom was sent to take its seat at Jerusalem. The second half

---

18

Chapter 1

In praise of wisdom, which comes from God, and brings peace and health to those who seek her. The basic quality of all wisdom is fear and reverence of the Lord, expressed in obedience to the Law.

18

Chapter 2

Trust in the Lord and have faith in the Lord during times of trial.

18

Chapter 3

Duties to parents, especially in their old age. Reflections on humility and pride.

18

Chapter 4

Generosity towards the poor and needy. The search for wisdom and for true self-knowledge and evaluation of oneself.

Chapter 1: **Commentary**

Each of the first four sections of the book begins with a poem on the origin of wisdom with God. However human the advice given and the proverbs listed may seem, the thought runs through the book that all wisdom comes from God. 'Fear of the Lord' is mentioned more than 60 times in the course of the book; it signifies reverence and awe rather than terror.

Chapter 2: **Commentary**

Fear or reverence of the Lord is its own reward. Somehow virtue will be rewarded and vice punished. The author is a traditionalist, and has hardly a word on life after death (perhaps 48:11), although a few years later, at the Maccabean persecution, we meet teaching on the resurrection of the dead, and, in the Greek sphere, immortality of the soul. Such teaching was only beginning to emerge.

Sirach teaching his wisdom to a group of people
Although Sirach was a city-dweller, many of his wisdom sayings draw on the world of nature.

ends with a paean of praise for the ancestors, climaxing in an enthusiastic description of the great high priest Simon (220–195 BC), whom the author obviously remembers.

The order of the arrangement of topics follows no further pattern; we seem to slide from one topic to another. Many of the passages are exactly 22 lines long, the number of letters in the Hebrew alphabet. The author is stern and strict on such matters as discipline and punishment, though he can be humorous as well. About women he is decidedly mistrustful and even cynical; he grants women no rights of their own, and would have them rigidly controlled by men. He is clear that virtue is rewarded and vice is punished, but he has no conception of life after death.

18

Chapter

5

Punishment from the Lord is deserved and cannot be avoided. The harm done by malicious talk.

18

Chapter

6

How to attract new, lasting and deserved friendships. The discipline needed to acquire wisdom, but the rewards for serving under her yoke.

18

Chapter

7

Various advice about personal relationships between friends, and with children, parents and the poor.

18

Chapter

8

How to avoid unnecessary quarrels, and people who are likely to get you into trouble.

18

Chapter

9

The dangers of sexual attraction, and of preoccupation with female beauty. Some reflections on true friendship.

18

Chapter

10

Qualities required by people in authority, and the folly of being carried away with self-importance and pride.

18

Chapter

11

The dangers of judging by appearances, and of making hasty and ill-considered judgements. God alone deserves absolute trust.

18

Chapter

12

True and false friends, whom to trust and whom not to trust, and the danger of false friends.

The deceptiveness of appearances
One of Sirach's wise sayings discourages people from judging based on appearances: 'The bee is small among flying creatures, but what it produces is the best of sweet things.'

Chapter 15: Commentary

This passage clearly teaches that sin is the result of human free will. Two other theories were also current in Judaism, that sin was brought to humanity by the fallen angels, and that God implanted in human beings two spirits, good and evil. It is striking that there is no reference here to the story of Adam and Eve.

There is a rebuke that is untimely, and there is the person who is wise enough to keep silent. How much better it is to rebuke than to fume! And one who admits his fault will be kept from failure. Like a eunuch lusting to violate a girl is the person who does right under compulsion.

Sirach 20:1–4

18

The perils of getting above yourself and associating with people who are too grand: keep to your own station.

Chapter
13

18

Envy and greed, and the folly of storing up wealth for yourself. True happiness lies in wisdom and self-knowledge.

Chapter
14

18

The Law as the source of true wisdom, and the importance of taking responsibility for your own decisions.

Chapter
15

18

The Lord ensures that everyone gets their due rewards and punishments; there is no escape.

Chapter
16

18

The Lord created all things and gave them a variety of gifts and talents. He continues to watch over them and encourage them to repent while there is still time.

Chapter
17

18

The unfathomable greatness of God, and his patience and compassion for human beings. The harm that can be done by thoughtless speech, and how to avoid this.

Chapter
18

18

The dangers of drink and sex. Some wise advice on communication with others and the folly of gossip. Some rules of thumb for spotting people who are trustworthy and those who are not.

Chapter
19

18

Paradoxical reflections on different sorts of people, and how to avoid getting into a mess, especially by careless talk.

Chapter
20

18

Chapter **21**

Pithy two-liners about wise and stupid ways of behaving towards other people, and the sort of people to avoid.

18

Chapter **22**

How to avoid fools and getting caught up in their folly. How to keep friends and value them.

18

Chapter **23**

The dangers of careless oaths, of calling God to witness everything and of coarse language. The dangers of sexual indiscipline, especially since God sees everything.

12 **18**

Chapter **24**

A hymn in praise of Wisdom: how Wisdom has chosen Zion for her dwelling, and brought with her every kind of loveliness and splendour. Wisdom as the source of living water.

18

Chapter **25**

Some numerical proverbs about different kinds of people. The dangers of women and their failings.

18

Chapter **26**

Miscellaneous observations, chiefly about the failings of women, but also on feminine virtues and values.

18

Chapter **27**

Warnings about commercial dishonesty, and on how to tell a person by their speech, honesty, trustworthiness and flattery in speech.

18

Chapter **28**

The evils of resentment, moodiness and quarrelling. The daunting consequences of careless gossip.

The importance of God's Laws
Sirach compares the Law planted in Jerusalem to several kinds of exotic trees growing in rich soil.

Chapter 24: **Commentary**

This eulogy of Wisdom concludes the first part of the book. It sums up the wisdom poems in chapters 4, 6 and 14. It transcends the earlier poems in Job 28 and Proverbs 8 on the divine origin of Wisdom, and prepares for the sublime statement of Wisdom 7. The personification of Wisdom prepares for the New Testament teaching on the divine origin of the Word of God.

Before the ages, in the beginning, he created me, and for all the ages I shall not cease to be. In the holy tent I ministered before him, and so I was established in Zion. Thus in the beloved city he gave me a resting-place, and in Jerusalem was my domain.

Sirach 24:9–11

18

Use of money: the dangers of lending, the importance of generosity towards people in need. Some useful rules for guests, on how to avoid making themselves unpopular.

Chapter **29**

18

How to train children. The importance of health and a positive attitude to life.

Chapter **30**

18

The dangers of excessive greed for money: it will make you sick. Some useful rules for behaviour at the dinner table, and especially about sensible drinking habits.

Chapter **31**

18

How to behave at a grand dinner. How to accept correction and to take care over observing the Law.

Chapter **32**

18

Inequality as a fact of life: we are all made differently. Guard your own independence. How to treat slaves.

Chapter **33**

Chapter 33: **Commentary**

In the ancient world slaves were merely chattels with no rights, deserving no sympathy or human consideration. Here the author breaks the mould by advising the reader to treat a single slave like a brother. In 7:21 he also advises humane treatment. It was many centuries before Christians applied the biblical teaching about human dignity to slavery.

18

Various counsels about taking notice of dreams, about successful travelling and about authentic sacrifices.

Chapter **34**

Chapter 35: **Commentary**

This criticism of sacrifices without integrity is unique in the wisdom literature, though a common theme in the earlier prophets. Increasingly within Judaism, fulfilment of the Law came to be regarded as equivalent to sacrifice, especially after the destruction of the Temple by the Romans.

18

The importance of genuineness and real generosity in worship. How God never fails to respond to prayer. How God judges the wicked sternly and yet with mercy.

Chapter **35**

12   **18**

A prayer for the protection of Zion and the People of God. The importance of marriage and making a family nest.

Chapter **36**

18

Chapter 37

False friends and advisers, trusting some people and not others, and how to tell the difference between them. The dangers of excess, particularly in food.

18

Chapter 38

Sickness – the busy doctor and the need for prayer. Mourning should be profound but brief. The brutalising effect of manual labour.

18

Chapter 39

The noble profession of the scribe; the great opportunity for wisdom and the blessing brought by a study of the Law.

18

Chapter 40

The nightmare of the prospect of death. The contrasts in life between good and bad, rich and poor.

18

Chapter 41

The bitterness of death to the peaceful, but the welcome death of the aged. The curse upon the wicked and the sense of shame that evil-doing brings.

18

Chapter 42

A list of maxims vital for success in life, and the worry of unmarried daughters.

18

Chapter 43

A great poem in praise of creation, the sun, the moon, the stars, the rainbow and other wonders of nature in creation.

18

Chapter 44

In praise of illustrious men: i. Enoch was taken up to heaven; ii. Noah was preserved from the flood; iii. Abraham observed the Law; iv. Isaac and Jacob continued his blessing.

Chapters 38–39: **Commentary**

The Greco-Roman world in general regarded manual labour as degrading and restrictive, no doubt because of its dependence on slave labour. After the satire on trades and crafts the author praises the scribe, who devotes himself to the three divisions of the Bible (Law, wisdom and prophecy) – surely an idealised self-portrait.

Chapter 42: **Commentary**

The book ends with a great call to praise God for his glory shown in creation and in the deeds of the ancestors.

Solomon reigned in an age of peace, because God made all his borders tranquil, so that he might build a house in his name and provide a sanctuary to stand for ever. How wise you were when you were young! You overflowed like the Nile with understanding.

Sirach 47:13–14

18 In praise of illustrious men: i. Moses received the Law; ii. Aaron initiated the priestly tradition; iii. Phinehas stood firm when the people rebelled.

Chapter **45**

18 In praise of illustrious men: i. Joshua led the battles of the Lord; ii. Caleb quelled a revolt; iii. The Judges were never disloyal; iv. Samuel instituted the kingship.

Chapter **46**

18 In praise of illustrious men: i. Nathan prophesied in David's time; ii. David brought song into the sanctuary; iii. Solomon built the Temple and amassed gold like tin; iv. Rehoboam and Jeroboam.

Chapter **47**

18 In praise of illustrious men: i. Elijah was taken in a fiery whirlwind; ii. Elisha was filled with Elijah's spirit but did not check sin; iii. Hezekiah built the water-tunnel and repelled Sennacherib; iv. Isaiah revealed the end of time.

Chapter **48**

18 In praise of illustrious men: i. Josiah reformed abuses. ii. The last kings of Juda. iii. Zerubbabel, Joshua and Nehemiah rebuilt the city and Temple.

Chapter **49**

18 In praise of illustrious men: Simon, son of Onias, the great high priest, officiated in the sanctuary in his ceremonial robes.

Chapter **50**

12 **17** A hymn of thanksgiving for the mercies of God, and a poem on the author's search for wisdom.

Chapter **51**

Enoch walked with God, and was taken up to heaven without suffering death
In early Jewish literature Enoch was often portrayed as the revealer of heavenly secrets.

Isaiah

Overview

In order that the prophetic writings may be understood, some basic, but perhaps unexpected, facts must be appreciated:

A modern reader expects that reading material will be presented more or less in chronological order. The prophetic books are not. The four 'great' prophets come first, that is, the four largest books, namely Isaiah, Jeremiah, Ezekiel and Daniel. To confuse matters, these four are – roughly speaking – in chronological order. Then follows the Book of the Twelve Prophets, whose order is not at all chronological.

The books of the prophets were not written by the figures who bear their names. The stories about them and sayings contained in the books were written down by those who heard them and were assembled by their disciples. Not all the sayings were in fact pronounced by these prophets. They are not in chronological order, but are linked together by a variety of different common threads. Biblical prophets are not primarily forecasters. The 'pro' in 'prophet' does not mean 'beforehand'. They were not prophesying what was going to happen, like weather forecasters. In fact, the 'pro' means 'on behalf of.' They speak on behalf of God, seeing a situation as God sees it, and voicing what God thinks of it. The prophets are the mouthpieces of God. However, since God uses human instruments humanly rather than mechanically, they are not

---

Chapter 1

Israel worships other gods and so the LORD has judged them. Don't bother with sacrifices: God wants obedience, justice, and the poor and orphans protected.

Chapter 1: **Commentary**

The ox and the ass of verse 3, contrasting with Israel's neglect, decorate many a Christmas crib. They do not feature in the New Testament.

Chapter 2

In the future, the LORD's Temple will be exalted and people from around the world will visit. But since God's people have turned to idolatry, for now they will suffer God's judgement.

Chapters 1–5: **Commentary**

Before the account of the call of Isaiah a series of key prophecies depicts the wicked condition of God's people in Jerusalem. Two post-exilic passages about the future restoration of a remnant (2:1–5 and 4:2–5) are also included.

mere divine loudspeakers, but each speaks the words of God in his own way. Since a major part of their ministry is to express God's displeasure at Israel's infidelity, they do forecast what will happen if Israel does not mend its ways.

There can be no mistaking the fact that the Book of Isaiah envisages historical situations that spread over at least two centuries. This is thought by some to be evidence of Isaiah's prophetic foresight. However, it is one of the firmest conclusions of critical biblical scholarship that the Book of Isaiah contains prophecies made in at least two entirely different periods. For convenience it is useful to envisage chapters 1–36 as belonging to the end of the eighth century BC, though some of this portion belongs to the latest period of Isaiah. A second, much more unified, part (chapters 40–55) was written as the Babylonian Exile was coming to an end in the mid-sixth century. A third part (chapters 56–66) reflects the period after the release from Exile, in 538 BC.

These prophecies of different periods are bound together by their import. Throughout the book runs the conception of God as the awesome Holy One of Israel who demands integrity and social justice, and who will redeem Israel and restore Jerusalem to its former glory by means of a messianic ruler.

Isaiah bears witness to the coming of the promised Messiah
The prophet Isaiah lived and worked in Jerusalem, surrounded by those who followed the other gods and goddesses of the ancient world.

The LORD rises to argue his case;
*   he stands to judge the peoples.*
The LORD enters into judgement
*   with the elders and princes of his people:*
'It is you who have devoured the vineyard;
*   the spoil of the poor is in your houses.*
What do you mean by crushing my people,
*   by grinding the face of the poor?' says the*
LORD God of hosts.

Isaiah 3:13–15

Ah, you who call evil good and good evil,
who put darkness for light and light for darkness,
who put bitter for sweet and sweet for bitter!

Isaiah 5:20

5	7	Chapter
Jerusalem and Judah are going to face God's judgement. The righteous will survive, but the wicked will suffer. The proud will all be brought low.		**3**

5	7	Chapter
Times will be desperate, especially for the women. But in the end, the city of Jerusalem will be cleansed and God will restore it. The survivors will prosper and be holy.		**4**

5	7	Chapter
Because of their injustice and their worship of gods other than the LORD, Israel and Judah are an unfruitful vineyard destined for invasion and destruction.		**5**

⑤	⑦	⑮

Chapter 6

In the year that the king of Judah, Uzziah, died, the LORD called Isaiah to be his prophet and showed him a vision of the heavenly throne room.

Chapter 6: **Commentary**

The vocation vision of Isaiah, his experience of the awesome holiness of the Holy One of Israel and its contrast with human sinfulness, sets the whole tone of the book.

⑤	⑦	⑰

Chapter 7

When Israel and Aram attacked Judah, Isaiah told Judah's king Ahaz to ask for a sign from God of victory. He refused, but God gave him a sign anyway: a child called Immanuel.

Chapters 7–12: **Commentary**

As danger threatens from Jerusalem's northern neighbours, and from Assyria, Isaiah promises that salvation lies in fidelity to the LORD rather than in military alliance, and foretells the birth of an heir to the messianic prophecies given to David.

The Tree of Jesse
Isaiah predicted that a future descendant of Jesse, the father of King David, would someday come to the throne as a worthy and righteous successor.

Chapter 8: **Commentary**

The sayings of the prophets were delivered orally. The prophet insists that this (verse 16) should be written down because its fulfilment will not be immediate.

5		7

Isaiah's son Maher-Shalal-Hash-Baz fulfils the prophecy: before he knows how to speak, Assyria destroys Aram and Israel. Isaiah warns about consulting psychics.

Chapter 8

---

*For all the boots of the tramping warriors
and all the garments rolled in blood
shall be burned as fuel for the fire.
For a child has been born for us,
a son given to us;
authority rests upon his shoulders;
and he is named Wonderful Counsellor,
Mighty God, Everlasting Father, Prince of Peace.*
Isaiah 9:5–6

5		7

Isaiah prophesies that the gloom facing Israel will eventually pass and that the Israelites will be restored to joy. But for now, they must suffer for their idolatry and wickedness.

Chapter 9

5		7

God pronounces disaster on those who oppress the poor and powerless. God promises judgement against the Assyrians. Afterwards, Israel's survivors will turn back to the LORD.

Chapter 10

---

*A shoot shall come out from the stock of Jesse,
and a branch shall grow out of his roots.
The spirit of the LORD shall rest on him,
the spirit of wisdom and understanding,
the spirit of counsel and might,
the spirit of knowledge and the fear of the LORD.*
Isaiah 11:1–3

5		7

The monarchy of David will be restored and the land of Israel will become prosperous, with all Israelites worshipping the LORD. They will return from their places of exile.

Chapter 11

5		7

When the people of Israel return to their Promised Land they will praise and thank the LORD, acknowledging their past infidelity, his restoration and his forgiveness.

Chapter 12

Chapters 13–23: **Commentary**

A series of prophecies against the nations who oppress Israel, headed by Babylon, the chief oppressor.

5		7

Isaiah prophesies against Babylon, predicting its conquest and destruction. Isaiah predicts that Babylon will never again be powerful or a threat to Israel.

Chapter 13

Chapter 14: **Commentary**

A brief prophecy of the return from Exile and a satirical lament on the arrival of the King of Babylon in Sheol, the abode of the dead.

5		7

God will restore Israel to its land and make it dominant over its neighbours. The Israelites will make fun of the king of Babylon's destruction. The Philistines will be defeated.

Chapter 14

5		7

Isaiah prophesies against Moab, predicting its defeat and destruction, listing the fate of various regions within the nation.

Chapter 15

5 | **7**

Chapter 16

Isaiah continues to describe Moab's defeat and destruction, the wailing and mourning of its people. He predicts that his prophecy will be fulfilled within three years.

5 | **7**

Chapter 17

Isaiah prophesies against the city of Damascus, predicting that it will become a heap of ruins. He also predicts a similar fate for Israel because of its idolatry.

On that day people will regard their Maker, and their eyes will look to the Holy One of Israel; they will not have regard for the altars, the work of their hands, and they will not look to what their own fingers have made, either the sacred poles or the altars of incense.

Isaiah 17:7–8

5 | **7**

Chapter 18

Isaiah prophesies against Cush, predicting its downfall. But then he promises that in the future, the people of Cush will worship the LORD and bring gifts to Jerusalem.

Chapter 19: **Commentary**

The prophecy against Egypt attracts a much later passage, which presupposes a Jewish settlement and sanctuary in Egypt and the conversion of the Egyptians.

5 | **7**

Chapter 19

Isaiah predicts civil war, conquest and famine in Egypt. But some day Egypt and Assyria will worship the LORD, becoming God's people as much as the Israelites.

The LORD will make himself known to the Egyptians; and the Egyptians will know the LORD on that day, and will worship with sacrifice and burnt-offering, and they will make vows to the LORD and perform them.
The LORD will strike Egypt, striking and healing; they will return to the LORD, and he will listen to their supplications and heal them.
On that day there will be a highway from Egypt to Assyria, and the Assyrian will come into Egypt, and the Egyptian into Assyria, and the Egyptians will worship with the Assyrians.
On that day Israel will be the third with Egypt and Assyria, a blessing in the midst of the earth, whom the LORD of hosts has blessed, saying, 'Blessed be Egypt my people, and Assyria the work of my hands, and Israel my heritage.'

Isaiah 19:21–25

7 | **17**

Chapter 20

By walking around naked for three years, Isaiah illustrates his prophecy that the Egyptians and the people of Cush will be taken away naked as captives to Assyria.

5 | **7**

Chapter 21

Isaiah prophesies about the fall of Babylon, predicting the siege by the Medes. He also predicts the downfall of Edom and Arabia.

5 | **7**

Chapter 22

Isaiah predicts that Jerusalem will suffer in the Valley of Vision. He prophesies that the palace steward Shebna will be deposed and die, while Eliakim will take his place.

Then the watcher called out:
'Upon a watch-tower I stand, O LORD, continually by day, and at my post I am stationed throughout the night.
Look, there they come, riders, horsemen in pairs!'
Then he responded,
'Fallen, fallen is Babylon; and all the images of her gods lie shattered on the ground.'

Isaiah 21:8–9

5 | **7**

Chapter 23

Isaiah predicts Tyre's destruction and the subsequent mourning among its trading partners. Though Tyre will rise again in 70 years, all its profits will go to the LORD.

Chapters 24–27: **Commentary**

Prophecies of cosmic disturbances and disasters sum up the threats against Israel's opponents. The LORD will lay waste to the earth, and re-establish Zion as a centre of world peace. This may celebrate the fall of the Assyrian Empire, or may be a much later, more general prophecy.

Chapter 25: **Commentary**

This chapter introduces the concept of an eschatological banquet, the symbol of peace and friendship, joy and merriment at the completion of time, when death will be no more. Jesus uses the image frequently in his parables. His welcome to sinners and feasting with them is an acted sign of the call to all people to join in this heavenly banquet.

*On this mountain the LORD of hosts will make for
  all peoples a feast of rich food, a feast of well-
  matured wines, of rich food filled with marrow,
  of well-matured wines strained clear.
And he will destroy on this mountain
  the shroud that is cast over all peoples,
  the sheet that is spread over all nations;
he will swallow up death for ever.
Then the LORD God will wipe away the tears from
  all faces, and the disgrace of his people he will
  take away from all the earth,
  for the LORD has spoken.*

Isaiah 25:6–8

⑤ **⑦**

The LORD is going to lay waste to the 'earth' – that is, to the land of Judah. All its inhabitants from highest to lowest will suffer equally.

Chapter **24**

⑤ **⑦**

When God forgives and restores the people of Israel, they will praise and thank him. They will rejoice over the destruction of their enemies. God is just, faithful and dependable.

Chapter **25**

⑤ **⑦**

They will praise God for forgiving Judah and destroying Judah's enemies. They will trust the LORD, obey him and worship him exclusively. He will grant them peace and prosperity.

Chapter **26**

⑤ **⑦**

God will punish the nations that attacked and oppressed his people. God will bring Israel back to its land and restore its prosperity. Israel will bless the rest of the world.

Chapter **27**

The concept of resurrection
One of the earliest references to the concept of resurrection appears in Isaiah 26, where the restoration of prosperity to the nation is compared to the resurrection of the dead.

5	7
Chapter **28**	The love of drinking will be replaced by the love of God. God will make sure that his people in Ephraim and Judah obey him.

5	7
Chapter **29**	Ariel – the city of Jerusalem – will be destroyed. Then, instead of just performing empty rituals, the Israelites, purged of their wickedness, will genuinely worship him.

5	7
Chapter **30**	Israel has turned to everything and everyone but God. Their hope of Egyptian help will prove futile. Only when they turn to God will they be rescued. Then they will praise God.

5	7
Chapter **31**	The Egyptians are merely mortals; they cannot be relied upon like God. The Israelites need to turn back to God and reject their idolatry. Some day they will repent.

5	7
Chapter **32**	A righteous king will come. Those who couldn't see the truth will suddenly see it. Before then, the women of Jerusalem will mourn until God's spirit comes and restores prosperity.

Chapter 29: **Commentary**

'Ariel' is a name given to Jerusalem; it means 'altar-hearth'. The destruction of Jerusalem is prophesied, and then its reversal.

The LORD said:
'Because these people draw near with their mouths
  and honour me with their lips,
    while their hearts are far from me,
and their worship of me is a human commandment
  learned by rote;
so I will again do
  amazing things with this people,
  shocking and amazing.
The wisdom of their wise shall perish,
  and the discernment of the discerning shall
  be hidden.
Ha! You who hide a plan too deep for the LORD,
  whose deeds are in the dark,
    and who say, "Who sees us? Who knows us?"
You turn things upside down!
  Shall the potter be regarded as the clay?
Shall the thing made say of its maker,
  "He did not make me";
or the thing formed say of the one who formed it,
  "He has no understanding"?'

Isaiah 29:13–16

See, a king will reign in righteousness,
  and princes will rule with justice.
Each will be like a hiding-place from the wind,
  a covert from the tempest,
like streams of water in a dry place,
  like the shade of a great rock in a weary land.
Then the eyes of those who have sight will not be
  closed, and the ears of those who have hearing
  will listen.
The minds of the rash will have good judgement,
  and the tongues of stammerers will speak readily
  and distinctly.
A fool will no longer be called noble,
  nor a villain be said to be honourable.

Isaiah 32:1–5

The great scroll of Isaiah
Among the Dead Sea Scrolls discovered in 1948 is a copy of the Book of Isaiah, the earliest complete copy of Isaiah's work in existence, dating from about 100 BC.

Chapters 34–35: **Commentary**

The dramatic and cosmic imagery of these chapters has earned them the title of the 'Little Apocalypse' of Isaiah. Chapter 35 pre-empts the restoration imagery of Second Isaiah.

Then the eyes of the blind shall be opened,
   and the ears of the deaf unstopped;
then the lame shall leap like a deer,
   and the tongue of the speechless sing for joy.
For waters shall break forth in the wilderness,
   and streams in the desert;
the burning sand shall become a pool,
   and the thirsty ground springs of water;
the haunt of jackals shall become a swamp,
   the grass shall become reeds and rushes.
                                    Isaiah 35:5–7

Chapters 36–39: **Commentary**

This historical appendix agrees almost exactly with the account in 2 Kings 18–20. It joins together three accounts, 36:1–37:9, and 37–38 is interwoven with 37:10–35. An independent explanation of Assyrian withdrawal is given in 37:36.

Chapters 40–55: **Commentary**

The second part of Isaiah is called 'The Book of Consolation'. It reflects the excited atmosphere of the prospect of the return to Jerusalem, a straight highway across the desert for our God, a second Exodus, a new creation. Far more unified than the earlier part of the book, it has large set-pieces on the majesty of the LORD, on the new Exodus, on mockery of Babylonian idolatry and on Cyrus the liberator as the anointed of the LORD. Its author is unknown.

A voice cries out:
'In the wilderness prepare the way of the LORD,
   make straight in the desert a highway for
   our God.
Every valley shall be lifted up,
   and every mountain and hill be made low;
the uneven ground shall become level,
   and the rough places a plain.
Then the glory of the LORD shall be revealed,
   and all people shall see it together,
   for the mouth of the LORD has spoken.'
                                    Isaiah 40:3–5

---

5   **7**

God is gracious and powerful. The wicked will be punished. Jerusalem will be restored and people will faithfully worship the LORD. Then Jerusalem will be secure and prosperous.

Chapter **33**

5   **7**

The nations surrounding Israel will be judged by God for their sins and for how they mistreated the Israelites. They will be destroyed.

Chapter **34**

5   **7**

The redeemed will rejoice. They will inhabit a peaceful and prosperous land without fear. The blind will see, the deaf will hear, the lame will walk, the mute will speak.

Chapter **35**

7   **17**

During the fourteenth year of Hezekiah, king of Judah, the Assyrian King Sennacherib attacks Jerusalem and tells the people to turn against Hezekiah. He promises to treat them well.

Chapter **36**

5   **7**   **17**

Isaiah tells Hezekiah that God will rescue Jerusalem. Then Sennacherib's army suddenly dies, forcing Sennacherib to leave. Back in Nineveh, two of his sons assassinate him.

Chapter **37**

5   **7**   **17**

Hezekiah becomes ill. Isaiah tells him he will not recover, but he prays and God grants him 15 more years of life. Hezekiah thanks God for his recovery.

Chapter **38**

7   **17**

Babylonians visit Jerusalem and Hezekiah reveals all his wealth to them. Isaiah predicts that the Babylonians will soon come back and strip Jerusalem of all that wealth.

Chapter **39**

5   **7**

God promises comfort, restoration and good news for the people of Israel. God is in charge, he made the universe, he is incomparable and he will restore hope and prosperity.

Chapter **40**

5 **7**

Chapter
41

God subdues the nations, but Israel is God's chosen servant, who has nothing to fear. Idols are powerless, unable to tell the future. Only the LORD tells the future.

5 **7**

Chapter
42

God's servant will be cared for and protected. God delights in his servant and has called him to righteousness. Israel was blind and deaf. They suffered because they had sinned.

5 **7**

Chapter
43

The LORD is Israel's only saviour. He will restore them: the blind will see and the deaf will hear. Despite Israel's unfaithfulness, God will rescue them from Babylon.

Cyrus the Great
Cyrus the Great, following his conquest of the Babylonian Empire, did just as the prophet Isaiah predicted and let the Jewish people return to their homeland.

5 **7**

Chapter
44

Israel is God's servant. He chose them for himself. Idols are nothing, simply powerless and useless statues, unlike the LORD the true God. Jerusalem will be re-inhabited.

5 **7**

Chapter
45

Cyrus is God's anointed and he will send the Israelites home. God is invisible but he is powerful. The visible idols are powerless. God knows the future. Idols don't. Trust God.

Chapter 42: **Commentary**

The opening verses give the first of four Songs of the Servant of the LORD (42:1–4; 49:1–6; 50:4–9; 52:13–53:12) whose persecution patiently borne will bring God's will to fulfilment. The Servant has been interpreted as the prophet himself, or as the personification of suffering Israel, but Christian tradition has always seen the Servant as Jesus.

> *Bring forth the people who are blind, yet have eyes,*
>   *who are deaf, yet have ears!*
> *Let all the nations gather together,*
>   *and let the peoples assemble.*
> *Who among them declared this,*
>   *and foretold to us the former things?*
> *Let them bring their witnesses to justify them,*
>   *and let them hear and say, 'It is true.'*
> *'You are my witnesses,' says the LORD,*
>   *'and my servant whom I have chosen,*
> *so that you may know and believe me*
>   *and understand that I am he.*
> *Before me no god was formed,*
>   *nor shall there be any after me.*
> *I, I am the LORD,*
>   *and besides me there is no saviour.'*
>
> **Isaiah 43:8–11**

Chapter 44: **Commentary**

The confrontation with the idols of Babylon brought an important new development to Israelite religion. Until then the Israelites had been henotheists, believing in the LORD as their God, but not excluding other gods for other people. Now they became monotheists, realising that the gods and idols of other nations were false and powerless. This part of Isaiah has several satires, mocking the false gods and their carved images.

> *Thus says the LORD, the King of Israel*
>   *and his Redeemer, the LORD of hosts:*
> *'I am the first and I am the last;*
>   *besides me there is no god.*
> *Who is like me? Let them proclaim it,*
>   *let them declare and set it forth before me.*
> *Who has announced from of old the things to come?*
>   *Let them tell us what is yet to be.*
> *Do not fear, or be afraid;*
>   *have I not told you from of old and declared it?*
>   *You are my witnesses!*
> *Is there any god besides me?*
>   *There is no other rock; I know not one.'*
>
> **Isaiah 44:6–8**

Chapter 47: **Commentary**

This description of the shame of Babylon is couched in the rhythm of a funeral poem. It is a mock dirge.

Chapter 48: **Commentary**

The Holy One of Israel is often described as the Redeemer of Israel. This stresses God's unfailing love. The word used for 'Redeemer' is the nearest male relative, who is bound by sacred family duty and love of the family to come to the rescue of the family member, no matter what it costs. By the covenant God has bound himself to Israel in the same way.

Thus says the LORD,
  your Redeemer, the Holy One of Israel:
'I am the LORD your God,
  who teaches you for your own good,
  who leads you in the way you should go.
O that you had paid attention to my
  commandments!
  Then your prosperity would have been
  like a river,
  and your success like the waves of the sea ...'

Isaiah 48:17–18

Chapter 51: **Commentary**

The re-established Jerusalem is seen as a new Eden, the source of the Law and of peace and salvation for all people. This second part of Isaiah stresses Israel's salvific role to the nations.

'I, I am he who comforts you;
  why then are you afraid of a mere mortal who
  must die, a human being who fades like grass?
You have forgotten the LORD, your Maker,
  who stretched out the heavens
  and laid the foundations of the earth.
You fear continually all day long
  because of the fury of the oppressor,
who is bent on destruction.
  But where is the fury of the oppressor?
The oppressed shall speedily be released;
  they shall not die and go down to the Pit,
  nor shall they lack bread.'

Isaiah 51:12–14

---

5 **7**

The Babylonian idols have to be carried by people who themselves will be carried into captivity. Remember what God has done in the past. He is still the same powerful God.

Chapter **46**

5 **7**

Babylon will fall and God will rescue his captive people. God was angry with his people, but he forgives them. Babylon will suffer for its idolatry, its pride and its trust in its wealth.

Chapter **47**

5 **7**

God warns Israel of the consequences of its idolatry. What happened to them was no surprise. But now, God will rescue them from Babylon and forgive them.

Chapter **48**

5 **7**

Before he was even born, God calls his servant to bring Israel back to the LORD and to make him a light to the Gentiles. Israel will once again be restored to its land.

Chapter **49**

5 **7**

Yes, Israel sinned and went into captivity; but God was not rejecting his people. God has the power to forgive and restore.

Chapter **50**

5 **7**

There is no reason to fear mortals. God is in charge, God is powerful and God will save. Jerusalem suffered, but soon the suffering will end. Those in bondage will be set free.

Chapter **51**

5	**7**
Chapter **52**	Jerusalem will be freed from its shackles. God is in control. He will give the Israelites reasons to sing. God will bring his people home. God's servant is wise, though disfigured.

5	**7**
Chapter **53**	God's servant will suffer for the sins of his people; he will be pierced and crushed for the iniquities of his people. He will go like a lamb to the slaughter, becoming an offering for sin.

5	**7**
Chapter **54**	Jerusalem is like a barren woman. God is like her husband, who rescues her and calls her back to himself after his anger has passed. God will never punish Jerusalem again.

5	**7**
Chapter **55**	God invites all those who are thirsty and hungry to come to him so he can satisfy their needs. He asks people to turn from their ways and to choose God's way instead.

5	**7**
Chapter **56**	God wants to see justice. No one should feel excluded. A relationship with God is available to everyone. But Israel's rulers only want to satisfy their own appetites.

5	**7**
Chapter **57**	The righteous suffer and die. Those who worship idols think their idols will save them. They won't. Only God can help. God will forgive and restore the wicked.

5	**7**
Chapter **58**	Religious ritual doesn't matter. What matters is rescuing the oppressed, feeding the hungry and helping the poor. Concern yourself with God's concerns if you want joy.

Chapter 53: **Commentary**

The Suffering Servant of the LORD may be seen as the nation of Israel or as an individual. The gospel Passion Narratives make several allusions to it, for Jesus' death was 'according to the scriptures'.

> Surely he has borne our infirmities
> and carried our diseases;
> yet we accounted him stricken,
> struck down by God, and afflicted.
> But he was wounded for our transgressions,
> crushed for our iniquities;
> upon him was the punishment that made us whole,
> and by his bruises we are healed.
> All we like sheep have gone astray;
> we have all turned to our own way,
> and the LORD has laid on him
> the iniquity of us all.

Isaiah 53:4–6

> Seek the LORD while he may be found,
> call upon him while he is near;
> let the wicked forsake their way,
> and the unrighteous their thoughts;
> let them return to the LORD, that he may have mercy
> on them,
> and to our God, for he will abundantly pardon.
> 'For my thoughts are not your thoughts,
> nor are your ways my ways,' says the LORD.
> 'For as the heavens are higher than the earth,
> so are my ways higher than your ways
> and my thoughts than your thoughts.'

Isaiah 55:6–9

Chapters 56–66: **Commentary**

Many would regard this section of the book as written by a different author than Second Isaiah. It envisages the situation after the return from the Exile, with the rebuilding of the Temple, the increasing welcome of foreigners into the covenant (and even Levitical and priestly office, 66:21) and also some criticism of slackness of observance.

Chapter 57: **Commentary**

A poem against abuses in worship: sacred prostitution, idols and child sacrifice cannot win God's favour.

The suffering servant
According to Isaiah, the suffering servant was pierced for our transgressions and crushed for our iniquities (Isaiah 53:5).

Chapters 60–62: **Commentary**

These chapters form a fitting climax to the message of the book. Chapters 60 and 62, on the resurrection of the Holy City, flank the climax of chapter 61 on the mission of the prophet.

Chapter 66: **Commentary**

The final verse of the book has given rise to much of the imagery of hell. In Jewish public reading this depressing ending is masked by ending with a repetition of verses 22–23.

'For as the new heavens and the new earth,
*   which I will make, shall remain before me,' says the*
LORD, 'so shall your descendants and your name
remain. From new moon to new moon, and from
sabbath to sabbath, all flesh shall come to worship
before me,' says the LORD.
'And they shall go out and look at the dead bodies of
the people who have rebelled against me; for their
worm shall not die, their fire shall not be quenched,
and they shall be an abhorrence to all flesh.'
                                    Isaiah 66:22–24

---

⑤ ⑦ Chapter 59
God has the power to rescue, but your sins get in the way. So turn back to God and he'll turn back to you. God understands that you can't rescue yourself; so he'll do the job for you.

⑤ ⑦ Chapter 60
The world will be attracted to the LORD. The nations will bring wealth and help rebuild Jerusalem. Those who do not serve Jerusalem will perish. God will be the light of Jerusalem.

⑤ ⑦ Chapter 61
Freedom for the captives has come; the city of Jerusalem will be rebuilt. God loves justice and he will save his people. God will make righteousness spring up before the world.

⑤ ⑦ Chapter 62
God will protect and watch over Jerusalem and its people. Israel's saviour is coming, bringing his reward. The Israelites will be a holy people, redeemed by God.

⑤ ⑦ Chapter 63
Israel suffered for a little while, but no more. God has saved his people and brought vengeance against their enemies. God is their saviour. When Israel suffered, he suffered.

⑤ ⑦ Chapter 64
Oh that God would come down and rescue his people! Even our best deeds are nothing but filthy rags. Please forgive us; Israel is a wasteland; the Temple has been destroyed.

⑤ ⑦ Chapter 65
God showed himself to people who didn't want him. Those who abandon God, God will abandon. But God will forgive them. Once again, the land will prosper and be at peace.

⑤ ⑦ Chapter 66
Sacrifices don't really matter. What matters is humility and contrition. Jerusalem can rejoice. The righteous will proclaim God's glory to the nations of the world.

Jeremiah

Overview

The Book of Jeremiah appears to the casual reader to be a jumble of unrelated fragments of prose and poetry. In fact, the pattern and purpose is clear, if it is read as an interpretation of the history of the Fall of Jerusalem, that traumatic event at the beginning of the sixth century BC. Israel's persistent failure to observe the covenant made with them by the LORD forced him to correct them by sending them into exile in Babylon, deprived of land and liberty, cult and covenant, Temple and king. The agony undergone by Jeremiah, the unwilling prophet, in his unenviable task of ramming home to them the inevitability of this correction, is but his part of the suffering they bore. But in the very centre of the drama comes the sign of hope: his prophetic purchase of a field on the edge of the doomed city, accompanied by the promise of a covenant (chapters 31–33). After this there remains only the historical account of the manhandling and ill-treatment of Jeremiah himself during the death-throes of the kingdom and the final triumphant blazoning of divine control of events in the prophecies of destruction of the persecutors.

It has been claimed that Jeremiah had little historical reality, but enough care is taken of historical detail to show that the authors or compilers of this intensely personal story are

---

Chapter 1: **Commentary**

From Moses to Isaiah and onwards God's messengers have always been loath to accept the commission. Jeremiah's dislike of his task is continually stressed.

Chapters 2–10: **Commentary**

The message of the book opens with a series of blistering threats. These poems may be a collection of Jeremiah's earliest sayings, reinforced by the prose passage, 7:1–8:3, rejecting any claim that appeal to the presence of the LORD in the Temple will save them. The images of Judah as a prostitute (the symbol of unfaithfulness) should shame the men, for it was their task to protect the purity of their women.

⑤	⑦	⑰

Chapter 1

God calls Jeremiah to be his prophet shortly before Judah goes into Babylonian captivity. No one will overcome Jeremiah, because God will be with him and will rescue him.

⑤	⑦

Chapter 2

God compares Israel to a wife having an affair, even though her husband is good and kind. Other nations are faithful to their gods, but Israel is not.

concerned with history. This is not to assert that all the words are necessarily those of Jeremiah himself, or even of his assistant, Baruch; some auxiliary passages may well have been brought in to complete the picture. But the tragedy was not fictional, and the martyrdom undergone by Jeremiah in fidelity to his task was real.

The world-historical background of the book is the inexorable expansion of the power of Babylon, established as the dominant power in the Near East at the Battle of Carchemish in 605 BC. The previous dominant power, Assyria, had gradually eaten up the little states of the Mediterranean coastline as far as Samaria. Now Babylon took over this role. In 598 BC, when King Jehoiachin attempted to break free, Nebuchadnezzar of Babylon pillaged all the treasure of the Temple and carried off a first tranche of the nobility and arms manufacturers to Babylon. Ten years later the puppet-king Zedekiah again rebelled, provoking further retaliation and the cruel deportation of the king and all the remaining population of any importance. Further feeble attempts at rebellion led to further deportations in 582. It was during these threatened and turbulent years that Jeremiah was prophesying, until finally he was carried off to Egypt by a group of dissident refugees.

'And when you have multiplied and increased in the land, in those days,' says the LORD, 'they shall no longer say, "The ark of the covenant of the LORD." It shall not come to mind, or be remembered, or missed; nor shall another one be made.'

Jeremiah 3:16

God speaks to Jeremiah
God told Jeremiah that he had decided to make him a prophet even before he was born.

5	7	Chapter 3
If a divorced woman remarries, will her first husband take her back? Judah is like a prostitute. She knows what happened to her sister Israel, but she isn't changing.		

5	7	Chapter 4
Even so, God asks for Israel and Judah to return to him. But if they won't, then a nation from the north is going to come and invade Judah and destroy Jerusalem.		

5	7	Chapter 5
Since everyone worships other gods, why should Yahweh forgive them? They chase other gods like a man chasing someone else's wife. But they wonder why God judged them.		

5	7	Chapter 6
Jerusalem will be besieged and destroyed, even though everyone seems convinced that it will never happen. The other prophets predict peace and prosperity that will never be.		

7

Chapter **7**

The Israelites worship idols and oppress the weak. God tells Jeremiah that no one will listen, so he should cut off his hair, throw it away and lament for the coming wrath.

5   **7**

Chapter **8**

The graves will be dug up and the corpses will be exposed before the sun, moon and stars that the Israelites worship. The living will go into captivity.

4   **5**   **7**

Chapter **9**

God mourns for the coming destruction of his people, broken-hearted over their rejection and their mistreatment of one another, and dismayed at the pain they will endure.

5   **7**

Chapter **10**

Don't be like the idolatrous nations. Idols are powerless, but God, the creator, has the power to punish. Jeremiah wants God to judge the nations who destroyed Israel.

5   **7**

Chapter **11**

God made a contract with Israel when he rescued them from Egypt. They broke it, so God is obligated to punish them. Some want Jeremiah to stop prophesying and plot to kill him.

5   **7**

Chapter **12**

Jeremiah complains to God, asking why the wicked prosper. He wants God to judge them. God tells him that even his own family will reject him, and Judah will be destroyed.

5   **7**

Chapter **13**

Jeremiah buries a loincloth. When he later digs it up, it is ruined. God says Israel is as worthless to God now as that loincloth. Israel will go into captivity because of its idolatry.

'The harvest is past, the summer is ended,
and we are not saved.'
For the hurt of my poor people I am hurt,
I mourn, and dismay has taken hold of me.
Is there no balm in Gilead?
Is there no physician there?
Why then has the health of my poor people
not been restored?
O that my head were a spring of water,
and my eyes a fountain of tears,
so that I might weep day and night
for the slain of my poor people!

Jeremiah 8:20–9:1

Thus says the LORD:
'Do not let the wise boast in their wisdom, do not let the mighty boast in their might, do not let the wealthy boast in their wealth; but let those who boast boast in this, that they understand and know me, that I am the LORD; I act with steadfast love, justice, and righteousness in the earth, for in these things I delight,' says the LORD.

Jeremiah 9:23–24

Chapters 11–20: **Commentary**

Jeremiah's searing complaints to the LORD spring from both his love of his own land – Anathoth is some 8 km (5 miles) north of Jerusalem – and his distaste for his pitiless task. They are reinforced by the prophet's own symbolic actions, the loincloth, his austere way of life, the broken jug, the baskets of figs. Such symbolic actions are frequently used by the prophets as graphic expressions of their message.

Chapter 13: **Commentary**

How could Jeremiah keep slipping off to the Euphrates ('Perat' in Hebrew), several hundred kilometres across the desert? More likely the lovely little stream of Parah, a few kilometres east of Jerusalem, is intended as the burial site.

An unhappy Jeremiah
Jeremiah complains to God about how the wicked are prospering while he, God's servant, is suffering unjustly.

The heart is devious above all else;
 it is perverse—
 who can understand it?
'I the LORD test the mind
 and search the heart,
to give to all according to their ways,
 according to the fruit of their doings.'
                    Jeremiah 17:9–10

Chapter 18: Commentary

What is meant by 'The word of the LORD came to Jeremiah'? Is it a voice from heaven? Is it words spoken in the wind? Is it words formed in the mind? Surely Jeremiah went for his afternoon walk, ended up at the pottery, and was suddenly aware that what happened to the pots was also happening to Israel. He realised that this was God's way of looking at Israel. The prophet sees reality as God sees it – clearly and often uncomfortably.

At one moment I may declare concerning a nation or a kingdom, that I will pluck up and break down and destroy it, but if that nation, concerning which I have spoken, turns from its evil, I will change my mind about the disaster that I intended to bring on it. And at another moment I may declare concerning a nation or a kingdom that I will build and plant it, but if it does evil in my sight, not listening to my voice, then I will change my mind about the good that I had intended to do to it.
                    Jeremiah 18:7–10

Cursed be the day on which I was born!
The day when my mother bore me,
 let it not be blessed!
Cursed be the man who brought the news to my
 father, saying,
'A child is born to you, a son', making him very glad.
Let that man be like the cities
 that the LORD overthrew without pity;
let him hear a cry in the morning
 and an alarm at noon,
because he did not kill me in the womb;
 so my mother would have been my grave,
 and her womb for ever great.
Why did I come forth from the womb
 to see toil and sorrow,
 and spend my days in shame?
                    Jeremiah 20:14–18

---

5 · **7**

God tells Jeremiah again not to pray for the well-being of the people: they are going into exile for their idolatry. Jeremiah prays that God has not rejected his people forever.

Chapter 14

5 · **7**

God tells Jeremiah that even if Moses and Samuel asked for the people to be forgiven, he wouldn't forgive them now. They must be punished. But God promises to protect Jeremiah.

Chapter 15

5 · **7**

God tells Jeremiah not to get married or to have any children. He tells him not to mourn for the dead or celebrate with the living. Someday Judah will be forgiven. But not now.

Chapter 16

5 · **7**

God describes Judah's idolatry. They have not kept the Sabbath. Those who trust in Yahweh will be blessed; those who trust in themselves will be cursed.

Chapter 17

5 · **7**

Just as a potter does what he wants with clay, so God does what he wants with Israel: unless they repent, judgement will fall. People plot against Jeremiah. He asks God to protect him.

Chapter 18

7

Yahweh tells Jeremiah to take some of the elders and priests to the Valley of Ben Hinnom. There, he smashes a clay jar and announces that God intends to smash Jerusalem.

Chapter 19

5 · **7** · **17**

The priest Pashhur has Jeremiah arrested, beaten and locked in stocks. Jeremiah says that he and his family will die in Babylon. Jeremiah wishes that he wasn't a prophet or even born.

Chapter 20

5   **7**   **17**

Chapter
21
Zedekiah, king of Judah, asks Jeremiah if maybe God would rescue them from Nebuchadnezzar. Jeremiah tells him no, only those who surrender to the Babylonians will live.

5   **7**

Chapter
22
The king, Jehoahaz, will never return. King Jehoiakim will have the burial of a donkey. His son, Jehoiachin will go into exile; none of his children will ever sit on David's throne.

5   **7**

Chapter
23
A righteous branch will come back from David's line to rule Judah and Israel and the captives will come home. The other prophets and priests offer false hope.

7

Chapter
24
After Jehoiachin and others had gone into exile, God showed Jeremiah two baskets of figs: one good, one bad. The exiles are the good figs, those still in Jerusalem, the bad ones.

5   **7**

Chapter
25
Jeremiah announces that the Jewish captivity in Babylon will last 70 years, but afterwards, God will destroy the Babylonian Empire. God will judge Egypt, Judah and others.

5   **7**   **17**

Chapter
26
After Jeremiah prophesies in the Temple courtyard, the religious establishment plans to kill him, until they remember a prophet named Micah who was never executed for similar words.

7   **17**

Chapter
27
Jeremiah wears a yoke to symbolise that Judah, Edom, Moab, Ammon, Tyre and Sidon will be conquered and oppressed by the Babylonians. Those who resist will be killed.

7   **17**

Chapter
28
The prophet Hananiah removes and breaks Jeremiah's yoke, predicting that within two years the power of Babylon will be broken. Jeremiah tells Hananiah he is wrong and will die.

Chapters 21–25: **Commentary**

Jeremiah continues his bitter invective against the leadership of the doomed city, its kings (21:11–22:30) and false prophets (23:9–40). The invective reaches its peak in the title 'my servant', given in 25:9 to the destroyer Nebuchadnezzar. The vision of the two baskets of figs (24) underlines that hope now lies in those already exiled to Babylon.

Chapter 22: **Commentary**

Here are collected together condemnations of a whole series of kings of Judah, then followed by a contrast, the messianic king in 23:1–8.

Chapters 26–36: **Commentary**

These chapters, framed by the two trials and rejections of Jeremiah's enduring message, and largely consisting of the prose accounts of Jeremiah's maltreatment by the political leaders of Jerusalem, circle around the two themes of hope in the exiles and doom for Jerusalem. The eventual restoration of Jerusalem is pegged out by Jeremiah's symbolic purchase of a field.

King Jehoiakim rejects Jeremiah
King Jehoiakim rejected Jeremiah and his prophecies and tried to destroy both Jeremiah and the words that he had written.

Chapters 30–31: **Commentary**

Poems of joy at the re-establishment of Jerusalem. In the more factual prose account (31:31–34) the new covenant differs by being interior (written on the heart) and individual, a covenant not merely with the nation as a whole but with each member.

'But this is the covenant that I will make with the house of Israel after those days,' says the LORD: 'I will put my law within them, and I will write it on their hearts; and I will be their God, and they shall be my people.

No longer shall they teach one another, or say to each other, "Know the LORD," for they shall all know me, from the least of them to the greatest,' says the LORD; 'for I will forgive their iniquity, and remember their sin no more.'

Jeremiah 31:33–34

Therefore, thus says the LORD: 'You have not obeyed me by granting a release to your neighbours and friends; I am going to grant a release to you,' says the LORD, '—a release to the sword, to pestilence, and to famine. I will make you a horror to all the kingdoms of the earth. And those who transgressed my covenant and did not keep the terms of the covenant that they made before me, I will make like the calf when they cut it in two and passed between its parts: the officials of Judah, the officials of Jerusalem, the eunuchs, the priests, and all the people of the land who passed between the parts of the calf shall be handed over to their enemies and to those who seek their lives. Their corpses shall become food for the birds of the air and the wild animals of the earth.'

Jeremiah 34:17–20

Then the king sent Jehudi to get the scroll, and he took it from the chamber of Elishama the secretary; and Jehudi read it to the king and all the officials who stood beside the king.

Now the king was sitting in his winter apartment (it was the ninth month), and there was a fire burning in the brazier before him.

As Jehudi read three or four columns, the king would cut them off with a penknife and throw them into the fire in the brazier, until the entire scroll was consumed in the fire that was in the brazier.

Jeremiah 36:21–23

7	17	
Jeremiah writes to the Babylonian exiles, encouraging them to settle down and make a new life for themselves. Shemaiah opposes Jeremiah, but will be punished as a false prophet.		Chapter **29**

5	7	
God promises to bring his people Israel and Judah back from captivity in Assyria and Babylonia. They do not need to fear. God's wrath is not forever.		Chapter **30**

5	7	
The Israelites' tears will turn to joy. God will make a new covenant with them, inscribing it on their hearts instead of on stone tablets. God can never reject his people Israel.		Chapter **31**

7	17	
As a sign that God will restore the people to their land, Jeremiah buys a field from his cousin Hanamel while the city of Jerusalem is besieged by the Babylonian army.		Chapter **32**

5	7	
In the future, God will bring the Israelites back to rebuild Jerusalem. God can no more break his covenant with David and the priests than the laws of physics can be broken.		Chapter **33**

7	17	
Jeremiah tells King Zedekiah that Jerusalem will be destroyed and he will be carried captive to Babylon. The rich are condemned for failing to free their slaves as promised.		Chapter **34**

7	17	
God contrasts the Rekabites' faithfulness to their ancestor's strange rules with the Israelites' failure to keep the reasonable rules of God. God blesses the Rekabites.		Chapter **35**

7	17	
Jehoiakim, the king, burns the words of Jeremiah's prophecies as they are read to him. But then God has Jeremiah write it all down again on another scroll.		Chapter **36**

7   **17**

Chapter
37

After being falsely accused of deserting to the Babylonians, Jeremiah is arrested. Jeremiah prophesies the destruction of Jerusalem and Zedekiah's exile.

7   **17**

Chapter
38

King Zedekiah allows Jeremiah to be put into a cistern for a while because Jeremiah is encouraging people to surrender to the Babylonians during the siege.

9   **17**

Chapter
39

The Babylonians destroy Jerusalem while Jeremiah is still imprisoned. Zedekiah sees his children executed. He is blinded, then taken to Babylon. The Temple is burnt.

17

Chapter
40

Released from prison, Jeremiah goes to Gedaliah, the governor appointed by Nebuchadnezzar. Gedaliah does not take seriously reports that Ishmael planned to assassinate him.

17

Chapter
41

Ishmael assassinates Gedaliah and his associates. Johanan, many soldiers, women, children and court officials want to flee to Egypt, afraid of Nebuchadnezzar's reaction.

7   **17**

Chapter
42

Johanan and the others then ask Jeremiah to enquire of God what they should do. They promise to obey God. Jeremiah tells them that God wants them to stay in Israel.

7   **17**

Chapter
43

Johanan and the rest tell Jeremiah he is lying. So they go to Egypt and take Jeremiah and his secretary Baruch with them. Jeremiah prophesies that Nebuchadnezzar will attack Egypt.

7   **17**

Chapter
44

Jeremiah tells them to abandon their idols. They reject Jeremiah's message, convinced that the reason they are suffering is that they have not been faithful enough to the gods.

Jeremiah weeps
Jeremiah, known as the weeping prophet, mourned the coming destruction of his nation, its capital and God's Temple.

So they took Jeremiah and threw him into the cistern of Malchiah, the king's son, which was in the court of the guard, letting Jeremiah down by ropes. Now there was no water in the cistern, but only mud, and Jeremiah sank in the mud.

Jeremiah 38:6

The king of Babylon slaughtered the sons of Zedekiah at Riblah before his eyes; also the king of Babylon slaughtered all the nobles of Judah. He put out the eyes of Zedekiah, and bound him in fetters to take him to Babylon.

Jeremiah 39:6–7

When Jeremiah finished speaking to all the people all these words of the LORD their God, with which the LORD their God had sent him to them, Azariah son of Hoshaiah and Johanan son of Kareah and all the other insolent men said to Jeremiah, 'You are telling a lie. The LORD our God did not send you to say, "Do not go to Egypt to settle there"; but Baruch son of Neriah is inciting you against us, to hand us over to the Chaldeans, in order that they may kill us or take us into exile in Babylon.'

Jeremiah 43:1–3

'But as for you, have no fear, my servant Jacob,
and do not be dismayed, O Israel;
for I am going to save you from far away,
and your offspring from the land of their captivity.
Jacob shall return and have quiet and ease,
and no one shall make him afraid.
As for you, have no fear, my servant Jacob,' says
the Lord, 'for I am with you.
I will make an end of all the nations
among which I have banished you,
but I will not make an end of you!
I will chastise you in just measure,
and I will by no means leave you unpunished.'

Jeremiah 46:27–28

Chapters 46–51: **Commentary**

These poems, taunting and mocking the destruction of
Israel's enemies, are gathered here in the Hebrew version
of the book. In the Greek text they occur after the
introduction at 25:38. The Greek text of Jeremiah differs
significantly from the Hebrew; the Hebrew probably adds
some explanations and additional material.

Flee from the midst of Babylon,
save your lives, each of you!
Do not perish because of her guilt,
for this is the time of the Lord's vengeance;
he is repaying her what is due.
Babylon was a golden cup in the Lord's hand,
making all the earth drunken;
the nations drank of her wine,
and so the nations went mad.

Jeremiah 51:6–7

Chapter 52: **Commentary**

This account of the destruction of Jerusalem in 589 BC
agrees almost entirely with that in 2 Kings 24:18–25:30.
The note on the eating arrangements for the blinded King
Jehoiachin is a polite way of saying that he was under
permanent house arrest.

(7) **(17)**

Jeremiah prophesies to Baruch, his secretary, that he
should not expect great things for himself. However,
he reassures him that God will protect him and spare
his life.

Chapter **45**

(5) **(7)**

Jeremiah's prophecy to Egypt: Nebuchadnezzar will
defeat Egypt, but in the future, Egypt will prosper.
He prophesies that Israel will be punished but
not destroyed.

Chapter **46**

(5) **(7)**

Jeremiah's prophecy to the Philistines: God says that
they will be attacked and destroyed all along the
coast, with their cities of Gaza and Ashkelon being
wiped out.

Chapter **47**

(5) **(7)**

Jeremiah's prophecy to Moab: their cities will be
destroyed and the people and their gods will be
taken away to exile. But someday their fortunes will
be restored.

Chapter **48**

(5) **(7)**

Israel will attack Amon, but someday their fortunes
will be restored. Edom will become uninhabited.
Damascus, Kedar, Hazor and Elam will be destroyed.

Chapter **49**

(5) **(7)**

Babylon will be attacked from the north and
overthrown because of what they did to the
Israelites. The Israelites will be forgiven and will
return to their homeland.

Chapter **50**

(5) **(7)**

Jeremiah warns that when Babylon is destroyed, the
people of Israel should flee. God, who made the
universe, is determined to repay Babylon for its
crimes against the Jewish people.

Chapter **51**

(16) **(17)**

An account of the destruction of Jerusalem: the
wealth stolen, and the people taken away into exile.
Jehoiachin king of Judah is granted a measure of
freedom in Babylon.

Chapter **52**

Lamentations

Overview

Lamentations is a series of five alphabetical poems lamenting the Fall of Jerusalem, written not long after that event in 586 BC. In the third poem each letter of the alphabet begins a line three consecutive times. The poems are likely to be anonymous, attributed by one ancient tradition to Jeremiah, perhaps because he was reputed to have written a lament for King Josiah (2 Chronicles 35:25), perhaps because of his laments in the Book of Jeremiah over the Fall of Jerusalem. However, some of the ideas clash with Jeremiah's own; Jeremiah could hardly have said that Jerusalem's prophets receive no vision from the LORD (Lamentations 2:9).

There are two remarkable aspects of these poems that deserve comment. Firstly, in Lamentations 1–2 a female voice is clear, as a mother mourning her children. This is one of the few occasions in the Bible when a truly female viewpoint is heard. The second notable point is the reproaches addressed to God for his dire punishment and failure to forgive. Although at the same time there is a clear recognition of guilt, the singer is angry and puzzled at God's refusal to forgive.

	4	5
Chapter 1	The great city of Jerusalem is deserted. She is weeping for all her children who have been taken away to Babylon. Jerusalem is guilty and so she now suffers for her crimes.	

	4	5
Chapter 2	God pours out his wrath on the city of Jerusalem. He has become Jerusalem's enemy and utterly destroyed it. God has never done anything like this before. Jerusalem mourns.	

	4	5
Chapter 3	God has unleashed his anger on Jerusalem, taking away everything that brought joy. We have sinned. All we can do is cry until God grants relief. Judge Babylon for what it did to us.	

	4	5
Chapter 4	God has done this to us because of our sins. He scattered the people among the nations. But someday the punishment will end. The exile in Babylon will not last long.	

	4	5
Chapter 5	God, don't forget our pain. We sinned. Please forgive us. Do not forget about us. Restore us – unless you really have rejected us for all time.	

Chapters 1–4: **Commentary**

Hebrew poetry has no rhymes at the ends of the lines. The balance and rhythm of poetry is given by a balance and parallelism of ideas. In addition, there is often an acrostic. That is, each verse (or each line) begins in turn with each of the successive letters of the Hebrew alphabet. This strict and artistic pattern is used in each of Lamentations 1–4. Other superb examples of the technique are Psalms 111, 112 and 119.

But you, O LORD, reign for ever;
  your throne endures to all generations.
Why have you forgotten us completely?
Why have you forsaken us these many days?
Restore us to yourself, O LORD, that we may
  be restored; renew our days as of old—
unless you have utterly rejected us,
  and are angry with us beyond measure.
Lamentations 5:19–22

Baruch

Overview

The Book of Baruch was written in Greek, so it was never part of the Hebrew Bible. So, though it is accepted by the Catholic and Greek Orthodox traditions, it is not included in the Protestant Bible. The attribution of its authorship to Baruch, Jeremiah's secretary, is fictional. To the main book is added the Letter of Jeremiah, which must have had a Hebrew original, since fragments of it have been found among the Dead Sea Scrolls.

Chapter 1: **Commentary**

The exiled People of Israel recognised that their infidelity to their God had resulted in the sack of Jerusalem, the loss of everything they valued and bitter, enslaved captivity in Babylon. As they reflected on their history, the prevailing spirit of writings at that time was one of guilt and repentance for their ingratitude.

Chapter 4: **Commentary**

After 70 years of exile in Babylon, King Cyrus set the Jews free and returned them to their homeland. The writings of the return from exile are full of joy and pride in Jerusalem. God will again bring them peace and protection. The prophets of this period begin to see that through them God will bring peace and happiness to the whole world: the nations will come to draw salvation from Jerusalem.

Letter of Jeremiah: **Commentary**

In their exile the Jews were confronted by the worship of all kinds of gods and idols carved by human hands. For them it was blasphemous to attempt to make any image of their God, and they exploded – as in this letter supposedly written by Jeremiah – in satire, mocking the absurdity of worshipping such statues.

Take off the garment of your sorrow and affliction, O Jerusalem, and put on for ever the beauty of the glory from God. Put on the robe of the righteousness that comes from God; put on your head the diadem of the glory of the Everlasting.

Baruch 5:1–2

2	17	
Introduction to the book and confession of sin. Israel has been disobedient to the Lord from the time the Lord brought them out from Egypt, and have brought the disasters upon themselves.		Chapter **1**

2		
Admission that Israel's infidelity deserved the punishment of exile, followed by appeal to the Lord's promise of forgiveness and a new heart, of a return to the land of their ancestors.		Chapter **2**

18		
God alone gives wisdom, and gives it to Israel. He has revealed it to Israel in the Book of the Law.		Chapter **3**

9	12	
Jerusalem, personified, prays for the return of her children, and predicts salvation and comfort for them, disaster and destruction for those who tormented them.		Chapter **4**

9	12	
An invitation to Jerusalem to prepare joyfully for the return of her children across the desert.		Chapter **5**

Ezekiel

Overview

The historical background to Ezekiel is similar to that of Jeremiah. Ezekiel was prophesying in the final years of the Kingdom of Judah, but from Babylon, among those who had already been exiled. He was a priest of the Jerusalem Temple. His task was to keep up the spirits of the exiles and show them that Israel's hope lay with them. The Fall of Jerusalem, the final destruction of city, monarchy and Temple, was inevitable. The great opening vision, which fills his horizon for the whole book, was of the awesome chariot of the LORD. The great tragedy of the book is worshippers bowing not to the Temple but to the rising sun; this is followed inevitably by the vision of the glory of the LORD leaving the Temple, going eastwards towards Babylon. The great hope of the book is the return of the glory of the LORD to the new Temple, prophesied in the vision of the new Jerusalem in the final chapters.

11	**15**	**17**

Chapter 1

Ezekiel sees four living creatures with four faces: human, lion, ox and eagle. Each has four wings. They stand beside wheels supporting a blue dome where the LORD sits on his throne.

7

Chapter 2

The LORD tells him to be a prophet to the Israelites, to never fear them and to never be rebellious like them. Then God has Ezekiel eat a scroll.

7

Chapter 3

The scroll tastes like honey. God tells Ezekiel to be a watchman for Israel. Ezekiel will be unable to speak except on those occasions when God speaks through him.

7	**9**

Chapter 4

Ezekiel draws the city of Jerusalem on a brick and lays siege to it, then must lie on his side next to it for over a year, eating bread he bakes over cow dung.

Chapter 1: **Commentary**

This awesome vision of the chariot-throne of God builds on previous visions of God enthroned (1 Kings 22, Isaiah 6), using also Mesopotamian elements, such as the huge stone caribou guarding the entrance to their temples. All the elements of these great beasts are symbolic, their aspects portraying intelligence, ferocity, power and penetration. The presence of God is not confined to the Temple, for God is omnipresent. God himself no human being can see, so only 'the likeness' of the glory is seen.

Chapters 4–5: **Commentary**

This mime is the first of Ezekiel's symbolic actions. Some of the mud bricks of the time are half a metre square. To cut the hair and beard is a sign of mourning (for the city), and of dispersal of the inhabitants.

I looked, and there was a figure that looked like a human being; below what appeared to be its loins it was fire, and above the loins it was like the appearance of brightness, like gleaming amber. It stretched out the form of a hand, and took me by a lock of my head; and the spirit lifted me up between earth and heaven, and brought me in visions of God to Jerusalem, to the entrance of the gateway of the inner court that faces north, to the seat of the image of jealousy, which provokes to jealousy. And the glory of the God of Israel was there, like the vision that I had seen in the valley.

Ezekiel 8:2–4

Chapters 8–11: **Commentary**

The defilement of the Temple by idols of animals, fertility symbols and by sun-worshippers, leads to its unavoidable consequence, the departure of the divine glory, leaving the Temple an empty and pointless shell.
The city is doomed.

These were the living creatures that I saw underneath the God of Israel by the river Chebar; and I knew that they were cherubim. Each had four faces, each four wings, and underneath their wings something like human hands. As for what their faces were like, they were the same faces whose appearance I had seen by the river Chebar. Each one moved straight ahead.

Ezekiel 10:20–22

The word of the LORD came to me: 'Mortal, the house of Israel is saying, "The vision that he sees is for many years ahead; he prophesies for distant times." Therefore say to them, "Thus says the LORD God: None of my words will be delayed any longer, but the word that I speak will be fulfilled, says the LORD God."'

Ezekiel 12:26–28

Chapter 12: **Commentary**

Another mime of exile. However, there remain false prophets and prophetesses in Jerusalem who mock Ezekiel's predictions of disaster (12:21).

---

7 | **9**

To symbolise the fate of the Judeans, Ezekiel shaves off his hair. He burns one third, he hits one third with a sword as he walks around the city, and the last third he scatters to the wind.

Chapter **5**

7 | **9**

Ezekiel prophesies doom and destruction for the mountains and hills of Israel and its inhabitants because of their soon-to-be destroyed idols.

Chapter **6**

5 | **7** | **9**

The end is now come upon the nation of Israel: God's anger is unleashed because of their idolatry. He will not pity them as they lose everything they have, including their lives.

Chapter **7**

7 | **9**

God's spirit shows Ezekiel that there is idolatry and the worship of other gods even in the LORD's Temple. For this, God tells Ezekiel, he is going to punish the people, without mercy.

Chapter **8**

7 | **9**

One man with the writing kit puts God's mark on the foreheads of those in Jerusalem that he finds mourning over idolatry. Six others then kill everyone without the mark.

Chapter **9**

7 | **9** | **15**

God's glory leaves the Temple, along with the four cherubs. The man with the writing kit takes the burning coals from the cherubs and scatters them over the city.

Chapter **10**

7 | **9**

Ezekiel prophesies against Pelatiah and all the leaders who predict prosperity. Pelatiah dies. Then Ezekiel prophesies that when the Israelites return from captivity, they will be free of idolatry.

Chapter **11**

7 | **9**

Ezekiel packs as if going into exile, then digs a hole through the wall of his house at dusk. This illustrates how the prince and people of Israel would soon be exiled.

Chapter **12**

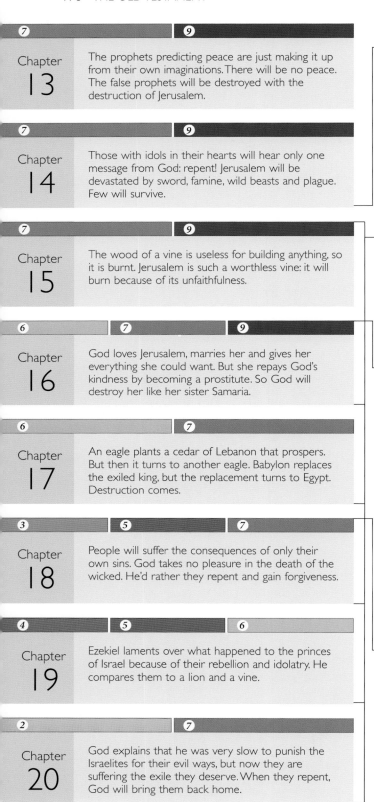

Chapter 13 7 9
The prophets predicting peace are just making it up from their own imaginations. There will be no peace. The false prophets will be destroyed with the destruction of Jerusalem.

Chapter 14 7 9
Those with idols in their hearts will hear only one message from God: repent! Jerusalem will be devastated by sword, famine, wild beasts and plague. Few will survive.

Chapter 15 7 9
The wood of a vine is useless for building anything, so it is burnt. Jerusalem is such a worthless vine: it will burn because of its unfaithfulness.

Chapter 16 6 7 9
God loves Jerusalem, marries her and gives her everything she could want. But she repays God's kindness by becoming a prostitute. So God will destroy her like her sister Samaria.

Chapter 17 6 7
An eagle plants a cedar of Lebanon that prospers. But then it turns to another eagle. Babylon replaces the exiled king, but the replacement turns to Egypt. Destruction comes.

Chapter 18 3 5 7
People will suffer the consequences of only their own sins. God takes no pleasure in the death of the wicked. He'd rather they repent and gain forgiveness.

Chapter 19 4 5 6
Ezekiel laments over what happened to the princes of Israel because of their rebellion and idolatry. He compares them to a lion and a vine.

Chapter 20 2 7
God explains that he was very slow to punish the Israelites for their evil ways, but now they are suffering the exile they deserve. When they repent, God will bring them back home.

Chapter 14: **Commentary**

One of the important points of Ezekiel's message is individual responsibility. Individuals can no longer rely on merely being members of the house of Israel, but each individual is responsible for his or her own personal relationship with God. The same message is taught in chapters 18 and 33.

Chapters 15–20: **Commentary**

Ezekiel takes the treasured symbols of Israel's national identity, negating each in turn. Israel is the vine of the LORD – it will be charred and shrivelled (chapters 15 and 17). Israel is the bride of the LORD – she turns into a harlot (chapters 16 and 23). Judah is a lion cub – it will be caged (chapter 19). The journey of the Exodus was no honeymoon of the LORD with his bride but a trail of rebellion (chapter 20).

You slaughtered my children and delivered them up as an offering to them. And in all your abominations and your whorings you did not remember the days of your youth, when you were naked and bare, flailing about in your blood.

After all your wickedness ('woe, woe to you!' says the LORD God), you built yourself a platform and made yourself a lofty place in every square; at the head of every street you built your lofty place and prostituted your beauty, offering yourself to every passer-by, and multiplying your whoring. You played the whore with the Egyptians, your lustful neighbours, multiplying your whoring, to provoke me to anger.

Ezekiel 16:21–26

'What do you mean by repeating this proverb concerning the land of Israel, "The parents have eaten sour grapes, and the children's teeth are set on edge"? As I live,' says the LORD God, 'this proverb shall no more be used by you in Israel. Know that all lives are mine; the life of the parent as well as the life of the child is mine: it is only the person who sins that shall die.'

Ezekiel 18:2–4

Chapter 21: **Commentary**

Prophecies are often joined together by an image or key word. Here three independent prophecies are joined by the image of a sword: a prose saying on the sword of the LORD, verses 1–12; a poetic threat, verse 13–22; the threatening sword of the King of Babylon, verses 23–32.

And the Babylonians came to her into the bed of love, and they defiled her with their lust; and after she defiled herself with them, she turned from them in disgust. When she carried on her whorings so openly and flaunted her nakedness, I turned in disgust from her, as I had turned from her sister. Yet she increased her whorings, remembering the days of her youth, when she played the whore in the land of Egypt and lusted after her paramours there, whose members were like those of donkeys, and whose emission was like that of stallions. Thus you longed for the lewdness of your youth, when the Egyptians fondled your bosom and caressed your young breasts.

Ezekiel 23:17–21

Chapter 24: **Commentary**

Ezekiel's personal tragedy mirrors that of the LORD. He loses his beloved bride. The stark prohibition of mourning images the pitiless destruction of Jerusalem.

Chapters 25–32: **Commentary**

The prophecies against the nations who delighted in the fate of Jerusalem are grouped between the threat and the realisation. Each nation must accept the LORD's vengeance for their share in the destruction.

Chapters 27–28: **Commentary**

Tyre was a great trading city on the coast of the Mediterranean, conquered only by Alexander the Great. Ezekiel mocks its claims to be invulnerable and to be divine, enthroned in a Garden of Eden and on the holy mountain.

⑤ ⑦ ⑨

Babylon is God's sword of judgement against the Israelites, punishing them for their rebellion, idolatry and lawlessness. They will suffer destruction.

Chapter
21

⑦ ⑨

Jerusalem is a city of bloodshed, filled with detestable practices: idolatry, the mistreatment of the poor and defenceless and general lawlessness. Therefore, Jerusalem will face judgement.

Chapter
22

⑤ ⑥ ⑦

Samaria and Jerusalem are sisters, Oholah and Oholibah. They are prostitutes committing adultery against their husband the LORD. God will punish them severely.

Chapter
23

⑤ ⑥ ⑦

Jerusalem is a cooking pot whose impurities will be burnt away. Ezekiel's wife dies but he can't mourn, illustrating how God himself will not mourn Jerusalem's destruction.

Chapter
24

⑦ ⑨

Ezekiel gives prophecies against Ammon, Moab, Edom and Philistia because they participated in and rejoiced over the destruction of Judah and Jerusalem.

Chapter
25

⑤ ⑦ ⑨

Ezekiel prophesies against the city of Tyre, predicting its destruction by Nebuchadnezzar, king of Babylon. It will be abandoned and left a ruin.

Chapter
26

④ ⑤ ⑦

Ezekiel sings a mock lament over the destruction of Tyre and what its destruction will mean to all those who traded with the city and depended upon it for their livelihood.

Chapter
27

⑤ ⑦ ⑨

Ezekiel prophesies against the king of Tyre, who imagines himself a god, but dies a mere mortal. The city of Sidon will also be destroyed and Israel will be safe at last.

Chapter
28

⑤   ⑦

Chapter 29

Ezekiel prophesies against the Pharaoh of Egypt, predicting that Nebuchadnezzar would conquer him. Because Nebuchadnezzar's battle against Tyre netted him no reward, God gives him Egypt in payment.

④   ⑤   ⑦

Chapter 30

Ezekiel laments over the destruction of Egypt and its dependent peoples by Nebuchadnezzar, king of Babylon.

⑤   ⑥   ⑦

Chapter 31

Assyria was once a mighty cedar, but it was cut down by Babylon. Egypt's Pharaoh is a mighty cedar and he too will be cut down by Babylon.

④   ⑦

Chapter 32

Ezekiel laments over Pharaoh, the king of Egypt, comparing him to a lion captured in a net. Babylon will destroy Pharaoh, who will die and be buried with the uncircumcised.

⑦

Chapter 33

God calls Ezekiel to serve as a watchman to warn the people of Israel. In the twelfth year of his exile, Ezekiel hears that Jerusalem has been destroyed for its idolatry and lawlessness.

Chapter 32: **Commentary**

In chapters 16 and 17 Ezekiel mocked Israel, taking their national religious symbols and stripping them down. Israel, the pure bride of the LORD, is vividly portrayed as a shameless whore. Israel as the great cedar tree; a vine is ripped to pieces by an eagle. Now it is Egypt's turn: the daunting crocodile, the king of the Nile, is humiliated by being netted, gutted and despoiled on the bank. Then we have a picture of the misery and shame of the nations in Sheol, suffering the powerless half-life of the dead.

Chapter 33: **Commentary**

The promises of restoration begin with a new account of the prophet's calling, the city's refusal to convert, its consequence, the continuing need to convert and the prophet's task. The message is expressed in a pattern so that the following lines are balanced: 1 and 5, 2 and 4, with 3 sitting centrally.

'Now you, mortal, say to the house of Israel, "Thus you have said: Our transgressions and our sins weigh upon us, and we waste away because of them; how then can we live?" Say to them, "As I live," says the LORD God, "I have no pleasure in the death of the wicked, but that the wicked turn from their ways and live; turn back, turn back from your evil ways; for why will you die, O house of Israel?"'
Ezekiel 33:10–11

Cherubim
The cherubim that appear in Ezekiel 1, 10 and elsewhere throughout the Bible were well known in the ancient world. This ivory plaque of an Egyptian deity was found at Samaria.

Chapter 34: **Commentary**

The imagery of God as a shepherd, and especially the shepherd of Israel, comes frequently in the Bible. Here the shepherd is 'my servant David', so God's representative, a messianic leader of the line of David. Sheep are unpredictable, silly creatures, and need careful guidance on the rocky, bare hills of Palestine, and protection from hungry predators. The image of Jesus as the Good Shepherd is taken up in the New Testament, especially in the Gospel of John.

Chapter 36: **Commentary**

The LORD's Name has been mocked by the nations for his failure to protect his people. By the liberation of his people and the return to Jerusalem his Name will be restored to holiness, 'hallowed be thy Name'.

Chapter 37: **Commentary**

Primarily this is a vision of the restoration to life of the dead bones of Israel by the Spirit of God, but both Jewish and Christian tradition see in it also a prophecy of individual restoration to life.

The hand of the LORD came upon me, and he brought me out by the spirit of the LORD and set me down in the middle of a valley; it was full of bones. He led me all round them; there were very many lying in the valley, and they were very dry.

Ezekiel 37:1–2

Chapter 38: **Commentary**

Gog and his country Magog are made-up names. This eschatological scene symbolises the cosmic defeat of Babylon. The imagery has contributed significantly to Christian imaginings of the final victory of the LORD.

Chapters 40–48: **Commentary**

The blueprint of the restored city provides the prophet's third vision of the LORD enthroned: as he had seen the divine glory leave the Temple, so he will see it return in 43:1–5. The name of the city is no longer 'Jerusalem' but 'The LORD is there' (48:35). The holiness surrounding the Temple is shown by the massive gates and inner courtyards. The entry-gates get narrower at each stage, as entry is increasingly restricted.

7

Ezekiel prophesies that God will become Israel's shepherd: he will seek the lost, heal the sick, strengthen the weak, make a covenant of peace with them and eliminate their enemies.

Chapter **34**

7 · **9**

Ezekiel prophesies against Edom: it will be destroyed and become a desolate wasteland because of how it treated the Israelites and rejoiced over their destruction.

Chapter **35**

2 · **7**

The mountains and hills will flourish, and the Israelites will be cleansed and restored to their homeland. Their heart of stone will be replaced with a heart of flesh, and God's Name will again be held holy.

Chapter **36**

6 · **7**

A valley of dry bones reassembles and comes back to life, symbolising the restoration of the nation. Judah and Israel will reunite and be ruled by one king, a descendant of David.

Chapter **37**

7 · **13**

When Israel is peaceful and prosperous, Gog will invade from the north, advancing like a cloud.

Chapter **38**

7 · **13**

God will destroy Gog and his army, feeding their flesh to the birds and animals. The Israelites will be restored to their land, where they will prosper and live securely.

Chapter **39**

7 · **16**

God gives Ezekiel a vision of a new Jerusalem and its Temple, where a man shining like bronze shows him its gates, inner court and inner rooms, measuring them all with a measuring rod.

Chapter **40**

7   **16**

Chapter
41

The man measures the rest of the new Temple, inside and out: the inner sanctuaries, entrances and main hall.

7   **16**

Chapter
42

The man shows Ezekiel the rooms for the priests, then measures all four sides of the area around the Temple.

7   **16**

Chapter
43

God's glory then returns to the Temple. The great altar is measured and God gives detailed instructions for performing the sacrifices.

7   **16**

Chapter
44

God gives detailed regulations for the Levites and priests. God warns that the Israelites must not disobey him again.

7   **16**

Chapter
45

A large section of the land of Israel around the Temple is designated a sacred district for the Levites. God gives additional regulations for sacrifices and Passover celebrations.

7   **16**

Chapter
46

God gives instructions for proper behaviour on the Sabbath and other appointed festivals. He also explains the proper sacrifices.

7   **16**

Chapter
47

A life-giving river, lined with fruit trees, flows from the Temple to the Dead Sea. The fruit is for food and the leaves are for healing. God describes the boundaries for the new land of Israel.

7   **16**

Chapter
48

Each of the 12 tribes receives a section of the new land of Israel. The new city of Jerusalem has three gates on each of its four sides, each named after a tribe of Israel.

Then he brought me to the gate, the gate facing east. And there, the glory of the God of Israel was coming from the east; the sound was like the sound of mighty waters; and the earth shone with his glory. The vision I saw was like the vision that I had seen when he came to destroy the city, and like the vision that I had seen by the river Chebar; and I fell upon my face. As the glory of the LORD entered the temple by the gate facing east ...

Ezekiel 43:1–4

...of the land. It is to be his property in Israel. And my princes shall no longer oppress my people; but they shall let the house of Israel have the land according to their tribes.

Thus says the LORD God: 'Enough, O princes of Israel! Put away violence and oppression, and do what is just and right. Cease your evictions of my people,' says the LORD God. 'You shall have honest balances, an honest ephah, and an honest bath.'

Ezekiel 45:8–10

Chapter 47: **Commentary**

The spring in the Temple is the source of life-giving water, which sweetens and brings fruitfulness even to the notorious Dead Sea. It recalls the rivers flowing from the Garden of Eden and the mythic paradise of legend.

He said to me, 'Mortal, have you seen this?'

Then he led me back along the bank of the river. As I came back, I saw on the bank of the river a great many trees on one side and on the other. He said to me, 'This water flows towards the eastern region and goes down into the Arabah; and when it enters the sea, the sea of stagnant waters, the water will become fresh. Wherever the river goes, every living creature that swarms will live, and there will be very many fish, once these waters reach there. It will become fresh; and everything will live where the river goes. People will stand fishing beside the sea from En-gedi to En-eglaim; it will be a place for the spreading of nets; its fish will be of a great many kinds, like the fish of the Great Sea. But its swamps and marshes will not become fresh; they are to be left for salt. On the banks, on both sides of the river, there will grow all kinds of trees for food. Their leaves will not wither nor their fruit fail, but they will bear fresh fruit every month, because the water for them flows from the sanctuary. Their fruit will be for food, and their leaves for healing.'

Ezekiel 47:6–12

Daniel

Overview

The Book of Daniel is an apocalypse, that is, a secret revelation. This type of literature became popular in Judaism during the persecutions. The purpose of such a book is to assure the persecuted that the LORD will deliver them triumphantly. The message of such an apocalypse is always in coded language, involving grand visions. An apocalypse is always anonymous, but often attributed to a great figure of the past. The visions in this book show that it was written at the time of the persecution of the Jews by the Syrian King Antiochus Epiphanes.

The visions occur in the second half of the book. The first half is devoted to establishing Daniel's credentials and showing the rewards of fidelity to the Jewish Law. The name Daniel is derived from that of an ancient wise sage named Danel, but the early chapters are set at the Persian court amid a confused historical background. The book is important in showing that this type of writing can also be a vehicle for God's message. For Christians it has a special value as background to the final book of the New Testament, and for the use of the expression 'Son of Man' in Daniel 7:13.

Chapter 1: **Commentary**

The young men show their mettle by insisting on observance of the food laws. At the time of writing, failure to observe them was equivalent to apostasy.

17

Daniel and his friends Shadrach, Meshach and Abednego are taken to Babylon, receive training in the language and literature of their captors and are assigned jobs in the bureaucracy.

Chapter
1

Chapter 2: **Commentary**

The stories from chapters 2–7 are arranged to balance: a series of kingdoms – idolatry – disaster for the king – disaster for the king – idolatry – a series of kingdoms (a-b-c-c-b-a). The allegories of chapters 2 and 7 describe the great empires that collapse successively and make way for the messianic kingdom. From 2:4 to 7:28 the language used is Aramaic, the court language of the Persian Empire, soon to be diffused over the Near East.

7 **17**

Daniel explains Nebuchadnezzar's dream of a statue representing current and future kingdoms in the Middle East. Nebuchadnezzar praises Daniel's God and rewards Daniel.

Chapter
2

Chapter 3: **Commentary**

The Prayer of Azariah and the Song of the Three Young Men does not appear in the Hebrew Bible, but is preserved in the Greek and Syriac Versions. It is not included in the Protestant Canon of Scripture.

15 **17**

Chapter **3**

Nebuchadnezzar builds a statue, then orders all to worship it. Shadrach, Meshach and Abednego refuse and are cast into a fiery furnace. They survive and Nebuchadnezzar rewards them.

1 **7** **17**

Chapter **4**

Nebuchadnezzar dreams of a tree being felled. Daniel explains that it means Nebuchadnezzar will go crazy. When he later returns to his senses, Nebuchadnezzar praises God for his deliverance.

Chapter 5: **Commentary**

This chapter includes plenty of minor historical inaccuracies: Belshazzar was son of Nabonidus, not Nebuchadnezzar. He was regent but never king. The words on the wall are *mana* (measure), *shaqal* (weigh) and *paras* (divide). 'As verses 26–28 explain, the writing predicts the fall of Belshazzar's kingdom

7 **9** **17**

Chapter **5**

King Belshazzar sees a hand write three words on the wall. Daniel explains that the Persians are going to conquer Babylon. That night, the Persians kill Belshazzar.

17

Chapter **6**

King Darius decrees that no one may pray to anyone but him for a month. Daniel refuses and is cast into a den of lions. He survives and Darius praises Daniel's God.

Then the conspirators came to the king and said to him, 'Know, O king, that it is a law of the Medes and Persians that no interdict or ordinance that the king establishes can be changed.'

Then the king gave the command, and Daniel was brought and thrown into the den of lions. The king said to Daniel, 'May your God, whom you faithfully serve, deliver you!'

Daniel 6:15–16

7 **13**

Chapter **7**

During the reign of Belshazzar, Daniel dreams of four powerful beasts. The angel Gabriel interprets them as four future kingdoms.

Chapter 7: **Commentary**

The four beasts represent the Babylonian, Median, Persian and Seleucid Empires. The ten horns are symbols of strength. But they all give way to the human figure, the 'son of man', who represents Judaism. Jesus may have alluded to this figure in his use of the expression 'son of man'.

7 **13**

Chapter **8**

Daniel has a vision of a goat destroying a ram. Gabriel explains that the ram is Persia and the goat is Greece. A small horn on the goat is a future evil king.

Chapter 8: **Commentary**

The ram represents the Persian Empire, but the goat represents Antiochus Epiphanes, who abolished the perpetual sacrifice in the Jerusalem Temple, and installed there a statue of Olympian Zeus.

7 **12** **13**

Chapter **9**

During the reign of Xerxes, Daniel confesses the sins of Israel in prayer. Gabriel explains that 70 'sevens' will end with desolation and an abomination in the Temple.

Chapters 10–11: **Commentary**

The interpreting angel summarises Greek history from Xerxes through Alexander the Great to Antiochus Epiphanes, but suddenly becomes vaguer after the date of writing. Michael, 'one of the chief princes' is protector of the Chosen People. His name means 'Who is like God?'

7 **13** **15**

Chapter **10**

During the reign of Cyrus, Daniel has a vision of a great war and mourns for three weeks. The angel Michael tells him not to be afraid and promises him an explanation.

Daniel in the lions' den
*Daniel was thrown to the lions
for refusing to worship alien
gods. He came to no harm.*

---

7 · **13** · **15**

Michael explains that there will be war between
Persia and Greece. A future mighty king will devastate
the people of Israel and God's Temple before he is
finally overthrown.

Chapter
11

---

7 · **13** · **15**

There will be a great period of distress and trouble,
but then the righteous will be resurrected. It will all
happen in the distant future.

Chapter
12

17

Susanna, the young wife of a Jew, resists the advances
of two elders. To cover themselves they accuse her of
being caught with a young man, but are foiled by
Daniel's cross-examination. They pay the penalty.

Chapter
13

17

A statue of a dragon is reputed to eat food. Daniel
prepares a meal which explodes inside it. As punishment
Daniel is dumped in the lions' den, where he is fed by
Habakkuk. After seven days he emerges unscathed.

Chapter
14

Chapter 13: **Commentary**

Appended to the Greek version of Daniel are two stories.
The first is this story of the triumph of female heroism
over male lust by means of the judgement of Daniel
the Wise.

Chapter 14: **Commentary**

The second appendix is two stories mocking idolatry.
The powerless Bel is a Babylonian god, mentioned in Isaiah
and Jeremiah.

Hosea

Overview

Hosea prophesied in the northern kingdom of Israel a couple of decades before Samaria was sacked by the Assyrians and the kingdom came to an end. His warnings went unheeded. The prophecy is dated in 1:1 to the years 743–716 BC. He was one of the first prophets whose words were collected and written down. He rebukes Israel for deserting the covenant by their idolatry, by turning to foreign alliances rather than to the LORD, and for their social injustice. But principally he is the prophet of God's

6	7	9

Chapter 1

To illustrate how Israel was treating God, God has Hosea marry a prostitute named Gomer. The names of his children signify the future judgement on Israel and Judah.

5	7	9

Chapter 2

God rebukes and punishes Israel for idolatry, comparing her to an adulteress. Nevertheless, God will someday be reconciled to the Israelites as his people.

2	6	7

Chapter 3

Hosea's wife had left him and been sold into slavery. He buys her back and reconciles with her, illustrating God's intentions for the Israelites.

5	7	9

Chapter 4

God brings his charges against the Israelites, accusing them of unfaithfulness, idolatry and law breaking. He tells them that they will be punished.

5	7	9

Chapter 5

God says that Ephraim will be destroyed and taken captive. The Israelites will feel the wrath of God: God will attack them as a lion attacks its prey.

5	7	9

Chapter 6

Israel is unrepentant. The Israelites outwardly practise their religion, but their hearts are not in it. Therefore, they will be judged.

Chapters 1–3: **Commentary**

The image of God's covenant with Israel as a marriage contract inspires the later prophets, the Song of Songs and eventually Ephesians 5. She was not necessarily a whore at the time of their marriage, but she turned out to be so. The prophecy looks back longingly to the honeymoon period in the desert, when Israel was entirely faithful to her spouse.

I will take you for my wife in faithfulness; and you shall know the LORD. On that day I will answer, says the LORD, I will answer the heavens and they shall answer the earth; and the earth shall answer the grain, the wine, and the oil, and they shall answer Jezreel ...

Hosea 2:20–22

Chapter 6: **Commentary**

The meaning of 'on the third day' (verse 2) is 'in a very short time'. This passage is understood by early Christian writers to be a prophecy of Christ's resurrection.

Gilead is a city of evil-doers, tracked with blood. As robbers lie in wait for someone, so the priests are banded together; they murder on the road to Shechem, they commit a monstrous crime. In the house of Israel I have seen a horrible thing; Ephraim's whoredom is there, Israel is defiled.

Hosea 6:8–10

love, for he sees his own unshakable love for his repeatedly unfaithful wife as an image of this love. It is perhaps for this reason that Hosea stands at the head of the Book of the Twelve Prophets.

For they sow the wind,
and they shall reap the whirlwind.
The standing grain has no heads,
it shall yield no meal;
if it were to yield,
foreigners would devour it.
Israel is swallowed up;
now they are among the nations
as a useless vessel.

Hosea 8:7–8

Chapter 11: **Commentary**

God's love for Israel is often described as *hesed*, the unfailing family love that will never abandon another family member. Hosea has imaged it as conjugal love, and now completes the picture with the love of parent for a young child.

Chapter 14: **Commentary**

A final prayer for repentance evokes a promise of forgiveness. The last verse of the book is a later addition in the wisdom style.

Those who are wise understand these things;
those who are discerning know them.
For the ways of the LORD are right,
and the upright walk in them,
but transgressors stumble in them.

Hosea 14:9

5   7   9

Whenever God thought about restoring Israel, they just sinned even more. The Israelites are foolish. God wants to restore them, but they have rejected him.

Chapter
7

5   7   9

Israel has rejected what is good. The Israelites follow idols and ignore all of God's commandments. As a result, God does not appreciate or accept their sacrifices.

Chapter
8

5   7   9

Israel has worshipped other gods besides the LORD, so the time of punishment is at hand for all their many sins. They will become wanderers among the nations.

Chapter
9

5   7   9

Israel has been deceitful and idolatrous. Instead of righteousness, they have sown wickedness. Therefore, they will harvest judgement.

Chapter
10

5   7   10

God loves Israel. He rescued them from Egypt. He made them prosperous. He would rather not punish them, but he must, since he is bound by the contract he made with them.

Chapter
11

5   7   9

The Israelites seek for help from everyone but God; they practise idolatry and break God's commandments, despite the warning of God's prophets.

Chapter
12

5   7   9

The Israelites have worshipped idols, even though God warned them since they left Egypt to worship only him. So God will judge them and destroy them.

Chapter
13

2   5   7

When the Israelites repent and turn back to God, then God will forgive them, heal them and bring them back home.

Chapter
14

Joel
Overview

I The Plague of Locusts 1:1–2:27

  a A Call to Repentance and Prayer 1:1–20

  b The Day of the LORD 2:1–17

  c The Prayer is Answered 2:18–27

II The Outpouring of the Spirit 2:28–3:3

  a The Judgement of the Nations 3:4–16

  b The Glory of Jerusalem 3:17–21

Nothing is known about the author of the prophecy or of the circumstances of its composition. The absence from the prophecy of any mention of king or Temple, and the emphasis on the nations of the world, suggest that the prophecy is post-exilic. It has been suggested that the first section (1:2–2:27) is a liturgical text for use in a liturgy of repentance. The prophecy of the outpouring of the Spirit is used as the basis of the apostle Peter's explanation of the happenings at Pentecost.

The chief theological emphasis of the prophecy is on the threat of the Day of the LORD, and this may have led to the positioning of the prophecy before Amos in the Book of the Twelve Prophets, as a preparation for and enhancement of the

The prophet Joel
The prophet Joel, son of Pethuel, is known only through the prophecy that bears his name. When he wrote, where he lived and what became of him remain a mystery.

Chapter 2: **Commentary**

Joel's prophecy of the outpouring of the Spirit is used by Peter in his speech at Pentecost to explain what has been happening, the tongues of fire and the speaking in strange tongues: 'I will pour out my Spirit on all flesh; your sons and your daughters shall prophesy. Then everyone who calls on the name of the LORD will be saved.'

④	⑤	⑦
Chapter 1	Joel prophesies about a plague of locusts that will come and devastate Israel like an army, stripping the land of all its crops. Israel will mourn.	

②	⑤	⑦
Chapter 2	The army of locusts devours the land like a fire. God asks for repentance and promises to replace what has been lost. He will pour his Spirit upon the people of Israel and deliver them.	

⑤	⑦	⑨
Chapter 3	God calls upon the Israelites to prepare for war against their enemies, whom they will successfully defeat. Israel's enemies will be destroyed on the day of the LORD.	

Proclaim this among the nations:
Prepare war, stir up the warriors.
Let all the soldiers draw near,
  let them come up.
Beat your ploughshares into swords,
  and your pruning-hooks into spears;
  let the weakling say, 'I am a warrior.'
Come quickly,
  all you nations all around,
  gather yourselves there.
Bring down your warriors, O LORD.

Joel 3:9–11

theme of the Day of the LORD in Amos. The early part of the prophecy is dominated by vivid images of destruction, devastation of the crops, lack of pasture or food, an invading army, cosmic turmoil – all leading up to a call for repentance and conversion. In the later part of the prophecy the same fierce, brutal and cosmic imagery continues, but now the great Day of the LORD will bring relief and peace to Mount Zion as well as destruction to the nations, which are to be judged in the Valley of Decision.

Constant throughout the prophecy is the daunting threat of an awesome Day of the LORD. This image appears first in the prophecy of Amos, but reaches perhaps its fullest vivid horror in Joel, with the stars losing their brilliance, the moon turned into blood and the LORD roaring from Zion (Joel 2:31; 3:16; Amos 1:2). It is a day when the world will be turned upside-down, a day of judgement, when at last the wicked will be punished and the righteous rewarded, when everything comfortably hidden will be hideously exposed. It is the hope of the humble and the woe of the wicked. Throughout the prophets the imagery of reversal becomes ever more terrible, while the peace and contentment promised to the humble of the LORD becomes ever more reassuring (Isaiah 2:6–12; Zephaniah 2:2–3; Zechariah 14:1–5; Malachi 4:1–30). In the New Testament the same imagery recurs in Paul's expectation of the heavenly triumphal procession of the Risen Christ (1 Thessalonians 4:16–17) and in the separation of the sheep and the goats at the Last Judgement (Matthew 25:31–46).

Amos

Overview

Like Hosea, Amos was one of the first of the prophets whose sayings were written down. He was no professional prophet, neither a court prophet nor a member of one of the groups of prophets, but was a tiller of sycamore-figs, who was unexpectedly plucked from Teqoa, a little village in the southern kingdom, to threaten the northern kingdom to correct their ways. He gave his message in the temple at Bethel some time between 783 and 740 BC, and was unceremoniously bustled out by the priest. His

The prophet Amos
Amos was a shepherd and keeper of sycamore-fig trees who came from the small village of Tekoa, about 10 km (6 miles) south of Bethlehem.

Chapters 1–2: **Commentary**

Amos' technique here is to rouse the righteous indignation of his hearers against these foreign nations and then turn it on themselves. Originally the seventh accusation, the climax, would have been against Israel, for the accusation against Judah (2:4–5) was inserted later. The stress on Law, and on Judah itself, does not fit Amos' message.

And he said:
'The LORD roars from Zion,
  and utters his voice from Jerusalem;
the pastures of the shepherds wither,
  and the top of Carmel dries up.'

Amos 1:2

Thus says the LORD:
For three transgressions of Israel, and for four, I will not revoke the punishment; because they sell the righteous for silver, and the needy for a pair of sandals – they who trample the head of the poor into the dust of the earth, and push the afflicted out of the way; father and son go in to the same girl, so that my holy name is profaned; they lay themselves down beside every altar on garments taken in pledge; and in the house of their God they drink wine bought with fines they imposed.

Amos 2:6–8

5	7	9

Chapter **1**

Amos describes God's coming judgement against Israel's neighbours. Damascus, Gaza, Tyre, Edom and Amon are judged for four sins: fire will consume them.

5	7	9

Chapter **2**

Amos describes God's coming judgement against Israel's neighbours. Moab and Judah will be judged for four sins. Then Amos announces that Israel, too, will be judged for four sins.

message is one of unmitigated disaster, for the promises of restoration given in the tailpiece are a subsequent addition (as are three little doxologies, added perhaps for liturgical use, 4:13, 5:8–9 and 9:5–6). Again like Hosea, he inveighs against their harsh commercial profiteering at the expense of the poor, against their luxurious lifestyle, against their empty sacrificing. They have forfeited their position as God's Chosen People (9:7–8).

Chapters 3–4: **Commentary**

Amos seems to think in sevens. In 3:3–8 Amos defends his prophesying by seven images to show that things do not happen without a cause. Then in 4:2–11 he gives a series of seven impending disasters: exile, famine, drought, blight, plague, slaughter, devastation. However in chapters 7–9 there are only four visions.

Chapter 5: **Commentary**

Verse 18 is the earliest mention of the Day of the LORD (see Joel). Amos' hearers expect it to be to their advantage, but Amos disillusions them. In 8:9 he begins to use the cosmic imagery that will be a feature of these prophecies.

Chapter 7: **Commentary**

The prose passage, 7:10–17, gives the only biographical information we have about Amos and his mission. A southerner denouncing the north at the heart of the northern sanctuary would not expect a friendly welcome.

Chapter 9: **Commentary**

The tailpiece, 9:11–15, is the only glimmer of hope. But it is a later addition to Amos' message, since it refers to Judah, not Israel, and presupposes the ruin of Jerusalem and the Exile.

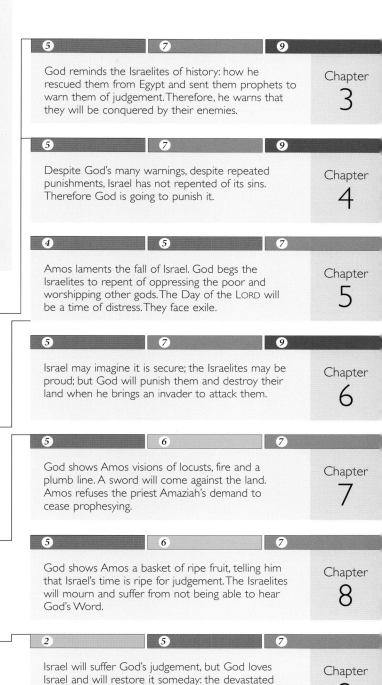

5 **7** **9**

God reminds the Israelites of history: how he rescued them from Egypt and sent them prophets to warn them of judgement. Therefore, he warns that they will be conquered by their enemies.

Chapter
3

5 **7** **9**

Despite God's many warnings, despite repeated punishments, Israel has not repented of its sins. Therefore God is going to punish it.

Chapter
4

4 **5** **7**

Amos laments the fall of Israel. God begs the Israelites to repent of oppressing the poor and worshipping other gods. The Day of the LORD will be a time of distress. They face exile.

Chapter
5

5 **7** **9**

Israel may imagine it is secure; the Israelites may be proud; but God will punish them and destroy their land when he brings an invader to attack them.

Chapter
6

5 **6** **7**

God shows Amos visions of locusts, fire and a plumb line. A sword will come against the land. Amos refuses the priest Amaziah's demand to cease prophesying.

Chapter
7

5 **6** **7**

God shows Amos a basket of ripe fruit, telling him that Israel's time is ripe for judgement. The Israelites will mourn and suffer from not being able to hear God's Word.

Chapter
8

2 **5** **7**

Israel will suffer God's judgement, but God loves Israel and will restore it someday: the devastated cities will be rebuilt, and Israel will never again be sent into exile.

Chapter
9

Obadiah

Overview

The prophet Obadiah
Obadiah's name was a popular one, used by at least 11 people in the Bible. But nothing definite is known of the prophet beyond his name.

The puzzle of the Book of Obadiah is why it is included in the Bible at all. It is the shortest book of the Bible. Nothing is known about the author. His name means 'Servant of the LORD', which may be no more than equivalent to 'Prophet of the LORD'.

Why did those who chose the sacred writings consider this to be of sufficient importance on its own? There are many other prophecies against Edom. Rivalry and war against Israel's eastern neighbour had been chronic from the earliest times. It was given a rationale in the story of the struggle between Isaac and his brother Edom/Esau (Genesis 25 and 27). Psalm 137 singles out the Edomites for punishment in revenge for their part in the destruction of Jerusalem. Much of the first poem here is already contained in Jeremiah 49. In the third poem Edom/Esau is mentioned as only one among many nations. Was the prophecy included simply to show that the enemies of the city of the LORD will not go unpunished?

Chapter 1: **Commentary**

These prophecies of Obadiah against Edom were fulfilled in 312 BC, when the territory of Edom to the east of the Dead Sea was completely overrun by the Nabateans. Edom as such disappears from history.

5	7	9

Chapter 1	Edom will be destroyed on account of its poor treatment of Israel. They will suffer as Israel suffered and their kingdom will become God's kingdom.

Jonah

Overview

I Jonah's Flight 1:1–17

II Jonah's Prayer 2:1–11

III Jonah's Obedience 3:1–10

IV Jonah's Petulance 4:1–11

The Book of Jonah is not intended as a true story, but neither is it a prophecy in the sense of foretelling the future. However, a message it certainly has, for it does speak of the ways of God with the world. It is a satire on Jewish self-righteousness, told with the humour typical of Jewish self-mocking stories. The contrast is clear between Jonah, the Jew, called to be a prophet and attempting to run away, and the citizens of Nineveh, who repent hugely the moment they are warned. Who are the Chosen People here? The 'prophet' disobeys God while the Gentiles respond with alacrity.

The date of the story is not easy to determine. Such attention to the salvation of the Gentiles must be post-exilic. The book is mentioned in Tobit, so it was probably written between the sixth and third centuries BC.

Jonah and the whale
When Jonah tried to run away from God, God sent a whale to swallow Jonah and bring him back.

Then they said to him, 'What shall we do to you, that the sea may quieten down for us?' For the sea was growing more and more tempestuous. He said to them, 'Pick me up and throw me into the sea; then the sea will quieten down for you; for I know it is because of me that this great storm has come upon you.'

Jonah 1:11–12

Chapters 1–4: **Commentary**

There are constant touches of humour. The prophet lies fast asleep while the Gentile sailors pray to their gods (1:5). The fish vomits up Jonah just as he prays 'Deliverance belongs to the LORD' (2:10). Even the animals wear sackcloth, refrain from drinking and cry to the LORD (3:7–8). The bush grows in a night and then withers as suddenly (4:6–7). God teases Jonah and Jonah rails at God for being too merciful (4:7–9).

⑦	⑰	
When God asks Jonah to go to Nineveh, he refuses and boards a ship going the other way. When a storm arises, Jonah tells the sailors to toss him overboard. A large fish swallows him.		Chapter **1**

⑤	⑫	
After three days in the large fish, Jonah prays for deliverance. God responds by having the fish vomit Jonah back up on the shore near where God first asked him to go to Nineveh.		Chapter **2**

⑦	⑰	
God once again asks Jonah to go to Nineveh. This time Jonah obeys. To his dismay, the people of Nineveh repent, so God forgives them.		Chapter **3**

③	⑩	⑰	
A disappointed Jonah sits down outside the city hoping that God will change his mind about Nineveh. God uses a bush that shelters Jonah but later dies to teach him that God loves everyone.			Chapter **4**

Micah

Overview

I   Judgement Against Jerusalem 1:1–3:12

II   Promises to Zion 4:1–5:15

III Reproaches to Israel 6:1–7:7

IV   Micah Intercedes for Zion 7:8–20

The superscription of the prophecy introduces Micah as coming from Moresheth, some 30 km (19 miles) southwest of Jerusalem, during the years 736–716 BC – that is, during the final years of the northern kingdom of Israel, conquered by Assyria in 722 BC. The prophecies alternate between harsh criticism of the injustices of the northern kingdom and promises to Jerusalem or Zion, some of which may be later insertions. However, as a whole the prophet could well have been a contemporary of Isaiah of Jerusalem: a passage about the destruction of towns in Judah (1:10–16) fits well the invasion of Sennacherib in 701, when only Jerusalem among the towns of Judah was spared. Particularly the promises of messianic peace and prosperity are held by some scholars to have been added after the exile. However, Micah 4:1–5 is duplicated in Isaiah 2:1–4, and they teach very similarly on the remnant of Israel and in other messianic passages (such as Micah 5:2–5 and Isaiah 7:16), so that it would be necessary to accept that these elements are or are not post-exilic in both prophets.

Chapter **1** — Micah predicts that God is going to judge Samaria and Jerusalem for their sins; the result will be much suffering and weeping.

Chapter **2** — The Israelites don't want to listen to Micah's warnings of judgement; they'd rather hear happy predictions of prosperity. But they will be forgiven and restored only after punishment.

Chapter **3** — God condemns Israel's leaders for their injustice and oppression and condemns the prophets who prophesied lies instead of the truth. Disaster is coming.

Chapter **4** — In the last days many nations will come to worship in Jerusalem. The exiles will all come home and live in peace and prosperity, worshipping the LORD faithfully.

Chapter **5** — A ruler for Israel will arise from Bethlehem. But Israel will go into exile for a while, to cleanse them of their idolatry. Then God will restore them and destroy Israel's enemies.

Chapter **6** — God calls on the mountains and foundations of the earth to bear witness to Israel's guilt. God wants to see repentance, justice and mercy, not animal sacrifices.

Chapter **7** — Israel is in misery; wickedness is rampant. But its sin will be forgiven and it will be restored to the land where it will once again find peace and prosperity.

Chapter 5: **Commentary**

The author of the New Testament Gospel of Matthew quotes Micah 5:1, which predicts that a man from Bethlehem will arise to rule over the nation of Israel. The author of the Gospel of Matthew believes that Jesus' birth in Bethlehem fulfilled that prediction (Matthew 2:6). In the New Testament, only the Gospels of Matthew and Luke describe Jesus' birth and locate it in Bethlehem.

Nahum

Overview

We know virtually nothing about the prophet Nahum – if indeed that was the name of the author, for the name could also have been a professional name. It means 'comforter' or 'consolation'. Besides the name we know only the name of his hometown or village, Elkosh, whose location is unknown. The prophecy is all about the fall of the great city of Nineveh, capital of the Assyrian Empire, conquered by the Babylonians in 612 BC. The only sure date is that it was written after the conquest of Thebes in Egypt by Assyria in 663 BC. However, whether the poems are a prediction of or a reflection on the fall of Nineveh is hard to say. The important message of the book is not a vengeful delight at the discomfiture of an enemy who was responsible for the fall of the northern kingdom of Israel and who had also fiercely ravaged Judah. It is rather a celebration of the mighty power of the LORD, the supreme controller of history, to whom even mighty empires are subject. This is the message of the poem or psalm that introduces the account of the destruction of Nineveh.

The prophecy consists of an alphabetical poem, whose lines begin successively with each letter of the alphabet (up to halfway through the alphabet), celebrating the awesome power of God over the world (1:1–8). After this follows (1:9–2.3) a promise of peace to Judah, which had been so threatened by Assyrian power. Then comes a vivid evocation of the terror and confusion of the assault on the city and its plundering, the ferocity of the attackers and the bewilderment and humiliation of the inhabitants, the pitiless slaughter of children, ending with a mockery of a funeral lament for the city. It is a powerful presentation of one of the great reversals of history.

Chapter 1: **Commentary**

'Belial' (verse 11) means 'worthless'. It occurs in the Bible also at 2 Corinthians 6:15, 'Has Christ anything to do with Belial?' It is a sort of nickname for the Devil ('nickname' itself really means 'abusive or mocking name', because the Devil has sometimes been named 'Old Nick'). The person referred to here could be Sennacherib, the Assyrian king who attacked Jerusalem, but then withdrew.

5	7	9	
The LORD is angry with Nineveh, the capital of the Assyrian Empire, for what the Assyrians did in destroying Israel. Therefore God will avenge his beloved people.			Chapter 1

5	7	9	
God is against Nineveh. An invader dressed in red, riding chariots, will attack and defeat Nineveh. Nineveh will be plundered and destroyed.			Chapter 2

5	7	9	
God is against Nineveh for its cruelty. It will suffer the fate of Cush, Egypt, Put and Libya: they were devastated; their infants were dashed to pieces. Nineveh will burn.			Chapter 3

Habakkuk

Overview

Trust in God
Habakkuk could not make sense of what God was planning to do, but trusted God would make it work out for the best.

This fragment of prophecy has proved difficult to interpret and there are issues of integrity. About the prophet nothing is known, though legend brings him into prominence again by the story of the miraculous feeding of Daniel in the lions' den (Bel and the Dragon, verses 33–39). A historical context for the prophecy can be gleaned from the imminent rise to power of the Chaldeans, – the Babylonians – (1:6), from about 615 BC onwards, and the mention of God 'in his holy temple', which must be before the destruction of the Temple in 589 BC.

Another issue is the integrity of the prophecy. A commentary on Habakkuk has been found among the scrolls of Qumran, which does not comment on chapter 3. Some have deduced that this shows that this chapter was not part of the work. However, it could also be that this poem was not considered relevant, and linguistic studies have shown that the same style of sound-play in words continues throughout the three chapters. The question posed by the book is how violence can seem to prevail. The initial frustrated complaint (1:1–4) gives way to the frightening view of the Chaldean hordes in full battle order (1:5–17). But then a solution is promised, so certain that it must be written down as a lasting and reliable record (2:1–4), and a series of five woes on the violent is detailed (2:5–20). Finally, a tranquil poem of confidence in the LORD rounds off the message.

5	7	9

Chapter 1

Habakkuk wants God to judge Israel's wickedness. God tells him that the Babylonians will destroy Israel. Habakkuk wonders how God can use the wicked to judge the more righteous.

5	7	9

Chapter 2

Habakkuk waits patiently for God's response. God tells him that although Israel will be judged for its idolatry and mistreatment of the poor, the Babylonians will also be judged.

1	5	7

Chapter 3

Habakkuk recognises God's power, acknowledges that he does not understand and affirms that he will rejoice in God even when everything is going wrong and makes no sense.

Chapter 2: **Commentary**

The famous verse 2:4, used by Paul in Romans 1:17 and Galatians 3:11, can be understood in various ways. Paul uses it of the saving *faith* of the individual believer. It could refer also to an individual's saving *fidelity*. In context the most likely original meaning was the *reliability* of the prophecy ('the righteous shall live by its reliability'). Paul often applies the scripture out of its context.

Zephaniah

Overview

The prophet Zephaniah is quite unknown, apart from the genealogy given at the head of his prophecy, and the fact that he prophesied during the reign of King Josiah, the great reformer at the end of the seventh century, killed at the battle of Carchemish in 609 BC. His prophecy has been taken at its face value as a single, coherent prophecy supporting the reforms of Josiah, encouraging conversion and predicting disaster at a great Day of the LORD for the proud and idolaters and for the nations opposing Jerusalem. It has also been seen as a composition completed only in exilic or post-exilic times, because of the threats against the nations and the ferocity of the presentation of the Day of the LORD. In more recent scholarship neither of these arguments has seemed cogent.

More important is Zephaniah's message on the poor and humble of the earth (2:3, 3:12–13), the remnant whose lowliness and reliance on the LORD rather than on any human power will win them the LORD's favour. This is the spirituality, prominent also in Isaiah 57:14–21, that will inspire and form the faithful in post-exilic times. In its turn this will issue in the humble expectation of those waiting for the Messiah, such as in Luke 1–2.

Chapter 1: **Commentary**

This poem is perhaps the most daunting of all the prophecies about the Day of the LORD, predicting the devastation that will strike Jerusalem. Verse 15 provides the basis for the medieval hymn 'Dies Irae' ('On the Day of Judgement'), often dramatically set to music. Other prophecies speak of a faithful remnant that will be left, but here everything is swept away in the wrath of the LORD. The poem would fit the context of a great reform movement such as that of King Josiah just before the end of the Kingdom of Judah.

5	7	9	Chapter 1
God says that he will sweep away everything from the land of Judah and Jerusalem, both people and animals, birds and fish – and the idols. He will punish the rulers of Judah.			

5	7	9	Chapter 2
God wants Judah to repent. Philistia, Moab and Ammon will be destroyed and turned over to the people of Judah. Cush and Assyria will be judged and destroyed.			

2	5	9	Chapter 3
Jerusalem's rulers, prophets and priests are unrighteous. Therefore, God will send them into exile. When they repent, he will restore them to their land.			

Haggai
Overview

I The LORD's Call to Rebuild the Temple 1:1–15

II The LORD's Promise to Restore the Glory 2:1–9

III The LORD's Blessings on a Defiled People 2:10–19

IV The LORD Makes Zerubbabel his Signet Ring 2:20–23

The prophet Haggai
Haggai was a prophet who encouraged the people to rebuild the Temple in Jerusalem.

The prophecy of Haggai consists of four short passages, encouraging those who had returned from the Babylonian Exile to make progress in rebuilding the Temple. The group who returned had speedily set about rebuilding the altar of the Temple and re-laying the foundations of the building, but there progress halted. It is clear from Haggai 1:4 that more secular buildings became more important. The Books of Ezra–Nehemiah also show that they were beset by opposition from the neighbouring Samaritans and from the local people, who no doubt resented this tight-knit band of returned exiles. When Darius came to the Persian throne (520 BC) the two prophets Haggai and Zechariah induced the Persian governor of the province of Yehud to search out the documentation in the royal archives decreeing that the Temple should be rebuilt. Accordingly, it was completed in five years.

Haggai's arguments are on the one hand that the drought and the meagre harvests are the result of the people's lassitude in rebuilding the Temple (1:7–11, 2:15–19), and that everything else is made unclean by the uncleanness of the unfinished building – ritual uncleanness is catching. On the other hand, when the Temple is completed, the glory of the LORD dwelling in it, and the blessings that this brings, will surpass the glory of the pre-exilic Temple (2:1–9).

---

⑦	
Chapter **1**	Haggai encourages the people who have returned from exile to rebuild God's Temple in Jerusalem.

⑦	
Chapter **2**	God promises to restore Israel's glory and he reassures Zerubbabel that he is doing what God wants to have done. In fact, he is like a signet ring on God's finger.

Chapters 1–2: **Commentary**

The Temple eventually built gives its name to the period of Jewish history, 'the Second Temple Period'. Materially it was less splendid than Solomon's Temple, but spiritually it was made just as important by the presence of God. This Temple was rebuilt by King Herod the Great at the time of Christ, and some portion of these walls still stand. The Roman author Pliny says that this Temple made Jerusalem 'far the most distinguished city of the East'.

Zechariah
Overview

The prophecy of Zechariah falls into two halves. The first half, chapters 1–8, pairs with Haggai, for both are prophets of the return from Exile, concerned with the rebuilding of the Temple and with the purity of the land. This part is internally dated to the years 520–518 BC (1:7 and 7:1). It consists of eight concentrically arranged visions, surrounded by an editorial framework. The two central visions (chapters 3–4) convey the stability of the rebuilt Temple and the purity of the two anointed ones, the high priest and Zerubbabel, the governor. The second part of Zechariah (chapters 9–14) is often classified as completely separate, a Deutero-Zechariah. It is much more strongly messianic and apocalyptic in tone. The book ends with an apocalyptic scene, the eschatological battle on the Mount of Olives, which will finally establish the rule of God over all nations.

Chapter 1: Commentary

Each of the visions is explained by an angel. Such angelic explanations of the meaning of a vision or an event are standard in the Bible and in Jewish literature of around the time of Christ. 'Angel' means 'messenger'. So in the New Testament the meaning of Mary's pregnancy is explained by the Angel Gabriel, and the meaning of the empty tomb of Jesus is also explained by an angel.

The men and horses among the myrtle trees signify God's concern for Jerusalem and the rebuilding of the Temple. The four horns represent the destruction of Israel's enemies.

Chapter **1**

A man with a measuring line measures Jerusalem, which will become a city without walls. Babylon will be destroyed. God will bless his people.

Chapter **2**

Satan makes accusations against the filthy, poorly clothed high priest Joshua. The angel of the LORD rebukes Satan, cleans up Joshua and grants him authority over the Temple. Judah is forgiven.

Chapter **3**

A gold lampstand with two olive trees next to it symbolises those anointed to serve the LORD of all the earth. Zerubbabel will complete the rebuilding of the Temple.

Chapter **4**

A flying scroll represents the curse against thieves and liars. A woman in a basket represents wickedness, which two winged women carry to Babylon.

Chapter **5**

Four chariots represent the four spirits of heaven going from God's presence out to the whole world. Zechariah had a crown made and placed it on the head of the high priest, Joshua.

Chapter **6**

God is not interested in fasting. He wants the people to administer justice, cease oppressing the poor and weak and stop planning evil against each other.

Chapter **7**

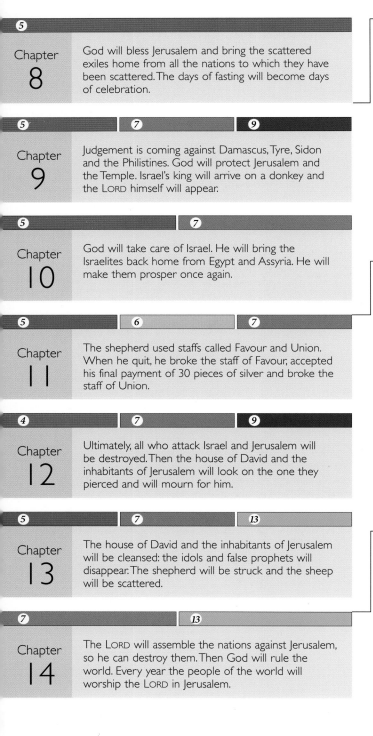

Chapter 8

God will bless Jerusalem and bring the scattered exiles home from all the nations to which they have been scattered. The days of fasting will become days of celebration.

Chapter 9

Judgement is coming against Damascus, Tyre, Sidon and the Philistines. God will protect Jerusalem and the Temple. Israel's king will arrive on a donkey and the LORD himself will appear.

Chapter 10

God will take care of Israel. He will bring the Israelites back home from Egypt and Assyria. He will make them prosper once again.

Chapter 11

The shepherd used staffs called Favour and Union. When he quit, he broke the staff of Favour, accepted his final payment of 30 pieces of silver and broke the staff of Union.

Chapter 12

Ultimately, all who attack Israel and Jerusalem will be destroyed. Then the house of David and the inhabitants of Jerusalem will look on the one they pierced and will mourn for him.

Chapter 13

The house of David and the inhabitants of Jerusalem will be cleansed: the idols and false prophets will disappear. The shepherd will be struck and the sheep will be scattered.

Chapter 14

The LORD will assemble the nations against Jerusalem, so he can destroy them. Then God will rule the world. Every year the people of the world will worship the LORD in Jerusalem.

Thus says the LORD of hosts: 'Peoples shall yet come, the inhabitants of many cities; the inhabitants of one city shall go to another, saying, "Come, let us go to entreat the favour of the LORD, and to seek the LORD of hosts; I myself am going." Many peoples and strong nations shall come to seek the LORD of hosts in Jerusalem, and to entreat the favour of the LORD.'

Thus says the LORD of hosts: 'In those days ten men from nations of every language shall take hold of a Jew, grasping his garment and saying, "Let us go with you, for we have heard that God is with you."'

Zechariah 8:20–23

Chapter 11: **Commentary**

The allegory of the shepherds. Shepherds often symbolise the leaders of the people. The prophet acts out an allegory about shepherds who care only about their own advantage and destroy the people. When he breaks the second staff, 'Union', this may symbolise the end of the union of the territories of Judah and Israel.

The prophet's allegorical play must be directed against contemporary rulers, but we do not know whom. The wages paid to the shepherd, 30 silver shekels, is an insultingly small sum, the price of a slave. This passage (verses 12–13), and the same insultingly small sum, is used by Matthew 27.3–9 to comment on Judas' betrayal of Jesus and his later remorse. There it is combined with a passage about Jeremiah's purchase of a field, and the whole passage is attributed to Jeremiah.

For I will gather all the nations against Jerusalem to battle, and the city shall be taken and the houses looted and the women raped; half the city shall go into exile, but the rest of the people shall not be cut off from the city. Then the LORD will go forth and fight against those nations as when he fights on a day of battle. On that day his feet shall stand on the Mount of Olives, which lies before Jerusalem on the east; and the Mount of Olives shall be split in two from east to west by a very wide valley; so that half of the Mount shall withdraw northwards, and the other half southwards. And you shall flee by the valley of the LORD's mountain, for the valley between the mountains shall reach to Azal; and you shall flee as you fled from the earthquake in the days of King Uzziah of Judah. Then the LORD my God will come, and all the holy ones with him.

Zechariah 14:2–5

Malachi

Overview

The name 'Malachi' means 'my messenger'; it may be a personal name, or may be taken from 3:1, 'I am going to send my messenger to prepare a way before me'. The book is consciously a preparation for the great Day of the coming of the LORD, and so to round off the book of the Twelve Prophets, celebrating the enduring love of the LORD through history (1:1–5), as Hosea celebrated it at the beginning of the Book. It is a spirituality based on the Temple and the Law, written during the Persian period, in order to recall the returned exiles to fidelity, at a time when the first enthusiasm of the return from exile had worn off. Each section of the prophecy rebukes a group for their lack of fidelity to the covenant and quotes their feeble excuses. The final appendix both looks backward to Moses, who gave them the Law and mediated the Covenant, and forward to the coming of Elijah, the final messenger. Jesus reiterates the same belief (Mark 9:11–13) regarding John the Baptist as this Elijah.

Chapter 2: **Commentary**

There are two teachings on marriage here. The first is against marrying 'the daughter of a foreign god'. This prohibition against mixed marriages was designed to prevent the loosening of the strict religious code of the returned exiles by the less strict way of life practised by the local people. Ezra 9 also has the same legislation for the post-exilic community. The second is against divorce. The only legislation in the Law was that if a divorce occurred it must be certified by a document (Deuteronomy 24:1); divorce itself was not forbidden. This new teaching is put forward also by Jesus.

Chapter 3: **Commentary**

The post-exilic community undertook (Nehemiah 10:37) to pay a tenth of their produce to the Levites, and they in turn a tenth to the priests, according to the legislation of Numbers 18:21–32. This was obviously being neglected.

3	7	
Israel questions whether God really loves them. He tells them they've shown him contempt by bringing him diseased and disfigured animals for sacrifice. They need to stop.		Chapter 1

3	7	
The prophet warns the priests to honour God and to listen to him. He wants them to teach what is good and true. He wants them to keep their promises. God hates divorce and injustice.		Chapter 2

3	7	
God will send his messenger to prepare his way. Though many Israelites have been unfaithful, there is a remnant that is obedient and who worship God.		Chapter 3

3	7	9	
A day of judgement is coming when God will destroy the wicked. But he will send the prophet Elijah before that dreadful Day of the LORD comes, so many people will repent.			Chapter 4

The New Testament

The earliest writings of the New Testament were probably the letters of Paul to Christian communities around the Eastern Mediterranean. Most of these Paul had founded himself, and they turned to him for enlightenment when they had problems, regarding him as their father in the faith. The letters to the Thessalonians touch on worries about the Second Coming of Christ. The First Letter to the Corinthians was sparked by a report of disorders brought by messengers from a deaconess of the troublesome and quarrelsome community he had founded at Corinth; they also brought a list of questions for him to solve. Perhaps the greatest of the letters was written to the Christian communities in Rome, a Church he had not founded, preparing to enlist their help for an apostolic mission to the far West. We do not know whether this mission ever took place.

It was only a decade or two after these letters that Mark, a brilliant storyteller, was invited to put together the stories about Jesus that had long been circulating in the Christian communities. He concentrated on showing the wonder of Jesus' personality, and Jesus' acceptance that it was only through suffering that he could reach the perfection of obedience to his Father. This must also have been an encouragement to the Christian communities who were already suffering some kind of persecution. If we accept the most usual theory of the origin of the Gospels, some years later two other catechists, whom we know as Matthew and Luke, were independently asked to combine with this account a collection of Jesus' sayings. Each had his own audience and his own special message. Matthew was writing to a community of Christians of Jewish origin, showing that Jesus was the fulfilment of all the hopes of Judaism. Luke, on the other hand, wrote his account for a richer, Gentile community, stressing the dangers of wealth and the need to use wealth wisely for the disadvantaged. The same author also wrote a second scroll, recounting how the faith spread from the first, ideal witnessing Christian community in Jerusalem to the capital of the Roman Empire 'at the ends of the earth'. In this he emphasised how every move in the spread of the faith beyond Judaism had been guided by the Spirit of Jesus, and how it was the stubborn rejection by the Jews that had repeatedly forced Paul to turn to the Gentiles.

Wholly independent of these accounts of the ministry, death and resurrection of Jesus is another account, based on the witness of the 'Beloved Disciple', whom tradition identifies with the apostle John. Whether it is earlier or later cannot now be established. Its theology is certainly more developed, and this has led many to hold that it is later than the other three Gospels. Here the emphasis is no longer on the proclamation of the rule of God. The focus has moved from message to messenger, for Jesus shimmers as a transcendent personality, at once wholly human and wholly divine, the Word of God through whom the world was made, and yet sharing with us fully human emotions and exhaustion. His humiliating death by crucifixion is seen as his own royal triumph, a climax over which he has complete control, leading to his first gift of the Spirit to the new Christian community formed by his mother and his Beloved Disciple.

The New Testament ends with some further letters. Among these is the great Letter to the Hebrews, which dwells on the superiority of the priesthood of Christ to the Law-based priesthood of Judaism and the superiority of the goal of Christian pilgrimage to the pilgrimage of the Exodus from Egypt. There follow seven so-called 'catholic' or 'universal' epistles, seemingly written by James, Peter, John and Jude (in descending order of length) about Christian morality and behaviour. Finally, the Book of Revelation, written to encourage Christians persecuted for standing out against Roman state idolatry, brings the message to a climax with its picture of the triumphant New Jerusalem, of which the Lord God and the Lamb are the light and the Temple.

Introduction to the Gospels (Matthew–John)

Jesus as saviour
The Gospels were written to explain that Jesus was the Messiah, the son of God, who died for the sins of the world and rose again.

The reader of the New Testament may wonder at the fact that there are four books, written by different authors, each of which describes the life of Christ. When one considers the nature and importance of parallelism in the Hebrew mind, perhaps the repetition is not as surprising. Where a Western writer would be concerned to present a single, unified account, the Jewish mind wished for a stereoscopic view; instead of relying on a single window into the life of Christ, the modern reader is able to view his life from more than one point of view, thereby getting a much clearer picture.

The careful reader of the Gospels will notice that the similarities between Matthew, Mark and Luke are much greater than simply three authors telling the same story. In fact, these three Gospels often have nearly identical wording, which raises at least three questions:

• Who wrote these Gospels?
• Were the writers dependent on each other, and if so, who depended on whom?
• What other sources did the authors of the Gospels make use of, that they might have had in common?

It seems clear that Matthew incorporated almost the entire Gospel of Mark into his narrative, although he condensed the accounts of the miracles, probably for thematic reasons. In addition to Mark, the author of Matthew inserted numerous sayings of Jesus, apparently taken from a source that both he and Luke had in common. This source is designated as 'Q' by scholars. Q is an abbreviation for *Quelle*, the German word for 'source'. The order of the Gospels is as follows:

1. Mark
2. Matthew, making use of Mark and Q.
3. Luke, making use of Mark, Q and other sources.
4. John, which apparently did not make reference to the earlier written Gospels, and is not, therefore, part of the synoptic problem.

Matthew

Overview

The Gospel according to Matthew builds on Mark, the first Gospel. Matthew adds some of the material that he shares with Luke, probably derived from the source Q, which no longer exists. He also adds some of his own material, and of course he presents the Gospel in his own way, with his own emphases. This may be regarded as five books (corresponding to the five books of Moses) with an introduction and a conclusion added. The most obvious feature is that he includes a great deal of Jesus' teaching, not given in Mark, building it into five great discourses in a balanced pattern:

The Sermon on the Mount: entry into the
    kingdom 5–7
The community on its mission 10
Images of the kingdom 13
The community together 18
Rewards and punishments: the kingdom
    completed 24–25

Matthew has been the favourite Gospel for many Christians throughout history. We do not know who the author was, but the Gospel was attached early to his name. Apart from the lists of the Twelve disciples, he is mentioned only in this Gospel: the story of the Call of Levi in Mark

---

15   **16**

Chapter 1

Acting on the message of an angel, Joseph adopts Jesus, miraculously conceived by Mary, making him a member of the royal house of David.

17

Chapter 2

Wise men are led by a star to Bethlehem. As Moses escaped from Pharaoh, so Jesus escapes Herod's attempt to kill this rival king of the Jews.

7   **17**

Chapter 3

John the Baptist proclaims that Jesus is the fulfilment of Isaiah's prophecy. The Spirit of God descends on Jesus as John baptises him in the Jordan.

Chapters 1–2: **Commentary**

The Gospel of Mark showed the Spirit descending on Jesus at his baptism, but what was he before then? These stories show that at birth he was adopted into the House of David. His story repeats that of Moses, so he is a second Moses. In both ways he fulfils the hopes of Judaism. Herod, the Jew, rejects Jesus while the Gentile Wise Men revere him – just as at the end the Jewish high priest rejects him and the Gentile Pilate declares him innocent.

When they saw that the star had stopped, they were overwhelmed with joy. On entering the house, they saw the child with Mary his mother; and they knelt down and paid him homage. Then, opening their treasure-chests, they offered him gifts of gold, frankincense, and myrrh. And having been warned in a dream not to return to Herod, they left for their own country by another road.

Matthew 2:10–12

recounts in Matthew the call of Matthew (9:9). Two characteristics of Matthew's teaching stand out: first, he puts things in order, gathering together a series of ten miracles, and arranging Jesus' teaching on particular subjects into five great matching sermons. Second, his use of imagery is superb: he uses plenty of images, often animal images, especially in contrasting pairs. Most of all, however, Matthew is the Gospel of Judaism: he writes for Christians sprung from Judaism, assuming that his audience know about Jewish customs and Jewish Law. He uses Jewish forms of teaching, and stresses that Christianity is the fulfilment of Judaism and all its hopes. Jesus is a second David and a new Moses, completing everything that was written in the scriptures about God's chosen servant. The Christian community, Jesus' own community, has come into the place of the community of God in the Old Testament; the Twelve chosen disciples are like the founders of the 12 tribes of Israel. Persecution of the followers of Jesus by Jews is to him the more bitter for that. Reflecting some years later than Mark, he also sees and shows more clearly the majesty of the Risen Christ even in the earthly Jesus, whom Peter names 'son of God'. He is also aware of the constant presence of Emmanuel, 'God with us' in the community Jesus founded on the apostles.

Chapters 5–7: **Commentary**

Like Moses, Jesus sits down on the mountain to teach his new Law. The eight Beatitudes teach basic Christian attitudes, then the six antitheses perfect the teachings of the Law, making some more strict (divorce), some more demanding (no revenge) and some more interior (forgiveness).

Chapters 8–9: **Commentary**

Matthew, the systematic teacher, collects a series of ten miracles to show Jesus fulfilling the messianic prophecies of the Old Testament. He stresses the importance of faith in Jesus for a miracle to happen.

8 · **15** Jesus is tested by the Devil in the desert for 40 days and 40 nights. He calls his first four disciples.		Chapter 4
3 · **5** The Sermon on the Mount: Jesus teaches the Beatitudes and completes the Jewish Law.		Chapter 5
3 The Sermon on the Mount: how Christians should give generously, pray and fast.		Chapter 6
3 The Sermon on the Mount: trust in God – the golden rule and the two ways, broad and narrow.		Chapter 7
8 · **15** Miracles of healing, the call of Matthew and the demands of following Jesus.		Chapter 8
8 More miracles, and Jesus eats with the outcasts and sinners.		Chapter 9
3 · **16** Instructions to the Twelve disciples on how to spread the Good News. The disciples need courage, generosity, perseverance and faith in the Spirit.		Chapter 10

1	9	12

Chapter 11

Jesus explains his mission to the Baptist: he is fulfilling the prophecies. He condemns those who reject him and welcomes those who accept his light yoke.

3	7	15

Chapter 12

Jesus is confronted by Pharisees who criticise him for failure to keep the Law. Even his own family reject him.

6

Chapter 13

Parables of the kingdom of heaven: the sower, the wheat, the mustard seed and the yeast, the treasure and the pearl, the net of fish.

8	17

Chapter 14

The death of John the Baptist, the feeding of the 5,000, Peter walks on the water to meet Jesus.

3	8

Chapter 15

Discussions about ritual purity, more healings, the feeding of the 4,000.

3	7

Chapter 16

Opposition from the Pharisees. Peter's recognition of Jesus as Messiah and son of God. He is the rock on which Jesus' community is built. But this leads on to the first prophecy of the Passion.

8

Chapter 17

The Transfiguration of Jesus and the second prophecy of the Passion.

'Come to me, all you that are weary and are carrying heavy burdens, and I will give you rest. Take my yoke upon you, and learn from me; for I am gentle and humble in heart, and you will find rest for your souls. For my yoke is easy, and my burden is light.'

Matthew 11:28–30

He came to his home town and began to teach the people in their synagogue, so that they were astounded and said,

'Where did this man get this wisdom and these deeds of power? Is not this the carpenter's son? Is not his mother called Mary? And are not his brothers James and Joseph and Simon and Judas? And are not all his sisters with us? Where then did this man get all this?' And they took offence at him.

But Jesus said to them, 'Prophets are not without honour except in their own country and in their own house.'

Matthew 13:54–57

Chapter 13: **Commentary**

Matthew adds other parables to those of Mark. Most of his parables are contrasts: good and bad wheat, good and bad fish. They all have the final judgement in view. Is the scribe of verse 52, mixing new and old, Matthew himself?

Chapter 15: **Commentary**

Jesus sweeps away hypocrisy and the Jewish use of tradition to avoid genuine, human obligations. Then he cures the daughter of a Gentile woman who believes in him as Lord and son of David. A second miraculous feeding (of 4,000) seems to be for the Gentiles.

And Jesus answered him, 'Blessed are you, Simon son of Jonah! For flesh and blood has not revealed this to you, but my Father in heaven. And I tell you, you are Peter, and on this rock I will build my church, and the gates of Hades will not prevail against it. I will give you the keys of the kingdom of heaven, and whatever you bind on earth will be bound in heaven, and whatever you loose on earth will be loosed in heaven.'

Matthew 16:17–19

At that time the disciples came to Jesus and asked, 'Who is the greatest in the kingdom of heaven?'

He called a child, whom he put among them, and said, 'Truly I tell you, unless you change and become like children, you will never enter the kingdom of heaven. Whoever becomes humble like this child is the greatest in the kingdom of heaven.'

Matthew 18:1–4

Chapter 18: **Commentary**

Jesus teaches about service within the Christian community, the need to search out the lost sheep, and especially the need for mutual forgiveness. He promises to stay with his disciples, and gives authority to his Church.

Then Peter came and said to him, 'Lord, if another member of the church sins against me, how often should I forgive? As many as seven times?' Jesus said to him, 'Not seven times, but, I tell you, seventy-seven times.'

Matthew 18:21–22

But Jesus called them to him and said, 'You know that the rulers of the Gentiles lord it over them, and their great ones are tyrants over them. It will not be so among you; but whoever wishes to be great among you must be your servant, and whoever wishes to be first among you must be your slave; just as the Son of Man came not to be served but to serve, and to give his life a ransom for many.'

Matthew 20:25–28

3		6
Instructions to the Twelve disciples on how to live in community.		Chapter **18**

3	
Jesus' teaching on divorce, celibacy and self-denial.	Chapter **19**

3		6		8
The parable of the vineyard labourers. The third prophecy of the Passion and teaching on leadership with service.				Chapter **20**

Feeding of the 4,000
Jesus miraculously provided food for 4,000 men starting with just a few fish and seven loaves of bread.

6 **8** **17**

Chapter 21

Jesus fulfils the prophecies by entering Jerusalem as son of David. When the elders question his authority he replies with two parables about the failure of the leaders.

3 **6** **10**

Chapter 22

Parable of the wedding feast and controversies about tribute to Caesar, resurrection of the dead and the greatest of all commandments.

3 **9**

Chapter 23

Final, sevenfold indictment of the scribes and Pharisees: do what they say, but do not follow their hypocritical example.

7

Chapter 24

The coming of the Son of Man – parables of readiness.

6

Chapter 25

The coming of the Son of Man – parables of the ten wedding attendants, the talents and the sheep and goats.

7 **17**

Chapter 26

Jesus' Last Supper with his disciples, his arrest and appearance before the Sanhedrin, and Peter's denials.

17

Chapter 27

Jesus is condemned to death by Pilate and is crucified.

8 **17**

Chapter 28

The empty tomb's significance is confirmed by an earthquake and a meeting of the Risen Christ with the women. Jesus' final blessing promises his presence in the Church. He sends the apostles to spread his word.

...and one of them, a lawyer, asked him a question to test him. 'Teacher, which commandment in the law is the greatest?'

He said to him, 'You shall love the Lord your God with all your heart, and with all your soul, and with all your mind. This is the greatest and first commandment. And a second is like it: You shall love your neighbour as yourself. On these two commandments hang all the law and the prophets.'
Matthew 22:35–40

Chapters 24–25: **Commentary**

Matthew fills out Mark's warning on the coming of the Son of Man. He adds four contrast parables about readiness for the final coming: some will be ready; some will be unready and will be taken off to eternal punishment. For Jesus the moment of decision was his own coming, the inauguration of the kingdom of God. For Matthew it is the final judgement before the Son of Man enthroned in glory.

Chapters 26–27: **Commentary**

Matthew stresses the part of the Jewish leaders in getting Jesus condemned. Judas commits suicide in fulfilment of the scriptures. Pilate three times declares Jesus innocent and washes his hands. The crowds accept responsibility for themselves and the next generation, and the chief priests and elders mock Jesus in the words of scripture. An earthquake and the resurrection of the sacred dead show that the crucifixion is the Day of the Lord.

But the chief priests, taking the pieces of silver, said, 'It is not lawful to put them into the treasury, since they are blood money.' After conferring together, they used them to buy the potter's field as a place to bury foreigners. For this reason that field has been called the Field of Blood to this day. Then was fulfilled what had been spoken through the prophet Jeremiah, 'And they took the thirty pieces of silver, the price of the one on whom a price had been set, on whom some of the people of Israel had set a price, and they gave them for the potter's field, as the Lord commanded me.'
Matthew 27:6–10

Chapter 28: **Commentary**

A major theme of this Gospel is the divine presence of Jesus in his Church. At the beginning he is named 'Emmanuel' (God with us), and the end he promises his strength as the Son of Man with power in heaven and on earth. This brackets the Gospel. In the middle (18:18–20) he promises his continued presence and authority.

Mark

Overview

Baptism of Jesus
Jesus was baptised in the River Jordan by his cousin, John the Baptist.

The Gospel of Mark was the first to be written. In it Mark retells the stories of Jesus that were circulating in the Christian community. He has the brilliant artistry of an oral storyteller with an eye for visual detail. He builds on a careful plan to show how difficult it was for the disciples to understand who Jesus was. In the introduction the reader (or listener) learns who Jesus is. The turning point is Peter's recognition that Jesus was the Messiah. After this Jesus begins to teach that he can reach his fulfilment only through suffering and death. Each of the two great revelations is symbolically preceded by a story of a blind man receiving his sight. The full revelation comes only when Jesus accepts the three titles before the high priest. Mark is interested above all in the personality of Jesus, his amazing power to attract, to heal, to reconcile and to forgive. He stresses also how slow the disciples are to understand: Jesus was an unexpected Messiah, and the message of suffering is never easy to accept.

We do not know the date when Mark wrote his Gospel. The concern of chapter 13 with the horrors of the Sack of Jerusalem in AD 70 has led many to think that it was composed within a few years of that event, which was either pending in the near future or reverberating in the recent past. An early tradition links Mark with the apostle Peter, but scholars are divided about the reliability of this tradition.

Chapter 2: Commentary

The hostility deepens as the chapter progresses, until finally in 3:6 comes the decision to eliminate Jesus. In fact the scribes and lawyers take no part in the death of Jesus. Were his disagreements with them really so fateful? Lawyers are perfectly used to arguing the interpretations of law, even if Jesus consistently favoured a different, gentler and more humane viewpoint. With the custodians of the Temple and Jesus' demonstration there it was a different matter.

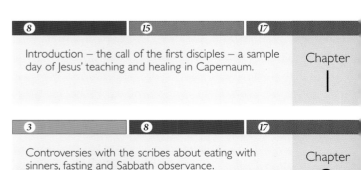

| 8 | 15 | 17 |

Introduction – the call of the first disciples – a sample day of Jesus' teaching and healing in Capernaum.

Chapter
1

| 3 | 8 | 17 |

Controversies with the scribes about eating with sinners, fasting and Sabbath observance.

Chapter
2

8	**15**	**17**

Chapter 3

More controversies: they decide to kill Jesus. Jesus appoints the Twelve disciples, but is rejected by the scribes and even by his own family.

6	**8**	**17**

Chapter 4

Parable of the sower: Jesus reflects on the meagre beginnings and great promise. Jesus calms a storm on the lake.

8	**15**	**17**

Chapter 5

Miracles: the Gerasene demoniac and the pigs; a woman with a haemorrhage and Jairus' 12-year-old daughter are restored to health.

3	**8**	**17**

Chapter 6

Jesus is rejected at Nazareth. The first mission of the Twelve disciples. John the Baptist is beheaded. Miracles at the lakeside.

3	**8**	**17**

Chapter 7

Controversies over clean and unclean food and the traditions of the Pharisees. Jesus cures a Gentile woman's daughter and ventures beyond Galilee.

3	**8**	**17**

Chapter 8

Feeding of the 4,000. The cure of a blind man at Bethsaida. Peter's recognises Jesus as Messiah and Jesus gives the first prophecy of his Passion.

...and the crowd came together again, so that they could not even eat. When his family heard it, they went out to restrain him, for people were saying, 'He has gone out of his mind.'

And the scribes who came down from Jerusalem said, 'He has Beelzebul, and by the ruler of the demons he casts out demons.'

Mark 3:20–22

He lived among the tombs; and no one could restrain him any more, even with a chain; for he had often been restrained with shackles and chains, but the chains he wrenched apart, and the shackles he broke in pieces; and no one had the strength to subdue him. Night and day among the tombs and on the mountains he was always howling and bruising himself with stones. When he saw Jesus from a distance, he ran and bowed down before him; and he shouted at the top of his voice, 'What have you to do with me, Jesus, Son of the Most High God? I adjure you by God, do not torment me.'

Mark 5:3–7

Jesus went on with his disciples to the villages of Caesarea Philippi; and on the way he asked his disciples, 'Who do people say that I am?' And they answered him, 'John the Baptist; and others, Elijah; and still others, one of the prophets.' He asked them, 'But who do you say that I am?' Peter answered him, 'You are the Messiah.' And he sternly ordered them not to tell anyone about him.

Mark 8:27–30

Chapter 8: **Commentary**

Peter's blurted acknowledgement is the turning point of the story. He realises that Jesus is the Messiah. But in Judaism the Messiah was a glorious warrior. The figure of the suffering servant of the Lord was never connected with the Messiah. It was difficult for the disciples to get their heads around this paradox – that the Messiah and his followers would reach their goal only through suffering and humiliation.

Transfiguration of Christ
Jesus took Peter, James and John up a mountain where they met Moses and Elijah and Jesus appeared glorified.

Chapter 13: **Commentary**

This chapter is of a different stamp to the rest of the Gospel, one single discourse instead of many little incidents. It is fenced in by warnings to 'watch out' and 'keep awake', since no one knows the time of the disaster. Two ruling scriptural quotations from Daniel are to be fulfilled: the *disastrous abomination* (verse 14=Daniel 9:27) and *the coming of the son of man* (verse 26=Daniel 7:13). The desecration of the Temple at the Sack in AD 70 is seen as the Day of the Lord. It was indeed a judgement on Israel, and a liberation for Christians because it meant that Jewish Christianity would no longer be able to dominate Christian practice.

Chapter 14: **Commentary**

We cannot now tell whether the Last Supper with Jesus was a regular Passover meal. We have only a partial account, two incidents, the identification of the betrayer and the institution of the Eucharist. Whether it was on Passover night or not, Jesus made it a celebration of his own new covenant with his disciples, which was to be perpetuated.

Peter said to him, 'Even though all become deserters, I will not.'

Jesus said to him, 'Truly I tell you, this day, this very night, before the cock crows twice, you will deny me three times.' But he said vehemently, 'Even though I must die with you, I will not deny you.' And all of them said the same.

Mark 14:29–31

Chapter 15: **Commentary**

The Romans alone had the right to impose the death penalty. Anyway, in the case of a provincial, the governor could simply order an execution, without any due trial. Pilate knew that he was out of his depth in the intricacies of Jewish Law. He was only a visiting outsider in Jerusalem, which was administered by the high priest. The high priest did not want a repetition of the scene in the Temple, particularly at a festival, so he concocted a political charge. For ten years the Jews had consistently outwitted Pilate. He may have smelt a rat, but he caved in to the high priest. Crucifixion was a humiliating, agonising death, which even the Romans considered barbaric.

Chapter 16: **Commentary**

The Gospel of Mark ends at verse 8. The rest, a resumé from other sources, in a wholly different style, was added later. When the other, later Gospels had given their meetings with the Risen Lord, it seemed that no Gospel was complete without them. The original Markan Gospel stopped open-ended, stressing the awe and terror of the women at this divine intervention, and wide open to many possibilities.

③	⑧	⑮

Jesus is seen in glory by the disciples. He cures an epileptic boy and prophesies the Passion for a second time. The disciples again misunderstand.

Chapter 9

③	⑧	⑰

Sayings on divorce and renunciation. The third prophecy of the Passion, again misunderstood. Blind Bartimaeus is given his sight at Jericho.

Chapter 10

③	⑧	⑰

Jesus arrives in Jerusalem and cleanses the Temple. The chief priests challenge his authority.

Chapter 11

③	⑥	⑰

The parable of the vineyard. Controversies with different groups about tribute, life after death, the greatest commandment and the Messiah.

Chapter 12

⑦

The eschatological discourse – reflections on the Day of the LORD and on the Sack of Jerusalem.

Chapter 13

⑰

The Last Supper, Jesus in Gethsemane, Jesus is arrested and appears before the Sanhedrin, Peter denies knowing him.

Chapter 14

⑰

Jesus condemned to death by Pilate, crucified and buried.

Chapter 15

⑧	⑰

Jesus' tomb is discovered empty by the women, who run away, terrified. A summary of meetings with the Risen Christ and their consequences.

Chapter 16

Luke

Overview

Luke accompanied Paul on many of his journeys, and wrote two volumes, not only an account of Jesus' ministry but also a record of the first expansion of the Christian community. His Gospel and the Acts of the Apostles share the same interests, and sophisticated style and vocabulary. His prefaces show that Luke moves in a grander world than the other Gospel-writers, a business world of bankers, creditors and swindlers. So Luke warns repeatedly of the dangers of wealth and considers especially the needs of the poor, the outcasts and oppressed. He is writing for the Gentiles around the Roman world, and stresses that Jesus came to save all peoples, men and women, Jews and Gentiles. He is also eager to show

Chapters 1–2: **Commentary**

Jesus is presented in parallel with his cousin John the Baptist, showing that, great as John is, Jesus is even greater: two annunciations, two births, two circumcisions. They both grow up in the world of Old Testament piety and devotion, where the promises to the poor and humble of Israel are to be fulfilled. No magi with gifts of gold, but only empty-handed shepherd boys in a stable. Already here Luke shows the equal importance of women with men, for they too are presented in parallel: Zechariah and Mary, Simeon and Anna. So later we will see Jesus raise to life a widow's son as well as a man's daughter, a man searching for a lost sheep and a woman for a lost coin, repentant Zacchaeus and the woman weeping at Jesus' feet.

5   **8**   **15**

Chapter
1

The parents of John the Baptist learn that he will be born. Gabriel tells Mary that she will give birth to the Messiah, even though she is a virgin. John the Baptist is born.

15   **17**

Chapter
2

Jesus is born in Bethlehem. Angels announce his birth to shepherds. Simeon blesses Jesus on the day of his circumcision. At the age of 12, Jesus stays behind at the Temple.

16   **17**

Chapter
3

John the Baptist baptises people and tells them that the Messiah is coming. John baptises Jesus. God announces that Jesus is his son. The genealogy of Jesus from Joseph to Adam.

Guided by the Spirit, Simeon came into the temple; and when the parents brought in the child Jesus, to do for him what was customary under the law, Simeon took him in his arms and praised God, saying, 'Master, now you are dismissing your servant in peace, according to your word; for my eyes have seen your salvation, which you have prepared in the presence of all peoples, a light for revelation to the Gentiles and for glory to your people Israel.'

Luke 2:27–32

that Rome and Christianity can live together in harmony. He presents a Jesus who is full of compassion, the final messenger of God, in the tradition of the prophets, full of the Spirit of God. Like Matthew, Luke follows the pattern of Mark, but adds more material about Jesus' teachings, particularly on prayer, poverty and perseverance. Some of the material is drawn from a source he shares with Matthew, some is unique to this Gospel. His parables are particularly full of insight, painting lively and complex characters who do the right thing for the wrong reason, and vividly express their joys and worries.

The Annunciation
The angels' Annunciation to the shepherds.

Chapter 4: **Commentary**

In the synagogue at Nazareth, full of the Spirit, Jesus gives his manifesto, parallel to the Sermon on the Mount in Matthew. Jesus fulfils the prophecies to the Gentile nations. So we shall hear the story of the grateful Samaritan leper, the parable of the Good Samaritan, the parable of the great feast to which Gentiles too are invited. This programme leads to the missions of the Acts of the Apostles.

Chapter 8: **Commentary**

Luke underlines the support of the women for Jesus (verses 1–3). Mary also has special prominence in this Gospel: in Mark 3:33–34 Jesus is hesitant towards his family; by contrast, here (and 11:27) Mary is the model of the disciple, just as at the Annunciation she is the model of hearing the word of God and keeping it. She will be present with the community in the upper room in Acts 1:14.

8	15	17

Jesus is tested by the Devil for 40 days in the desert. In the synagogue at Nazareth, filled with the Spirit, he lays out his programme as God's messenger to the poor and to Gentiles.

Chapter
4

3	8	17

Jesus calls his first disciples. He heals a leper and a paralysed man. He calls Matthew as his disciple and has dinner with tax collectors. Jesus is questioned about why his disciples don't fast.

Chapter
5

3	5	6

Jesus heals a man on the Sabbath, appoints 12 disciples and teaches four beatitudes to the poor. He teaches the need for compassion, generosity and integrity.

Chapter
6

8	17

Jesus heals a Roman centurion's servant and raises a widow's son to life. He praises John the Baptist. He forgives a sinful woman who weeps at his feet.

Chapter
7

6	8	15

Jesus tells the parables of the sower and the lamp. He calms the storm, and drives demons from a man and into a herd of pigs. Jesus heals a woman and raises a dead girl back to life.

Chapter
8

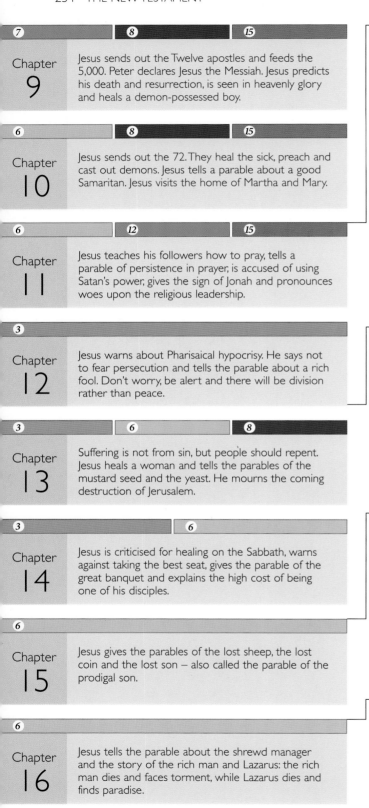

7 | **8** | **15**

Chapter
9

Jesus sends out the Twelve apostles and feeds the 5,000. Peter declares Jesus the Messiah. Jesus predicts his death and resurrection, is seen in heavenly glory and heals a demon-possessed boy.

6 | **8** | **15**

Chapter
10

Jesus sends out the 72. They heal the sick, preach and cast out demons. Jesus tells a parable about a good Samaritan. Jesus visits the home of Martha and Mary.

6 | **12** | **15**

Chapter
11

Jesus teaches his followers how to pray, tells a parable of persistence in prayer, is accused of using Satan's power, gives the sign of Jonah and pronounces woes upon the religious leadership.

3

Chapter
12

Jesus warns about Pharisaical hypocrisy. He says not to fear persecution and tells the parable about a rich fool. Don't worry, be alert and there will be division rather than peace.

3 | **6** | **8**

Chapter
13

Suffering is not from sin, but people should repent. Jesus heals a woman and tells the parables of the mustard seed and the yeast. He mourns the coming destruction of Jerusalem.

3 | **6**

Chapter
14

Jesus is criticised for healing on the Sabbath, warns against taking the best seat, gives the parable of the great banquet and explains the high cost of being one of his disciples.

6

Chapter
15

Jesus gives the parables of the lost sheep, the lost coin and the lost son – also called the parable of the prodigal son.

6

Chapter
16

Jesus tells the parable about the shrewd manager and the story of the rich man and Lazarus: the rich man dies and faces torment, while Lazarus dies and finds paradise.

He said to them, 'When you pray, say:
"Father, hallowed be your name.
Your kingdom come.
Give us each day our daily bread.
And forgive us our sins,
* for we ourselves forgive everyone indebted to us.*
And do not bring us to the time of trial."'

Luke 11:2–4

Someone in the crowd said to him, 'Teacher, tell my brother to divide the family inheritance with me.'
But he said to him, 'Friend, who set me to be a judge or arbitrator over you?' And he said to them, 'Take care! Be on your guard against all kinds of greed; for one's life does not consist in the abundance of possessions.'

Luke 12:13–15

Chapter 15: **Commentary**

Three parables underline Jesus' welcome to sinners. Conversion is crucial in Luke, with the woman weeping at Jesus' feet and Zacchaeus as examples. Jesus does not wait for sinners to come to him, but goes out to seek them. You cannot be a follower of Jesus without first admitting to being a sinner – even Peter in 5:1–11. The scene of the crucifixion is one of conversion: the women of Jerusalem weep, the executioners and the 'good thief' are forgiven and all depart beating their breasts. The way is open for the conversions of the Acts of the Apostles.

Chapter 16: **Commentary**

The parable of the rich man and Lazarus typifies the dreadful fate of the uncaring rich, just like the parable of the rich fool in 12:16–21. Writing for a well-to-do society, Luke underlines the need to use wealth well. Instead of Matthew's eight beatitudes about Christian spirituality, Luke has four blessings on those who are really poor (6:20–23) followed by four 'woes' on the rich. From the beginning of the Gospel, it is the poor who welcome Jesus.

The apostles said to the Lord, 'Increase our faith!'
The Lord replied, 'If you had faith the size of a
mustard seed, you could say to this mulberry
tree, "Be uprooted and planted in the sea", and it
would obey you.'

Luke 17:5–6

Chapter 19: **Commentary**

The entry into Jerusalem is the climax of this journey on which the disciples have learnt the difficulties of following Jesus. Jerusalem is the hinge-point of the mission, where Jesus dies, where he meets his disciples after the resurrection and from where his message spreads to the world. In prophetic phrases Jesus again weeps over unrepentant Jerusalem as he enters the city and as he leaves it for execution. Luke is writing after the horrors of the siege and Sack of Jerusalem in AD 70.

He looked up and saw rich people putting their gifts into the treasury; he also saw a poor widow put in two small copper coins. He said, 'Truly I tell you, this poor widow has put in more than all of them; for all of them have contributed out of their abundance, but she out of her poverty has put in all she had to live on.'

Luke 21:1–4

Chapter 22: **Commentary**

In Luke there is only one prayer in Gethsemane. It is no longer a Jesus beside himself in fear and distress. Rather a dignified Jesus prepares himself in prayer, giving an example of prayer to his disciples. We have seen Jesus praying at his baptism, his Transfiguration and when he teaches the disciples to pray. There are also the parables about prayer (the Pharisee and the tax collector) and perseverance in prayer (the widow and the unjust judge). Prayer will be stressed in the early community of Jerusalem too.

Chapter 24: **Commentary**

The journey to Emmaus is the paradigm of the Christian apostolate: the companions start open-minded but puzzled. The stranger explains to them the scriptures. They listen and in the Eucharist their eyes are opened and they really meet the Risen Christ. Then they return and carry on their own apostolate. The story is also told with beautiful symmetry: start at Jerusalem – eyes closed – meeting with Jesus – eyes opened – return to Jerusalem. A similar story is told of Philip and the Ethiopian in Acts 8:26–40.

③	⑧	
Jesus tells his disciples to forgive repeatedly and heals ten men with leprosy. He teaches that the kingdom of God is among them and that Jerusalem will be destroyed.		Chapter **17**

③	⑥	⑧
The parable of the unjust judge. The contrasting prayers of a Pharisee and a tax collector. Jesus blesses children. A rich man wants to enter God's kingdom. Jesus heals a blind beggar.		Chapter **18**

③	⑥	⑰
Jesus invites himself to dinner with Zacchaeus. A parable about a man who entrusts ten minas (one mina was worth three months' wages) to his servants. Jesus enters Jerusalem triumphantly. He expels the money-changers.		Chapter **19**

③	⑥	⑰
Jesus tells the parable of the tenants who killed the heir. Jesus answers a question about whether to pay taxes to Caesar. He warns against the hypocrisy of the teachers of the law.		Chapter **20**

③	⑦	
Jesus praises the generosity of the poor widow who gave all she had to the Temple. Jesus predicts the destruction of Jerusalem and the Temple.		Chapter **21**

⑰	
At the Last Supper, Jesus reveals that he will be betrayed. Jesus is arrested. Peter disowns Jesus three times and Jesus is condemned by the Sanhedrin.	Chapter **22**

⑰	
Jesus goes before Pilate, then before King Herod. Finally, Pilate condemns him to crucifixion. Jesus is crucified, dies and is buried in the tomb of Joseph of Arimathea.	Chapter **23**

⑧	⑰
On Sunday morning, some women go to the tomb and discover that Jesus has risen from the dead. His other disciples soon learn the news. Later, Jesus is taken up into heaven.	Chapter **24**

John
Overview

The wedding in Cana
The first miracle Jesus performed was at a party in Cana celebrating a wedding. When they ran out of wine, Jesus made more.

The Gospel according to John does not follow the same plan or pattern as the other three. It has no parables, no mention of scribes or Sadducees (Jesus' opponents are simply 'the Jews') and many fewer incidents or healings. John's technique is to give a few 'signs', whose sign-value is then developed by a long reflection by Jesus or the evangelist. There is not just one visit to Jerusalem at the end of Jesus' ministry, but four visits, beginning with the cleansing of the Temple, which in the other Gospels comes at the end. The figure of Jesus also is different: in the other Gospels Jesus proclaims the Kingship of God; here he proclaims himself in terms that those who refuse to accept him find blasphemous. Instead of the pithy, short sayings of Jesus we have long meditations in the same style as the author of the Gospel.

Who is the author of this unique work? We are deliberately kept in the dark. It is the tradition of the Beloved Disciple, who is carefully left unidentified, but who is next to Jesus at his Last Supper, accompanies Jesus' mother at the foot of the cross, recognises the meaning of the empty tomb, and hands on the tradition. This is a portrait of any disciple whom Jesus loves. The message is the same throughout, and the same literary style pervades the whole gospel, marked by puzzled questions, irony and teasing and deliberate ambiguities – what is 'living water' or 'bread from heaven'? What is the

Chapter 1: **Commentary**

The Gospel of Mark starts with the baptism of Jesus. Matthew and Luke add a prefatory couple of chapters to show that Jesus had his special quality and task from the beginning of his life. John goes further back, to the beginning of all things, when the word already was. The first words, 'In the beginning' are also the first words of Genesis. The prologue is symmetrical: it begins and ends with the living contact of the word with the Father. At the centre the word became flesh; on either side are acceptance and rejection; beyond that, the passages about John the Baptist. The word of God is the wisdom of God, God's agent in creation. The word is not the Father, and yet is divine, in life-giving union with and dependence on the Father.

Chapter

1

God becomes a human being named Jesus. John the Baptist announces Jesus is the Messiah. Andrew and John become Jesus' first disciples, followed by Peter, Philip and Nathanael.

'hour of Jesus'? On the other hand some of the Gospel seems to be assembled from independent blocks: the story of the raising of Lazarus is independent of its surroundings; there are three different versions of the discourse after the Last Supper; the final chapter follows a concluding paragraph (20:30–31); some series of sayings seem to be repeated (5:19–25 and 5:26–31); the story of the adulterous woman (7:53–8:11) is an extreme case.

The date when the Gospel of John was finally written is strongly disputed. Some would put it as the earliest Gospel. More general opinion is that it is the latest of the Gospels. It is not possible to show that John was written either to supplement or to correct the other three Gospels; in this matter they are entirely independent. Some of the sayings may be in a more primitive state, that is, nearer to the original sayings of Jesus, than in the other Gospels, but this is certainly not universally the case. The opinion that John is the latest is founded on the fact that in a way the theology is the most developed. Certainly the Christology is the highest Christology, more aware of the exalted status of Jesus than any of the other Gospels. This does not demand that it be later than the others, just the product of another theologian, who was differently inspired or thought differently.

Nicodemus
Nicodemus was a member of the Sanhedrin who visited Jesus at night to learn more about him. He became a disciple of Jesus.

Chapter 4: Commentary

This delightful dialogue with the Samaritan is typical of John. It is as though they are teasing each other, Jesus deliberately misleading her with ambiguities, and she cheekily responds to Jesus. Gradually she grows to understand and value him, until she, in her turn, runs off to summon her compatriots. Since water is the symbol of the life-giving Law, Jesus is claiming to be the source of true life and true worship in the Spirit.

8	17	
At the reception following a wedding, they run out of wine. At the urging of his mother, Jesus turns water into wine. Jesus drives the money-changers out of the Temple in Jerusalem.		Chapter 2

3	17	
Nicodemus approaches Jesus at night to learn more about him. Jesus explains that he came to save humanity from its sins. John the Baptist testifies that Jesus is the Messiah.		Chapter 3

3	8	17	
Jesus talks to a Samaritan woman by a well. Many Samaritans believe that he is the Messiah. Jesus heals the son of a royal official.			Chapter 4

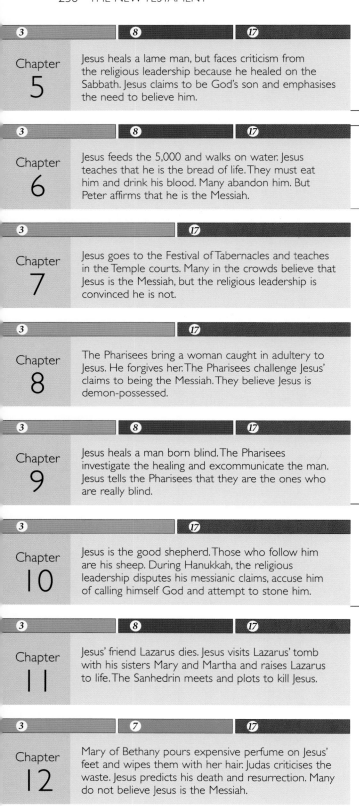

3 | **8** | **17**

Chapter 5

Jesus heals a lame man, but faces criticism from the religious leadership because he healed on the Sabbath. Jesus claims to be God's son and emphasises the need to believe him.

3 | **8** | **17**

Chapter 6

Jesus feeds the 5,000 and walks on water. Jesus teaches that he is the bread of life. They must eat him and drink his blood. Many abandon him. But Peter affirms that he is the Messiah.

3 | **17**

Chapter 7

Jesus goes to the Festival of Tabernacles and teaches in the Temple courts. Many in the crowds believe that Jesus is the Messiah, but the religious leadership is convinced he is not.

3 | **17**

Chapter 8

The Pharisees bring a woman caught in adultery to Jesus. He forgives her. The Pharisees challenge Jesus' claims to being the Messiah. They believe Jesus is demon-possessed.

3 | **8** | **17**

Chapter 9

Jesus heals a man born blind. The Pharisees investigate the healing and excommunicate the man. Jesus tells the Pharisees that they are the ones who are really blind.

3 | **17**

Chapter 10

Jesus is the good shepherd. Those who follow him are his sheep. During Hanukkah, the religious leadership disputes his messianic claims, accuse him of calling himself God and attempt to stone him.

3 | **8** | **17**

Chapter 11

Jesus' friend Lazarus dies. Jesus visits Lazarus' tomb with his sisters Mary and Martha and raises Lazarus to life. The Sanhedrin meets and plots to kill Jesus.

3 | **7** | **17**

Chapter 12

Mary of Bethany pours expensive perfume on Jesus' feet and wipes them with her hair. Judas criticises the waste. Jesus predicts his death and resurrection. Many do not believe Jesus is the Messiah.

Chapter 5: **Commentary**

John's Christology is different from that of the first three Gospels. There Jesus is seen as a mysterious figure who fits no expected messianic category and concentrates on the kingdom of his Father. In John he proclaims himself, but nowhere so clearly as in 5:19–31, in which he details his relationship to the Father. Is Jesus God? These verses make sense of an answer.

Chapter 6: **Commentary**

The bread of life discourse, a sermon given in the synagogue at Capernaum, building on the miraculous feeding in the desert, shows how Jesus perfects the symbols of Judaism. He is the true bread from heaven, providing true nourishment. In the earlier part of the discourse the bread is the revelation of Jesus, which is to be believed. In verses 51–58 Jesus is the Eucharistic bread, to be eaten. John has no account of the institution of the Eucharist – for him the sacraments begin only after the death of Jesus – and this is his equivalent.

'Not that anyone has seen the Father except the one who is from God; he has seen the Father. Very truly, I tell you, whoever believes has eternal life. I am the bread of life. Your ancestors ate the manna in the wilderness, and they died. This is the bread that comes down from heaven, so that one may eat of it and not die. I am the living bread that came down from heaven. Whoever eats of this bread will live for ever; and the bread that I will give for the life of the world is my flesh.'

John 6:46–51

Chapter 9: **Commentary**

The healing of the man born blind is a fine example of Johannine irony. The contrast is between the blind man who can see and the sighted officials who are blind. The more they try to push the man away from Jesus, the more insistent he becomes, and the closer to Jesus, until he finally acknowledges Jesus fully. His parents timidly opt out because, by the time John was writing, to acknowledge Jesus in this way entailed exclusion from the synagogue.

Jesus replied, 'I have shown you many good works from the Father. For which of these are you going to stone me?' The Jews answered, 'It is not for a good work that we are going to stone you, but for blasphemy, because you, though only a human being, are making yourself God.'

John 10:32–33

'You call me Teacher and Lord – and you are right, for that is what I am. So if I, your Lord and Teacher, have washed your feet, you also ought to wash one another's feet. For I have set you an example, that you also should do as I have done to you. Very truly, I tell you, servants are not greater than their master, nor are messengers greater than the one who sent them. If you know these things, you are blessed if you do them.'

John 13:13–17

Chapters 13–17: **Commentary**

John has no account of the institution of the Eucharist, for the sacraments come only after Jesus' death. Jesus begins with an acted parable of the ultimate service, which he is to perform for his followers. The discourse after supper, preparing the disciples for the future community, seems to be in three versions: chapter 14, chapters 15–16 and chapter 17. A crucial factor is the presence of Christ through his Spirit, the Advocate whom the Father will send, to witness to him and to lead the disciples into all truth. Chapter 17 is a priestly blessing, a meditation modelled on the Lord's Prayer.

Chapter 18: **Commentary**

The Johannine Passion Narrative gives a different angle to those of the other Gospels. It is the triumph of Jesus. From the beginning the divinity of Jesus shines through: the arresting soldiers fall back in worship as Jesus claims the divine title 'I am' (verse 5). There is no agony in the garden, no humiliating interrogation by the Sanhedrin; before Annas Jesus merely continues his teaching. At the Pilate trial the Jewish leaders condemn not Jesus, but themselves before Jesus, crowned as king and enthroned on the judgement seat, when they say 'We have no king but Caesar.'

3	7	17	
During the Last Supper, Jesus washes his disciples' feet, predicts Judas' betrayal and warns Peter that he will deny he knows Jesus.			**Chapter 13**

3	7	17	
Jesus comforts his disciples and tells them that he is the way, the truth and the life. He promises that when he returns to his Father, the Holy Spirit will come to them.			**Chapter 14**

3	17	
Jesus tells his disciples that he is the vine and that they are the branches. He tells them that just as the world has hated Jesus, so the world will hate them.		**Chapter 15**

3	7	17	
The Holy Spirit will teach the disciples and convict the world of sin. The disciples' grief will soon turn to joy. Jesus offers them peace during the trouble they will experience.			**Chapter 16**

3	12	17	
Jesus prays that he will be glorified. He prays for all who will ever follow him: that God will love them, protect them, make them holy and guide them.			**Chapter 17**

3	17	
Jesus is arrested and taken to the Sanhedrin. Peter denies Jesus three times. Jesus faces the Roman governor Pilate. Jesus tells Pilate that his kingdom is not of this world.		**Chapter 18**

Woman caught in adultery
Jesus forgave a woman who committed adultery and shamed those men who accused her.

17

Chapter

19

Pilate sentences Jesus to death. Jesus is crucified, dies and is buried in the tomb of Joseph of Arimathea.

After this, when Jesus knew that all was now finished, he said (in order to fulfil the scripture), 'I am thirsty.' A jar full of sour wine was standing there. So they put a sponge full of the wine on a branch of hyssop and held it to his mouth. When Jesus had received the wine, he said, 'It is finished.' Then he bowed his head and gave up his spirit.

John 19:28–30

Chapter 19: **Commentary**

The crucified Jesus, acknowledged as king, dies only when he has finished his task. He unites his mother and the Beloved Disciple to form the first Christian community. Only then do blood and water flow from his side, which Christian tradition has understood as symbolic of the sacraments of Eucharist and baptism.

Mary Magdalene
Mary Magdalene was the first person Jesus visited after his resurrection.

Chapter 20: **Commentary**

There is no Pentecost scene in John. In the upper room Jesus already fulfils the promises of the final discourse by giving them peace, joy and the Spirit for their mission. This is also the gift of complete authority. Only by Thomas and in the prologue (1:1) is Jesus so clearly given the title of 'God'.

3   **8**   **17**

Chapter

20

Mary Magdalene and the other women find the tomb empty and tell Jesus' disciples. John and Peter visit the empty tomb. Jesus appears to Mary, other disciples and, last of all, to Thomas.

Now Jesus did many other signs in the presence of his disciples, which are not written in this book. But these are written so that you may come to believe that Jesus is the Messiah, the Son of God, and that through believing you may have life in his name.

John 20:30–31

3   **8**   **17**

Chapter

21

Jesus appears to his disciples in Galilee, where they catch an unusually large number of fish. Jesus forgives Peter. Peter affirms his love for Jesus.

Chapter 21: **Commentary**

This epilogue has some strongly Johannine features and some utterly unJohannine ones. Peter and the Beloved Disciple always occur together. Peter's forgiveness is symbolised by his triple acknowledgement, and the Beloved Disciple is noted as the vehicle of the tradition that will continue until Jesus comes again.

Acts

Overview

The programme for this second volume of Luke is given by Jesus in Acts 1:8: the disciples are to bear witness to Jesus in Jerusalem, then in Judea and Samaria, then to 'the ends of the earth', a Jewish cryptogram for Rome. It is a story told with all the zest of a Hellenistic historian who wishes to 'entertain as well as edify', for there are plenty of racy tales of journeys, danger, riots, escapes, court scenes and shipwrecks. The author is thoroughly conversant with the geographical and political details of the area. The sudden intrusion of 'We-passages' ('we set sail…') suggests that the author accompanied Paul on many of his voyages. In the Hellenistic manner, the commentary is given largely by speeches that explain what is going on (Peter at Pentecost, Stephen at the end of the Jerusalem mission; later, Peter and Paul). Throughout the story the reader is aware that the spread of the Church and the witness of the disciples is being led by the Spirit of Christ, who inspires their life in Jerusalem and guides them about when and where they should move. The disciples are carrying on the work of Jesus by their teaching, miracles and witness even to martyrdom, so that the life of the Church is still the life of Jesus. In this there is a strong parallel between the apostles Peter and Paul, whose miracles and preaching show a careful balance. The Book of the Acts plays out the strong interest in the Gentiles seen already in Luke's Gospel, for a major theme is the openness of the Roman authorities to Christianity. Any clashes that do occur, such as the trials and imprisonments of Paul, are due to hostility on the part of the Jews.

Chapter 2: **Commentary**

The coming of the Spirit is the birthday of the Christian community, for Jesus had warned them to do nothing until the Spirit should come. It is pictured in terms that recall the descent of fire from heaven when God appeared to Moses on Mt Sinai (Exodus 19:18). Peter then explains its significance in terms of the eschatological coming of the Spirit in Joel 3. He similarly explains the resurrection of Jesus as fulfilling the scriptures.

15	17	
Jesus gives his disciples final instructions to take the Good News to the world and then is taken up into heaven. The remaining 11 apostles select Matthias to replace Judas.		Chapter **1**

3	5	12	
On the day of Pentecost, the Holy Spirit comes upon the disciples gathered in an upper room in Jerusalem. Peter preaches to a crowd that gathers; 3,000 become Christians.			Chapter **2**

3	8	17	
Peter and John go to the Temple. Peter heals a lame beggar, then speaks to the crowd about Jesus.			Chapter **3**

③	⑫	⑰

Chapter 4

Peter and John are brought before the Sanhedrin because they are preaching about Jesus. They are warned to stop it. The believers share their possessions with one another.

⑧	⑮	⑰

Chapter 5

Ananias and his wife Sapphira die after lying to the Church. An angel frees the apostles who were arrested and the Sanhedrin discusses what to do about followers of Jesus.

③		⑰

Chapter 6

Because of disagreements between Hebraic and Hellenised Jews, the apostles select seven Hellenised Jews as deacons. One, Stephen, is arrested by the Sanhedrin for blasphemy.

Chapter 4: **Commentary**

Maltreatment at the hands of the Jewish authorities is welcomed as an honour for the sake of Christ, whose witnesses they are. This is one important element in the descriptions (2:42; 4:32; 5:12) of the community at Jerusalem as the ideal Christian community, praying together and sharing their resources as each had need.

Then he said to them, 'Fellow-Israelites, consider carefully what you propose to do to these men. For some time ago Theudas rose up, claiming to be somebody, and a number of men, about four hundred, joined him; but he was killed, and all who followed him were dispersed and disappeared. After him Judas the Galilean rose up at the time of the census and got people to follow him; he also perished, and all who followed him were scattered. So in the present case, I tell you, keep away from these men and let them alone; because if this plan or this undertaking is of human origin, it will fail; but if it is of God, you will not be able to overthrow them—in that case you may even be found fighting against God!'

Acts 5:35–39

Stephen's martyrdom
Stephen, one of the first deacons, became the first Christian to die for his faith.

Chapter 7: **Commentary**

Stephen's speech marks the end of Jerusalem's second chance to embrace the message of Jesus. He underlines that their failure is consonant with their whole history. The account of his martyrdom is consciously modelled on that of Christ to whom he is witnessing.

But they covered their ears, and with a loud shout all rushed together against him. Then they dragged him out of the city and began to stone him; and the witnesses laid their coats at the feet of a young man named Saul. While they were stoning Stephen, he prayed, 'Lord Jesus, receive my spirit.' Then he knelt down and cried out in a loud voice, 'Lord, do not hold this sin against them.' When he had said this, he died.

Acts 7:57–60

Chapter 9: **Commentary**

This account of Paul's vocation to belief in Christ and to apostleship is given three times (also 22:4–16; 26:9–18) with slight variations for the occasion. The account is modelled on the conversion of a persecutor in 2 Maccabees 3:13–40. The account of a vision given by Paul in 2 Corinthians 12:2–4 may be an interior account of the same event. Whether it should be called a conversion is doubtful, for Paul did not turn his back on Judaism, but saw Christ as the completion of the Jewish hope.

Meanwhile Saul, still breathing threats and murder against the disciples of the Lord, went to the high priest and asked him for letters to the synagogues at Damascus, so that if he found any who belonged to the Way, men or women, he might bring them bound to Jerusalem. Now as he was going along and approaching Damascus, suddenly a light from heaven flashed around him. He fell to the ground and heard a voice saying to him, 'Saul, Saul, why do you persecute me?' He asked, 'Who are you, Lord?' The reply came, 'I am Jesus, whom you are persecuting. But get up and enter the city, and you will be told what you are to do.'

Acts 9:1–6

Chapter 10: **Commentary**

The conversion of Cornelius is significant as being the entry of the first Gentile – and a Roman official at that – into the Christian community. It is preceded by the vision abolishing food restrictions, and thus making the entry of Gentiles a real possibility. It was important to show that this was no individual initiative by Peter: the Spirit came on Cornelius before Peter had finished speaking. Like Paul's vocation story, it is repeated three times for emphasis.

3	17	Chapter 7
In his defence, Stephen summarises Jewish history and affirms that Jesus is the Messiah. The Sanhedrin condemns him, so a mob stones him to death, while Saul watches and approves of the martyrdom.		

8	15	17	Chapter 8
The Christians of Jerusalem are persecuted and flee, except for the apostles. Philip preaches in Samaria. Simon the Sorcerer converts. Philip baptises an Ethiopian eunuch.			

8	17	Chapter 9
Saul persecutes Christians until stopped in his tracks by a vision of Christ on the road to Damascus. Healed of blindness, he begins preaching the gospel. Peter heals a paralysed man and raises a dead woman.		

8	12	17	Chapter 10
The centurion Cornelius of Caesarea hears the Gospel from Peter after Peter's vision of being commanded to eat unclean animals. He and his family believe and receive the Holy Spirit and baptism.			

8	12	17	Chapter 11
Peter argues that the conversion of Cornelius demonstrates that Gentiles may also become Christians. The church in Antioch sends Barnabas and Paul to Judea with aid.			

8	12	15	Chapter 12
King Herod kills James, the brother of John, then arrests Peter. An angel comes and frees Peter while the Church prays for his release. Herod is later struck down by an angel and is eaten by worms.			

3	8	17	Chapter 13
The church in Antioch sends Barnabas and Saul to preach about Jesus around the Roman world. In Paphos they blind a sorcerer. In Pisidian Antioch they preach to Gentiles.			

3 **8** **17**

Chapter 14

Paul and Barnabas preach in Iconium. In Lystra, Paul heals a lame man. Some decide Paul and Barnabas are gods. Paul is stoned but survives. After Derbe, they return to Antioch.

3 **17**

Chapter 15

Some Jewish Christians preach that Gentiles must be circumcised. The Jerusalem Council decides this is unnecessary. Paul and Barnabas split up. Barnabas goes to Cyprus. Paul goes through Syria and Cilicia.

8 **15** **17**

Chapter 16

Paul, Silas and Timothy go to Philippi. Lydia converts. After casting a demon from a girl, they are imprisoned. An earthquake frees them and the jailer converts to Christianity.

3 **17**

Chapter 17

In Thessalonica, a mob starts a riot and so Paul and Silas go first to Berea, and then to Athens, where Paul uses Greek poetry and philosophers to preach about Jesus.

3 **17**

Chapter 18

In Corinth, Paul preaches in the synagogue and to the Gentiles. He works as a tentmaker with Priscilla and Aquila, who teach Apollos. Apollos goes on to preach in Achaia.

8 **15** **17**

Chapter 19

In Ephesus, Paul teaches first in a synagogue, then in a lecture hall for two years. Opposition arises from idol makers who fear losing business. They nearly start a riot.

3 **8** **17**

Chapter 20

Paul goes through Macedonia, Greece, and then leaves Ephesus to return to Jerusalem. Paul preaches a farewell sermon to the people of Ephesus and raises the dead Eutychus.

7 **17**

Chapter 21

In Caesarea, a prophet warns Paul of arrest in Jerusalem. Paul goes to the Temple, where a mob tries to kill him. Rescued by the Romans, Paul asks to speak to the crowd.

Chapter 15: **Commentary**

This meeting at Jerusalem removed a potential obstacle to the free entry of Gentiles into the Christian community. The account does not altogether make sense, for the circumcision issue with which it began is never solved. Possibly Luke has joined together two issues: first, whether Gentile converts must observe the full Law, and second, how Gentile converts could avoid upsetting observant Jewish Christians. The letter, verses 23–29, concerns only the latter. The decision-making process is important also, and the awareness of the presence of the Spirit.

Chapter 16: **Commentary**

As a Roman citizen Paul could not be flogged or imprisoned without trial. It is odd that he left his protest until the next morning. Perhaps the drama of the tale has been somewhat heightened.

About midnight Paul and Silas were praying and singing hymns to God, and the prisoners were listening to them. Suddenly there was an earthquake, so violent that the foundations of the prison were shaken; and immediately all the doors were opened and everyone's chains were unfastened. When the jailer woke up and saw the prison doors wide open, he drew his sword and was about to kill himself, since he supposed that the prisoners had escaped. But Paul shouted in a loud voice, 'Do not harm yourself, for we are all here.'

Acts 16:25–28

Chapter 17: **Commentary**

Paul's speech is a masterpiece of rhetoric, with plenty of classical allusions. It may well represent Paul's own thought, for it has strong links to what he wrote in Romans 1:19–23. In fact he is also playing with them sarcastically, for the word translated 'religious' in verse 22 can also mean 'superstitious'.

Then some itinerant Jewish exorcists tried to use the name of the Lord Jesus over those who had evil spirits, saying, 'I adjure you by the Jesus whom Paul proclaims.' Seven sons of a Jewish high priest named Sceva were doing this. But the evil spirit said to them in reply, 'Jesus I know, and Paul I know; but who are you?' Then the man with the evil spirit leapt on them, mastered them all, and so overpowered them that they fled out of the house naked and wounded.

Acts 19:13–16

Chapter 22: **Commentary**

Paul retells the story of his Damascus road experience with slight adjustments for his audience, stressing his Jewish pedigree, for Gamaliel II was one of the leading Rabbis of the time. Again he is saved by his Roman citizenship, but just in the nick of time.

Paul on trial
Paul was arrested when he visited Jerusalem. He defended himself before the Roman governor, Felix.

Chapter 26: **Commentary**

A third retelling of the story, delicately adjusted to the presence of royalty. Paul uses the classic opening of compliments and includes a classical quip as well as a quotation from Jeremiah.

Chapter 27: **Commentary**

The story of the shipwreck is a combination of a straightforward story, following the correct nautical procedure for shipwreck, with interludes of prisoner Paul acting as a prophet, or, more specifically, the prophet Jonah, to save them (verses 21–25 and 33–36).

Chapter 28: **Commentary**

The story comes to an end in Rome, as Paul has reached 'the ends of the earth' (as Rome is called in some Jewish texts). We do not know what happened after this, and the theory that Paul had to be released if he was not charged within two years has no foundation. It is also the third time that Paul solemnly notes that he has been rejected by the Jews and so forced to turn to the Gentiles. This had occurred before in Asia Minor (13:46) and in Greece (18:6). On those occasions Paul marked it by turning away with a biblical rejection; here he marks it by a quotation of Isaiah, which occurs elsewhere with this sense.

---

3 — **17**

Paul explains how he came to be a Christian. When he tells them that God asked him to preach to the Gentiles, they become enraged. The Romans arrest Paul, then send him to the Sanhedrin.

Chapter **22**

3 — **17**

Paul addresses the Sanhedrin, which splits and argues. After a death threat, the Romans move Paul to Caesarea. He meets the Roman governor Felix, then is placed under guard in Herod's palace.

Chapter **23**

3 — **17**

The high priest Ananias and other elders go to Caesarea to level charges against Paul. Paul makes his defence. Two years later, when Festus replaces Felix, Paul is still imprisoned.

Chapter **24**

3 — **17**

Paul makes a defence before Festus, who asks Paul to stand trial in Jerusalem. Paul refuses and appeals to Caesar. King Agrippa and his wife arrive and decide to meet with Paul.

Chapter **25**

3 — **17**

Paul tells Agrippa about how he came to be a Christian. Agrippa agrees with Festus that Paul is guilty of nothing and that had he not appealed to Caesar he could have been released.

Chapter **26**

3 — **7** — **17**

Paul sails for Rome and reaches Crete. It is late in the season, but it is not a good place to winter so they sail on. A storm sinks the ship, but Paul and the crew reach dry land.

Chapter **27**

3 — **8** — **17**

They discover they have landed on Malta. Paul survives a snakebite. After three months, they finally reach Rome. Paul is under house arrest for two years and preaches.

Chapter **28**

3

Chapter
1

Paul writes to Christians in Rome, expressing his desire to visit them. The Good News is for all humanity. Righteousness comes from faith. God's judgement is the consequence of sin.

3

Chapter
2

God's judgement is righteous. Those living by the Law will be judged by it, while those without it will be judged by their consciences. Righteousness is from the Spirit, not from laws.

3   **5**

Chapter
3

Jewish people have the Word of God, which gives them an advantage. But in the end, no human being is really righteous. Righteousness comes from faith, rather than from good works.

3

Chapter
4

A meditation on Abraham's faith. We can do nothing ourselves, but can only hang on desperately to God's promises in trust.

2   **3**

Chapter
5

A fuller explanation of Christ's work: Adam's disobedience ruins everything. The loving obedience of the Second Adam annuls this. As Adam started off on the wrong track, so Christ puts us back on track.

2   **3**

Chapter
6

We were crucified with Jesus and died with him; likewise, we rose from the dead with him. Therefore, where before we were slaves to sin, now we are slaves to righteousness.

2   **3**

Chapter
7

When people die they are free from the Law. The Law taught me I was failing, but I still could not fulfil it.

2   **3**   **10**

Chapter
8

We are being renewed, as is the whole of creation, by the Spirit of Christ. We should live according to the Spirit, casting aside humanity's disobedient ways. God loves us and his Spirit will triumph over all difficulties.

Romans
Overview

I   Salvation by Faith 1:1–11:36

II   God's Justice 1:1–4:25

    a God's Wrath on Jew and Gentile 1:18–3:20

    b Faith and God's Righteousness 3:21–31

    c The Example of Abraham 4:1–25

III Salvation 5:1–8:29

    a The Obedience of Christ 5:12–21

    b Baptism into Christ 6:1–23

    c The Law is Powerless 7:1–25

    d Life in the Spirit 8:1–29

IV The Place of Israel 9:1–11:36

V   Exhortation 12:1–15:13

VI Epilogue 15:14–16:27

Chapters 1–3: **Commentary**

After introducing the letter Paul sets out to show that the whole world is sunk in evil and failure, Gentile and Jew alike. There is only one possible remedy: the sacrifice of atonement in Christ (3:25). Paul gives here the ritual solution. Another explanation comes in 5:12–21: Christ's obedience annuls Adam's disobedience. Adam is the paradigm or image of disobedience, whereas Christ's obedience puts people right with God.

Chapters 4–5: **Commentary**

The idea of 'righteousness' or 'justification' is crucial. This is nothing to do with any human behaviour or any merits gained by good actions. God alone is righteous because he sticks by his promises to Abraham. Abraham didn't earn God's blessing, but he trusted in God and received it as a gift. So now Christ has put everything right by his obedience, and we can only put our trust in that.

Chapter 6: **Commentary**

Paul invents a series of words to show how we share in Christ by being dipped (baptised) into Christ's death and in him rising to his new life. We were buried in his burial, and we have grown into him, like two ends of a broken bone growing together. Once we have been dipped into Christ we share his risen life; his resurrection is our resurrection.

Why did Paul write to the Romans? Several reasons have been put forward, not all of them incompatible.

• Paul was planning a journey to Spain; he may not have known Latin, and he certainly did not know Spain, so he wanted help from Christians at Rome.
• According to Acts, Paul thought it unnecessary for Christians to obey Jewish Law, but he did allow observance of it. In order to win help from the Jews he needed to make clear what his attitude to the Law was. He did not sweep away the Law.
• Evidence exists that a group of Jews were expelled from Rome for disorderly behaviour connected with someone named 'Chrestos'. Is this person Christos (Christ)? Was Paul trying to heal a rift by showing each group that it needed the other?
• The letter is the fullest statement of how salvation in Christ works. Perhaps Paul wanted to send it to Rome ahead of time as an example of his teaching and a letter of introduction.

Chapters 9–11: **Commentary**

The Mystery of Israel: Paul is tortured by the failure of his brother Jews to accept what he sees as the logical climax of their history as the Chosen People of God. He searches the scripture to explain this, and sees that it was inevitable that they would reject their Messiah. Then he uses the image of an olive tree. He sees that this does not work horticulturally, so ends with a hymn to God's unendingly merciful love.

Chapters 12–15: **Commentary**

Paul's letters include a section on how to live the Christian life and its difficulties. Here he insists on working with the civil authorities. This must be before official persecutions began, for they were largely motivated by Christian refusal to worship Rome and the emperor as divine.

Chapter 16: **Commentary**

The Roman churches seem to have had no overarching authority or unity. Paul greets several different house-churches. Note the importance of women, especially Junia, who is 'prominent among the apostles'. The 'family/household of Aristobulus' may have been the first Christians in Rome, for Aristobulus, grandson of King Herod, died in Rome in the late 40s. He may have had Christians among his slaves.

Paul loves the Jewish people and wants them to accept Jesus as the Messiah. God is just. For now, the Gentiles are believing in Jesus more than the Jewish people.	Chapter 9
But Paul's great desire and prayer to God is that his own people, the Jewish people, would accept that Jesus is the Messiah. All who call on his name will be saved.	Chapter 10
God has not rejected his people Israel. In fact, someday all of the Jewish people will be saved. The Jewish people are God's people forever and nothing can change that.	Chapter 11
All Christians should devote themselves fully to God. Each individual is important and has a role to play. We should love each other and everyone else, whether friend or foe.	Chapter 12
Obey the government and be good citizens. All the laws in the Bible can be summarised by the command to love others. So don't focus just on yourself. Focus on helping others.	Chapter 13
Don't quarrel over disputable matters. Something you think is fine may be sinful for someone else and vice versa. So don't judge and don't do things that cause problems for others.	Chapter 14
Encourage one another and help each other. Accept each other just as Jesus accepted you. Paul expresses his desire to visit and minister to the people in Rome.	Chapter 15
Paul ends with personal greetings to people in Rome that he knows. He urges them to work together and to stay away from divisive people.	Chapter 16

I Corinthians

Overview

Corinth was an international trading city, with two ports and a biennial 'Olympic'-style games, a seething population of rich and poor, dockers, sailors, passing tradesmen, Jews and Greeks and upwardly mobile fraudsters. At one time it had been notorious for its sexual immorality. Paul spent 18 months there, bringing the Good News of Christ. His stay there provides us with our only firm date for his career: he was there during Gallio's proconsulate in AD 51/52 (Acts 18:12). It was a troublesome community, divided and fractious. It seems to have had no human leaders, but relied entirely on the Spirit as guide. Paul wrote to the Corinthians several times, and this 'First Corinthians' is in fact the second of his letters – the first has disappeared. He was at Ephesus and had heard from 'Chloe's people' of all kinds of misbehaviour; they also brought him some written questions about how they should behave. In this letter he first deals with the divisions and scandals he has heard; this part is full of sarcasm, which would have been quite wounding when the letter was read out in the community. Then he goes on to answer the questions more gently. Finally he teaches about the Spirit and the final transformation of those who die in the Spirit. Beyond the answers, the value of the letter lies in the principles on which Paul bases his decisions.

---

③

Chapter

1

Paul warns the Christian community in Corinth against following personalities. Jesus' death on the cross is God's power and true wisdom and Christians have nothing to boast about except the Lord.

③

Chapter

2

Paul claims no great wisdom or charisma; he simply preaches about Jesus dying on the cross. The message of the Good News comes from God, not from human reasoning.

Chapters 1–3: **Commentary**

The trouble was disunity, each group choosing its own way of following Christ. 'Cephas' is Aramaic for 'Peter'; these were probably people who wanted to keep to Jewish customs. Apollos was an Alexandrian Jew, perhaps a philosopher. The Greeks prided themselves on being philosophers, but Paul insists that true wisdom belongs to God. In the Old Testament God's creative Wisdom is personified, and Paul sees Jesus as Wisdom itself, as John 1:1 sees Christ as the Logos, or Word of God. Christ is also the Power of God. Both these ideas will be developed in the later Pauline writings. Paul attempts to defuse their pretensions by sarcasm.

For no one can lay any foundation other than the one that has been laid; that foundation is Jesus Christ. Now if anyone builds on the foundation with gold, silver, precious stones, wood, hay, straw – the work of each builder will become visible, for the Day will disclose it, because it will be revealed with fire, and the fire will test what sort of work each has done. If what has been built on the foundation survives, the builder will receive a reward. If the work is burned, the builder will suffer loss; the builder will be saved, but only as through fire.

1 Corinthians 3:11–15

Chapter 7: **Commentary**

In the second half of the letter Paul is replying to questions put to him; he is less sarcastic in this part. His advice on sex is largely determined by his view that the Day of the Lord is imminent: there is no point in bringing children into a world threatened by cataclysm. He gives a series of rulings of different strength, from the Lord (verse 10), from the Spirit (verse 40) and in his own opinion (verse 28). In a male-dominated age his insistence on the parity of women's sexual rights is remarkable.

Chapter 8: **Commentary**

Verse 6 gives precious teaching on Christ. Paul takes the basic confession of Jewish faith and worship, 'The Lord our God is one Lord' (Deuteronomy 6:4), and splits it to include Christ: for Christians 'there is one God, the Father… and one Lord, Jesus Christ, through whom…'. The Father is the origin, for whom we exist, but we exist through Jesus Christ. Again, this is Old Testament teaching on divine wisdom through whom God created everything (Proverbs 8:22; Wisdom 7:25).

③ God is the one who is building the ministry and work of the Church, not special people. God uses the inconsequential people to confound the self-important.	Chapter **3**
③ True apostles are servants of Jesus, not masters. Paul speaks of his suffering and persecution and sarcastically speaks of how great the Corinthians must be in contrast.	Chapter **4**
③ ⑨ Paul criticises the assembly in Corinth for tolerating a member of their fellowship who has taken his father's wife as his own. He tells them they should expel him.	Chapter **5**
③ ⑨ Paul criticises the assembly in Corinth for suing one another. They instead should settle their differences among themselves. Although we are free in Christ, we shouldn't use our freedom to behave badly.	Chapter **6**
③ Given the problems facing Christians from the Roman Empire, staying single might be wise. Nevertheless, marriage is good and divorce should be avoided if possible.	Chapter **7**
③ Idols are nothing, so eating food sacrificed to them shouldn't bother you. But if it does, or if it would harm another's conscience, then refrain. Don't lead people to sin against their own consciences.	Chapter **8**

Roman courtroom
Paul believed that Christians should not bring lawsuits against one another. Instead, disagreements between Christians were to be settled by the Church.

3

Chapter

9

Although Paul, as an apostle, has certain rights, he has chosen not to exercise them. He's more concerned with the needs of others than with his own needs. Be self-disciplined.

3

Chapter

10

God can give us victory over temptations. As a believer, you have the right to do anything you want, but not everything is beneficial. Whatever you do, do it to God's glory.

3   **11**

Chapter

11

It is traditional for women to cover their heads in worship when they pray or prophesy. Celebrate the Lord's supper together. Remember it's not about satisfying your hunger.

3   **11**

Chapter

12

Every Christian has been given a spiritual gift from God for the purpose of helping the Church. Therefore, all Christians are important and should exercise their gifts to benefit all.

Women's conduct
Paul encouraged all women to cover their heads when praying or prophesying in church.

Who at any time pays the expenses for doing military service? Who plants a vineyard and does not eat any of its fruit? Or who tends a flock and does not get any of its milk?

Do I say this on human authority? Does not the law also say the same? For it is written in the law of Moses, 'You shall not muzzle an ox while it is treading out the grain.' Is it for oxen that God is concerned? Or does he not speak entirely for our sake? It was indeed written for our sake, for whoever ploughs should plough in hope and whoever threshes should thresh in hope of a share in the crop. If we have sown spiritual good among you, is it too much if we reap your material benefits? If others share this rightful claim on you, do not we still more?

Nevertheless, we have not made use of this right, but we endure anything rather than put an obstacle in the way of the gospel of Christ.

1 Corinthians 9:7–12

Chapter 11: **Commentary**

In verses 23–25 Paul gives us the oldest tradition about the Lord's Supper, almost identical with Mark's tradition, but handed down in Greek rather than Aramaic. However, he warns the Corinthians that the Eucharist must be a celebration of a community united in love and care. By 'the body' he means both the Eucharistic bread and the Eucharistic community.

Chapters 12–14: **Commentary**

Paul's teaching on the Spirit in the community is at the heart of this letter. The Christian community is one body, enlivened by the Spirit of Christ, which manifests itself in rich ways, all of which must serve the community in different ways. None is superior to any other, and none should give grounds for superiority. These are still the gifts of the Christian community, all necessary for the good functioning of the body, and all belonging to the community rather than to the individual. The image of the body as a political organism is common enough in the ancient world, but this teaching that it is the body of a person, namely Christ, is specifically Pauline.

For just as the body is one and has many members, and all the members of the body, though many, are one body, so it is with Christ. For in the one Spirit we were all baptized into one body – Jews or Greeks, slaves or free – and we were all made to drink of one Spirit.

Indeed, the body does not consist of one member but of many.

1 Corinthians 12:12–14

Love is patient; love is kind; love is not envious or boastful or arrogant or rude. It does not insist on its own way; it is not irritable or resentful; it does not rejoice in wrongdoing, but rejoices in the truth. It bears all things, believes all things, hopes all things, endures all things.

Love never ends. But as for prophecies, they will come to an end; as for tongues, they will cease; as for knowledge, it will come to an end.

1 Corinthians 13:4–8

Chapter 14: **Commentary**

Verses 34–35 are often cited as examples of Paul's anti-feminine bias. The prohibition on women speaking contradicts 11:5, which gives regulations for dress for women speaking in the assembly. Perhaps the prohibition is against garrulous women interrupting the liturgy.

Chapter 15: **Commentary**

The Corinthians seem to have concentrated so much on the Spirit that they denied the bodily resurrection, perhaps misled by a Platonic contempt for the body. So Paul first quotes the very ancient tradition of Christ's resurrection and then explains. He refuses to discuss what the risen body is (verse 35), but basically says it is transformed into the sphere of the divine, taking on divine imperishability, glory and power, and animated no longer by the soul but by the Spirit of God (verses 42–44).

And if Christ has not been raised, then our proclamation has been in vain and your faith has been in vain. We are even found to be misrepresenting God, because we testified of God that he raised Christ – whom he did not raise if it is true that the dead are not raised. For if the dead are not raised, then Christ has not been raised. If Christ has not been raised, your faith is futile and you are still in your sins. Then those also who have died in Christ have perished. If for this life only we have hoped in Christ, we are of all people most to be pitied.

1 Corinthians 15:14–19

The resurrection
Paul pointed out that if Jesus did not come back to life after crucifixion, then Christianity was meaningless, worthless and wrong.

③ **⑩** **⑪**

Love is more important than anything else: it is patient, trusting and never fails. It is concerned only with others. Everything else will fade, but love will endure forever.

Chapter
13

③ **⑪**

God is an orderly God, not a God of confusion. Therefore, if everything is confused, God isn't the cause. Conduct your worship services in an orderly and intelligible way.

Chapter
14

③ **⑧**

The Good News is that Jesus died for our sins and rose again. If Jesus did not rise from the dead, then Christianity is a lie. Just as Jesus rose from the dead, so shall we.

Chapter
15

③

Paul explains that he is taking up a collection for the needy in Jerusalem. He gives other personal requests. He tells them to do everything in love and to greet one another with a kiss.

Chapter
16

2 Corinthians

Overview

Paul's fierce sarcasm in First Corinthians obviously upset the recipients, for relations continued to be stormy. His next visit to them was 'painful', after which the representative he sent to them was insulted. Paul then wrote a rebuke that won them over. After that comes Second Corinthians, or at least the first part of it, which is gentle and conciliatory, or even apologetic. Some scholars think that Second Corinthians is an amalgamation of several letters. The chief richness of Second Corinthians is Paul's reflection on the office of apostle as a ministry of light and selfless endurance in the service of Christ.

Chapter 1

Paul explains that as much as he had hoped to return to Corinth again, his situation was such as to prevent him from making it yet, but that was all for the best.

Chapter 2

Paul tells the Corinthian congregation that they should forgive the man they expelled now that he has repented. Paul explains his opportunities for ministry in Troas and Macedonia.

Chapter 3

We don't sell God's word for profit. The old covenant of Moses was glorious, but the new covenant of the Spirit is even better. The old covenant brought death. The new one brings life.

Chapter 4

Despite the current persecution, suffering and rejection of the message of Good News, still, we don't give up. God renews our spirit, because we keep an eternal perspective.

Chapter 5

We look forward to the resurrection and our new bodies, which will never decay. In the meantime, we attempt to persuade people to believe the message of the Good News.

Chapter 1: Commentary

The thanksgiving concentrates on Paul's own sufferings for Christ, which he will detail in 13:21–29. In I Corinthians 15:32 he mentions fighting wild beasts at Ephesus, perhaps figuratively. He also mentions (12:7) a 'thorn in the flesh' that tormented him – this was, perhaps, a recurrent sickness. He saw that these sufferings made him the servant of the Lord Christ, as Jesus had been the Servant of the Lord God. This endurance of suffering won him authority greater than the so-called 'super-apostles'.

Chapter 3: Commentary

The expression 'Old Testament' or 'old covenant' occurs in the Bible only here, at verse 14. The new covenant is heralded by Jeremiah 31:31, and is instituted by Jesus at the Last Supper.

Chapter 4: Commentary

Paul sees his apostolate as a 'ministry of light', drawing perhaps on the light that Moses needed to keep veiled after his experience of God on Sinai (3:8, 14), but also on his own experience of Christ as light on the road to Damascus. He sees Christ as the image or icon of God, as the personification of Wisdom, sharing the glory of God.

Chapter 5: Commentary

This passage about looking forward to being united with the Lord is unique in Paul for its use of the Greek philosophical language of body and soul, in which the body can be stripped off. Elsewhere he regards a person as an enlivened body, to be transformed at death after the model of Christ's resurrection (I Corinthians 15). He is eager to be taken up into life and to make his home with the Lord.

Paul arrested
*While in Corinth, Paul was arrested and brought
to the Bema to stand trial, but the charges were
dismissed by Gallio, proconsul of Achaia.*

Chapter 6: **Commentary**

The passage 6:13–7:1 against compromise with idolatry
breaks the sequence of thought, which continues at 7:2. It
has been suggested that this is the 'lost' early letter to the
Corinthians mentioned in 1 Corinthians 5:9. Others
consider it a later insertion, not by Paul.

Chapters 8–9: **Commentary**

Paul was very concerned about a monetary collection for
the poor of the church of Jerusalem. He considered it an
act of homage and gratitude to the community where the
church had originated. It would also be a much-needed
reassurance of his own loyalty to the mother Church. In
fact, when he took the money to Jerusalem it was accepted
only conditionally on his using some of it to pay for the
performance of a vow in the Temple (Acts 21:23–24).
Chapter 8, addressed to the Corinthians, may have been
inserted here because of the mention of Titus in 7:14 and
8:6, and drawn in with it the more general letter, chapter 9,
to the whole province of Achaia.

Chapters 10–12: **Commentary**

We learn more about Paul's person and life story, as his
letters are the primary source. He is obviously proud of his
Jewish pedigree, and the claim that he was educated by
Gamaliel (in Acts 22) is borne out by the skill in rabbinic
argument shown in his letters. Here we learn also of his
mystical experience of Christ and of things that cannot be
expressed in words (12:4). He underwent the toils,
privations and dangers of seafaring in ancient times, and of
solitary travel in rough, inhospitable country. He mentions
flogging by the Jews (perhaps for his claims for Jesus) and
being beaten with rods, perhaps for refusing to acknowledge
the emperor as 'Lord', and of course the worries of the
apostolate. He makes clear also that he had to put up with
abuse and gibes from the Corinthians themselves.

---

3   **5**

Paul describes his sufferings. Thanks to God's help, he
has managed to keep going despite it all. He warns
the Christians in Corinth against idolatry.

Chapter **6**

---

3   **4**

Paul is happy that his previous letter led the church
to repent. Though that letter hurt them, it was for
their own good. He tells them how much Titus
enjoyed his stay with them.

Chapter **7**

3

Paul talks about how generous the Macedonian
church was in their collection for the needy in
Jerusalem. He encourages them to also be generous.
Titus will pick up their generous donation.

Chapter **8**

3

Paul knows how eager they are to help. Those who
sow sparingly will reap sparingly. Those who sow
abundantly will reap abundantly. But giving must be
done voluntarily.

Chapter **9**

3

Paul defends his ministry with them. He's no different
in person than he is in his letters. Don't take his
outer 'timidity' as an indication that inside he's
anything other than bold.

Chapter **10**

3

Paul reluctantly lists his accomplishments, since they
are so concerned with status. What they should really
be impressed with is simply the message of God,
regardless of the messenger.

Chapter **11**

---

3   **15**

Paul admits he is less than perfect. He is concerned
about how easily the Corinthians let people take
advantage of them. They should avoid gossip,
arrogance, disorder and other sins.

Chapter **12**

3

Paul issues final warnings. He encourages the
Corinthian believers to remain faithful to Jesus and
the message of the Good News.

Chapter **13**

Galatians

Overview

Hagar and Sarah
*Paul compared the slave Hagar to the Law,
and Abraham's wife, Sarah, to the Gospel
(Galatians 4:21–27).*

Paul's letter to the Galatians is rough and raw. He leaves out all the customary politenesses and calls them 'fools' and 'mad'. Some Jewish Christians from Jerusalem came to the Christian converts in these Jewish communities and told them they must still observe the Jewish Law. Paul is furious: did you receive the Spirit by which you work miracles through Christ or through the Law? He tells the story of a previous confrontation over the matter between himself and Peter, in which he rebuked Peter to his face. Christianity is still founded on the promises to Abraham, fulfilled in Jesus Christ. It may well have been this issue that changed Christianity from being just one tendency within Judaism to being a separate way of life. Apart from showing us Paul at his most forceful, the letter is still valuable to us for its teaching on the basics of Christian salvation. We can do nothing to save ourselves; we can only trust in God's promises. No exterior compulsion can help us; we must be motivated by the inspiration of God's Spirit.

Chapter 1: **Commentary**

In all his other letters Paul observes the usual courteous forms of his time, starting with a greeting and going on to a blessing or thanksgiving. Here he is so furious that he merely identifies himself, stressing his authority. He omits any blessing and expresses his disgust at their listening to such unacceptable teaching. This was a radical challenge: what is the basis of following Christ, a belief or a code of conduct? We can easily stick to our old ways of behaving even when they no longer make sense. Circumcision and the other Jewish practices bound the people together, but was this necessary for those who welcomed Christ as Saviour?

Chapter 2: **Commentary**

Like all profound changes, the implications of Christian belief took a long time and a series of confrontations to sink in, especially since the practical way of life was so integral to Judaism. First there was the conversion of Cornelius, then the decision and letter from the community in Jerusalem (Acts 15). Even then, even Peter adhered to the old ways. Were some practices of Judaism necessary? Were some merely helpful?

③

Chapter **1**   Paul is amazed that the Galatians have abandoned the Good News for something that isn't good news at all: legalism. Paul's message comes from Jesus, not human reasoning.

②   ③

Chapter **2**   Paul meets the apostles in Jerusalem, but what he preaches comes from Jesus, not them. He once criticised Peter. If righteousness comes from following the Law, then why did Jesus die?

Chapter 3: **Commentary**

Paul is obviously writing for Jews. He shows his skill in rabbinic arguing. First he gives the basis of all Judaism, the promises to Abraham (verse 6, quoting Genesis 15:6). Then he makes a complicated, artificial argument based on two uses of the word 'cursed' in Deuteronomy (verses 10 and 13). Next he uses two careful arguments that turn Judaism upside-down: the promise envisaged Christ, not all Abraham's race (verse 16), and the mediation of angels was not an enhancement but a restriction on the importance of the Law (verse 19).

You foolish Galatians! Who has bewitched you? It was before your eyes that Jesus Christ was publicly exhibited as crucified! The only thing I want to learn from you is this: Did you receive the Spirit by doing the works of the law or by believing what you heard? Are you so foolish? Having started with the Spirit, are you now ending with the flesh? Did you experience so much for nothing? – if it really was for nothing. Well then, does God supply you with the Spirit and work miracles among you by your doing the works of the law, or by your believing what you heard?

Just as Abraham 'believed God, and it was reckoned to him as righteousness'...

Galatians 3:1–6

Chapter 4: **Commentary**

This chapter is all about Christians as sons. All Christians are sons of God and sons of Abraham, even female sons, for in Jewish Law only sons, and not daughters, could be heirs. So all Christians are heirs and are adopted as sons. This inheritance is deep in our hearts and enables us to cry 'Abba'. It is striking that this Aramaic expression, which Jesus must have used, is retained even in the Greek. It is not a baby-name like 'Daddy', but is the name used by an affectionate adult. In the passage on the two covenants Paul neatly reverses the usual Jewish interpretation, making Jerusalem the slave city, and Christians the heirs to the free and heavenly Jerusalem.

Chapter 5: **Commentary**

The murky list of works of the flesh and the inspiring list of works of the Spirit show that 'of the flesh' does not mean simply 'sensual'. It includes other results of human self-indulgence and frailty, such as idolatry and envy. Whereas the Law is an external check, the Spirit gives an internal impetus, which does not inhibit but enhances liberty.

3

The Galatians have the Holy Spirit because they believed, not because they followed the Law. We have been freed from the Law. As children of God, we live by faith.

Chapter
3

3

Before you knew God, you were enslaved to false gods. Don't go back to lies. Hagar, the slave woman, represents the Law. Sarah, the free woman, represents the Good News.

Chapter
4

2   **3**   **10**

We have been freed from the Law thanks to Jesus' sacrifice. Those old regulations don't matter. The whole Law is summed up by the command to love others.

Chapter
5

2   **3**

Look out for one another; restore those caught in sin. Do good to everyone. Remember, circumcision doesn't matter. What matters is the new life in Jesus.

Chapter
6

The confrontation
Paul confronted Peter for his hypocrisy and publicly criticised him over his treatment of Gentile Christians.

Ephesians
Overview

Many regard this letter as written by a follower of Paul who well understood his thought but developed it using many phrases drawn from his other letters. The thought has entered a new phase. The struggles with Judaism are passed, the wall between the two has been broken down, allowing Jews and Gentiles to be joined in one Lord, one faith, one baptism, sharing in the privileges of Israel. The supremacy of Christ, the mystery to be revealed at the end of time, now embraces the whole universe.

3	12

Chapter 1

Paul praises God and thanks him for all the blessings he and the Church have in Jesus. He prays they will understand the hope and glory that Jesus has given them.

Chapter 1: **Commentary**

This letter, beginning with this magnificent sevenfold blessing of God's plan in Christ, may be circular. There is no response to particular questions or situations, as in the earlier Pauline letters. The words 'in Ephesus' (verse 1) are missing in some manuscripts, and may have been inserted later. On the other hand, the letter bears strong similarities to the letter to the Colossians, not far from Ephesus.

2	3

Chapter 2

Our sins have all been forgiven thanks to what Jesus did on the cross. He brought the Jewish people and the Gentiles together, making them one body in Christ.

Chapter 2: **Commentary**

In the earlier Pauline letters salvation is still in the future. We have been reconciled, but we will be saved. In this letter we have already been saved and have a place with Christ in heaven, which is only still waiting to be revealed. The dividing wall between Jews and Gentiles (verse 14) may be a reminiscence of the barrier in the Temple marking off the Court of the Gentiles, which no Gentile might cross, on pain of death.

2	3

Chapter 3

Thanks to what Jesus did on the cross, the Gentiles are able to join the nation of Israel and with Israel become one body in Jesus. God can do more for us than we can imagine or ask.

3	11

Chapter 4

The imprisoned Paul urges the Ephesians to be united. Jesus gives the Church apostles, prophets, evangelists, pastors and teachers. Renew your minds in Jesus and avoid evil.

Chapter 5: **Commentary**

In Roman society a wife was the property of her husband. It is therefore remarkable that the husband is bidden to mutual obedience with his wife. Remarkable also is the image of husband as selfless lover, giving himself for his bride. The love of husband for wife is an image of Christ's love for the Church, the one as enduring as the other. Parents are also put under an obligation to their children, who normally had no rights in the ancient world.

3	10

Chapter 5

There should be no bad behaviour among Christians. You'll no longer be slaves to your selfish desires. Instead, submit to each other and work for the good of one another.

Chapter 6: **Commentary**

Paul often uses images from the games (boxing, running, wrestling) and from gladiatorial contests, which then held the public interest as football does today. Here, however, the images are of a real contest with the powers of evil, feared or revered in the Hellenistic world.

3	12	15

Chapter 6

Put on the armour of God. Your battle is not with people, but with spiritual forces. Don't use human means in the war of ideas. Don't ever stop praying.

Philippians

Overview

Paul had a special affection for the Philippi community. It was the first city he visited in Europe, and the only community from which he accepted gifts of money – for which he thanks them in this letter. It was originally a military colony, founded for retired soldiers. Its magistrates were called 'generals'. Here (in 1:1) we meet for the first time the officials, *episcopoi* in Greek, who will eventually be called 'bishops'. It is an intimate and joyful letter, in which Paul openly speaks of his desire to be gone and to be with Christ, but also of his willingness to stay to serve the Church. Paul is writing from prison, but where he was imprisoned we do not know – possibly Ephesus. Acts tells us that he spent over two years in Ephesus, but has little to say of his long-term activity there, perhaps remaining silent about an imprisonment.

Chapter 1: **Commentary**

Paul writes movingly of his yearning to be wholly joined with Christ. He is already living with the life of Christ, but this would be a completion. However, he recognises that he has a task to do for Christ.

Chapter 2: **Commentary**

The hymn to Christ may be an early Christian hymn that Paul picked up and used. It is unusually balanced and formal for Paul himself, four three-line stanzas, to which Paul added some characteristic touches. It is perhaps contrasting the second with the first Adam: both were made in the image of God, but the first Adam tried to be equal to God and would not obey, so was humbled. By contrast Paul applies to Christ the strictly monotheistic passage of Isaiah 45:23, implying that the worship due to God alone is given to Christ, and that this is to the glory of God the Father. This is perhaps the strongest of Paul's statements about the divinity of Christ, for 'Lord', *kyrios*, is properly a divine title.

Chapter 3: **Commentary**

In another moving and intimate passage, while asserting his own Jewishness, Paul turns back on the Jews the injurious name 'dogs', used to mean Gentiles, and mocks circumcision as a mutilation. Just as Christ set aside his divine privileges, so Paul set aside the privileges of Judaism.

3

Paul thanks God for the Philippians. His imprisonment has served to advance the message of the Good News. He encourages them to live a life worthy of the Good News.

Chapter **1**

---

2   **3**   **5**

Christians should imitate Jesus. Although he was God, he chose to become human so he could die for our sins. Don't complain. God is working for his glory and purposes.

Chapter **2**

---

2   **3**

Paul warns against those who believe that Christians must follow the Law and get circumcised. Paul encourages Christians to follow his example.

Chapter **3**

---

1   **3**

Christians should work together in unity. They should remain steadfast in their faith. They should always rejoice because they belong to Jesus forever. Paul thanks the Philippians for their help.

Chapter **4**

Colossians

Overview

Colossae was a large Jewish city in the Lycus Valley of central Turkey. It was evangelised either by Paul himself or by his helper Epaphras. This letter shows a considerable development from the previous Pauline letters. The style is more rhetorical and it uses a number of phrases drawn from Paul's earlier writings. Some have thought that it was written by a devoted follower of Paul, presenting what Paul would have said in the circumstances. Both style and theology are similar to those of Ephesians, and Ephesians uses a number of phrases drawn from Colossians. It has a more exalted view of the majesty of Christ, for Christ is seen as divine Wisdom, the icon of God and the model by which God created all things, superior to any other supernatural powers. In the main Pauline letters the Church is the body of Christ; here Christ is the head of the body which is the Church, so the source of direction, authority and nourishment.

3

Chapter 1

Paul thanks God for the Christians in Colossae. Jesus is God. He is the creator of the universe. He has reconciled us to the Father by his death on the cross.

2 · **3**

Chapter 2

Paul warns against focusing on rules and regulations. Rules are the way of the world, not the way of Christ. Righteousness comes from Jesus' death on the cross, not our behaviour.

2 · **3** · **10**

Chapter 3

Since we rose with Jesus, we should set our attention on spiritual things. We've started new lives thanks to Jesus. So love each other and submit to each other.

3 · **12**

Chapter 4

Paul encourages the Christians in Colossae to devote themselves to prayer. He thanks them for their help. He adds greetings from those who are with him.

Chapter 1: **Commentary**

The hymn to Christ (verses 15–20) is in two parallel stanzas. The first presents Christ as the Wisdom of God, the firstborn of creation; it leans heavily on Wisdom 7:22. This new development is perhaps the result of reflection on the comparison between Christ and the heavenly powers. The second stanza presents him as the firstborn from the dead and the principle of resurrection, reconciling the whole human race. It is surprising that at the end of the first stanza the Church is the body of Christ. It would be more expected that the whole of creation is his body, but two ideas are being combined.

Chapter 2: **Commentary**

A polemical development against various Jewish beliefs and practices, such as circumcision, Jewish festivals, extreme reverence for angels and rules of purity. The hostility towards Judaism stands in stark contrast to the warm approach towards Judaism in Ephesians.

Chapter 4: **Commentary**

The letter to Laodicea (a few kilometres from Colossae and also one of the seven churches of the Book of Revelation), mentioned in verse 16, has disappeared. It is informative that the letters were passed around from one church to another.

I Thessalonians

Overview

This is the first of Paul's letters that we possess. Thessalonica was a small port town in the north of Greece. No doubt there was a Jewish community there, which had welcomed Paul. But the scarcity of allusion to scripture suggests that most of the Christian community had come from paganism. The letter gives a picture of a united community, getting on with their lives together. However, they were worried about Christians who had died, for Paul had taught them that Christ has conquered death. So Paul gives his first important teaching about the Second Coming of Christ.

Chapter 1: **Commentary**

Paul stresses that they broke with idolatry, which suggests that the majority of the community were of pagan origin. It was not a rich community; Paul says he worked night and day in order not to be a burden to them, and encourages them to go on working with their own hands (4:11). Conversion to Christianity would cut them off from many social activities that were associated with pagan cults, even the games and the theatre. This would inevitably result in some isolation and even unpopularity. They would need some 'joy in the Spirit' in order to persevere.

Chapters 4–5: **Commentary**

If Christ had conquered death, how was it that some of their community had died? Paul gives them a picture of Christ's Second Coming in terms of the triumphal procession of a Roman general after a great victory. This is an interpretation of the Jewish idea of the Day of the Lord. It is clear that he was expecting it to happen soon, for some of those hearing the letter read out would still be alive, and in that triumphal procession would go to join their friends who had already died.

For the Lord himself, with a cry of command, with the archangel's call and with the sound of God's trumpet, will descend from heaven, and the dead in Christ will rise first. Then we who are alive, who are left, will be caught up in the clouds together with them to meet the Lord in the air; and so we will be with the Lord for ever. Therefore encourage one another with these words.

1 Thessalonians 4:16–18

---

3 Paul thanks God for the faith of the Christians in Thessalonica. They have become imitators of Paul and the Lord, becoming models for Christians in Macedonia and Achaia.

Chapter **1**

3 Paul reminisces about his time in Thessalonica, and how its people have remained faithful to Jesus. Paul expresses how much he'd like to come back and see them again.

Chapter **2**

3 Paul shares all the positive news that Timothy brought him about the Thessalonian believers and how encouraged he was to learn that they have remained faithful to God.

Chapter **3**

3   **7**   **10**

Christians should continue living lives that please God. When Jesus returns, those who have died will be resurrected. They will live with Jesus forever.

Chapter **4**

3   **7**

The Day of the Lord is coming without warning. So be prepared: live lives pleasing to God instead of in debauchery. Encourage each other to love and in doing good deeds.

Chapter **5**

2 Thessalonians

Overview

A church in Thessalonica
Paul wrote to the Christian community in Thessalonica, which has thrived and endured for centuries. He helped establish a church there.

The first letter to the Thessalonians was peaceful and warm. Paul writes to them warning that the Second Coming of Christ will occur suddenly, like a thief in the night. The community to which the second letter is addressed is clearly under considerable pressure and persecution, and they are warned that fierce persecution, a 'rebellion' led by 'the lawless one' must precede the Second Coming; they should not be surprised at persecution. The circumstances and worries of the community have changed. Has the author of the letter? Many of the phrases used here occur also in 1 Thessalonians, but there is not the same warmth and friendliness of tone. The author warns against a letter implying that the Day of the Lord is already present; it would be a bold forger who denounced as a forgery the letter he was imitating! There are many examples of anonymous writings of the time attributed to distinguished persons in order to give the writing authority. The authorship is therefore a puzzle, but it cannot be ruled out that this second letter is anonymous and merely attributed to Paul.

3		12	

Chapter 1

Paul thanks God for the believers in Thessalonica. Wherever he goes, he tells others about their strength and perseverance during persecution. And he prays for them all the time.

3		7		13	

Chapter 2

Jesus hasn't returned yet. Before he does, there will be a rebellion: a lawless man will exalt himself and proclaim himself to be God. So stand firm in the faith.

3		12	

Chapter 3

Paul asks Christians to pray for the rapid spread of the Good News. Pray to be delivered from evil people. God will give Christians strength to endure. Keep busy and work hard.

Chapter 2: **Commentary**

The imagery of the prelude to the Second Coming of Christ is highly developed, a rebellion and a lawless one, claiming to be God and working for Satan. The main import, however, is that the Second Coming cannot occur until there has been a period of turmoil and trial. The message is opposite, but not contradictory, to the message of 1 Thessalonians, as though the hearers had been so struck by 1 Thessalonians that they simply stopped working and waited for the end.

Chapter 3: **Commentary**

Paul normally dictated his letters, but he often ends them with a personal signature. This is, however, usually an expression of affection rather than a guarantee of authenticity. This makes the present signature slightly suspicious.

1 Timothy

Overview

The three letters to Timothy and Titus address two lieutenants of Paul, instructing them about setting up the organisation in Christian communities. These 'pastoral letters' are normally considered pseudonymous, that is, they were falsely attributed to Paul by their author in order to give them authority.

The saying is sure and worthy of full acceptance, that Christ Jesus came into the world to save sinners – of whom I am the foremost. But for that very reason I received mercy, so that in me, as the foremost, Jesus Christ might display the utmost patience, making me an example to those who would come to believe in him for eternal life.

1 Timothy 1:15–16

Chapter 2: **Commentary**

These letters are mistrustful of women, and have led to accusations of anti-feminism. However, women played an important part in the early Christian community, as Acts shows repeatedly. Lydia, a woman, was the first European Christian. In Romans 16 Paul greets several female leaders of house-churches at Rome. The letter was carried to Rome by a deaconess, Phoebe. There were female catechists and an order of widows that required regular enrolment. Paul merely lays down rules for modesty of dress to be observed by women who speak in the assembly. The teaching on women of these Pastoral Epistles is more to conform to social attitudes of the day.

Chapter 4: **Commentary**

The Jewish communities around the Mediterranean were ruled by a body of elders presided over by an elected foreman (or woman). Timothy is said to have received his office by a blessing in the laying on of hands by the prophets and elders (verse 14), but he does seem to have some leading role in making the appointments (5:19–22). This may well be a special delegation by Paul. The appointment of elders, including one who presides, was Titus' first task in Crete. It is not known when the threefold structure of bishop–presbyter–deacon, apparent at Antioch in AD 108, began, or when it became standard.

3

Paul encourages Timothy to oppose false teachers. Paul thanks God for giving him strength. To encourage him, Paul reminds Timothy of the prophecies given about him.

Chapter 1

---

3 | **11**

Paul gives Timothy instructions on how to conduct worship services, including prayer, proper dress and the role of men and women in the service.

Chapter 2

---

3 | **5** | **11**

Paul explains the qualifications of overseers and deacons. He hopes to come and see Timothy soon, but he wanted Timothy to have this information now, in case he is delayed.

Chapter 3

3

Paul warns Timothy that there will be those who abandon the faith and instead teach odd rules and regulations. Everything God made is good. Preach the Good News diligently.

Chapter 4

3

Paul tells him how to treat the people in his congregation, especially widows. Christians who work in the church deserve to be paid for their time.

Chapter 5

3

He encourages Christian slaves to respect their masters. Beware of false teachers. Do not get distracted by the pursuit of wealth. Instead, focus on God and serving him.

Chapter 6

2 Timothy

Overview

Paul in prison
Tradition has it that Paul wrote his second letter to Timothy while he was in prison awaiting his execution.

3

Chapter
1

Paul wishes he could visit Timothy, who must continue preaching the Good News. Paul complains about those who have abandoned him, but praises those who have stuck by him.

3

Chapter
2

Paul encourages Timothy to stand firm in the faith. He explains how to deal with false teachers who quarrel about inconsequential matters that are a waste of time.

3

Chapter
3

Dark days are coming, when people will love themselves and money more than God. Paul reminds Timothy of his faithfulness to God and the Good News.

3

Chapter
4

Timothy must continue preaching the Good News. Paul is in prison and will be executed soon. He hopes to see Timothy before he dies. He complains about those who mistreated him.

Second Timothy is printed second because it is shorter than 1 Timothy; not necessarily because it is later. However, it reuses a number of phrases and ideas from 1 Timothy: old men often repeat themselves! It is the most personal of the Pastoral Epistles, both in its tone and in the personal news of Paul and his requests at the end. It is personal also in giving named examples of good and bad conduct – especially the latter. It is a valedictory letter, the letter of an elder who is imprisoned, seemingly at Rome. He is awaiting trial, which he expects will bring him safe to the heavenly kingdom, rather than to liberty. Indeed, he reckons that he has already been poured out as a sacred libation. He is preparing his young successor to guard his inheritance, and sees his own life and work coming to an end. Nevertheless, the same concern for good order and fidelity to tradition is evident as in 1 Timothy. Personally he is at peace, but he is none too optimistic about the future, warning that there will be false teaching and unnecessary wrangling about words, accompanied by a general breakdown of morality as the last days approach. He is still concerned with the details of living, with a touch of an old man's fussiness (the cloak and the scrolls of 4:13). Typical perhaps of an old man's mentality is that he gives all kinds of pieces of advice helter-skelter, not delaying for long on any one topic and using very rich and varied imagery. The constant movement from one topic to another makes it difficult to give a coherent outline of the letter.

Chapter 1: **Commentary**

The fact that Timothy's mother and grandmother are represented as Christians may indicate that he is a third-generation Christian. This would suggest a late date, though of course all three generations could have become Christians in quick succession.

The saying is sure: If we have died with him, we will also live with him; if we endure, we will also reign with him; if we deny him, he will also deny us; if we are faithless, he remains faithful – for he cannot deny himself.

2 Timothy 2:11–13

Titus

Overview

Titus, as a Gentile Christian, had been chosen to accompany Paul for the negotiations at Jerusalem over observance of the Jewish Law (Galatians 2:3), and Paul again chose him to soothe the Corinthian community after Paul's ferocious letter, First Corinthians (as stated in 2 Corinthians 7:13–16). He must have been a skilled negotiator. This letter is addressed to him for guidance in organising 'with full authority' the Christian community in Crete.

The letter assumes that there are communities in several towns, for elders are to be appointed 'in every town'; one of them is to be the 'overseer'. The Greek word for this, *episcopos*, is the word that later corrupted in English to 'bishop', but the community may not yet have been sufficiently structured for the word 'bishop' to be appropriate in translation. The same term is used in Titus 1:7 as in 1 Timothy 3:2. The majority of the advice is concerned with good behaviour according to the canons of the Hellenistic morality of the time, in order to secure a good reputation for the community. Family morality is very important, as is giving a good example. If an elder is to lead the Christian community effectively he must first be able to lead his own family effectively. Advice is given to elders, to older men and women, and to younger men and women.

Chapter 1: **Commentary**

An important advance in Christology is in the use of the term 'Saviour', which is rarely used in the rest of the New Testament; twice by Luke. In the Old Testament God is the Saviour, in the context of delivering Israel from Egypt or from the Babylonian Captivity. In this letter God is called 'Saviour' in 1:3, 2:10 and 3:4, but Christ is also called 'Saviour' in 1:4, 2:13 and 3:6. It is as though they are deliberately put in parallel. In 2:13 the passage can be understood as calling Christ Jesus 'our God and Saviour'; it would be one of the very few passages in the New Testament where Jesus is called 'God'.

But when the goodness and loving-kindness of God our Saviour appeared, he saved us, not because of any works of righteousness that we had done, but according to his mercy, through the water of rebirth and renewal by the Holy Spirit. This Spirit he poured out on us richly through Jesus Christ our Saviour, so that, having been justified by his grace, we might become heirs according to the hope of eternal life.

Titus 3:4–7

3	**11**	
Paul describes the qualities of those who should be chosen as elders in the church. He criticises Christians who are rebellious and lazy.		Chapter 1

3	
Paul encourages Titus to teach sound doctrine. He should adapt his message to each age group, gender and socioeconomic level of his congregation.	Chapter 2

3	
Christians must obey and respect those in authority. Jesus rescued them from their sins so they could do good to others, not so they could satisfy their own selfish desires.	Chapter 3

Philemon

Overview

This little letter to Philemon is hardly more than a note (25 verses) from Paul in prison about Philemon's slave, Onesimus. There are two possible interpretations. Either Onesimus had run away and taken refuge with Paul, so Paul is asking Philemon to forgive him and take him back without punishment, since a runaway slave was normally put to death with a maximum of brutality. Or Philemon had sent Onesimus to help Paul for a fixed period, now expired, and Paul is asking for an extension of his helpful presence. It is full of affection and light-hearted word-play, for the name 'Onesimus' means 'useful'. Onesimus has become a Christian, and Paul asks Philemon to treat him like a brother, hinting that he should free him from slavery. In the Roman world this was a shocking idea, for slaves were treated as mere inhuman chattels. It was many centuries before Christians would come to see that the letter already has the germ of the ideas that would outlaw slavery in Christianity.

We do not know when it was written or where Paul was imprisoned. If it was in Ephesus (as suggested in the Overview to Philippians), the journey to Philemon at Colossae would not be very far. From Rome it would be a daunting distance.

Hand-lettered page
The Letter to Philemon was quickly accepted as scripture by the Christian community and was copied by hand before the invention of the printing press.

Chapter 1: **Commentary**

The sense of brotherhood was especially strong among the early Christians, in the awareness that all Christians form one family. In the earliest community at Jerusalem they pooled their resources, prayed together and owned everything in common. They were soon to be welded even more closely together by persecution. So Paul sees the new Christian Onesimus as his brother and urges Philemon to do the same.

2	3

Chapter

1

Onesimus was an escaped slave who Paul converted to Christianity. Paul sends him back to his Christian owner Philemon and asks Philemon to set him free.

Hebrews

Overview

This anonymous letter, placed immediately after the letters of Paul, was entitled (in the second century) 'To the Hebrews' because it would be apt as a letter to Christian Jewish priests who still hankered after the old Jewish rituals. It uses scriptural passages and Jewish patterns of interpretation to show that the sacrifice and covenant of Christ fulfil God's promises and bring the faithful to perfection, contrasting them with those of the old dispensation. It contains a rich theology not only of Christ's effective priesthood but also of his divine and human nature, a human nature that enabled him to share in and sympathise with the agonies of human suffering.

Explanations of Christ's priesthood alternate with passages of moral exhortation and warnings. The author stresses that the pilgrimage of the Israelites through the desert was only an image of the Christian pilgrimage to the final place of rest, and that the faith of the great patriarchs was a model for Christian faith and perseverance.

Focus on Jewish ritual need not imply that the letter was written before the destruction of the Temple in AD 70, for there had been temporary interruptions of the ceremonial on previous occasions, and the author might well guess that the ritual would eventually resume.

Chapter 1: **Commentary**

This is a magnificent presentation of the position of Christ. He is heir to the Father (as in Paul's letter to the Romans 5–6), the light of God's glory (as in Wisdom 7:25–26). Verse 8 is one of the very few passages in the New Testament where Jesus is given the title of 'God', but the whole chapter, especially the contrast with the angels, explains what is meant by this. Angels played an important part in Jewish theology and devotion, but Christ is vastly more than these awesome powers of God.

Chapter 2: **Commentary**

Writing to Jewish priests, the author uses Jewish methods of interpretation, explaining Jesus' position in terms of Psalm 8. The argument is that the obedience of Jesus could put right human sinfulness only if Jesus was in every way a member of the human race, sharing human sorrows and suffering. Thus Jesus is the one who sanctifies. Reconciliation or atonement is always God's own work, not a human work; but, by being both God and man, Jesus is the one who reconciles.

3	5	15	
Jesus is superior to everything in creation, even to the angels, because Jesus is God. Everyone in heaven and on earth must worship him.			Chapter 1

3	5	15	
Jesus became a human being, so he could make human beings holy. Human beings are now his brothers and sisters. Jesus suffered and was tempted like all of us.			Chapter 2

3	5	
Jesus is also greater than Moses. Believe today that Jesus is the Messiah. Don't reject him as the Israelites rejected God after leaving Egypt. They had to wander for 40 years.		Chapter 3

muluig: modis. olim ds loquens patrib; in ppheus: nouif sime dieb; istis locutus e nobis in

The new covenant
The author of the Book of Hebrews argues that with the death, burial and resurrection of Jesus, God has made a new covenant with his people.

3		5

Chapter
4

Those who rejected God never entered into a place of rest with God. Today, God offers that rest in Jesus: God has rested from his work of creation. We too will reach a place of rest.

3		5

Chapter
5

Jesus is the great high priest in the order of Melchizedek. He was tempted and yet did not sin. He was obedient to God and has become the source of eternal salvation.

3		9

Chapter
6

Don't fall away. It is impossible for those who fall away to ever repent again. Instead, all they have to look forward to is God's judgement. Jesus is our high priest forever.

3

Chapter
7

Abraham, the ancestor of the Levites, paid a tithe to Melchizedek. Thus, Melchizedek is superior to the Levites and Jesus, a priest like Melchizedek, is also superior to the Levites.

2		3		5

Chapter
8

Through Jesus, we have entered into a new covenant with God. The covenant is written on our hearts rather than on stone tablets. This new covenant is superior to the old one.

Chapter 4: **Commentary**

Again interpreting a Psalm, the author shows that God's promise of rest was not fulfilled at the Exodus, but it is still a promise that remains to be perfectly fulfilled for God's people. This is the foundation of the view of the Christian people as a people still on pilgrimage. It is also another view of the eternal Christian goal: heaven is not 'up there', but is God's perfect peace, the fulfilment of every desire in God.

Chapter 5: **Commentary**

Christ's priesthood is the heart of this letter. Here it is explained in terms of Psalm 110, a kingly priesthood, like that of the legendary Melchizedek. We are also given a different tradition of Jesus' prayer before the Passion. The key point of the prayer and of the Passion itself is Jesus' loving obedience to his Father, annulling the disobedience of Adam. As a human being he learned obedience progressively to perfect acceptance, and it was this that made him the source of eternal salvation.

Chapter 7: **Commentary**

Again a piece of Jewish interpretation of scripture: since Melchizedek's ancestry is not mentioned, it may be presumed that he had none and that his life had no beginning or end. The priesthood of Christ is a permanent priesthood: the sacrifices of the old Law were designed to deal with separate sins, but were ineffective, whereas Christ's sacrifice deals with all sins, once and for all time. The author goes on to contrast Christ's entry into the sanctuary of heaven once and for all with the high priest's repeated entry into the Holy of Holies on each annual Day of Atonement.

But Jesus has now obtained a more excellent ministry, and to that degree he is the mediator of a better covenant, which has been enacted through better promises. For if that first covenant had been faultless, there would have been no need to look for a second one.
God finds fault with them when he says:
'The days are surely coming, says the Lord, when I will establish a new covenant with the house of Israel and with the house of Judah...'

Hebrews 8:6–8

Chapter 9: **Commentary**

The new covenant had to be sealed in blood – again, a comparison with the covenant made on Sinai. Blood is the sign of life; when blood runs out, there is no more life. So blood is sacred because it belongs to God, the author of life. To sprinkle the people with blood was to sanctify them and give them the blessing of God's gift of life. How much more effective would be the blood of Christ, also the symbol of his total dedication to God?

Chapter 11: **Commentary**

Why this long list of ancestors? As the little quotation at the end of chapter 10 shows, now, after Christ's sacrifice, all we need is the endurance to hang on in faith and trust. In this chapter faith is not just an intellectual matter of believing, but is the act of gritting the teeth and 'hanging on in there' in the conviction that God will not renege on his promises. God can be relied on, just as Jesus relied on him and took his place at God's right hand.

Chapter 12: **Commentary**

In the final comparison of the two covenants the two themes of the letter, the effectiveness of Christ's sacrifice and the pilgrimage of the Christian, come together: the covenant at the beginning of the great Exodus journey was awesome and frightening, but the new covenant in Christ will bring us home.

Endure trials for the sake of discipline. God is treating you as children; for what child is there whom a parent does not discipline? If you do not have that discipline in which all children share, then you are illegitimate and not his children. Moreover, we had human parents to discipline us, and we respected them. Should we not be even more willing to be subject to the Father of spirits and live? For they disciplined us for a short time as seemed best to them, but he disciplines us for our good, in order that we may share his holiness. Now, discipline always seems painful rather than pleasant at the time, but later it yields the peaceful fruit of righteousness to those who have been trained by it.

Hebrews 12:7–11

Keep your lives free from the love of money, and be content with what you have; for he has said, 'I will never leave you or forsake you.' So we can say with confidence,

'The Lord is my helper; I will not be afraid. What can anyone do to me?'

Hebrews 13:5–6

②		③	

In the Temple, sacrifices must be offered regularly for sin. But the sacrifice of Jesus on the cross is a one-time sacrifice that does away with all sins forever.

Chapter **9**

②		③		⑤

The Law is merely the shadow of what Jesus did on the cross. Do not give up. Jesus has cleansed us of sins forever, making us pure and holy. We live by faith.

Chapter **10**

③		⑰	

Living by faith is nothing new. Look at all the people in the Old Testament who lived by faith, from Abel, Noah and Abraham through Samuel and David.

Chapter **11**

②		③		⑨

God disciplines people to make them better. Discipline is unpleasant, but ultimately beneficial. So live in hope and joy: God's kingdom is coming and you're a part of it.

Chapter **12**

①		③		⑩

Keep on loving one another, submit to the authority of your leaders and offer praise to Jesus. Pray for us and greet one another warmly.

Chapter **13**

Offering up Isaac
By faith, Abraham was prepared to offer up Isaac, knowing that God could resurrect him and still fulfil his promise.

James
Overview

After the letters of Paul, are printed seven letters to all Christians. Between these two groups comes the Letter to the Hebrews, which at one time was thought to be by Paul. These letters are sometimes called the 'catholic' epistles because they are addressed to the whole Church ('catholic' means 'everywhere, all over the world'). Each of them except the first, attributed to James the brother of the Lord, is claimed as written by one of the 12 disciples. In each case this attribution has been questioned, but they have been accepted as part of the normative body of scripture on which the Christian Church is built. It was a tradition within Judaism to attribute a work to an important figure of the past; this was a claim that it was what that figure would have said in the circumstances.

The Letter of James is a fine example of Christian wisdom writing, modelled on the Jewish wisdom literature. In the knowledge that all true wisdom comes from God, and using a rich stock of Hellenistic imagery, it offers a series of neat aphorisms about true Christian behaviour. It is essentially a practical rather than a theoretical wisdom. There is special concern for the poor, for control of the tongue, for perseverance and for prayer.

3	18

Chapter 1

Don't let trouble get you down. Remember that when you are tempted it is never God who is tempting you. Listen to God and then do what he says.

3	18

Chapter 2

Don't show favouritism for any reason. Words are cheap. It is actions that count. If your claim to faith isn't demonstrated by your actions, then you really don't have any faith.

3	18

Chapter 3

The hardest thing to control is what you say. If you can control your tongue, then you really do have self-control. Wisdom is demonstrated by actions.

3	15	18

Chapter 4

Submit yourself to God's will. God is in control of your life and everything that happens to you. So don't be arrogant.

3	18

Chapter 5

Don't trust in your wealth. It won't last. If you take advantage of others, God will judge you. Suffering is hard, but God will see you through. God will answer your prayers.

Chapter 1: **Commentary**

The greeting to the 12 tribes of the dispersion shows an interest already in the wider world than Jerusalem. Is it a sign that the letter was written later than the traditional martyrdom of James? Both God and Christ are addressed indiscriminately as 'the Lord', which seems to show a well-developed view of the divinity of Christ.

Chapter 2: **Commentary**

Is salvation by faith in Christ or by works? Paul insists on the former. James insists on the latter. Is there opposition between the two? James is teaching that the mere assertion of faith is unreal if it has no effect on behaviour. How you behave demonstrates what you believe. So Abraham showed his trust in God by his willingness to sacrifice his son, Isaac, and his faith was increased by what he did. There is opposition between Paul and James only if James is understood as teaching that Abraham earned his salvation by his willingness to sacrifice Isaac.

I Peter

Overview

This letter is addressed to Christians in several of the provinces of Asia Minor, encouraging them to stand firm in hardship. There is, however, no mention of bloody persecution, though we know from Roman sources that this was taking place in those provinces in the early second century. It reminds Christians of their dignity as living stones, built on Christ as foundation stone. They are strangers in the world, but their suffering is linked to that of Christ, who was rejected. It outlines the generosity with which they should behave in an alien world, and the reward that awaits them.

The apostle Peter
Peter spent the years after Jesus' resurrection teaching and preaching.

Chapter 2: **Commentary**

It does not seem to have been part of the early Christian mission to shake the structure of society. So obedience to the civil authorities and to the emperor is here enjoined, and there is no question of opposition to slavery. All the evidence suggests that slaves constituted a large proportion of the first generations of Christians. On the other hand, the human equality of all is stressed: slaves too have been ransomed by Christ. A very different Christian attitude to the idolatry of the Roman state is shown in the Book of Revelation.

Chapter 3: **Commentary**

The early Christian tradition that Christ descended into hell or the underworld, in order to bring up from there the sacred dead, has minimal support from verses 18–19. It is more grounded on ideas in the apocalyptic tradition. The 'spirits in prison' of verse 19 may be a reference to a myth about the evil spirits that at one time dominated the world. Christ's preaching to them is here placed after, not before, the resurrection.

1	3	5

Praise God for giving us a new birth through Jesus' resurrection. Set your hope, therefore, on the Good News and the fact that you will live forever with Jesus.

Chapter 1

3	5

Get rid of bad behaviour. Work together, live well among the non-believers and give them no reason to criticise: be good obedient citizens and behave as Jesus behaved.

Chapter 2

3	5	10

Submit yourselves to those around you; don't give them any cause to speak badly of you. If you suffer for doing what's right, you are blessed. Keep your conscience clear.

Chapter 3

3

Live for God, not for yourself. The end is near, so be alert and love one another. God will be with you through suffering. Don't let trouble keep you from doing the right thing.

Chapter 4

3	15

Leaders should be good shepherds and watch over those that God has put into their care. Be alert and watch out for the trouble Satan might try to bring. You're not alone in suffering.

Chapter 5

2 Peter

Overview

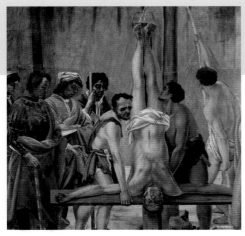

Peter's martyrdom
According to tradition, Peter was crucified upside-down at his request. He didn't believe he deserved to die like Jesus.

Second Peter is written in the style of a valedictory letter, that is, a final letter of instruction from a teacher to his disciples before departure or death. It seems to be contradicting a claim that there will be no judgement on the wicked, that the Second Coming of Christ will never occur and that greed and particularly sexual debauchery will go unpunished. The author cites his own witness of the majestic glory of Christ at the Transfiguration as evidence that the Second Coming will occur, and details the punishment that awaits false prophets, such as those who say it will never come. Impatience is out of place, for God's sense of time is not the same as ours: 'with the Lord one day is like a thousand years, and a thousand years are like one day' (3:8).

Despite the claim to have witnessed the Transfiguration, it is unlikely that the letter was in fact written by the apostle Peter. Such a claim is part of the conventions of pseudonymity. The rhetoric (such as the chain of virtues in 1:5–7) is far too sophisticated for the uneducated Galilean fisherman. The writing presupposes that a collection of Pauline letters is already in existence and in circulation (3:16). 'Peter's' own expectation of death according to Jesus' prediction (1:14) most likely presupposes the Gospel of John (21:18). Most cogent of all, a question about the delay of the Day of the Lord could never have occurred before some years after the destruction of Jerusalem in AD 70.

3	10

Chapter 1 — God has given you everything you need to live for him. Pay attention to God's words from the prophets: you can depend on what God has said.

3	9	15

Chapter 2 — Just as there were false prophets in the past, so today, beware of them. They are arrogant, they don't know what they are talking about and God will judge them.

7	9	13

Chapter 3 — The Day of the Lord is coming. Just because there is a delay, doesn't mean that it isn't going to happen. So do the right thing. Live holy lives so you'll be ready when that day finally arrives.

Chapter 2: **Commentary**

There is a close relationship between this letter and Jude 4–18. Both letters use the fall of the angels, Sodom and Gomorrah, and Balaam as examples of behaviour that will be punished. These are common examples in Jewish writing of the period.

I John

Overview

This First Letter of John is no ordinary letter, for it lacks the usual opening and concluding greetings. Perhaps it would be better classified as a sermon or exhortation, although it has always been part of the collection of catholic or universal epistles. It is closely related to the Gospel of John, particularly on the centrality of love, for its morality is built entirely on the importance of the new commandment of love. Nevertheless, there are some clear differences: it lacks some key concepts of that Gospel, such as glory and Holy Spirit. Despite the similarities it is unlikely that the letter was written by the same person as the Gospel.

Chapter 1: **Commentary**

The opening verses strongly recall the prologue of the Gospel of John. However, instead of the stress on the pre-existence of the word, the emphasis is on the humanity of the word, that we have seen and heard and touched with out hands. Throughout the letter the stress is on the human work of Christ rather than on his divinity.

Chapter 2: **Commentary**

The mysterious figure of the Antichrist (verse 18) appears only in 1–2 John, but may perhaps be identified with the Enemy of 2 Thessalonians 2:4, who is to appear before the final Day of the Lord. The emphasis of the letter on the last days is one of the differences from the Gospel of John, which stresses rather the presence of the Spirit in the community now, when eternal life has already begun. The error of the Antichrist is to deny the true relationship of the Son to the Father, which is at the heart of all the Johannine writings.

3

We proclaim Jesus, a human being we knew and touched. He gives light. Those in the dark don't belong to him. Everyone sins. If you claim otherwise, you're lying.

Chapter **1**

3 **5** **10**

There is one old command: love each other. If you love others, you're in the light. If you don't, you're in the dark. Those who deny Jesus is the Messiah are anti-Messiahs.

Chapter **2**

2 **3** **10**

God has made us his children. Jesus has taken away our sins, so that we don't have to sin anymore. This is love: Jesus died for us. Jesus' commandment is to love each other.

Chapter **3**

2 **3** **10**

If you deny Jesus came from God and became human, then you don't know God. God is love. If we say we love God and then hate someone, we really don't love God.

Chapter **4**

2 **3**

Whoever believes Jesus is the Messiah has eternal life. If you don't believe Jesus is the Messiah, then you don't have eternal life. We are the children of God.

Chapter **5**

2 John

Overview

John's letters
*Either the Second or the Third Letter of John could be
a covering note to the First Letter of John, introducing
it to the community to which it was sent.*

The Second and Third Letters of John, unlike the First, are typical of the short papyrus letters of the time.

This letter is obviously related to the First Letter, since it mentions the new commandment of love, which is so central to the First Letter, and to the Gospel of John. It also mentions the danger of deception by the Antichrist, a name used nowhere else in the literature of the time. However, whereas the Gospel and the First Letter do not specify their author, here the author is designated 'the Elder'. Many of the earliest churches were led by a group of elders, as were also the Jewish communities of the diaspora, but who is meant by 'the Elder'? Papias, the early Bishop of Hierapolis in Asia Minor, mentions a 'John the Elder' at Ephesus, which opens many possibilities.

There is a remarkable contrast in the letter between the warmth of most of the letter and the harshness of the reaction to those with whom the author disagrees. The letter is very gently addressed to 'the Lady, the Chosen One' and to her children; this is a delicate way of indicating a letter from one community to another. The letter itself is full of love and joy until it comes to verses 9–10. Such a contrast makes the severity of the exclusion all the stronger, and shows the acuteness of the danger in the author's estimation. The purpose of the letter was obviously to issue this warning, and presumably the author had someone specific in mind, whom he does not name. In the second century there were many variations of those who revered Jesus, but did not think that he was a fully authentic human being. He merely seemed to be human or was a human being inhabited by the divinity, who left him before the crucifixion. The doctrine of the Incarnation is so paradoxical that many attempted to avoid it or explain it away.

Chapter 1: **Commentary**

These two short letters are sent by 'the Elder'. The Jewish communities around the Mediterranean were each ruled by a council of elders, one of whom was elected for a limited period as chair (man or woman). The word can also be used simply to describe an old man, so here it may designate either an official or an old person, possibly John.

③

Chapter

1

John is happy to hear that the Christian community is walking in the truth. Watch out for false teachers who deny Jesus was a human being. Anyone like that is the Antichrist.

3 John

Overview

This brief little note has similarities to the Second Letter. It is also from 'the Elder' whom we cannot identify. This, too, could be a covering note for the First Letter, which lacks the formalities of a letter. It is linked to the other Johannine writings by several small touches, such as the typically Johannine notion of 'walking in the truth' (verses 3–4). Apart from the brief sally against Diotrephes, the chief point of the letter seems to be a recommendation for the friends (verses 5–6), neatly tacked on by the word-play of 'walking'. Before the days of email and telephone, such letters of introduction were important for travellers. It is valuable as showing the friendship between different Christian communities. In the first centuries of Christianity the churches around the Mediterranean formed a fellowship, staying in touch with one another by frequent letters detailing news and appointments

It is similar also in that it is warm and loving, apart from one sally against Diotrephes, who has been spreading false charges against the author. By the standards of the time the rebuke to him is notably mild, for written controversy in those days was unchecked by any notion of political correctness.

We know nothing about any of the personalities mentioned in the letter. Gaius is no doubt the leader of the recipient community. It is also a reasonable guess that Demetrius was the leader of the travelling brothers. The same difficulties about dating the letter exist as for the First and Second Letters.

John's death
According to tradition, the apostle John, alone among Jesus' 12 disciples, died a peaceful death of old age.

Chapter 1: Commentary

'Truth' (verse 4) is always a keyword in the Johannine writings. Jesus describes himself as 'the Way, the Truth and Life' (John 14:6). He prays that his Father will sanctify his followers in the Truth, and promises that his Spirit, the Spirit of Truth, will guide them into all Truth. So to walk in the Truth is to walk in Christ.

3

John hopes Gaius is well and praises him for his hospitality. He warns about Diotrephes and praises Demetrius. He'd like to write more, but he'll save it for when he sees him.

Chapter
1

Jude
Overview

Jesus' half-brother
According to tradition, Jude was one of Jesus' half-brothers.

This short letter has been considered a gem of early Judaeo-Christian interpretation of the scripture. It uses the method of interpretation known to us from the contemporary documents of the Dead Sea Scrolls. Basically it is an appeal to the readers to strengthen some Christians against 'ungodly' people. Several times in the letter licentiousness and lust are mentioned, which opens the possibility that the way these 'ungodly' people were misleading Christians was by anti-nomianism, that is, the doctrine that faith is sufficient for salvation. That is, if you believe, it does not matter what you do, since you are free not just of the Jewish Law but of all moral law. This is certainly a possible distortion of the Christian message, and a distortion that would make some sense to Christians who were issuing from Judaism.

Many have considered this letter too to be pseudepigraphical. A good case can, however, be made out that it is a genuine letter from Jude. A pseudepigrapher adopting this title would probably have made the stronger claim that he was 'Jude, brother of the Lord', instead of the humbler claim 'Jude, a servant of Jesus Christ and brother of James'. The use of the scripture fits well with contemporary exegesis. The Greek style is quite, but not impossibly, sophisticated; it could well be within the range of a Galilean preacher who had spent some time proclaiming the message in a Greek environment. It could therefore be one of the earliest writings of the New Testament.

Chapter 1: Commentary

| 3 | 9 | 15 |

Chapter 1

Jude writes about the sin and coming doom of ungodly false teachers who reject authority. He calls upon Christians to persevere through the hard times. He praises God.

The author's method of combating this view is to present four warnings, consisting of texts with interpretation: verses 5–7 three Old Testament groups: the rebels at the Exodus, the wicked angels, Sodom and Gomorrah; verse 11 three Old Testament individuals: Cain, Balaam and Korah; verse 14 a prophecy of Enoch (this is not canonical scripture, but was at the time certainly considered a sacred writing); verse 17 predictions of the Apostles. These are followed by the appeal to help the waverers.

Revelation

Overview

The Revelation to John is a splendid example of an apocalyptic writing (for apocalyptic writing see introduction to Daniel, p. 201). It was written to reassure Christians that they would eventually be delivered from the persecutions they were undergoing from the power of Rome.

Chapter 1: **Commentary**

The seven letters to seven churches may be the latest part of the book (prefaces often are). They show from the beginning that the Risen Lord, of whom the splendid vision stands before them, is the Lord of all history. The churches are all communities in the Lycus Valley, a valley running roughly east–west along the middle of Turkey. There were large Jewish communities there, of which presumably a number of members became Christian. The letters play neatly on salient characteristics of the communities. They are the first of several sevens in the book: seven seals, seven trumpets, seven plagues, seven bowls, seven times 'I am coming', seven times 'Christ', twice seven (14) times 'Jesus'.

I reprove and discipline those whom I love. Be earnest, therefore, and repent. Listen! I am standing at the door, knocking; if you hear my voice and open the door, I will come in to you and eat with you, and you with me. To the one who conquers I will give a place with me on my throne, just as I myself conquered and sat down with my Father on his throne.

Revelation 3:19–21

Chapters 4–5: **Commentary**

Like all the descriptions and scenes in this book, the imagery builds richly on biblical symbolism, and cannot be appreciated without reference to it. This magnificent vision of the Lord builds on the succession of visions of God in 1 Kings 22, Isaiah 6, Ezekiel 1 and Daniel 7. At one time God, at another the Lamb, seems to be seated on the throne and to be worshipped by the whole of creation. The Lamb combines the imagery of the victorious Paschal Lamb and a lordly young ram, as he holds the scroll showing his control of history.

3	5

John writes to the seven churches in the Roman province of Asia. Like them, he has suffered and he has had a vision of Jesus who told him to write a message to the seven churches.

Chapter **1**

3	9

Ephesus must continue to persevere. Smyrna must remain faithful during persecution. Pergamum must reject false teachings. Thyatira must endure suffering and reject immorality.

Chapter **2**

3	9

He warns Sardis to remember what they were taught. Philadelphia must hold on to what they have. Laodicea must stop depending on their wealth.

Chapter **3**

11	13	15

John sees the heavenly throne room. God sits on his throne and 24 elders and four cherubs continuously praise him, the one who created the universe.

Chapter **4**

11	13	15

God has a scroll sealed with seven seals. The Lamb takes the scroll. The elders and the cherubs worship the Lamb, who is worthy to open the seals because he died for everyone's sins.

Chapter **5**

9	13	15

The Lamb opens the seals, releasing judgements represented by horsemen: conquest, war, famine and death. Martyrs wait for vengeance. There is an earthquake and falling stars.

Chapter **6**

11	13	15

Chapter 7

Four angels hold back the four winds. Another angel places a seal on the foreheads of 144,000 from the 12 tribes of Israel. A multitude in white robes praise God and the Lamb.

9	13	15

Chapter 8

The seventh seal opens: there is a half-hour of silence. Seven angels blow trumpets: hail and fire burn the land, a burning mountain bloodies the sea, fish die and the sun darkens.

9	13	15

Chapter 9

The fifth trumpet: a star falls, opening the abyss. Its smoke becomes locusts that sting those without God's seal on their foreheads. Angels from the Euphrates kill a third of humanity.

9	13	15

Chapter 10

An angel plants his right foot on the sea and his left on the land. He shouts and seven thunders rumble. John is told to eat a little scroll. Then he is told to prophesy.

9	13	15

Chapter 11

John measures God's Temple. The beast of the abyss kills the two witnesses. They rise from the dead. An earthquake devastates Jerusalem. The kingdoms of the world become the kingdom of God.

9	13	15

Chapter 12

A woman bears a male child. God protects him from the dragon, Satan. Michael and his angels defeat Satan and his angels. God protects the woman from Satan, who then attacks Christians.

9	13	15

Chapter 13

A ten-horned beast with seven heads arises, attacks God's people, rules the world and is worshipped. A second beast forces all to take the mark of the beast on their hands or foreheads.

9	13	15

Chapter 14

The 144,000 did not worship the beast. One angel announces judgement, a second the fall of Babylon, the third, judgement on those with the beast's mark. The beast's worshippers are destroyed.

Chapter 7: **Commentary**

The delay between the sixth and seventh seals signifies the delay of the Day of the Lord, so that the conquering army of the Lamb can be sealed to show protective ownership by the Lamb. As all the numbers in the book, these numbers are symbolic: 12 tribes squared and multiplied by a thousand, and then a numberless mass.

Chapter 8: **Commentary**

Silence in heaven is the immediate prelude to divine judgement. It also enables the prayers of the saints to be heard in heaven. Then the trumpets of the Holy War herald God's judgement, and the destruction of a third of earth, sea, fresh water and stars is a warning to repent.

Chapter 11: **Commentary**

Two witnesses are required for valid testimony. These two are also reminiscent of Moses and Elijah, who were able to produce plague as a punishment on unrepentant sinners. The measuring rod is a guarantee of permanence of the Temple.

Chapter 12: **Commentary**

The conflict between the dragon and the woman repeats that of the Garden of Eden. Combined is the myth of Apollo, whose mother was threatened by the serpent, later to be slain by Apollo. The 12 stars designate the woman as the People of Israel. Christian tradition has interpreted the woman as Mary, the mother of the Lord.

Chapter 13: **Commentary**

In Hebrew, letters are used for numbers. The letters of 'Nero Caesar' add up to 666, which is also a triangular number, and triply short of the perfect number, 777, so in every way a symbol of evil.

Chapter 14: **Commentary**

As in Joel 4:12–13 the two harvests are positive and negative: the first harvest is gathered in from the nations, then the unconverted are harvested into the wine-press of God's wrath. This is followed by the destruction of the whole cosmos.

And I saw three foul spirits like frogs coming from the mouth of the dragon, from the mouth of the beast, and from the mouth of the false prophet. These are demonic spirits, performing signs, who go abroad to the kings of the whole world, to assemble them for battle on the great day of God the Almighty. ('See, I am coming like a thief! Blessed is the one who stays awake and is clothed, not going about naked and exposed to shame.') And they assembled them at the place that in Hebrew is called Harmagedon.

Revelation 16:13–16

Chapters 17–18: **Commentary**

Prostitution is the standard image of the infidelity of idolatry. The Great Prostitute is Rome, on seven hills, her feet by the River Tiber, with seven emperors. Her cult (the cult of the emperor and Rome) is the symbol of all evil. Her amazing and shameful imports will be detailed (18:12–13) amid satirical mourning songs from the merchants of the world.

Chapter 20: **Commentary**

Evil must be chained up for a very long time, emerging only for a last futile battle. However, in early Christianity many interpreted this thousand years as literally an earthly rule of Christ.

Chapter 21: **Commentary**

The city descending like a bride is the virginal, i.e. faithful, People of God, counting 12 squared and multiplied by 1000, the largest number used by the Greeks. It is cubed, like the *debir* of the Temple, but vast. The precious stones are those of the high priest's breastplate. The Lord God and the Lamb *is* the light and the temple, whose servants worship *him* (the singular verb with the plural subject indicates a single divinity).

Chapter 22: **Commentary**

The final 'Come, Lord' is the Greek translation of a very ancient Aramaic prayer, followed by an epistolary conclusion to balance the seven letters at the beginning of the book.

9	13	15

Seven angels come with the seven last plagues in seven bowls, the wrath of God, while those who had been faithful to God sing praises to God.

Chapter 15

9	13	15

God's wrath from seven bowls: festering sores, sea of blood, rivers of blood, scorching sun, darkness and the battle at Armageddon. An earthquake devastates the city and hailstones fall.

Chapter 16

9	13	15

The Whore of Babylon, drunk with the blood of God's people, rides the beast with seven heads and ten horns. She is the great city that rules over the earth. She will be destroyed.

Chapter 17

9	13	15

A lament over the fall and destruction of Babylon. She is judged and destroyed for what she did to God's people. Though merchants mourn the loss of trade, God's people rejoice.

Chapter 18

9	13	15

Babylon's destruction brings rejoicing. The wedding of the Lamb arrives. Jesus defeats the beast and his armies with the sword coming from his mouth: the Word of God.

Chapter 19

9	13	15

Satan is locked away for 1,000 years, then released. He leads an army against Jesus and God's people, but is annihilated. Satan is cast into the lake of fire and the dead are judged.

Chapter 20

13	15

A new heaven and new earth appear; the new Jerusalem, the Lamb's bride, descends from heaven. Only those whose names are written in the Book of Life are in it.

Chapter 21

13	15

A river of the water of life flows from the throne of God and the Lamb. Beside it grows the tree of life. God's people will live with him forever. Jesus is returning soon.

Chapter 22

INDEX

Page numbers in italics refer to
illustration captions.
Entries in bold refer to books of
the Bible.

O

Obadiah, Book of 210
Obed 61
Obed-Edom the Gittite 83
obedience 49, 50, 51, 64
occult practices 36
Oded 91
offerings 34–35, 43, 44, 50, 51
Og 46
Oholiab 32, 33
Old Testament 15–17
Omri 75
Onesimus 264
Onias 114
Origen 111
Othniel 56

P

Pagnini, Santes 10
Paphos 243
parables of Jesus
  persistence in prayer 234
  the failure of the leaders 228
  the great banquet 234
  the kingdom of heaven 226
  the labourers in the vineyard 227
  the lamp 233
  the lost coin 234
  the lost sheep 234
  the net of fish 226
  the Pharisee and the tax collector 235
  the prodigal son 234
  the rich fool 234
  the rich man and Lazarus 234
  the servants and the minas 235
  the sheep and the goats 228
  the shrewd manager 234
  the sower and the seed 226, 230, 233
  the talents 228
  the ten wedding attendants 228
  the tenants and the heir 235
  the treasure and the pearl 226
  the unjust judge 235
  the vineyard 231
  the wedding feast 227
Pashhur 187
Passion of Jesus 226, 227, 230, 231
Passover 29, 37, 40, 43, 44, 53, 80, 81,
  92, 200

Paul 244–246, 262
  confrontation with Peter 255
  letter to Philemon 264
  letter to the Colossians 258
  letter to the Ephesians 256
  letter to the Galatians 254–255
  letter to the Philippians 257
  letter to the Romans 246–247
  letter to Titus 263
  letters to the Corinthians 248–251,
    252–253
  letters to the Thessalonians 259, 260
  letters to Timothy 261, 262
  road to Damascus 243
Pekah 79, 80
Pekahiah 79
Pelatiah 195
Pentecost 241
Pergamum 275
Persia 105, 202, 203
Peter 206, 226, 236, 240, 241–242,
  243, 255
  death 270
  denies Jesus 228, 231, 235, 239
  freed from prison by angel 243
  heals lame man 241
  heals paralysed man 243
  raises dead woman 243
  recognizes Jesus as Messiah 230, 234, 238
  teachings 269–270
Peter 1 269
Peter 2 270
Pethuel 206
Pharisees 226, 227, 230, 235, 238
Philadelphia 275
Philemon 264
Philip 236, 243
Philippi 244
Philippians 257
Philistia 197, 215
Philistines 56, 58–59, 69, 175, 191, 218
  Ark of the Covenant 62–63
  war with Israelites under Saul 64–67
Phinehas 43
Pilate 228, 231, 235, 239–240
Potiphar's wife 24
priests of Israel 32, 33, 34, 35, 37, 40,
  49, 200
Priscilla 244
Promised Land 39, 46, 51, 175

prophets 49, 74
Proverbs 150–151
  ch 1 150
  ch 2–5 151
  ch 6–10 152
  ch 11–17 153
  ch 18–24 154
  ch 25–31 155
Psalms 124–125
  1 124
  2–3 125
  4–11 126
  12–14 127
  15–22 128
  23–30 129
  31–34 130
  35–41 131
  42–48 132
  49–52 133
  53–59 134
  60–66 135
  67–72 136
  73–77 137
  78–81 138
  82–89 139
  90–93 140
  94–100 141
  101–106 142
  107–110 143
  111–115 144
  116–120 145
  121–128 146
  129–136 147
  137–143 148
  144–150 149
Ptolemais 112
Put 213

R

Rachel 23
Rahab 52, *53*
Ramoth 44
Ramoth Gilead 75, 89
Ramses II 27
Raphael, Archangel 103, 104
Razis 115
Rebecca, wife of Isaac 21, 22
Red Sea, parting of *1*, 30, *30*
Rehoboam 73, 74, 88–89

FURTHER READING

General

Barton, John
The Biblical World
Routledge, 2002

Barton, John
Oxford Bible Commentary
OUP Oxford, 2007

Brown, Raymond E.
New Jerome Biblical Commentary
Continuum, 2003

Ehrman, Bart
Misquoting Jesus
HarperOne, 2007

Fitzmyer, Joseph
The Interpretation of Scripture
Paulist Press, 2008

McKenzie, John
Dictionary of the Bible
Touchstone, 1995

Old Testament

Alter, Robert
The Art of Biblical Narrative
Basic Books, 1983

Alter, Robert
The Art of Biblical Poetry
Basic Books, 1987

Anderson, Bernhard
The Living World of the Old Testament
Longman, 1988

Blenkinsopp, Joseph
The Pentateuch
Anchor Bible, 2000

Boadt, Lawrence
Reading the Old Testament: An Introduction
Paulist Press, 1984

New Testament General

Brown, Raymond
Introduction to the New Testament
Yale University Press, 1997

Dunn, James D.G.
Christology in the Making
SCM Press, 2003

Ehrman, Bart
Misquoting Jesus
HarperOne, 2007

Hooker, Morna
Studying the New
Epworth Press,

Johnson, Luke T
The Writings of t
Fortress Press, 2

Ratzinger, Joseph
Jesus of Nazareth
Doubleday Relig

Gospels

Bauckham, Richa
Jesus and the Eye
Wm. B. Eerdma

Brown, Raymon
Birth of the Mess
Anchor Bible, 1

Brown, Raymon
Death of the Me
Yale University

Burridge, Richar
Four Gospels, On
Wm. B. Eerdma

Conzelmann, H
Theology of Luke
Harper Collins,

Dawes, Gregory
The Historical Je
Westminster Jol

Dodd, Charles
The Founder of (
Macmillan, 1970

Edwards, Ruth
Discovering John
SPCK Publishing

Fitzmyer, Joseph
Luke the Theolog
Wipf & Stock P

France, R.T.
Matthew, Evange
Wipf & Stock P

Harrington, Wil
John: Spiritual Th
Columba Press,

FOLD-OUT FLAP

Fold out this flap to find an at-a-glance key to the colour and number system used to identify the Bible themes. Keep this flap open as you use this book, or until you become familiar with the key.

Isaiah bears witness to the coming of the promised Messiah
The prophet Isaiah lived and worked in Jerusalem, surrounded by those who followed the other gods and goddesses of the ancient world.

CREDITS

Quarto would like to thank the following agencies for supplying images for inclusion in this book:

AKG London, pp.27, 145
Alamy, pp.127, 170
Art Archive, pp.7, 14, 19, 25, 26, 28, 41, 47, 60, 63, 66, 74, 141, 144, 183, 211, 216, 223, 227, 230, 236, 242, 249, 250, 253, 254, 262, 267, 269, 270
Bridgeman, pp.2, 10t, 10b, 22, 29, 30, 33, 38, 39, 43, 44, 45, 48, 50, 53, 57, 59, 61, 65, 71, 73, 77, 78, 87, 88, 92, 97, 99, 130, 107, 109, 111, 114, 118, 122, 123, 125, 130, 133, 137, 138, 140, 143, 149, 152, 159, 174, 178, 188, 190, 198, 207, 208, 210, 233, 237, 239, 251, 255, 260, 264, 266, 272, 273, 274, 173
Dover pp.203, 100, 94, 121, 185, 186,
Mary Evans pp.36, 79, 80, 90, 91, 93, 95, 96, 151, 163, 166/167, 177, 180, 214, 229, 240, 245
Pitts Theology Library, Candler School of Theology, Emory University p.165

While every effort has been made to credit contributors, Quarto would like to apologise should there have been any omissions or errors—and would be pleased to make the appropriate correction for future editions of the book.

About the paintings

Allori, Cristofano (1577–1621) (after), p.107
Arpo, Guariento di (fl.1350–1400), p.10b
Assyrian School, p.198
Bartolo di Fredi, also Manfredi de Battilori (1330–1410), p.122
Bassano, Jacopo (Jacopo da Ponte) (1510–92), p.48
Bassano, Leandro da Ponte (1557–1622), p.183
Bellini, Giovanni (1430–1516), p.230
Bendixen, Siegfried Detler (1786–1864), pp.2, 10t
Blake, William (1757–1827), p.123
Brueghel, Pieter the Elder (1525–69), p.66
Buonarroti, Michelangelo (1475–1564), p.207
Caravaggio, Michelangelo (1571–1610) (follower of), p.59
Carracci, Annibale (1560–1609), p.242
Cavallino, Bernardo (1616–54), p.71
Claeissens, Anthuenis (1536–1613) (studio of), p.109
Coli, G. (1643–81) and Gherardi, F. (1643–1704) (circle of), p.78
Correggio, Antonio Allegri (1489–1534), p.240
Cranach, Lucas, the Elder (1472–1553), p.175
Dutch School, (16th century), p.92
Eeckhout, Gerbrandt van den (1621–74), p.63
English School, (12th century), pp.125, 143, 149, 266
English School, (14th century), p.130
English School, (19th century), p.38
English School, (20th century), p.188
Fetti or Feti, Domenico (1589–1624), p.274
Fouquet, Jean (c.1420–80) and studio, p.111
Fragonard, Jean-Honore (1732–1806), p.73
French School, (15th century), p.22, 210
French School, (19th century), p.87
German School, (15th century), p.43, 45, 50, 97
German School, (19th century), p.77
Ghirlandaio, Ridolfo (Bigordi), Il (1483–1561), p.255
Guiart Desmoulins, Douce, p.145
Hemessen, Jan Sanders van (c.1504–66), p.239
Hermann, Franz George II (1692–1768), p.152
Hole, William Brassey (1846–1917), p.99
Italian School, (15th century), p.264

Italian School, (17th century), p.53
Jaquerio, Giacomo (fl.1403–53), p.273
Jordaens, Jacob (1593–1678), p.237
Jordan, L. (20th century) (after), p.39
Juan de Borgona, (c.1470–c.1535), p.208
Kronberg, Julius (1850–1921), p.65
Lairesse, Gerard de (1640–1711), p.114
Letin, Jacques de (1597–1661), p.47
Leyden, Lucas van (1494–1533), p.227
Martin, John (1789–1854), p.144
Massys or Metsys, Jan (1509–75), p.103
Moreau, Gustave (1826–98), p.159
Murillo, Bartolome Esteban (1618–82), p.236
Orsel, Victor (1795–1850), p.254
Raphael (Raffaello Sanzio of Urbino) (1483–1520) (after), p.88
Rembrandt Harmenszoon van Rijn (1606–69), pp.33, 190, 262
Romanian School, (17th century), p.140
Sassoferato (1609–85), p.250
Scheits, Matthias (c.1630–c.1700), p.133
Scorel, Jan van (1495–1562) (follower of), p.61
Serra, Pedro (fl.1375–1408), p.269
Solimena, Francesco (1657–1747), p.57
Surikov, Vasilij Ivanovic (1848–1916), p.137
Texier, Charles Felix Marie (1802–71) (after), p.260
Tiepolo, Giambattista (1696–1770), p.267
Tissot, James (1836–1902), pp.28, 41, 60, 216
Trevisani, Francesco (1656–1746), p.251
Uffizien, Florenz, Italien, p.151
Vincent, Francois Andre (1746–1816), 118
Wet or Wett, Jacob Willemsz de (c.1610–72), pp.30, 233
Zurbaran, Francisco de (1598–1664) (follower of), p.272